THE MIND AND SPIRIT
OF EARLY AMERICA

THE MIND AND SPIRIT OF EARLY AMERICA

Sources in American History
1607-1789

Edited by

Richard Walsh
Georgetown University

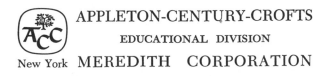

APPLETON-CENTURY-CROFTS
EDUCATIONAL DIVISION
New York MEREDITH CORPORATION

Cover: A view of the State House in Boston.
Courtesy of The New York Historical Society,
New York City.

PRINTED IN THE UNITED STATES OF AMERICA

390–91556–4

To
B. J.
J. M.
B. R.
E. A. & L. J.

Contents

ONE   The Seventeenth Century, 1607–1708

TWO   Provincial Society, 1713–63

THREE   The Revolutionary Era, 1763–89

Preface

The purpose of this book is to examine the attitudes and social institutions of the first Americans through studying their writings. The selection of materials is based not so much on political institutions as on ideas. For ideas make events. In assembling the following documents, I have made few concessions to the twentieth-century reader. The texts have not been modernized. I have interpolated explanations where necessary, but sparingly for fear of muddling a piece of writing. A place name has been added here, a first name there, but throughout I have tried to render the sources as faithfully as possible. Any changes in the texts which I have made have been explained in the footnotes. Annotation has been kept to a minimum, but a bibliography of important studies and additional secondary sources has been listed after the three major sections.

Except in the brief introductory paragraphs, I have not provided biographical identification of the men and women who appear in the readings. The *Dictionary of American Biography*, 20 volumes and supplements (1930–1958), and the *Dictionary of National Biography*, 21 volumes and supplement (1919–   ), fill the need far better than could a cryptic line in this work. Also, the definition of obsolete words may be readily found in *Webster's New International Dictionary of the English Language* (1958), or better still, the magnificent *Oxford English Dictionary*, 17 volumes (1933).

No single volume could possibly include all the source materials available for study. Local archives and societies (which this volume has purposely sampled), university and city libraries, and national depositories are rich in early Americana. This work, therefore, is highly selective in the materials on which it draws and the number of documents it presents. My hope is that it will nevertheless beckon the reader toward a further search for the mind and spirit of early America.

Georgetown University   R. W.

Acknowledgments

This book was formed in the classroom. I owe a special debt of gratitude to the many undergraduate and graduate students who, since 1960, have studied the primary sources with me in a course on the colonial mind. Their reactions to the material and men of the period, and sometimes their direct aid in transcribing documents or pursuing facts for me is deeply appreciated, as are the comments of numerous of my colleagues. Some of these good scholars are Dr. Dorothy Brown of Georgetown University; Dr. Louis Magazine of Misericordia College; Dr. Joan Maloney, Salem College, Massachusetts; Dr. Edward Roddy of Merrimac College, Massachusetts; Anthony Nicolosi of the Rutgers University Library; Dr. David Skaggs of Bowling Green State University; Dr. Albert Abbott of Fairfield University; the Rev. Dr. Thomas O. Hanley, S.J., of Marquette University; and Malcolm Clark of the College of Charleston. Linda Marion Arnold, Warren E. Stickle,† and Janet A. Lane, my more recent assistants, have also performed valuable services. Also William C. Filby of the Maryland Historical Society and Carl L. Chamberlain, Curator of the John Gilmary Shea Collection of Rare Books at Georgetown University Library were most helpful. Dr. Alden T. Vaughan of Columbia University made useful suggestions which affected not only improvement in this book but also in the above-mentioned course. I thank Robin Friedheim of Georgetown University Press for her editorial assistance. But none of these good people is responsible for any unwanted errors which I may have committed in the following work.

†Now of Purdue University.

ONE

The Seventeenth Century
1607–1708

INTRODUCTION

In 1632, Father Andrew White, promoting Lord Baltimore's projected colony of Maryland, gave Englishmen some good reasons for going to the New World. White directed his words toward men who were already alert to the advantages of colonization. He pointed out to the patriots of England who would willingly increase her holdings overseas that "the empire of the realm [would] be more widely extended." He assured the land-hungry yeomen, townsmen, and gentlemen who aspired to improve their lot by investment or emigration that all who went would be admitted "to a participation" of "profits and honor." He reminded the Christians that they could carry "the light of the Gospel and of Truth . . . where no knowledge of the True God has shone"; and he indicated that persecuted sects could practice their religion without fear in America.

By 1689, there were over 200,000 people settled in British North America, in colonies stretching along the Atlantic coast from Maine to South Carolina. The colonists had survived the "starving times," adjusted to the American climate, dispossessed the Indian tribes of their forests and hunting grounds, and established farms, plantations, and towns from which they prosperously exported a growing volume of lumber, naval stores, rice, tobacco, fish, and furs. In turn they bought necessary manufactured goods and even luxuries from England. The seventeenth century had been one of amazing accomplishment.

The founding of the English colonies began one of the greatest migrations in human history. Englishmen, who formed the bulk of the early migrants, brought with them concepts of social organization and a body of thought reflecting their experience in their mother country, but they adapted them to the demands of their new environment. Seventeenth-century England was a nation of clashing political and religious ideals and interests. In America the conflicting groups produced contrasting minds and societies—mainly Puritan, Quaker, Anglo-Dutch, and Cavalier—possessing no unity except that which was derived from their attachment to their mother country. In the New World each society built something tangibly distinctive from what existed in the Old World. Each contributed to laying the basis for American life and thought, making knowledge of the seventeenth century essential to the understanding of the colonial past.

1

Promoters and Founders

1. JOHN SMITH, *A TRUE RELATION*, 1607[*]

John Smith (1580–1631), son of a small farmer of Lincolnshire, England, won the title "Gentleman and Captain" for his military exploits as a soldier of fortune in Eastern Europe where he fought against the Turks. Captured and released by the "heathen," he returned to England when plans were afoot to colonize Virginia, and through his influential connections he became a councillor for the new enterprise.

In his A True Relation, *the first book written in America and an invaluable source book for life in the Jamestown settlement, he displays the characteristics of his age: militant patriotism, adventurousness, and religiosity. In a vigorous, Elizabethan style he describes the precarious life of the first settlers, who were menaced by Indians, plagued by illness, and threatened by starvation.*

Smith, who was the center of political dissensions, took over the leadership of the colony and by his account saved it from disaster. In 1609 he suffered severe wounds from an accidental explosion of gunpowder and had to be brought back to England. He never returned to Virginia, but went on exploratory trips to the New England coast, describing and mapping it and promoting colonization there. The Pilgrims and Massachusetts settlers used the information Smith gathered to establish Plymouth and Boston.

. . . The instant change of the winde being faire [for our ship] . . . we repaired to the fort with all speed where the first we heard was that 400. Indians the day before had assalted the fort, and supprised it, had

[*] Edward Arber, ed., *Capt. John Smith . . . Works* (Westminster: Archibald Constable and Co., 1895), vol., I, pp. 7–13. [I have changed the *u* to *v*, *viz.*: fiue = five, and substituted *i* and *j* to modernize words.—Editor's Note]

not God (beyond al their expectations) by meanes of the shippes (at whom they shot with their Ordinances and Muskets) caused them to retire[;] they had entred the fort with our own men, which were then busied in setting Corne, their armes beeing then in driefats [casks] and few ready but certain Gentlemen of their own, in which conflict, most of the Counsel was hurt, a boy slaine in the Pinnas, and thirteene or fourteene more hurt.

With all speede we palisadoed our Fort: (each other day) for sixe or seaven daies we had alarums by ambuscadoes, and four or five cruelly wounded by being abroad: the Indians losse wee know not, but as they report three were slain and divers hurt.

Captaine *Newport* having set things in order, set saile for England that 22 of June [1607] leaving provision for 13. or 14 weeks.

The day before the Ships departure, the King of *Pamanuke* [Opechancanough] sent the Indian that had met us before in our discoverie, to assure us peace; our fort being then palisadoed round, and all our men in good health and comfort, albeit, that throgh some discontented humors, it did not so long · continue. For the President and Captaine *Gosnold*, with the rest of the Counsell, being for the moste part discontented with one another, in so much, that things were neither carried with that discretion nor any busines effected in such good sort as wisdome would, nor our owne good and safetie required, wherby, and through the hard dealing of our President, the rest of the counsell beeing diverslie affected through his audacious commaund; and for Captaine *Martin*, (albeit verie honest) and wishing the best good, yet so sicke and weake; and my selfe so disgrac'd through others mallice: through which disorder God (being angrie with us) plagued us with such famin and sicknes, that the living were scarce able to bury the dead: our want of sufficient and good victualls, with continuall watching, foure or five each night at three Bulwarkes, being the chiefe cause: onely of Sturgion wee had great store, whereon our men would so greedily surfet, as it cost manye their lives: the Sack, Aquauitie [brandy] and other preservatives for our health, being kept onely in the Presidents hands, for his owne diet, and his few associates.

Shortly after Captaine *Gosnold* fell sicke, and within three weekes died. Captaine *Ratcliffe* being then also verie sicke and weake, and my selfe having also tasted of the extremitie therof, but by Gods assistance being well recovered. *Kendall* about this time, for divers reasons deposed from being of the Councell: and shortly after it pleased God (in our extremity) to move the Indians to bring us Corne, ere it was halfe ripe, to refresh us, when we rather expected when they would destroy us.

About the tenth of September there was about 46. of our men dead, at which time Captaine *Wingfield* having ordred the affaires in such sort that he was generally hated of all, in which respect with one consent he was deposed from his presidencie, and Captaine *Ratcliffe* according to his course was elected.

Our provision being now within twentie dayes spent, the Indians brought us great store both of Corne and bread ready made: and also there came such aboundance of Fowles into the Rivers, as greatly refreshed our weake estates, whereuppon many of our weake men were presently able to goe abroad.

As yet we had no houses to cover us, our Tents were rotten, and our Cabbins worse then nought: our best commoditie was Yron which we made into little chissels.

The president['s] and Captaine *Martins* sicknes, constrayned me to be Cape Marchant, and yet to spare no paines in making houses for the company; who notwithstanding our misery, little ceased their mallice, grudging, and muttering.

As at this time were most of our chiefest men either sicke or discontented, the rest being in such dispaire, as they would rather starve and rot with idlenes, then be perswaded to do any thing for their owne reliefe without constraint: our victualles being now within eighteene dayes spent, and the Indians trade decreasing, I was sent to the mouth of the river, to *Kegquouhtan* an Indian Towne, to trade for Corne, and try the river for Fish, but our fishing we could not effect by reason of the stormy weather. The Indians thinking us neare famished, with carelesse kindnes, offred us little pieces of bread and small handfulls of beanes or wheat, for a hatchet or a piece of copper: In like maner I entertained their kindnes, and in like scorne offered them like commodities, but the Children, or any that shewed extraordinary kindnes, I liberally contented with free gifte, [of] such trifles as well contented them.

Finding this colde comfort, I anchored before the Towne, and the next day returned to trade, but God (the absolute disposer of all heartes) altered their conceits, for now they were no lesse desirous of our commodities then we of their Corne: under colour to fetch fresh water, I sent a man to discover the Towne, their Corne, and force, to trie their intent, in that they desired me up to their houses: which well understanding, with foure shot I visited them. With fish, oysters, bread, and deere, they kindly traded with me and my men, beeing no lesse in doubt of my intent, then I of theirs; for well I might with twentie men have fraighted a Shippe with Corne: The Towne conteineth eighteene houses, pleasantly seated upon three acres of ground, uppon a plaine, halfe invironed with a great Bay of the great River, the other parte with a Baye of the other River falling into the great Baye, with a little Ile fit for a Castle in the mouth thereof, the Towne adjoyning to the maine by a necke of Land of sixtie yardes.

With sixteene bushells of Corne I returned towards our Forte: by the way I encountred with two Canowes of Indians, who came aboord me, being the inhabitants of *waroskoyack*, a kingdome on the south side of the river, which is in breadth 5. miles and 20 mile or neare from the mouth: With these I traded, who having but their hunting provision, requested me to returne to their Towne, where I should load my boat with corne: and with near thirtie bushells I returned to the fort, the very name whereof gave great comfort to our despa[i]ring company:

Time thus passing away, and having not above 14. daies victuals left, some motions were made about our presidents [Captain John Ratcliffe] and Captaine *Archers* going for England, to procure a supply: in which meane time we had reasonably fitted us with houses. And our President and Captaine *Martin* being able to walk abroad, with much adoe it was concluded, that the pinnace and barge should goe towards *Powhatan*, to trade for corne:

Lotts were cast who should go in her, the chance was mine; and while she was a rigging, I made a voiage to *Topohanack*, where arriving, there was but certain women and children who fled from their houses, yet at last I drew them to draw neere; truck they durst not, corne they had plenty, and to spoile I had no commission:

In my returne to *Paspahegh*, I traded with that churlish and trecherous nation: having loaded 10 or 12 bushels of corne, they offred to take our pieces and swords, yet by stelth, but [we] seeming to dislike it, they were ready to assault us: yet standing upon our guard, in coasting the shore, divers out of the woods would meet with us with corn and trade. But least we should be constrained, either to indure overmuch wrong or directly fal to revenge, seeing them dog us, from place to place, it being night, and our necessitie not fit for warres, we tooke occasion to returne with 10 bushells of corne:

Captaine *Martin* after made 2 journies to that nation of *Paspahegh*, but eache time returned with 8. or 10. bushells.

All things being now ready for my journey to *Powhatan*, for the performance thereof, I had 8. men and my selfe for the barge, as well for discoverie as trading; the Pinnace, 5. Marriners, and 2. landmen to take in our ladings at convenient places.

The 9 of November I set forward for the discovery of the country of *Chik[a]hamania*, leaving the pinnace the next tide to followe, and stay for my comming at *Point weanock*, 20 miles from our fort: the mouth of this river falleth into the great river at *Paspahegh*, 8 miles above our fort:

That afternoone I stayed the eb in the bay of *Paspahegh* with the Indians: towards the evening certaine Indians haled me, one of them being of *Chikahamania*, offred to conduct me to his country, the

Paspahegheans grudged therat: along we went by moonelight; at midnight he brought us before his Towne, desiring one of our men to go up with him, whom he kindely intertained, and returned back to the barge:

The next morning I went up to the towne, and shewed them what copper and hatchets they shold have for corne, each family seeking to give me most content: so long they caused me to stay that 100 at least was expecting my comming by the river, with corne. What I liked, I bought; and least they should perceive my too great want, I went higher up the river:

This place is called *Manosquosick*, a quarter of a mile from the river, conteining thirtie or fortie houses, uppon an exceeding high land: at the foote of the hill towards the river, is a plaine wood, watered with many springes, which fall twentie yardes right downe into the river. Right against the same is a great marsh, of 4. or 5. miles circuit, divided in 2 Ilands, by the parting of the river, abounding with fish and foule of all sorts:

A mile from thence is a Towne called *Oraniocke*. I further discovered the Townes of *Mansa, Apanaock, Werawahone,* and *Mamanahunt,* at eche place kindely used: especially at the last, being the hart of the Country; where were assembled 200. people with such abundance of corne, as having laded our barge, as also I might have laded a ship:

I returned to *Paspahhegh*, and considering the want of Corne at our Fort, it being night, with the ebb, by midnight I arived at our fort, where I found our Pinn[a]is run aground:

The next morning I unladed seaven hogsheds into our store.

The next morning I returned againe: the second day I arived at *Mamanahunt,* wher the people having heard of coming, were ready with 3 or 400. baskets litle and great, of which having laded my barge, with many signes of great kindnes I returned:

At my departure they requested me to hear our pieces, being in the midst of the river; which in regard of the eccho seemed a peale of ordnance. Many birds and fowles they see us dayly kil that much feared them. So desirous of trade wer[e] they, that they would follow me with their canowes; and for any thing, give it me, rather then returne it back: So I unladed again 7 or 8. hogsheads at our fort.

Having thus by Gods assistance gotten good store of corne, notwithstanding some bad spirits not content with Gods providence, still grew mutinous; in so much, that our president having occasion to chide the smith [James Read, the Blacksmith] for his misdeamenour, he not only gave him bad language, but also offred to strike him with some of his tooles. For which rebellious act, the smith was by a jury condemned to be hanged, but being uppon the ladder, continuing very obstinate as hoping upon a rescue, when he saw no other way but death with him, he became penitent, and declared a dangerous conspiracy: for which, Captaine *Kendall*, as principal, was by a Jury condemned, and shot to death.

This conspiracy appeased, I set forward for the discovery of the River *Checka Hamania*. This third time I discovered the Townes of *Matapamient, Morinogh, Ascacap, moysenock, Righkahauck, Nechanichock, Mattalunt, Attamuspincke,* and divers others: their plenty of corne I found decreased, yet lading the barge, I returned to our fort:

Our store being now indifferently wel provided with corne, there was much adoe for to have the pinace goe for England, against which Captain *Martin* and my selfe stood chiefly against it: and in fine after many debatings *pro et contra*, it was resolved to stay a further resolution:

This matter also quieted, I set forward to finish this discovery, which as yet I had neglected in regard of the necessitie we had to take in provision whilst it was to be had.

2. GEORGE PERCY, *OBSERVATIONS* OF JAMESTOWN, 1607*

George Percy (1580–1632), a typical English "second son," or gentleman without fortune, became a soldier and sailed on the first crossing to the Virginia colony. He recorded the details of the voyage, the landing, and the initial explorations; and in stoic fashion, as though reporting battle casualties, he listed those who had died and were dying from the hardships of the first year.

On April 12, 1612, he left the colony and never returned. He continued in the service of the king and was wounded at the head of a company operating in the Netherlands during the war with Spain.

This River [the James] which wee have discovered is one of the famousest Rivers that ever was found by any Christian. It ebbs and flowes a hundred and threescore miles, where ships of great burthen may harbour in safetie. Wheresoever we landed upon this River, wee saw the goodliest Woods as Beech, Oke, Cedar, Cypresse, Wal-nuts, Sassafras, and Vines in great abundance, which hang in great clusters on many Trees, and other Trees unknowne; and all the grounds bespred with many sweet and delicate flowres of divers colours and kindes. There are also many fruites as Strawberries, Mulberries, Rasberries, and Fruites unknowne. There are many branches of this River, which runne flowing through the Woods with great plentie of fish of all kindes; as for Sturgeon, all the World cannot be compared to it. In this Countrey I

* Samuel Purchas, *Hakluytus Posthumus or Purchas His Pilgrimes* (New York: Macmillan, 1905–7), Vol. XVIII, pp. 415–19.

have seene many great and large Medowes having excellent good pasture for any Cattle. There is also great store of Deere both Red and Fallow. There are Beares, Foxes, Otters, Bevers, Muskats, and wild beasts un-knowne.

The foure and twentieth day [May, 1607] wee set up a Crosse at the head of this River, naming it Kings River, where we proclaimed James King of England to have the most right unto it. When wee had finished and set up our Crosse, we shipt our men and made for James Fort. By the way, wee came to Pohatans Towre, where the Captaine went on shore suffering none to goe with him. Hee presented the Commander of this place, with a Hatchet which hee tooke joyfully, and was well pleased.

But yet the Savages murmured at our planting in the Countrie, whereupon this Werowance made answere againe very wisely of a Savage, Why should you bee offended with them as long as they hurt you not, nor take any thing away by force. They take but a litle waste ground, which doth you nor any of us any good.

I saw Bread made by their women, which doe all their drugerie. The men takes their pleasure in hunting and their warres, which they are in continually, one Kingdome against another. The manner of baking of bread is thus. After they pound their wheat into flowre, with hote water they make it into paste, and worke it into round balls and Cakes, then they put it into a pot of seething water: when it is sod throughly, they lay it on a smooth stone, there they harden it as well as in an oven.

There is notice to be taken to know married women from Maids. The Maids you shall alwayes see the fore part of their head and sides shaven close, the hinder part very long, which they tie in a pleate hanging downe to their hips. The married women weares their haire all of a length, and is tied of that fashion that the Maids are. The women kinde in this Countrey doth pounce and race their bodies, legges, thighes, armes and faces with a sharpe Iron, which makes a stampe in curious knots, and drawes the proportion of Fowles, Fish, or Beasts; then with paintings of sundry lively colours, they rub it into the stampe which will never be taken away, because it is dried into the flesh where it is sered.

The Savages beare their yeeres well, for when wee were at Pamonkies, wee saw a Savage by their report was above eight score yeeres of age. His eyes were sunke into his head, having never a tooth in his mouth, his haire all gray with a reasonable bigge beard, which was as white as any snow. It is a Miracle to see a Savage have any haire on their faces. I never saw, read, nor heard, any have the like before. This Savage was as lusty and went as fast as any of us, which was strange to behold.

The fifteenth of June we had built and finished our Fort, which was triangle wise, having three Bulwarkes, at every corner, like a halfe

Moone, and foure or five pieces of Artillerie mounted in them. We had made our selves sufficiently strong for these Savages. We had also sowne most of our Corne on two Mountaines. It sprang a mans height from the ground. This Countrey is a fruitfull soile, bearing many goodly and fruitfull Trees, as Mulberries, Cherries, Walnuts, Cedars, Cypresse, Sassafras, and Vines in great abundance.

Munday the two and twentieth of June, in the morning, Captaine Newport in the Admirall departed from James Port for England.

Captaine Newport being gone for England, leaving us (one hundred and foure persons) verie bare and scantie of victualls, furthermore in warres and in danger of the Savages, we hoped after a supply which Captaine Newport promised within twentie weekes. But if the beginners of this action doe carefully further us, the Country being so fruitfull, it would be as great a profit to the Realme of England, as the Indies to the King of Spaine. If this River which wee have found had been discovered in the time of warre with Spaine, it would have beene a commoditie to our Realme, and a great annoyance to our enemies.

The seven and twentieth of July the King of Rapahanna demanded a Canoa, which was restored, lifted up his hand to the Sunne (which they worship as their God), besides he laid his hand on his heart, that he would be our speciall friend. It is a generall rule of these people, when they swere by their God which is the Sunne, no Christian will keep their Oath better upon this promise. These people have a great reverence to the Sunne above all other things: at the rising and setting of the same, they sit downe lifting up their hands and eyes to the Sunne, making a round Circle on the ground with dried Tobacco; then they began to pray, making many Devillish gestures with a Hellish noise, foming at the mouth, staring with their eyes, wagging their heads and hands in such a fashion and deformitie as it was monstrous to behold.

The sixt of August there died John Asbie of the bloudie Fluxe. The ninth day died George Flowre of the swelling. The tenth day died William Bruster Gentleman, of a wound given by the Savages, and was buried the eleventh day.

The fourteenth day, Jerome Alikock, Ancient, died of a wound, the same day, Francis Midwinter, Edward Moris Corporall died suddenly.

The fifteenth day, there died Edward Browne and Stephen Galthorpe. The sixteenth day, there died Thomas Gower Gentleman. The seventeenth day, there died Thomas Mounslic. The eighteenth day, there died Robert Pennington, and John Martine Gentleman. The nineteenth day, died Drue Piggase Gentleman. The two and twentieth day of August, there died Captaine Bartholomew Gosnold, one of our Councell: he was honourably buried, having all the Ordnance in the Fort shot off, with many vollies of small shot.

After Captaine Gosnol[d]s death, the Councell could hardly agree by the dissention of Captaine Kendall, which afterwards was committed about hainous matters which was proved against him.

The foure and twentieth day, died Edward Harington and George Walker, and were buried the same day. The six and twentieth day, died Kenelme Throgmortine. The seven and twentieth day died William Roods. The eight and twentieth day died Thomas Stoodie, Cape Merchant.

The fourth day of September died Thomas Jacob Sergeant. The fift day, there died Benjamin Beast. Our men were destroyed with cruell diseases, as Swellings, Flixes, Burning Fevers, and by warres, and some departed suddenly, but for the most part they died of meere famine. There were never Englishmen left in a forreigne Countrey in such miserie as wee were in this new discovered Virginia. Wee watched every three nights, lying on the bare cold ground, what weather soever came, warded all the next day, which brought our men to bee most feeble wretches. Our food was but a small Can of Barlie sod in water, to five men a day, our drinke cold water taken out of the River, which was at a floud verie salt, at a low tide full of slime and filth, which was the destruction of many of our men. Thus we lived for the space of five moneths in this miserable distresse, not having five able men to man our Bulwarkes upon any occasion. If it had not pleased God to have put a terrour in the Savages hearts, we had all perished by those wild and cruell Pagans, being in that weake estate as we were; our men night and day groaning in every corner of the Fort most pittifull to heare. If there were any conscience in men, it would make their harts to bleed to heare the pittifull murmurings and out-cries of our sick men without reliefe, every night and day, for the space of sixe weekes, some departing out of the World, many times three or foure in a night; in the morning, their bodies trailed out of their Cabines like Dogges to be buried. In this sort did I see the mortalitie of divers of our people.

It pleased God, after a while, to send those people which were our mortall enemies to releeve us with victuals, as Bread, Corne, Fish, and Flesh in great plentie, which was the setting up of our feeble men, otherwise wee had all perished. Also we were frequented by divers Kings in the Countrie, bringing us store of provision to our great comfort.

The eleventh day there was certaine Articles laid against Master [Edward Maria] Wingfield which was then President; thereupon he was not only displaced out of his President ship, but also from being of the Councell. Afterwards Captaine John Ratcliffe was chosen President.

The eighteenth day, died one Ellis Kinistone which was starved to death with cold. The same day at night, died one Richard Simmons. The nineteenth day, there died one Thomas Mouton.

3. WILLIAM BRADFORD, *OF PLYMOUTH PLANTATIONS*, 1606–20*

William Bradford (1590–1657) was a leader of the separatists who made the first permanent settlement in New England, beginning the Puritan exodus to the New World. Largely self-educated, Bradford wrote Of Plymouth Plantations *in the best seventeenth-century "plaine style." A classic of American literature, it resembles the Old Testament, since it also describes the history of a "chosen" people—the hardships and trials of their expatriation to Holland and their suffering and triumph in the American wilderness.* Of Plymouth Plantations *has a lasting human appeal: these humble folk were not adventurers seeking wealth, but poor men with their families searching for peace and freedom from bigotry.*

[Ano. 1602–6]

But that I may come more near my intendments; when as by the travell & diligence of some godly & zealous preachers, & Gods blessing on their labours, as in other places of the land, so in the North parts [of England] many became inlightened by the word of God, and had their ignorance & sins discovered unto them, and begane by his grace to reforme their lives, and make conscience of their wayes, the worke of God was no sooner manifest in them, but presently they were both scoffed and scorned by the prophane multitude, and the ministers urged with the yoak of subscription, or els must be silenced; and the poore people were so vexed with apparators, & pursuants, & the comissarie courts, as truly their affliction was not smale; which, notwithstanding, they bore sundrie years with much patience, till they were occasioned (by the continuance & encrease of these troubls, and other means which the Lord raised up in those days) to see further into things by the light of the word of God. How not only these base and beggerly ceremonies [of the Anglicans] were unlawfull, but also that the lordly & tiranous power of the prelats ought not to be submitted unto; which thus, contrary to the freedome of the gospell, would load & burden mens consciences, and by their compulsive power make a prophane mixture of persons & things in the worship of God. And that their offices & calings, courts &

---

* *Bradford's History "Of Plymouth Planations" from the Original Manuscript* (Boston: Massachusetts General Court, 1898), pp. 11–17, 20–21, 29–33, 109–15. This edition is of historical importance since it is the first printing from the original after Great Britain's return of the original to the United States. It resided in Great Britain for more than a century, apparently having been carried there during the American Revolution. The best edited version is W. C. Ford's *History of Plymouth Plantation, 1620–1647 by William Bradford* (Boston: Massachusetts Historical Society, 1912).

cannons, &c. were unlawfull and antichristian; being such as have no warrante in the word of God; but the same that were used in poperie, & still retained. At the coming of king James into England; *The new king (saith he) found their established the reformed religion, according to the reformed religion of king Edward the 6. Retaining, or keeping still the spirituall state of the Bishops, &c. after the ould maner, much varying & differing from the reformed churches in Scotland, France, & the Neatherlands, Embden, Geneva, &c. whose reformation is cut, or shapen much nerer the first Christian churches, as it was used in the Apostles times.* . . .

So many therfore of these proffessors as saw the evill of these things, in thes[e] parts, and whose harts the Lord had touched wth heavenly zeale for his trueth, they shooke of this yoake of antichristian bondage, and as the Lords free people, joyned them selves (by a covenant of the Lord) into a church estate, in the fellowship of the gospell, to walke in all his wayes, made known, or to be made known unto them, according to their best endeavours, whatsoever it should cost them, the Lord assisting them. And that it cost them something this ensewing historie will declare.

These people became 2 distincte bodys or churches, & in regarde of distance of place did congregate severally; for they were of sundrie townes & vilages, some in Notingamshire, some of Lincollinshire, and some of Yorkshire, wher they border nearest togeather. In one of these churches (besids others of note) was Mr. John Smith, a man of able gifts, & a good preacher, who afterwards was chosen their pastor. But these afterwards falling into some errours in the Low Countries, ther (for the most part) buried them selves, & their names.

But in this other church (wch must be the subjecte of our discourse) besids other worthy men, was Mr. Richard Clifton, a grave & revered preacher, who by his paines and dilligens had done much good, and under God had ben a means of the conversion of many. And also that famous and worthy man Mr. John Robinson, who afterwards was their pastor for many years, till the Lord tooke him away by death. Also Mr. William Brewster a reverent man, who afterwards was chosen an elder of the church and lived with them till old age.

But after these things they could not long continue in any peaceable condition, but were hunted & persecuted on every side, so as their former afflictions were but as flea-bitings in comparison of these which now came upon them. For some were taken & clapt up in prison, others had their houses besett & watcht night and day, & hardly escaped their hands; and the most were faine to flie & leave their howses & habitations, and the means of their livelehood. Yet these & many other sharper things which aftterward befell them, were no other then they looked for, and therfore were the better prepared to bear them by the assistance of

Gods grace & spirite. Yet seeing them selves thus molested, and that ther was no hope of their continuance ther, by a joynte consente they resolved to goe into the Low-Countries, wher they heard was freedome of Religion for all men; as also how sundrie from London, & other parts of the land, had been exiled and persecuted for the same cause, & were gone thither, and lived at Amsterdam, & in other places of the land. So affter they had continued togeither aboute a year, and kept their meetings every Saboth in one place or other, exercising the worship of God amongst them selves, notwithstanding all the dilligence & malice of their adverssaries, they seeing they could no longer continue in that condition, they resolved to get over into Hollād as they could; which was in the year 1607. & 1608. . . .

Being thus constrained to leave their native soyle and countrie, their lands & livings, and all their friends & famillier acquaintance, it was much, and thought marvelous by many. But to goe into a countrie they knew not (but by hearsay), wher they must learne a new language, and get their livings they knew not how, it being a dear place, & subjecte to the misseries of warr, it was by many thought an adventure almost desperate, a case intolerable, & a misserie worse then death. Espetially seeing they were not aquainted with trads nor traffique, (by which that countrie doth subsiste,) but had only been used to a plaine countrie life, & the inocente trade of husbandrey. But these things did not dismay them (though they did some times trouble them) for their desires were sett on the ways of God; & to injoye his ordinances; but they rested on his providence, & knew whom they had beleeved. Yet this was not all, for though they could not stay, yet were they not suffered to goe, but the ports & havens were shut against them, so as they were faine to seeke secrete means of conveance, & to bribe & fee the mariners, & give exterordinarie rates for their passages. And yet were they often times betrayed (many of them), and both they & their goods intercepted & surprised, and therby put to great trouble & charge. . . .

Ther was a large companie of them purposed to get passage at Boston in Lincoln-shire, and for that end had hired a shipe wholy to them selves, & made agreement with the maister to be ready at a certaine day, and take them and their goods in, at a conveniente place, wher they accordingly would all attende in readines. So after long waiting, & large expences, though he kepte not day with them, yet he came at length & tooke them in, in the night. But when he had them & their goods abord, he betrayed them, haveing before hand complotted with the serchers & other officers so to doe; who tooke them, and put them into open boats, & ther rifled & ransaked them, searching them to their shirts for money, yea even the women furder then became modestie; and then caried them back into the towne, & made them a spectackle & wonder to the multitude, which came flocking on all sids to behould

them. Being thus first, by the chatchpoule officers, rifled, & stripte of
their money, books, and much other goods, they were presented to the
magestrates, and messengers sente to informe the lords of the Counsell
of them; and so they were comited to ward. Indeed the magestrats
used them courteously, and shewed them what favour they could; but
could not deliver them, till order came from the Counsell-table. But the
issue was that after a months imprisonments, the greatest parte were
dismiste, & sent to the places from whence they came; but 7 of the
principall were still kept in prison, and bound over to the Assises.

. . . .

The rest of the men that were in greatest danger, made shift to
escape away before the troope could surprise them; those only staying
that best might, to be assistante unto the women. But pitifull it was
to see the heavie case of these poore women in this distress; what
weeping & crying on every side, some for their husbands, that [were
separated from them] . . . others not knowing what should become of
them, & their litle ones; others againe melted in teares, seeing their poore
litle ones hanging aboute them, crying for feare, and quaking with
could. Being thus aprehended, they were hurried from one place to
another, and from one justice to another, till in the ende they knew
not what to doe with them; for to imprison so many women & innocent
children for no other cause (many of them) but that they must goe with
their husbands, semed to be unreasonable and all would crie out of
them; and to send them home againe was as difficult, for they aledged,
as the trueth was, they had no homes to goe to, for they had either sould,
or otherwise disposed of their houses & livings. To be shorte, after they
had been thus turmoyled a good while, and conveyed from one constable
to another, they [the constables] were glad to be ridd of them in the end
upon any termes; for all were wearied & tired with them. Though in the
mean time they (poore soules) indured miserie enough; and thus in the
end necessitie forste a way for them.
But that I be not tedious in these things, I will omitte the rest,
though I might relate many other notable passages and troubles which
they endured & underwente in these their wanderings & travells both at
land & sea; but I hast to other things. Yet I may not omitte the fruite
that came hearby, for by these so publick troubls, in so many eminente
places, their cause became famouss, & occasioned many to looke into
the same; and their godly cariage & Christian behaviour was such as
left a deep impression in the minds of many. And though some few
shrunk at these first conflicts & sharp beginings, (as it was no marvell,)
yet many more came on with fresh courage, & greatly animated others.
And in the end, notwithstanding all these stormes of oppossition, they
all gatt over at length, some at one time & some at an other, and some

in one place & some in an other, and mette togeather againe according to their desires, with no small rejoycing.

Being now come into the Low Countries, they saw many goodly & fortified cities, strongly walled and garded with troopes of armed men. Also they heard a strange & uncouth language, and beheld the differente maners & customes of the people, with their strange fashons and attires; all so farre differing from that of their plaine countrie villages (wherin they were bred, & had so longe lived) as it seemed they were come into a new world. But these were not the things they much looked on, or long tooke up their thoughts; for they had other work in hand, & an other kind of warr to wage & maintaine. For though they saw faire & bewtifull cities, flowing with abundance of all sorts of welth & riches, yet it was not longe before they saw the grime & grisly face of povertie coming upon them like an armed man, with whom they must bukle & incounter, and from whom they could not flye; but they were armed with faith & patience against him, and all his encounters; and though they were sometimes foyled, yet by Gods assistance they prevailed and got the victorie.

Now when Mr. Robinson, Mr. Brewster, & other principall members were come over, (for they were of the last, & stayed to help the weakest over before them,) such things were thought on as were necessarie for their setling and best ordering of the church affairs. And when they had lived at Amsterdam aboute a year, Mr. Robinson, their pastor, and some others of best discerning, seeing how Mr. John Smith and his companie was allready fallen in to contention with the church that was ther before them, & no means they could use would doe any good to cure the same, and also that the flames of contention were like to breake out in that anciente church it selfe (as affterwards lamentably came to pass); which things they prudently foreseeing, thought it was best to remove, before they were any way engaged with the same; though they well knew it would be much to the prejudice of their outward estats, both at presente & in licklyhood in the future; as indeed it proved to be.

For these & some other reasons they removed to Leyden, a fair & bewtifull citie, and of a sweete situation, but made more famous by the universitie wherwith it is adorned, in which of late had been so many learned men. But wanting that traffike by sea which Amsterdam injoyes, it was not so beneficiall for their outward means of living & estats. But being now hear pitchet they well to such trads & imployments as they best could; valewing peace & their spirituall comforte above any other riches whatsoever. And at [length] they came to raise a competente & comforteable living, but with hard and continuall labor. . . .

After they had lived in this citie about some 11 or 12 years, (which is the more observable being the whole time of that famose truce between that state & the Spaniards,) and sundrie of them [the Puritans] were taken away by death, & many others begane to be well striken in years, the grave mistris Experience haveing taught them many things, those prudent governours with sundrie of the sagest members begane both deeply to apprehend their present dangers, & wisely to foresee the future, & thinke of timly remedy. In the agitation of their thoughts, and much discours of things hear aboute, at length they began to incline to this conclusion, of remooval to some other place. Not out of any new-fanglednes, or other such like giddie humor, by which men are often-times transported to their great hurt & danger, but for sundrie weightie & solid reasons; some of the cheefe of which I will hear breefly touch. And first, they saw & found by experience the hardnes of the place & countrie to be such, as few in comparison would come to them, and fewer that would bide it out, and continew with them. For many that came to them, and many more that desired to be with them, could not endure that great labor and hard fare, with other inconveniences which they underwent & were contented with. But though they loved their persons, approved their cause, and honoured their sufferings, yet they left them as it weer weeping, as Orpah did her mother in law Naomie, or as those Romans did Cato in Utica, who desired to be excused & borne with, though they could not all be Catoes. For many, though they desired to injoye the ordinances of God in their puritie, and the libertie of the gospell with them, yet, alass, they admitted of bondage, with danger of conscience, rather then to indure these hardships; yea, some preferred & chose the prisons in England, rather then this libertie in Holland, with these afflictions. But it was thought that if a better and easier place of living could be had, it would draw many, & take away these discour-agments. Yea, their pastor would often say, that many of those who both wrate & preached now against them, if they were in a place wher they might have libertie and live comfortably, they would then practise as they did.

They saw that though the people generally bore all these diffi-culties very cherfully, & with a resolute courage, being in the best & strength of their years, yet old age began to steale on many of them, (and their great & continuall labours, with other crosses and sorrows, hastened it before the time,) so as it was not only probably thought, but apparently seen, that within a few years more they would be in danger to scatter, by necessities pressing them, or sinke under their burdens, or both. And therefore according to the devine proverb, that a wise man seeth the plague when it cometh, & hideth him selfe, Pro. 22. 3, so they like skillfull & beaten souldiers were fearfull either to be intrapped or surrounded by their enimies, so as they should neither be able to fight nor flie; and therfor thought it better to dislodge betimes to some place of better advantage & less danger, if any such could be found. Thirdly;

as necessitie was a taskmaster over them, so they were forced to be such, not only to their servants, but in a sorte, to their dearest chilldren; the which as it did not a litle wound the tender harts of many a loving father & mother, so it produced likwise sundrie sad & sorowful effects. For many of their children, that were of best dispositions and gracious inclinations, haveing lernde to bear the yoake in their youth, and willing to bear parte of their parents burden, were, often times, so oppressed with their hevie labours, that though their minds were free and willing, yet their bodies bowed under the weight of the same, and became decreped in their early youth; the vigor of nature being consumed in the very budd as it were. But that which was more lamentable, and of all sorowes most heavie to be borne, was that many of their children, by these occasions, and the great licentiousnes of youth in that countrie, and the manifold temptations of the place, were drawne away by evill examples into extravagante & dangerous courses, getting the raines off their neks, & departing from their parents. Some became souldiers others tooke upon them farr viages by sea, and other some worse courses, tending to dissolutnes & the danger of their soules, to the great greefe of their parents and dishonour of God. So that they saw their posteritie would be in danger to degenerate & be corrupted.

Lastly, (and which was not least,) a great hope & inward zeall they had of laying some good foundation, or at least to make some way therunto, for the propagating & advancing the gospell of the kingdom of Christ in those remote parts of the world; yea, though they should be but even as stepping-stones unto others for the performing of so great a work.

These, & some other like reasons, moved them to undertake this resolution of their removall; the which they afterward prosecuted with so great difficulties, as by the sequell will appeare.

The place they had thoughts on was some of those vast & unpeopled countries of America, which are frutfull & fitt for habitation, being devoyd of all civill inhabitants, wher ther are only salvage & brutish men, which range up and downe, litle otherwise then the wild beast of the same. . . .

[Ano. 1620]

I shall a litle returne backe and begine with a combination made by them before they came ashore, [in America] being the first foundation of their govermente in this place; occasioned partly by the discontented & mutinous speeches that some of the strangers amongst them had let fall from them in the ship—That when they came a shore they would use their owne libertie; for none had power to comand them, the patente they had being for Virginia, and not for New-england, which belonged to an other Goverment, with which the Virginia Company had nothing to doe. And partly that shuch an acte by them done (this their condition considered) might be as firme as any patent, and in some respects more sure.

The forme was as followeth.

In the name of God, Amen. We whose names are underwritten, the loyall subjects of our dread soveraigne Lord, King James, by the grace of God, of Great Britaine, Franc, & Irland king, defender of the faith, &c., haveing undertaken, for the glorie of God, and advancemente of the Christian faith, and honour of our king & countrie, a voyage to plant the first colonie in the Northerne parts of Virginia, doe by these presents solemnly & mutually in the presence of God, and one of another covenant & combine our selves togeather into a civill body politick, for our better ordering & preservation & furtherance of the ends aforesaid; and by vertue hearof to enacte, constitute, and frame such just & equall lawes, ordinances, acts, constitutions, & offices, from time to time, as shall be thought most meete & convenient for the general good of the colonie, unto which we promise all due submission and obedience. In witness wherof we have hereunder subscribed our names at Cap-Codd the 11 of November, in the year of the raigne of our soveraigne lord, King James, of England, France, & Ireland the eighteenth, and of Scotland the fiftie fourth. Ano: Dom. 1620.

After this they chose, or rather confirmed, Mr. John Carver (a man godly & well approved amongst them) their Governour for that year. And after they had provided a place for their goods, or comone store, (which were long in unlading for want of boats, foulnes of winter weather, and sicknes of diverce,) and begune some small cottages for their habitation, as time would admitte, they mette and consulted of lawes & orders, both for their civill & military Govermente, as the necessitie of their condition did require, still adding therunto as urgent occasion in severall times, and as cases did require.

In these hard & difficulte beginings they found some discontents & murmurings arise amongst some, and mutinous speeches & carriags in other; but they were soone quelled & overcome by the wisdome, patience, and just & equall carrage of things by the Govr and better part, wch clave faithfully togeather in the maine. But that which was most sadd & lamentable was, that in 2 or 3 moneths time halfe of their company dyed, espetialy in Jan: & February, being the depth of winter, and wanting houses & other comforts: being infected with the scurvie & other diseases, which this long vioage & their inacomodate condition had brought upon them; so as ther dyed some times 2 or 3 of a day, in the foresaid time; that of 100 & odd persons, scarce 50 remained. And of these in the time of most distres, ther was but 6 or 7 sound persons, who, to their great comendations be it spoken, spared no pains, night nor day, but with abundance of toyle and hazard of their owne health, fetched them woode, made them fires, drest them meat, made their beads, washed their lothsome cloaths, cloathed & uncloathed them; in a word, did all the homly & necessarie offices for them wch dainty & quesie stomacks cannot endure to hear named; and all this willingly & cherfully, without any grudging in the least, shewing herein their true love unto their freinds & bretheren. A rare example & worthy to be remembred. Tow of these 7 were Mr. William Brewster, ther reverend Elder, & Myles Standish, ther Captein & military comander, unto whom my selfe, & many others, were much beholden in our low & sicke condition. And yet the Lord so upheld these persons, as in this generall calamity they were not at all infected either with sicknes, or lamnes. And what I have said of these, I may say of many others who dyed in this generall vissitation, & others yet living, that whilst they had health, yea, or any strength continuing, they were not wanting to any that had need of them. And I doute not but their recompence is with the Lord.

But I may not hear pass by an other remarkable passage not to be forgotten. As this calamitie fell among the passengers that were to be left here to plant, and were hasted a shore and made to drinke water, that the sea-men might have the more bear, and one (which was this author him selfe) in his sicknes desiring but a small cann of beere, it was answered, that if he were their owne father he should have none; the disease begane to fall amongst them also, so as allmost halfe of their company dyed before they went away, and many of their officers and lustyest men, as the boatson, gunner, 3 quartermaisters, the cooke, & others. At wch the mr. [master] was something strucken and sent to the sick a shore and tould the Govr he should send for beer for them that had need of it, though he drunke water homward bound. But now amongst his company ther was farr another kind of carriage in this miserie then amongst the passengers; for they that before had been boone companions in drinking & joyllity in the time of their health & wellfare, begane now to deserte one another in this calamitie, saing they would not hasard ther lives for them, they should be infected by coming to help them in their cabins, and so, after they came to dye by it, would doe litle or nothing for them, but if they dyed let them dye. But shuch of the passengers as were yet abord shewed them what mercy they could wch made some of their harts relente, as the boatson (& some others), who was a prowd yonge man, and would often curse & scofe at the passengers; but when he grew weak, they had compassion on him and helped him; then he confessed he did not deserve it at their hands, he had abused them in word & deed. O! saith he, you, I now see, shew your love like Christians indeed one to another, but we let one another lye & dye like doggs. Another lay cursing his wife, saing if it had not ben for her he had never come this unlucky viage, and anone cursing his felows, saing he had done this & that, for some of them, he had spente so much, & so much, amongst them, and they were now weary of him, and did not help him, having need. Another gave his companion all he had, if he died, to help him in his weaknes; he went and got a litle spise & made him a mess of meat once or twise, and because he dyed not so soone as he expected, he went amonst his fellows, & swore the rogue would cousen him, he would see him choaked before he made him any more meate; and yet the pore fellow dyed before morning.

All this while the Indians came skulking about them, and would sometimes show them selves aloofe of, but when any aproached near them, they would rune away. And once they stoale away their tools wher they had been at worke, & were gone to diner. But about the 16 of *March* a certaine Indian came bouldly amongst them, and spoke to them in broken English, which they could well understand, but marvelled at it. At length they understood by discourse with him, that he was not of these parts, but belonged to the eastrene parts, wher some English-ships came to fish, with whom he was acquainted, & could name sundrie of them by their names, amongst whom he had gott his language. He became profitable to them in aquainting them with many things concerning the state of the cuntry in the east-parts wher he lived, which was afterwards profitable unto them; as also of the people hear, of their names, number, & strength; of their situation & distance from this place, and who was cheefe amongst them. His name was *Samaset*; he tould them also of another Indian whos name was *Squanto*, a native of this place, who had been in England & could speake better English then him selfe. Being, after some time of entertainmente & gifts, dismist, a while after he came againe, & 5 more with him, & they brought againe all the tooles that were stolen away before, and made way for the coming of their great Sachem, called *Massasoyt*; who, about *4 or 5 days after*, came with the cheefe of his freinds & other attendance, with the aforesaid *Squanto*. With whom, after frendly entertainment, & some gifts given him, they made a peace with him (which hath now continued this 24 years). . . .

4. ANDREW WHITE, *A RELATION OF THE COLONY OF THE LORD BARON OF BALTIMORE*, 1633*

Andrew White (1579–1656) was a London-born Jesuit who accompanied the first settlers to Maryland as a missionary. He originally wrote

* From William McSherry, S.J., "A Relation . . . by Father Andrew White," *Woodstock Letters* (Woodstock, Md. 1872), Vol. I, pp. 12–21. This source has the Latin text in the footnotes; see also Clayton Colman Hall, ed., *Original Narratives of Early American History: Narratives of Early Maryland: 1633–1684* (New York: Charles Scribner's Sons, 1910), pp. 3–10.

the following as Declaratio Coloniae Domini Baronis de Baltimore. *Ceci-
lius Calvert translated, revised, and circulated it to promote colonization.
Typical of such tracts, it emphasized the natural resources and potential
wealth of the New World.*

The province is near the English colony in Virginia, which, in
honor of his wife Maria, his most serene majesty of England wished to
be called Maryland, or the Land of Maria. This province, his most
serene majesty, in his munificence, lately, in the month of June, 1632,
gave to the Lord Baron of Baltimore and his heirs forever; which donation he secured, and has confirmed by the public seal of the whole realm.
Therefore the most illustrious Baron has resolved immediately to lead
a colony into that region; first, and especially, that into the same and
the neighboring places he may carry the light of the Gospel and of
truth where it has been found out that hitherto no knowledge of the true
God has shone; then, furthermore, with the design, that all the companions of his voyage and labors may be admitted to a participation of
the profits and honor, and that the empire of the realm may be more
widely extended.

For this enterprise, with all haste and diligence, he seeks companions of his voyage—as well those who have pledged themselves to
share his fortunes as others also. For the whole affair being carefully
considered, and the counsel of men eminent for experience and prudence
being called in, he has now weighed carefully and studiously all the
advantages and disadvantages which hitherto advanced or impeded
other colonies, and found nothing which does not greatly approve his
design and promise the most happy success.

For both the writings which his most noble father [George
Calvert] left behind him, an eye-witness, a gentleman of means, and
most worthy of credit, the uniform account of those who daily come and
go to us from thence, or not far from thence, as well as the things which
Captain Smith, who first discovered that country, most veritably wrote
and published, contain statements truly wonderful and almost unheard
of, in relation to the fertility and excellence of its soil. There is added
to this also, the common consent and testimony of innumerable men who
are here at London, and who are about to return to those parts from
which they sometimes since have come, who with one accord verify and
confirm what Smith has committed to writing.

Wherefore the most noble Baron, about to make sail, God help-
ing, unto those parts; and to those whom he shall obtain as companions
and supporters in an undertaking so illustrious, he makes the most ample
and liberal promises, of which this is first and especial, (to omit the titles
of honor and rank which are granted to fidelity, virtue, bravery and illustrious services,) that such gentlemen as shall pay down one hundred

pounds English to convey five men, (which sum shall be sufficient for arms and implements, for clothes and other necessary articles) whether it shall please them to join our company themselves, or otherwise accredit their men and money, to those who shall be charged with this duty or to any person whom they may commission to look after them and receive their division of lands,—to them and to their heirs forever, shall be assigned a possession of two thousand acres of good land. Besides these emoluments, if they offer themselves as companions in the first expedition, furthering our project, they shall obtain their share by no means small, in a profitable trade, (of which more hereafter,) with other privileges;—concerning all which things, when they come to the aforesaid Baron, they shall be made acquainted. But what has been before said of the one hundred pounds English, this may be also understood of a smaller or greater sum of money in proportion, whether from one person separately, or collected together and contributed by many.

The first and chief object of the illustrious Baron (which also ought to be the object of others who may be in the same ship) is, that in a land so fruitful shall be sown not so much the seeds of grain and fruit trees as of religion and piety; a design truly worthy of Christians, worthy of angels, worthy of Angles [Englishmen] than which England, renowned for so many ancient victories, has undertaken nothing more noble or more glorious. Behold the regions are white unto the harvest, prepared to receive into their fruitful bosom the seed of the Gospel. From thence they are sending, on all sides, messengers to seek for suitable men who may instruct the inhabitants in the doctrine of salvation and regenerate them in the sacred font.

There are present at this very time in the city, those who state that they have seen at Jamestown, in Virginia, messengers sent from their chiefs for this purpose, and infants carried to New England, that they might be washed in the waters of salvation. Who then can have a doubt, but that by this one work so glorious, many thousand souls may be led to Christ? I call the rescue and salvation of souls a glorious work, for that was the work of Christ the King of Glory. But since there are not to all the same ardor of mind and elevation of soul, so as to regard nothing but divine things, esteem nothing but heavenly things—inasmuch as most men regard rather pleasures, honors and wealth, as if in love with them—it has happened by some unseen power, or rather by the manifest remarkable wisdom of the Deity, that this one undertaking should embrace all inducements that affect men—emoluments of every kind.

It is admitted that the natural position of the country is the best and the most advantageous; for it extends towards the north to the thirty-eighth or fortieth degree of latitude, in the same position of place as Seville, Sicily and Jerusalem, and not unlike the best portions and

climate of Arabia Felix. The air is serene and mild, neither exposed to
the burning heat of Florida or ancient Virginia, nor withered by the
cold of New England, but has a medium temperature between the two—
enjoys the advantages of each, and is free from their inconveniences. On
the east it is washed by the ocean: on the west it adjoins an almost
boundless continent, which extends to the China sea.

There are two large arms of the sea, one on each side—bays
most abundant in fish. The one whose name is Chesapeake, is twelve
miles broad, and flowing between two regions, rolls from south to north
one hundred and sixty miles, is able to contain great navies, and is
marked by various large islands fit for grazing, where they fish actively
for shad. They call the other the Delaware, where, the entire year, there
is fishing for codfish, but not so profitable, except during the cold months,
as those which are rather warm prevent their being cured with salt, and
indeed this great plenty of fishing arises from this: the wind which sets
continually from the Canaries, between the north and the east, rolls the
earth and the fish with it to the Gulf of Mexico, where since it can
neither return again to the east nor the south, it is driven violently towards the north and sweeps in its tide, along the coast of Florida,
Virginia, Maryland and New England, a great multitude of fish which,
as they avoid the *cetacea*, fly to the shoal places where they are more
easily taken by the fishermen.

There are various and noble rivers, the chief of which they
call Patowomek, suitable for navigation, flowing one hundred and forty
miles towards the east, where a trade with the Indians is so profitable,
that a certain merchant, the last year, shipped beaver skins at a price,
of forty thousand pieces of gold, and the labor of traffic is compensated
by thirty-fold profit.

In the level and champagne country, there is a great abundance
of grass; but the region is for the most part shaded with forests; oaks and
walnut trees are the most common, and the oaks are so straight and
tall that beams can be made from them, sixty feet long, and two feet
and a half thick. Cypress trees will shoot up eighty feet before they
send forth branches, and three men with extended arms, scarcely en-
compassed them. The mulberry that feed the silk worms, are very common. There is also found an Indian grain which the Portuguese call
l'ove de l'hierva. Alders, ash trees and chestnuts, not inferior to those
which Spain, Italy and Gaul produce—cedars equal to those which
Lebanon boasts. What shall I say of the pine, laurel, fir, sassafras and
others, with various trees also which yield balsam and odoriferous gum,
—trees for all the most useful purposes—for architecture, for nautical
uses, for planks, for resin, pitch and terebinth, for mustard, for perfumes,
and for making cataplasms? But the woods are passable, not rough with

an undergrowth of thorns and shrubs, but formed by nature to afford food to beasts, and pleasure to men. There are grapes in abundance, from which wine can be pressed; some resemble cherries and have a thick and unctuous juice. The inhabitants call them chesamines. There are cherries equal to Damascus plums, and gages very much like ours. There are three kinds of plums. Mulberries, chesnuts, and walnuts are so abundant that they are used in various ways for food. Strawberries and esculent blackberries you will in like manner, find.

Of fishes, the following are already familiar: sturgeon, herrings, porpoises, craw-fish, torpedoes, trout, mullets of three kinds, urchins, roach, white salmon, periwinkles and others of that kind, of innumerable names, and unknown species. But so great is the abundance of swine and deer that they are rather troublesome than profitable. Cows, also, are innumerable and oxen suitable for bearing burdens or for food; besides five other kinds of large beasts unknown to us, which our neighbors use for the table. Sheep will have to be taken from the Canaries: asses, also, and mules. The neighboring forests are full of wild horses, bulls and cows, of which five or six hundred thousand are annually carried to Seville from the part of the country which lies towards New Mexico. As many goats as you wish can be obtained from the neighboring people. Add to this, muskrats, squirrels, beavers, ferrets and weasels, not however, destructive as with us to eggs and hens. Of the birds, the eagle is the most ravenous. Of hawks, there are various kinds which live in a great measure on fish. There are partridges, not larger than our quails, but almost infinite in number. Innumerable wild turkeys, which are double the size of our tame and domestic ones. There are also blackbirds, thrushes and a great many little birds of which there are various kinds, some red, some blue etc. The winter is plenteous in swans, geese, cranes, herons, ducks, creepers, green parrots, and many other birds unknown to our part of the world.

Lemons and quinces of the best quality grow there. Apricots are so abundant that an honest gentleman, and worthy of credit, positively affirmed he had cast, last year, an hundred bushels of them to the hogs. What shall I say of the lupines, beans, garden roots etc., most excellent in quality, when even the peas, in these places, grow in ten days, to a height of fourteen inches? The country is so fruitful in corn that, in the most barren places, it returns the seed twice an hundred fold; but in other places and generally, one grain yields five or six hundred grains. In the more productive years, there is a yield of from fifteen hundred to sixteen hundred fold, and this indeed during one harvesting, whereas the fertility of the soil affords three harvests. That I may presently draw to a close, it is very likely that the soil is adapted to all the fruits of Italy— figs, pomegranates, golden olives, etc.

Nor are there wanting things that may be of use to fullers and apothecaries; there is plently, also, of tin, iron, hemp and flax. There is hope, too, of finding gold; for the neighboring people wear bracelets of unwrought gold and long strings of pearls. Other advantages, both numerous and lucrative may be expected, which sagacious industry and long acquaintance will discover.

2

Religious Writings

5. JOHN COTTON, *TREATISE UPON CHURCH GOVERNMENT*, 1634*

John Cotton (1584–1652) was the beloved teacher and minister of the Massachusetts Bay Colony. Trained at Trinity College, Cambridge, he held the post of pastor to the Puritans of St. Botolph's Lincolnshire, but was forced to flee to America in 1633 because of his nonconformist practices. In Massachusetts he became one of the leading advisors to the government, and his catechism, Spiritual Milk for Babes, *enjoyed a wide reading in New England.*

His more formal writings were voluminous and difficult; they are replete with numerous citations in Greek, Hebrew, and Latin. The following selection, however, is more related to his catechism and is descriptive of the Anglican-Puritan mind. Cotton, like many of his contemporaries, wanted to reform the Church of England but remain within it. Thus, he outlined for Puritan communicants the church's organization and service, as he saw them.

Questions and Answers upon Church Government: 1634

Q. *What is the Church of God Ordained and Established in the New Testament?*

A. The Church of God is a Mystical Body, whereof Christ is the Head, and the Members be Saints, united together, in one Congregation, by

* John Cotton, *A Treatise of Faith . . . Questions and Answers upon Church Government* (Boston: B. Green, 1713), Part IV, pp. 19–28. The characteristically voluminous biblical citations have been deleted from this piece.

an Holy Covenant, to worship the Lord, & to Edify one another, in all his Holy Ordinances. . . .

Q. *What sorts of Members hath God set in his Church?*

A. Some of them are Ministers and Officers of the Church; others of them are commonly called by the general name of Brethren & Saints. . . .

Q. *What sorts of Ministers, or Officers, hath God set in his Church?*

A. The Ministers and Officers of the Church, are some of them Extraordinary, as Apostles, Prophets, Evangelists; some Ordinary, as Bishops, and Deacons. . . .

Q. *What sorts of Bishops, hath God Ordained in his Church?*

A. There are three sorts of them, according as there be three sorts of Elders in the Church, though under two heads; some Pastors, some Teachers, some Ruling Elders; that is to say, such Elders as labour in Word and Doctrine; and such as Rule the Church of God.

Q. *What manner of persons hath God Appointed to be called to the Office of a Bishop, or Elders, in the Church?*

A. A Bishop, or Elder, in the Church, must be himself blameless for Holiness and Righteousness, and of a clean heart from passions and lusts; at least blameless for passions and lust; also a vigilant man, and of good behaviour; also in his family of good government, and of good hospitality; in his Name of good report, of them that are without; in his Profession, not a young Plant, a young Christian; but holding forth the word of truth, apt to teach it, and to maintain it. . . .

Q. *What is the Work and Office of Pastors and Teachers?*

A. The Office of a Pastor, is to attend to Exhortation, and therein to Dispense a word of Wisdom. The Teacher is to attend unto Doctrine, and therein to attend to a word of Knowledge. . . .

Q. *What is the Office or Work of the Ruling Elder?*

A. Seeing the Kingdom of Christ is not of this World, but Heavenly and Spiritual; and the Government of his Kingdom is not Lordly, but Stewardly and Ministerial, and to labour in Administration of Exhortation and Doctrine, is the proper work of Pastor & Teacher: It remains to be the Office of the Ruling Elder, to assist the Pastor & Teacher, in all other Acts of Rule . . . besides, as becomes those Stewards of the Household of God. And therefore to put Instances: As, first, To open & shut the doors of God's House, by Admission of Members, by Ordination of Officers, by Excommunication of . . . obstinate Offenders. Secondly, To help those in the Church live inordinately without a Calling, or idly in their Calling. Thirdly, To prevent or heal Offences, either in Life or Doctrine, that might corrupt their own Church, or other Churches also, if their Counsel be required. Fourthly, to prepare Matters for the Church ['s] Consideration, and to moderate the carriage of things in the Church Assemblies; as to . . . Matters to the Church, and order [and] of Speech and Silence. Fifthly, to feed the Flock of God with a word of Admonition; and as they shall be called, to Visit and Pray over their Sick Brethren.

Q. *What manner of men hath God appointed to the Deacon Office?*

A. Men of Gravity, and of good Report; not given to disinhumnation, [*sic*] not to Wine, nor to Coveteousness; *Men full of the Holy Ghost and Wisdoms; and holding the Mystery of the Faith in a good Conscience, keeping their Household in a good Rule*; and injoyning, or having such Wives, as may neither dishonour, nor corrupt their Callings; no slanderers, but grave and sober, and faithful in all things, . . .

Q. *What is the Office of the Deacons?*

A. To Receive the Offerings of the Church which are brought into them, and laid down before them, and therewith to serve Tables, to distribute with simplicity, not only to the Ministers of the Church, but to any other of the brethren, that shall have use or need, . . .

Q. *But is it not also the Deacons Office to apply mercy with chearfulness?*

A. Yes, verily, to their Brethren in Misery; But that part of their Office, they chiefly perform by the hand of the Widows, which are Chosen into their number, who are therefore called Deaconess, or Servant of the Church, . . .

Q. *What manner of Widows hath God allowed to be Chosen into this number?*

A. Ancient Women, of Sixty Years of Age, well reported of for good works, for nursing their Children, lodging Strangers, washing the Saints Feet, for Relieving the Afflicted, and following diligently every good work, . . .

Q. *What manner of men are they whom God hath appointed to be received as Brethren and Members of the Church?*

A. Such as are Called of God out of the World, unto the Fellowship of Jesus Christ; and do willingly offer and joyn themselves, first to the Lord, and then to the Church, by Confession of their Sins, by profession of their Faith, and by laying hold of his Covenant, . . .

Q. *What is the Office of the Members or Brethren of the Church one toward another: Or, What is the Office or Duty God calls Brethren unto, the Members of the Church, as he is a Member which God calls all the Brethren unto.*

A. Brotherly Love, and the fruits thereof, Brotherly Unity, and Brotherly Equality; and Brotherly Communion.

Q. *Wherein stands that Brotherly Unity which the Members are to hold one with another?*

A. To be prefectly joyned together in one mind and one Judgment, and one speech, in one Truth; and when we cannot be of one Judgment, yet still to be of one heart, not provoking nor envying one another, but forbearing, and forgiving, not judging or despising one another, in differences of weakness; but so far as we are come to walk together, by the same Rule, and to teach and learn one another, the way of God more perfectly, . . . we all grow up in the unity of the faith, unto a perfect man in Christ Jesus, . . .

Q. *Wherein stands that Brotherly Equality we are to hold one with another?*

A. In submitting our selves alike to all the Ordinances of God and in Enjoying alike all Christian Liberties, in preferring others above ourselves, and in seeking one another's welfare, and feeling their Estate, as our own, in bearing one another's burdens in equal proportion; the summ is, Brotherly Equality stands in equal submission to all Gods Ordinances; in equal fruition of all Christian Liberties, in giving mutual honour alike, in seeking one another's welfare, equally in feeling one another's Estate as our own; and finally in applying our selves to one another's burthens as our own.

Q. *Wherein stands the Brotherly Communion the Members are to hold one with another?*

A. In being steadfast in the Apostles Doctrine & Worship and Ministration, and for this end to dwell together, to watch over one another, to Report together, to the Publick Assemblies, and there to joyn together in Holy Duties with one accord, and as God hath prospered them to lay up in store every Lords-Day, for the Supply of the Saints. . . .

Q. *What Worship and what part of it is first to be Administered when the Church is Assembled?*

A. The Apostles exhort first of all, All manner of Prayers to be made for all men, for Kings, and all that are in Authority; that we may lead a quiet and peaceable life, in all Godliness and Honesty, . . .

Q. *Whether are Forms of Publick Prayer Devised & Ordained by men, an acceptabel Service unto God?*

A. If such Forms of Prayer had been an Ordinance of the Lord, and an acceptable Service to him, doubtless *Paul* himself, or some of the Apostles would not have held back that part of God's Worship from the Church. Again, Publick Prayer is a part of Publick Ministry, as well as Prophesying, and the Form of the one, no more to be taught by the Precepts of men, than the other; & besides, both of them are alike, the Gift of the Holy Ghost, to whom it belongs as well to teach us what to Pray, as how to Pray: Nor will it well stand with the Holy gesture of Prayer, which is to lift up the Eyes to Heaven, to call down the Eyes in Prayer upon a Book.

Q. *What part of Gods Worship is next to be Administered after Prayer?*

A. Before Prophesying, it will be necessary to Sing a Psalm, and then by some of the Teaching Elders to read the Word, and with all Preaching to give the sense, and applying the use, in dispensing whereof the Ministers were wont to stand above all the people in a Pulpit of Wood, and the Elders on both sides, while the people hearkened to them with Reverence and Attention, and they may Prophesie by two or three, and let the other Judge. Also the Elders may call upon any of their Brethren, whether of their own Church or other Churches to speak a word of Exhortation to the People; and for the better Edifying a mans self or others, it may be lawful for any young or old, save only for women to ask questions at the mouth of the Minister. . . .

Q. *After the Ministry of the Word; what other part of God's Worship is next to be Administered?*

A. After the Word, which is the Covenant of God, the Seals of the Covenant are next to be administred, & as for Baptism, it is to be dispensed by a Minister of the Gospel, unto a Believer professing his Repentance and his Faith, being a Member of the same Church-Body, and likewise to his Seed, presented by the Parent, unto the Lord and his Church. At which time the Minister in God's room calleth upon the Parent, to Renew his Covenant with God, for himself and his Seed, and calleth upon God as the nature of the Ordinance requireth, for the pardon of Original Sin, and the Sin of the Parent, and likewise for a Blessing upon the Sacrament, and the Infant, and then calling the Child by that name the Parents hath given it, for their own Edification and the Childs; he baptizeth it, whether by dipping or sprinkling, in the Name of the Father, and of the Son, and of the Holy Ghost.

Q. *In what manner the Supper of the LORD is to be Administered?*

A. The Lord's Supper is to be Dispensed by a Minister of the Word, unto the Faithful of the same Body; or commended to them from a like Body; having examined & judged themselves and sitting down with them at the Lords Table, before whom the Minister breaks the Bread and blesseth it, taketh it, and giveth it to all the Brethren, with this Command, once for all, to take it, and eat it as the Body of Christ broken for them, and this to do in Remembrance of Christ: In like manner, he taketh the Cup, and having given thanks, he poureth it forth, and giveth it to them once for all, to take and drink it, as the Blood of Christ shed for them, and this do in Remembrance of Christ; after all he ends his Thanksgiving with Singing a Psalm.

Q. *How is the Collection for the Saints to be Administered?*

A. The Collection for the Saints is by the Apostles, ordered to be made for the time, every Lords Day for the measure as God hath prospered

every one, for manner not of Complaint, but willingly bro't as an
Offering to God, he laid down as at first before the Apostles; so after-
wards before the Deacons: And to be laid up as in a Common
Treasury, and by them, to be Distributed to the Supply of the
Ministers and poor Saints, according to their need, and all the Out-
ward Service of the Church. . . .

Q. *What Duty of God's Worship is to be Administered in the Dismissing
of the Assembly?*

A. After all the parts of God's Publick Worship have been Administered,
the Minister, or any of the Prophets is to Dismiss the Assembly with
a word of Blessing, offering Blessing unto the Lord, and putting a
Blessing upon his People. . . .

Q. *In what manner are the Publick Duties of God's Worship to be Administered in the Assemblies of the Saints in the Church?*

A. In Spiritual Simplicity, without affectation of Legal Shadows, or
Worldly Pomp, or Carnal Excellency, decently and in order, and to
Edification.

6. NATHANIEL WARD, *THE SIMPLE COBBLER OF AGGAWAM*, 1647[*]

*Nathaniel Ward (c. 1578–1652), lawyer and Puritan minister, was
educated in the law at Emmanuel College, Cambridge. His pastoral
calling came after thirteen years of legal practice. Dismissed from the
ministry by Archbishop Laud, he moved to Massachusetts in 1633, where
he quickly became one of the colony's most outstanding preachers and
scholars. He was responsible for the final version of the Massachusetts
code of laws, the "Body of Liberties." In 1647, Ward published* The
Simple Cobbler, *from which the following is taken. It reflects Massachusetts' growing alarm at the developing religious pluralism in the
mother country. Written in a vigorous style, its legal logic would have
done justice to John Calvin, also a lawyer turned theologian. The work
was influential in America, but not particularly so in England, where it
was chiefly aimed.*

*Ward's strictures on ladies' styles probably had little influence
anywhere.*

On Toleration

[Those who] have given or taken any unfriendly reports of us
New English, should doe well to recollect themselves. We have been

---

[*] Theodore de la Guard (Nathaniel Ward), *The Simple Cobbler of Agga-
wam in America* . . . , 5th ed. (Boston: Daniel Henchman, 1713), pp. 3–13, 29–31.
See reading selection #20, Roger Williams' *The Bloudy Tenent.* . . .

reputed [to be] a Collovies [gathering of filth] of wild Opinionists, swarmed into a remote wilderness to find elbow-room for our Phanatick Doctrines and Practises: I trust our diligence past, and constant sedulity against such persons and courses, will plead better things for us. I dare take upon me, to be the Herauld of *New-England* so far, as to proclaim to the World, in the name of our Colony, that all Familists, Antinomians, Anabaptists, and other Enthusiasts shall have free liberty to keep away from us, and such as will come to be gone as fast as they can, the sooner the better.

Secondly, I dare aver, that God doth no where in his word tolerate Christian States, to give Tolerations to such adversaries of his Truth, if they have power in their hands to suppress them.

Here is lately brought us an Extract of a *Magna Charta*, so called, compiled between the Sub planters of a *West-Indian* Island; whereof the first Article of constipulation, firmly provides free stable-room and litter for all kind of Consciences, be they never so dirty or jadish; making it actionable, yea, treasonable, to disturb any man in his Religion, or to dis-commend it, whatever it be. We are very sorry to see such professed Prophaneness in *English* Professors, as industriously to lay their Religious foundations on the ruine of true Religion; which thirdly binds every Conscience *to contend earnestly for the Truth: to preserve unity of Spirit, Faith and Ordinances, to be all like minded, of one accord; every man to take his Brother into his Christian care, to stand fast with one Spirit, with one mind, striving together for the faith of the Gospel;* and by no means to permit Heresies or Erronious Opinions: But God ab-horring such loathsome beverages, hath in his righteous judgment blasted that enterprize, which might otherwise have prospered well, for ought I know; I presume their case is generally known ere this.

If the Devil might have his free option, I believe he would ask nothing else, but liberty to enfrancize all false Religions, and to em-bondage the true; nor should he need: It is much to be feared, that lax Tolerations upon State-pretences and planting necessities, will be the next subtle Strategem he will spread to diflate the Truth of God, and supplant the Peace of the Churches. Tolerations in things tolerable, ex-quisitely drawn out by the lines of the Scripture, and pencil of the Spirit, are the sacred favours of Truth, the due latitudes of Love, the fair Compartments of Christian fraternity: but irregular dispensations, dealt forth by the facilities of men, are the frontiers of error, the re-doubts of Schisme, the perilous irricaments [wrath?] of carnal and spiritual enmity.

My heart hath naturally tested four things: The Standing of the Apocrypha in the Bible; Forainers dwelling in my Country, to crowd out Native Subjects into the corners of the Earth; Alchymized Coines; Tolerations of divers Religions, or of one Religion in segregant shapes;

He that willingly assents to the last, if he examines his heart by day-light, his Conscience will tell him, he is either an Atheist, or an Heretick, or an Hypocrite, or at best a captive to some Lust: Poly-piety is the greatest impiety in the World. True Religion is *Ignis probitatis*, which doth *congregare homogenea & egregare heterogenea.* [True Religion is a fire of testing, which doth bring together what is compatible and separate what is not.]

Not to tolerate things meerly indifferent to weak Consciences, argues a Conscience too strong: pressed uniformity in these, causes much disunity: To tolerate more than indifferents, is not to deal indifferently with God: He that doth it, takes his Scepter out of his hand, and bids him stand by. Who hath to do to institute Religion but God. The power of all Religion and Ordinances, lies in their Purity: their Purity in their Simplicity: then are mixtures pernicious. I lived in a City, where a Papist Preached in one Church, a Lutheran in another, a Calvinist in a third; a Lutheran one part of the day, a Calvinist the other, in the same Pulpit: the Religion of that Place was but motly and meagre, their affections Leopard-like.

If the whole Creature should conspire to do the Creator a mischief, or offer him an insolency, it would be in nothing more, than in erecting untruths against his Truth, or by sophisticating his Truths with humane medleys: the removing of some one iota in Scripture, may draw out all the life, and traverse all the Truth of the whole Bible: but to authorise an untruth, by a Toleration of State, is to build a Sconce against the walls of Heaven, to better God out of his Chair: To tell a practical lye, is a great Sin, but yet transient; but to set up a Theor[et]ical untruth, is to warrant every lye that lyes from its root to the top of every branch it hath, which are not few.

I would willingly hope that no Member of the Parliament hath skilfully ingratiated himself into the hearts of the House, that he might watch a time to Midwife out some ungracious Toleration for his own turn, and for the sake of that, some other, I would also hope that a word of general caution should not be particularly misapplied. I am the freer to suggest it, because I know not one many of that mind, my aim is general, and I desire may so be accepted. Yet good Gentlemen, look well about you, and remember how *Tiberias* pla'd the Fox with the Senate of *Rome*, and how *Fabius Maximus* cropt his ears for his cunning.

That State is wise, that will improve all pains and patience rather to compose, than tolerate differences in Religion. There is no divine Truth, but hath much Coelestial fire in it from the Spirit of Truth: nor no irreligious untruth without its propositions of antifire from the spirit of Error to contradict it: the zeal of the one, the virulency of the other, must necessarily kindle combustions. Fiery diseases seated in the Spirit, imbroil the whole frame of the body: others more external and cool, are less dangerous. They which divide in Religion, divide in God; they who divide in him, divide beyond *Genus Generalissimum*, where there is no reconciliation, without atonement; that is, without uniting in him, who is One, and in his Truth which is also one.

Wise are those men who will be perswaded rather to live within the pale of Truth, where they may be quiet, than in the purlieves, where they are sure to be hunted ever and anon, do Authority what it can. Every singular Opinion, hath a singular opinion of it self, and he that holds it a singular opinion of himself, and a simple opinion of all contra-sentients: he that confutes them, must confute all three at once, or else he does nothing; which will not be done without more stir than the Peace of the State or Church can indure.

And prudent are those Christians, that will rather give what may be given, than hazard all by yielding nothing. To sell all Peace of Country, to buy some Peace of Conscience unseasonably, is more avarice than thrift, imprudence than patience: they deal not equally, that set any Truth of God at such a rate; but they deal wisely that will stay till the Market is fallen.

My Prognostics deceive me not a little, if once within three seven years, Peace prove not such a Penny-worth at most Marts in Christendom, that he that would not lay down his Money, his Lust, his Opinion, his Will, I had almost said the best flower of his Crown for it, while he might have had it; will tell his own heart, he plaid the very ill Husband.

Concerning Tolerations, I may further assert.

That Persecution of true Religion, and Toleration of false, are the *Jannes* and *Jambres* to the Kingdom of Christ, whereof the last is far the worst. *Augustines* Tongue had not owed his Mouth one Penny-rent though he had never spake word more in it, but his, *Nullum malum pagus libertate errandi.* [There is no evil worse (*peius* for *pagus*) than the freedom to err.]

Frederick Duke of *Saxon*, spake not one foot beyond the mark when he said. He had rather the Earth should swallow him up quick, than he should give a toleration to any Opinion against any Truth of God.

He that is willing to tolerate any Religion, or discrepant way of Religion, besides his own, unless it be in matters meerly indifferent, either doubts of his own, or is not sincere in it.

He that is willing to tolerate any unfound Opinion, that his own may also be tolerated, though never so sound, will for a need hand Gods Bible at the Devils girdle.

Every Toleration of false Religions, or Opinions hath as many Errors and Sins in it, as all the false Religions and Opinions it tolerates, and one found one more.

That State that will give Liberty of Conscience in matters of Religion, must give Liberty of Conscence and Conversation in their Moral Laws, or else Fiddle will be out of Tune, and some of the strings crack.

He that will rather make an irreligious quarrel with other Religions than try the Truth of his own by valuable Arguments, and peaceable sufferings; either his Religion, or himself is irreligious.

Experience will teach Churches and Christians, that it is far better to live in a State united, though a little Corrupt, than in a State, whereof some Part is incorrupt, and all the rest divided.

I am not altogether ignorant of the eight Rules given by Orthodox Divines about giving Tolerations, yet with their favour I dare affirm.

That there is no Rule given by God for any State to Give an affirmative Toleration to any false Religion, or Opinion whatsoever; they must connive in some Cases, but may not concede in any.

That the State of *England* (so far as my Intelligence serves) might in time have prevented with ease, and may yet without any great difficulty deny both Toleration, and irregular conivences *salva Republica*. [With proper regard for the Republic.]

That if the State of *England* shall either willingly Tolerate, or weakly connive at such Courses, the Church of that Kingdom will sooner become the Devils dancing-School, than Gods Temple: The Civil State a Bear-garden, than an Exchange: the whole Realm a Pais base[r] than an *England*. And what pity it is, that that Country which hath been the Staple of Truth to all Christendom, should now become the Aviary of Errors to the whole World, let every fearing heart judge.

I take Liberty of Conscience to be nothing but a freedom from Sin, and Error. *Conscientia in tantum libera, inquantum ab errore liberata.* [Conscience is free in so far as it is free from error.] And Liberty of Error nothing but a Prison for Conscience. Then small will be the kindness of a State to build such Prisons for their Subjects.

The Scripture saith, there is nothing makes free but Truth, and Truth Saith, there is no Truth but one: If the States of the World would make it their sum-operous Care to preserve this One Truth in its purity and Authority, it would ease you of all other Political cares. I am sure Satan makes it his grand, if not only task, to adulterate Truth; Falshood is his sole Scepter, whereby he first ruffles, and ever since ruined the World.

If Truth be but One, methinks all the Opinionists in *England* should not be all in that One Truth, Some of them I doubt are out. He that can extract an unity out of such a disparity, or contract such a disparity into an unity; had need be a better Artist, than ever was Drebell.

If two Centers (as we may suppose) be in one Circle, and lines drawn from both to all the points of the Compass they will certainly cross one another, and probably cut through the Centers themselves.

There is talk of an universal Toleration, I would talk as loud as I could against it, did I know what more apt and reasonable Sacrifice *England* could offer to God for his late performing all his heavenly Truths than an universal Toleration of all hellish Errors, or how they shall make an universal Reformation, but by making Christ's Academy the Devils University, where any man may commence Heretick *per falsum*; [By a false doctrine] where he that is *Filius Diabolicus* [A son of the devil], or *simpliciter* [evil itself] . . . , may have his grace to go to Hell *cum Publico Privilegio* [by State Concession]; and carry as many after him as he can.

Religio docenda est, non coercenda [Religion must be taught, not forced] is a pretty piece of *album Latinum* [doctrine] for some kind of throats that are willingly sore, but *Haeresis dedocenda est non per mittenda* [teaching heresy must not be permitted], will be found a far better Diamoron for the Gargarismes this Age wants, if timely and thoroughly applyed.

If there be room in England for

Religious Men, but pernicious Hereticks	Good Spirits, but very Devils.
Familists	*Manes*
Libertines	*Lemures*
Erastians	*Dryades*
Antitrinitarians	*Homadryades*
Anabaptists	*Potamides*
Antiscripturists	*Naiades*
Arminians	*Hinnides*
Manifestarians	*Picrides*
Millinarians	*Nereides*
Antinomians	*Pales*
Socinians	*Anonides*
Arrians	*Parcades*
Perfectists	*Castalides*
Brownists	*Monides*
Mortalians	*Charites*
Seekers	*Heliconides*
Enthusiasts,	*Pegafides.*
&c.	&c.

In a word room for Hell above ground.
It is said, Though a man have light enough himself to see the

Truth, yet if he hath not enough to enlighten others, he is bound to tolerate them, I will engage my self, that all the Devils in *Britanie* shall sell themselves to their shirts, to purchase a Lease of this Position for three of their Lives, under the Seal of the Parliament.

It is said, That Men ought to have Liberty of their Conscience, and that it is Persecution to debar them of it: I can rather stand amazed than reply to this: it is an astonishment to think that the braines of men should be parboyl'd in such impious ignorance. . . .

On Women's Fashions

Should I not keep Promise in speaking a little to Women's fashions, they would take it unkindly. I was loath to pester better matter with such stuff; I rather thought it meet to let them stand by themselves, like the *Quae Genus* in the Grammar, being Deficients, or Redundants, not to be brought under any Rule: I shall therefore make bold for this once to borrow a little of their loose-tongued liberty, and mispend a word or two upon their long-waisted but short-skirted patience. A little use of my stirrup will do no harm.

Ridentem dicere verum, quid prohibet? [What is to prevent speaking the truth with a smile?]

> *Gray gravity itself can well beteam*
> *That language be adapted to the theme.*
> *He that to parrots speaks, must parrotize;*
> *He that instructs a fool, may act th' unwise.*

It is known more than enough that I am neither Niggard nor cinick to the due bravery of the true Gentry; if any man mislikes a bullimong drassock more than I, let him take her for his labor; I honour the Woman that can honour herself with her attire; a good Text always deserves a fair Margent; I am not much offended if I see a trimme far trimmer than she that wears it; in a word, whatever Christianity or Civility will allow, I can afford with *London* measure. But when I hear a nugiperous Gentledame inquire what dress the Queen is in this week, what the nudiustertian fashion of the court, with edge to be in it in all haste, whatever it be; I look at her as the very gizzard of a trifle, the product of a quarter of a cipher, the epitome of nothing, fitter to be kickt, if she were of a kickable substance, than either honor'd or humor'd.

To speak moderately, I truly confess it is beyond the ken of my understanding to conceive how those Women should have any true Grace or valuable virtue that have so little wit as to disfigure themselves with such exotic garbs as not only dismantles their native lovely lustre but transclouts them into gantbar-geese, ill-shapen, shotten shellfish, Egyptian Hyeroglyphicks, or at the best into French flirts of the pastry, which a proper English Woman should scorn with her heels: it is no marvel they wear drails on the hinder part of their heads, having nothing as it seems in the fore part but a few Squirr'ls' brains to help them frisk from one ill-favored fashion to another.

> These whim-crowned shes, these fashion-
> fancying wits,
> Are empty thin-brained shells and fiddling
> kits.

The very troublers and impoverishers of mankind; I can hardly forbear to commend to the World a saying of a Lady living sometime with the Queen of *Bohemia;* I know not where she found it, but it is pity it should be lost.

> The world is full of care, much like unto a
> bubble,
> Women and care, and care and Women, and
> Women and care and trouble.

7. WILLIAM PENN, *SOME FRUITS OF SOLITUDE*, 1693*

William Penn (1644–1718) was an intellectual, minister, imperialist, and Quaker; Some Fruits of Solitude *shows him in several of these roles. It offers insights into the reflections and attitudes of Quakers (also called Friends), and it presents a method of developing the pious life—the "Inner Plantation," as George Fox had termed it. Penn's work not only brought the English Friends to America but also appealed directly to the pietistic and mystical sects of Europe, particularly the Germans of the Palatinate and Würtemburg—Mennonites and Moravians who, oppressed by Catholic overlords, repaired for sanctuary to Pennsylvania, founded by Penn in 1681. Penn's writings, while deeply religious, also prescribe a practical mode of conduct for worldly affairs which made the Quakers incomparable businessmen. His maxims, composed during the period when he had temporarily lost the proprietorship of his colony because of his friendship with the deposed Stuarts, have a practical tone which anticipates the naturalism of the eighteenth century.*

Reflections and Maxims Relating to the Conduct of Human Life

1. *Ignorance.* It is admirable to consider how many *Millions* of People come into, and go out of the World, *Ignorant of themselves,* and of the World they have lived in.

* William Penn, *Some Fruits of Solitude* (Boston: H. M. Caldwell, 1903), pp. 33–46, 53–62.

2. If one went to see *Windsor-Castle*, or *Hampton-Court*, it would be strange not to observe and remember the Situation, the Building, the Gardens, Fountains, &c. that make up the Beauty and Pleasure of such a Seat: And yet few People know *themselves*; No, not their *own Bodies*, the *Houses* of their Minds; The *Most curious* Structure of the World; a *living Walking* Tabernacle: Nor the *World* of which it was made, and out of which it is fed, which would be so much our Benefit, as well our Pleasure, to know. We cannot Doubt of this when we are told that the *Invisible Things of God are brought to light by the Things that are seen*; and consequently we read our Duty in them, as often as we look upon them, to him that is the Great and Wise Author of them if we look as we should do.

3. The *World* is certainly a great and stately *Volume* of natural Things; and may be not improperly stiled the *Hieroglyphicks* of a better; But, alas! how very few Leaves of it doe we seriously turn over! This ought to be the *Subject* of the Education of our *Youth*, who, at Twenty, when they should be fit for Business, know little or nothing of it.

4. *Education.* We are in Pain to make them Scholars, but not *Men*! To talk, rather than to know; which is true *Canting*.

5. The first Thing obvious to Children is what is *sensible*; and that we make no Part of their Rudiments.

6. We press their Memory too soon, and puzzle, strain and load them with Words and Rules; to know *Grammar* and *Rhetorick*, and a strange Tongue or two, that is ten to one may never be useful to them; leaving their natural *Genius* to *Mechanical* and *Physical* or natural Knowledge uncultivated and neglected; which would be of exceeding Use and Pleasure to them through the whole Course of their Life.

7. To be sure, Languages are not to be despised or neglected. But Things are still to be preferred.

8. Children had rather be making of *Tools* and *Instruments* of Play; *Shaping, Drawing, Framing* and *Building*, &c., than getting some Rules of Propriety of Speech by Heart: And those also would follow with more Judgment, and less Trouble and Time.

9. It were Happy if we studied Nature more in natural Things; and acted according to Nature; whose Rules are *few, plain and most reasonable.*

10. Let us begin where she begins, go her Pace, and close always where she ends, and we cannot miss of being good *Naturalists.*

11. The Creation would not be longer a Riddle to us: The *Heavens, Earth* and *Waters*, with their respective, various and numerous Inhabitants: Their Productions, Natures, Seasons, Sympathies and Antipathies; their Use, Benefit and Pleasure, would be better under-

stood by us: And an *Eternal Wisdom, Power, Majesty* and *Goodness,* very *conspicuous* to us; thro' those sensible and passing Forms: The World wearing the *Mark* of it's Maker, whose Stamp is every where *visible,* and the *Characters* very *legible* to the Children of *Wisdom.*

12. And it would go a great Way to caution and direct People in their Use of the World, that they were better studied and knowing in the Creation of it.

13. For how could Man find the Confidence to abuse it, while they should see the Great Creator stare them in the Face, in all and every Part thereof?

14. Therefore Ignorance makes them insensible, and that Insensibility hardly in misusing this noble Creation, that has the Stamp and Voice of a Deity every where, and in every Thing, to the Observing.

15. It is pity therefore that Books have not been composed for *Youth,* by some curious and careful *Naturalists,* and also *Mechanicks,* in the *Latin* tongue, to be used in Schools, that they might learn Things with Words: Things *obvious* and *familiar* to them, and which would make the Tongue easier to be attained by them.

16. Many able *Gardeners* and *Husbandmen* are yet ignorant of the *Reason* of their Calling; as most *Artificers* are of the Reason of their own Rules that govern their excellent Workmanship. But a Naturalist and Mechanick of this Sort, is *Master* of the Reason of both, and might be of the Practice too, if his Industry kept Pace with his Speculation; which were very commendable; and without which he cannot be said to be a *complete* Naturalist or Mechanick.

17. Finally, if Man be the *Index* or *Epitomy* of the World, as *Philosophers* tell us, we have only to read our *selves* well to be *learned* in it. But because there is nothing we less regard than the *Characters* of the Power that made us, which are so clearly written upon us and the World he has given us, and can best tell us what we are and should be, we are even Strangers to our own *Genius*: The *Glass* in which we should see that true instructing and agreeable Variety, which is to be observed in Nature, to the Admiration of that Wisdom and Adoration of that Power which made us all.

18. *Pride.* And yet we are very apt to be *full* of our selves, instead of *Him* that made what we so much value; and, but for whom we can have no Reason to value our selves. For we have nothing that we can call our own; no, not our selves: For we are all but *Tenants,* and at *Will* too, of the great Lord of our selves, and the rest of this great Farm, the World that we live upon.

19. But methinks we cannot answer it to our Selves as well as our Maker, that we should live and die ignorant of our Selves, and thereby of Him and the Obligations we are under to Him for our Selves.

20. If the worth of a Gift sets the Obligation, and directs the Return of the Party that receives it: he that is ignorant of it, will be at a loss to value it and the Giver, for it.

21. Here is Man in his Ignorance of himself. He knows not how to estimate his Creator, because he knows not how to value his Creation. If we consider his Make, and lovely Compositure; the several stories of his lovely Structure. His divers Members, their Order, Function and Dependency: The Instruments of Food, the Vessels of Digestion, the several Transmutations it passes. And how Nourishment is carried and difused throughout the whole Body, by most innate and imperceptible Passages. How the Animal Spirit is thereby refreshed, and with an unspeakable Dexterity and Motion sets all Parts at work to feed themselves. And last of all, how the Rational Soul is seated in the Animal, as its proper House, as is the Animal in the Body; I say, if this rare Fabrick alone were but considered by us, with all the rest by which it is fed and comforted, surely Man would have a more reverent Sense of the Power, Wisdom and Goodness of God, and of that Duty he owes to Him for it. But if he would be acquainted with his own Soul, its noble Faculties, its Union with the Body, its Nature and End, and the Providences by which the whole Frame of Humanity is preserved, he would Admire and Adore his Good and Great God. But Man is become a strange *Contradiction* to himself; but it is of himself: Not being by Constitution, but *Corruption* such.

22. He would have others obey him, even his own kind; but he will not obey God, that is so much above him, and who made him.

23. He will lose none of his Authority; no, not bate an Ace of it; He is humorous to his Wife, he beats his Children, is angry with his Servants, strict with his Neighbours, revenges all Affronts to Extremity; but, alas forgets all the while that *he is the Man*; and is more in *Arrear* to God, that is so very patient with him, than they are to him with whom he is so strict and impatient.

24. He is curious to *wash, dress* and *perfume* his Body, but *careless* of his Soul. The one shall have many Hours, the other not so many Minutes. This shall have three or four new Suits in a Year, but that must wear *its old Cloaths* still.

25. If he be to receive or see a great Man, how nice and anxious is he that all Things be in Order? And with what Respect and Address does he approach and make his Court? but to God, how *dry* and *formal* and *constrained* in his Devotion?

26. In his Prayers he says, *Thy Will be done*: But means his own: At least acts so.

27. It is too frequent to begin with God and end with the *World*. But He is the good Man's *Beginning* and *End*; His *Alpha* and *Omega*.

28. *Luxury.* Such is now become our Delicacy, that we will not eat ordinary Meat, nor drink small, pall'd Liquor; we must have the best, and the best cook'd for our Bodies, while our Souls feed on *empty* or *corrupted* Things.

29. In short, Man is *spending* all upon a *bare* House, and hath little or no Furniture within to recommend it; which is preferring the Cabinet before the Jewel, a Lease of seven Years before an Inheritance. So *absurd* a thing is Man, after all his proud Pretences to Wit and Understanding. . . .

47. *Bounds of Charity.* Lend not *beyond* thy Ability, nor *refuse* to lend out of thy Ability: especially when it will help others *more than it can hurt thee.*

48. If thy Debtor be honest and capable, thou hast thy mony again, if not with Encrease, with Praise; if he prove insolvent, don't ruin him to get that, *which it will not ruin thee to lose*: For thou art but a *Steward*, and another is thy Owner, Master and Judge.

49. The more merciful Acts thou dost, the more Mercy thou wilt *receive*; and if with a *charitable* Imployment of thy Temporal Riches, thou gainest *Eternal* Treasure, thy Purchase is *infinite*: Thou wilt have found the Art of *Multiplying* indeed.

50. *Frugality or Bounty. Frugality* is good, if *Liberality* be joyn'd with it. The first is *leaving off* superfluous Expences; the last *bestowing* them to the *Benefit* of others that need. The first without the last *begins Covetousness*; the last without the first begins *Prodigality*: Both together make an *excellent Temper.* Happy the Place where-ever that is found.

51. Were it universal, we should be Cur'd of two Extreams, *Want* and *Excess*: And the one would supply the other, and so bring both nearer to a *Mean*; the just Degree of earthly Happiness.

52. It is a Reproach to Religion and Government to suffer so much Poverty and Excess.

53. Were the *Superfluities* of a Nation valued, and made a perpetual Tax or *Benevolence*, there would be more Alms-houses than Poor; Schools than Scholars; and *enough to spare* for Government besides.

54. Hospitality is good, if the poorer Sort are the *Subjects* of our Bounty; else too near a superfluity. . . .

57. *Industry.* Love *Labour*: For if thou dost not want it for Food, thou mayest it for *Physick*. It is *wholesom*, for thy *Body*, and good for the Mind. It *prevents* the Fruits of Idleness, which many times comes of nothing to do, and leads too many to do what is *worse* than nothing.

58. A *Garden, an Elaboratory*, a *Work-house, Improvements* and *Breeding*, are pleasant, and profitable Diversions to the Idle and the Ingenious: For here they *miss* Ill Company, and converse with *Na-*

ture and *Art*; whose Variety are equally grateful and instructing; and preserve a good *Constitution* of Body and Mind.

59. *Temperance.* To this a *spare* Diet contributes much. Eat therefore to *live*, and do not live to eat. That's like a *Man*, but this below a *Beast.*

60. Have wholesome, but not *costly* Food, and be rather cleanly than *dainty* in ordering it.

61. The *Receipts* of Cookery are swell'd to a Volume, but a *good Stomach* excels them all; to which nothing contributes more than *Industry* and *Temperance.*

62. It is a cruel Folly to offer up to *Ostentation* so many Lives of Creatures, as make up the State of our Treats; as it is a prodigal one to spend more in *Sawce* than in Meat.

63. The Proverb says, *That enough is as good as a Feast*: But it is certainly better, if Superfluity be a Fault, which never fails to be at Festivals.

64. If thou rise with an Appetite, thou are sure never to sit down without one.

65. Rarely drink but when thou art *dry*; not then, between Meals, if it can be avoided.

66. The *smaller* the Drink, the *clearer* the Head, and the *cooler* the Blood; which are great Benefits in Temper and Business.

67. Strong Liquors are good at some Times, and in small Proportions; being better for *Physick* than Food, for *Cordials* than common Use.

68. The most *common* Things are the most *useful*; which shews both the *Wisdom* and *Goodness* of the Great Lord of the Family of the World.

69. What therefore he has made rare, don't thou use *too commonly*; Lest thou shouldest invert the Use and Order of things; become Wanton and Voluptuous; and thy Blessings prove a *Curse.*

70. *Let nothing be lost*, said our Saviour. But that is *lost* that is *misused.*

71. Neither urge another to that thou wouldst be unwilling to do thyself, nor do thy self what looks to thee *unseemly*, and intemperate in another.

72. All Excess is ill; but *Drunkenness* is of the worst Sort: It *spoils* Health, *dismounts* the Mind, and unmans Men: It *reveals Secrets*, is *Quarrelsome, Lascivious, Imprudent, Dangerous* and *Mad*; In fine, he that is Drunk is not a Man; Because he is so long void of *Reason*, that distinguishes a Man from a Beast.

73. *Apparel.* Excess in Apparel is another costly Folly. The very Trimming of the vain World would cloath all the *naked* One.

74. Chuse thy Cloaths by thine own Eyes, not anothers. The more plain

and simple they are, the better. Neither unshapely nor fantastical, and for Use and Decency, and not for Pride.

75. If thou art clean and warm, it is sufficient; for more doth but rob the *Poor*, and please the *Wanton*.

76. It is said of the true Church, *The King's Daughter is all glorious within*. Let our Care therefore be of our Minds more than of our Bodies, if we would be of her Communion.

77. We are told with Truth, that *Meekness* and *Modesty* are the Rich and Charming Attire of the Soul: And the plainer the Dress, the more distinctly, and with greater Lustre, their Beauty shines. . . .

3

Education

8. THE MASSACHUSETTS SCHOOL LAWS OF 1642 AND 1647*

In 1642, the Massachusetts General Court enacted the earliest known law on education in the American colonies. This and later laws established the community's responsibility to educate the young. The act of 1647, known as the "old deluder Satan" law, was especially aimed against heresy, which Puritans believed originated in ignorance, and was the model for a number of similar bills in the New England colonies.

Law of 1642

This Cort, taking into consideration the great neglect of many parents & masters in training up their children in learning, & labor, & other implyments which may be proffitable to the common wealth, do hereupon order and decree, that in every towne the chosen men appointed for managing the prudentiall affaires of the same shall henceforth stand charged with the care of the redresse of this evill, so as they shall bee sufficiently punished by fines for the neglect thereof, upon presentment of the grand jury, or other information or complaint in any Court within this jurisdiction; and for this end they, or the greater number of them, shall have power to take account from time to time of all parents and masters, and of their children, concerning their calling and implyment of their children, especially of their ability to read and understand the principles of religion & the capitall laws of this country, and to impose fines upon such as shall refuse to render such accounts to

* *Records of the Governor and Company of Massachusetts Bay in New England*, Nathaniel B. Shurtleff, ed. (Boston: W. White, 1853–54), Vol. II, pp. 8–9, 203.

them when they shall be required; and they shall have power, with consent of any Court or the magistrate, to put forth apprentices the children of such as they shall find not to be able & fitt to imploy and bring them up, nor shall take courses to dispose of them themselves; & they are to take care that such as are to set to keep cattle bee set to some other impliment withall, as spinning up on the rock, knitting weveing tape, . . . & that boyes and girles be not suffered to converse together, so as may occasion any wanton, dishonest, or immodest behaviour; & for their better performance of this trust committed to them, they may divide the towne amongst them, appointing to every of the said townesmen a certaine number of families to have special oversight of. They are also to provide that a sufficient quantity of materialls, as hemp, flaxe, ecra, may be raised in their severall townes, & tooles & implements provided for working out the same; & for their assistance in this so needfull and beneficiall imploymt, if they meete with any difficulty or opposition wch they cannot well master by their own power, they may have recorse to some of the matrats, [magistrates] who shall take such course for their help and incuragmt as the occasion shall require according to justice; & the said townesmen, at the next Cort in those limits, after the end of their year, shall give a briefe account in writing of their proceedings herein, provided that they have bene so required by some Cort or magistrate a month at least before; & this order to continew for two yeares, & till the Cort shall take further order.

Law of 1647

It being one cheife project of the ould deluder, Satan, to keepe men from the knowledge of the Scriptures, as in former times by keeping them in an unknowne tongue, so in these latter times by perswading from the use of tongues, that so at least the true sence and meaning of the originall might be clouded by false glosses of saint seeming deceivers, that learning may not be buried in the grave of or fathrs in the church and commonwealth, the Lord assisting or endeavors.

It is therefore ordred, that evry towneship in this jurisdiction, after the Lord hath increased the number to 50 householdrs, shall then forthwith appoint one wth in their towne to teach all such children as shall resort to him to write & reade, whose wages shall be paid eithr by the parents or mastrs of such childen, or by the inhabitants in genrall, by way of supply as provided, those that send their children be not oppressed by paying much more than they can have them taught for in othr townes; & it is furthr ordered, that where any towne shall increase to the numbr of 100 familes or householdrs, they shall set up a grammar schoole, the mr thereof being able to instruct youth so farr as they shall be fited for the university, provided that if any town neglect the

performance hereof abouve one yeare, that every such towne shall pay
5£ to the next schoole till they shall performe this order.

9. *THE NEW ENGLAND PRIMER, 1683*[*]

*Every English and colonial youngster began his school life with
the hornbook, a sheet printed with the alphabet, the Lord's Prayer, and
Roman numerals mounted upon a board with a handle. The little scholars
started with this challenge to mind and bottom as early as two years of
age. Other books used for elementary learning were a speller and a catechism, doubtless Cotton's* Spiritual Milk for Babes. *But by far the most
popular teaching tool was the primer, first mentioned in an English bookseller's list of 1683. Hundreds of editions were printed and circulated in
Puritan as well as non-Puritan colonies, each community of parents revising the work in accordance with its own particular beliefs and needs. The
following is an early eighteenth-century edition in which remnants of
older editions persist.*

The Alphabet

A   In Adam's Fall
      We Sinned All.

B   Thy Life to Mend
      This Book Attend.

F   The Idle Fool
      Is whipt at School.

J   Job feels the Rod
      Yet blesses God.

K   Queens and KINGS
      Are gaudy things.

P   Peter denies
      His Lord and cries.

T   Time cuts down all
      Both great and small.

U   Uriah's beauteous wife
      Made David seek his life.

Z   Zacheus he
      Did climb the Tree
      His Lord to see.

[*] *The New England Primer Enlarged* (Boston: S. Kneeland & T. Green,
1727). This edition was not paginated.

The Dutiful Child's Promise

Now the child being entred in his letters and spelling, let him learn these and such like Sentences by Heart, whereby he will be both instructed in his Duty, and encouraged in his Learning.

I will fear GOD and honour the KING.

I will honour my Father and Mother.

I will obey my Superiors.

I will submit to my Elders.

I will Love my Friends.

I will hate no Man.

I will forgive my enemies, and Pray to God for them.

I will as much as in me lies keep all God's Holy Commandments.

10. *NEW ENGLAND'S FIRST FRUITS,* HARVARD COLLEGE, 1643*

This piece was part of a promotional tract to encourage Puritan migration to Massachusetts by describing the great strides the colony had made in higher education. It is generally acknowledged to have been written by Henry Dunster (1609–59?), the second president of Harvard, who had fled England in 1640, and it outlines the curriculum of the college in its infancy.

Educated at Magdalene College, Cambridge, Dunster was much admired by the Puritans for his teaching and scholarship. His capable administration of Harvard—he secured its present charter in 1650—and his generosity to the college insured its survival. But, in 1653, Dunster converted to Baptism and the Board of Overseers condemned his heresy and removed him from the presidency.

1. In Respect of the Colledge, and the Proceedings of *Learning* Therein

1. After God had carried us safe to *New England,* and wee had builded our houses, provided necessaries for our liveli-hood, rear'd convenient places for Gods worship, and setled the Civill Government: One of the next things we longed for, and looked after was to advance *Learning* and perpetuate it to Posterity; dreading to leave an illiterate

* *Old South Leaflets,* General Series (Boston: Directors of the Old South Work, [1896–19   ]), Vol. III, No. 51, pp. 1–6.

Ministery to the Churches, when our present Ministers shall lie in the Dust. And as wee were thinking and consulting how to effect this great Work; it pleased God to stir up the heart of one Mr. *Harvard* (a godly Gentleman, and a lover of learning, there living amongst us) to give the one halfe of his Estate (it being in all about 1700 £.) towards the erecting of a Colledge, and all his Library: after him another gave 300 £. others after them cast in more, and the publique hand of the State added the rest: the Colledge was, by common consent, appointed to be at *Cambridge,* (a place very pleasant and accomodate) and is called (according to the name of the first founder) *Harvard Colledge.*

The Edifice is very faire and comely within and without, having in it a spacious Hall; (where they daily meet at Common Lectures) Exercises, and a large Library with some Bookes to it, the gifts of diverse of our friends, their Chambers and studies also fitted for, and possessed by the Students, and all other roomes of Office necessary and convenient, with all needfull, Offices thereto belonging: And by the side of the Colledge a faire *Grammar* Schoole, for the training up of young Schollars, and fitting of them for *Academicall Learning*, that still as they are judges ripe, they may be received into the Colledge of this Schoole: Master *Corlet* is the Mr., who hath very well approved himselfe for his abilities, dexterity and painfulness, in teaching and education of the youth under him.

Over the Colledge is master *Dunster* placed, as President, a learned conscionable and industrious man, who hath so trained up, his Pupills in the tongues and Arts, and so seasoned them with the principles of Divinity and Christianity, that we have to our great comfort, (and in truth) beyond our hopes, beheld their progresse in Learning and godlinesse also; the former of these hath apeared in their publique declamations in *Latine* and *Greeke*, and Disputation Logicall and Philosophicall, which they have beene wonted (besides their ordinary Exercises in the Colledge-Hall) in the audience of the Magistrates, Ministers, and other Schollars, for the probation of their growth in Learning, upon set dayes, constantly once every moneth to make and uphold: The latter hath been manifested in sundry of them by the savoury breathings of their Spirits in their godly conversation. Insomuch that we are confident, if these early blossomes may be cherished and warmed with the influence of the friends of Learning and lovers of this pious worke, they will be the help of God, come to happy maturity in a short time.

Over the Colledge are twelve Overseers chosen by the generall Court, six of them are of the Magistrates, the other six of the Ministers, who are to promote the best good of it, and (having a power of influence into all persons in it) are to see that every one be diligent and proficient in his proper place.

2. Rules, and Precepts that are observed in the Colledge

1. When any Schollare is able to understand *Tully*, or such like classical Latine Author *extempore*, and make and speake true Latine in Verse and Prose, *suo ut aiunt Marte*; And decline perfectly the Paradigm's of *Nounes* and *Verbes* in the *Greek* tongue: Let him then and not before be capable of admission into the Colledge.

2. Let every Student be plainly instructed, and earnestly pressed to consider well, the maine end of his life and studies is, *to know God and Jesus Christ which is eternall life*, Joh. 17. 3. and therefore to lay *Christ* in the bottome, as the only foundation of all sound knowledge and Learning.

And seeing the Lord only giveth wisedome, Let every one seriously set himselfe by prayer in secret to seeke it of him Prov. 2, 3.

3. Every one shall so exercise himselfe in reading the Scriptures twice a day, that he shall be ready to give such an account of his proficiency therein, both in *Theoreticall* observations of the Language, and *Logick*, and in *Practicall* and spirituall truths, as his Tutor shall require, according to his ability; seeing *the entrance of the word giveth light, it giveth understanding to the simple, Psalm.* 119. 130.

4. That they eshewing all profanation of Gods Name, Attributes, Word, Ordinances and times of Worship, doe studie with good conscience, carefully to retaine God, and the love of his truth in their mindes, also let them know, that (notwithstanding their Learning) God may give them up *to strong delusions*, and in the end *to a reprobate minde*, 2 thes. 2. 11, 12. Rom. I. 28

5. That they studiously redeeme the time; observe the generall houres appointed for all the Students, and the speciall houres for their owne *Classes*: and then diligently attend the Lectures, without any disturbance by word or gesture. And if in anything they doubt, they shall enquire, as to their fellowes, so, (in case of *Non satisfaction*) modestly of their Tutors.

6. None shall under any pretence whatsoever, frequent the company and society of such men as lead an unfit, and dissolute life.

Nor shall any without his Tutors leave, or (in his absence) the call of Parents or Guardians, goe abroad to other Townes.

7. Every Schollar shall be present in his Tutors chamber at the 7th. houre in the morning, immediately after the sound of the Bell, at his opening the Scripture and prayer, so also at the 5th. houre at night, and then give account of his owne private reading, as aforesaid in Particular the third, and constantly attend Lectures in the Hall at the houres

appointed. But if any (without necessary impediment) shall absent himself from prayer or Lectures, he shall bee lyable to Admonition, if he offend above once a week.

8. If any Schollar shall be found to transgresse any of the Lawes of God, or the Schoole, after twice Admonition, he shall be lyable, if not adultus, to correction, if adultus, his name shall be given up to the Overseers of the Colledge, that he may bee admonished at the publick monthely Act.

3. The times and order of their Studies, unlesse experience shall shew cause to alter

The second and third day of the weeke, read Lectures, as followeth.

To the first yeare at 8th. of the clock in the morning *Logick*, the first three quarters, *Physicks* the last quarter.

To the second yeare at the 9th. houre, *Ethicks* and *Politicks*, at convenient distances of time.

To the third yeare at the 10th. *Arithmetick* and *Geometry*, the three first quarters, *Astronomy* the last.

Afternoone

The first yeare disputes at the second houre.
The 2d. yeare at the 3d. houre.
The 3d. yeare at the 4th. every one in his Art.

The 4th. day reads Greeke

To the first yeare the *Etymologie* and *Syntax* at the eigth houre.
To the 2d. at the 9th. houre, *Prosodia* and *Dialects*.

Afternoone

The first yeare at 2d houre practice the precepts of *Grammar* in such Authors as have variety of words.

The 2d. yeare at 3d. houre practice in *Poësy, Nonnus, Duport,* or the like.

The 3d yeare perfect their *Theory* before noone, and exercise *Style, Composition, Imitation, Epitome,* both in Prose and Verse, afternoone.

The fift day reads Hebrew, and the Easterne Tongues

Grammar to the first yeare houre the 8th.
To the 2d. *Chaldee* at the 9th. houre.
To the 3d. *Syriack* at the 10th. houre.

Afternoone

The first yeare practice in the Bible at the 2d. houre.
The 2d. in *Ezra* and *Danel* at the 3d. houre.
The 3d. at the 4th. houre in *Trestius* New Testament.

The 6th. day reads Rhetorick to all at the 8th. houre

Declamations at the 9th. So ordered that every Scholler may de-
claime once a moneth. The rest of the day *vacat Rhetoricis studiis.*

The 7th. day reads Divinity Catecheticall at the 8th houre,
Common places at the 9th. houre.
Afternoone

The first houre reads history in the Winter,
The nature of plants in the Summer.
The summe of every Lecture shall be examined before the new
Lecture be read.
Every Schollar that on proofe is found able to read the Originalls
of the *Old* and *New Testament* into the Latine tongue, and to resolve
them *Logically*; withall being of godly life and conversation; And at any
publick Act hath the Approbation of the Overseers and Master of the
Colledge, is fit to be dignified with his first Degree.
Every Schollar that giveth up in writing a *System*, or *Synopsis*,
or summe of *Logick*, Naturall and Morall *Phylosophy, Arithmetick, Geometry* and *Astronomy*: and is ready to defend his *Theses* or positions:
withall skilled in the Originalls as abovesaid: and of godly life & conversation: and so approved by the Overseers and Master of the Colledge,
at any publique *Act*, is fit to be dignified with his 2d. Degree.

11. INSTRUCTIONS FOR ANGLICAN SCHOOLMASTERS, 1706*

*The Society for the Propagation of the Gospel in Foreign Parts,
founded in 1701 by the Reverend Thomas Bray, was the missionary arm
of the Anglican Church in colonial America. Although Bray's original
intention was to convert the Indians, he soon discovered that the more
pressing need lay with the Christians, for the ministry, with few exceptions throughout the 17th century, was inattentive to duties and without
discipline, and the education of the young was haphazard at best. On a
visit to Maryland, Bray was appalled at the state of education and*

* From *A Collection of Papers Printed by order of the Society for the
Propagation of the Gospel in Foreign Parts* (London: E. Owen, 1741), pp. 20–22.
See also C. F. Pascoe, *Two Hundred Years of the S.P.G.* (London: S.P.G., 1901),
pp. 844–45.

religious instruction there. Bray and the S.P.G. were responsible for the establishment of libraries in the Anglican colonies of Maryland, Virginia, and the Carolinas. Carefully chosen ministers were also sent to America. The S.P.G.'s greatest educational contribution, however, was rendered at the level of the parish school. The following report evidences the nature of elementary instruction in the non-Puritan colonies.

I. THAT they will consider the End for which they are employed by the Society, *viz*. The instructing and disposing Children to believe and live as Christians.

II. In order to this End, that they teach them to read truly and distinctly, that they may be capable of reading the Holy Scriptures, and other pious and usefule Books, for informing their Understandings, and regulating their Manners.

III. That they instruct them thoroughly in the Church-Catechism; teach them first to read it distinctly and exactly, then to learn it perfectly by Heart; endeavouring to make them understand the Sense and Meaning of it, by the help of such Expositions as the Society shall send over.

IV. That they teach them to Write a plain and legible Hand, in order to the fitting them for useful Employment; with as much Arithmetick, as shall be necessary to the same purpose.

V. That they be industrious, and give constant Attenda[n]ce at proper School-Hours.

VI. That they daily use, Morning and Evening, the Prayers composed for their Use in this Collection with their Scholars in the School, and teach them the Prayers and Graces composed for their Use at Home.

VII. That they oblige their Scholars to be constant at Church on the Lord's-Day, Morning and Afternoon, and at all other Times of Publick Worship; that they cause them to carry their Bibles and Prayer Books with them, instructing them how to use them there and how to demean themselves in the several Parts of Worship; that they be there present with them, taking Care of their reverent and decent Behaviour, and examine them afterwards, as to what they have heard and learn'd.

VIII. That when any of their Scholars are fit for it, they recommend them to the Minister of the Parish, to be publickly Catechized in the Church.

IX. That they take especial Care of their Manners, both in their Schools and out of them; warning them seriously of those Vices to which Children are most liable; teaching them to abhor Lying and Falsehood, and to avoid all Sorts of Evil-speaking; to love Truth and Honesty; to be Modest, Gentle, Well-behaved, Just and Affable, and Courteous to all, their Companions; respectful to their Superiors, particularly towards all that minister in holy Things, and especially to the

Minister of their Parish; and all this from a Sense and Fear of Almighty God; endeavouring to bring them in their tender years to that Sense of Religion, which may render it the constant Principle of the Lives and Actions.

X. That they use all kind and gentle Methods in the Government of their Scholars, that they may be loved as well as fear'd by them; and that when Correction is necessary, they make the Children understand, that it is given them out of Kindness, for their Good, bringing them to a Sense of their Fault, as well as of their Punishment.

XI. That they frequently consult with the Minister of the Parish, in which they dwell, about the Methods of managing their Schools, and be ready to be advised by him.

XII. That they do in their whole Conversation shew themselves Examples of Piety and Virtue to their Scholars, and to all with whom they shall converse.

XIII. That they may be ready, as they have Opportunity, to teach and instruct the *Indians* and *Negroes*, and their Children.

XIV. That they send to the Secretary of the Society, once in every six months, an Account of the State of their respective Schools, the Number of their Scholars, with the Methods and Success of their Teaching.

NOTITIA SCOLASTICA; *or an Account to be sent every Six Months to* the SOCIETY *by each* Schoolmaster, *concerning the State of their respective Schools.*

1. Attendance daily given.
2. Number of Children taught in the School.
3. Number of Children baptized in the Church of England.
4. Number of *Indian* and Negroe Children.
5. Number of Children born of Dissenting Parents.
6. Other Schools in or near the Place.
7. Of what Denomination.
8. Other Employments of the Schoolmaster.

. . . .

12. HUGH JONES, *THE PRESENT STATE OF VIRGINIA*, 1693–1721*

Hugh Jones (c. 1670–1760), a graduate of Oxford, came to Virginia in 1716 and was appointed the following year to the Chair of Mathe-

---

* From Hugh Jones, *The Present State of Virginia* (London: J. Clarke, 1724), pp. 26–28, 83–94. See also *The Present State of Virginia . . .* by Hugh Jones, Richard L. Morton, ed. (Chapel Hill): Published for the Virginia Historical Society by the University of North Carolina Press, 1956.

matics at the College of William and Mary. Of an intelligent and zealously religious nature, he soon took an active part in the affairs of Williamsburg, serving as chaplain to the House of Burgesses and lecturer in Bruton parish church. He published several textbooks, including the first English grammar written in America, A Short English Grammar, an Accidence to the English Tongue.

In 1721 Jones sailed for England, where he wrote the following Present State of Virginia. A highly personalized account of the Old Dominion, it is most valuable for the sections on the College of William and Mary, which had been founded in 1693 through the efforts of the Reverend James Blair (1655–1743). The college greatly reflected the Cavalier atmosphere of Virginia and Maryland—perhaps too greatly, for its students were noted more for their drinking and gaming than for erudition. Still, the school produced two Presidents of the United States and scores of provincial leaders. Hugh Jones finally settled in Maryland where he became a noteworthy Anglican churchman and an intractable opponent of the Catholics of that colony.

The College of William and Mary

Publick Buildings here [in Williamsburg] of Note, are the College, the Capitol, the Governor's House, and the Church. The Latitude of the *College* at Williamsburgh, to the best of my Observation, is 37° .21′ *North*.

The Front which looks due *East* is double, and is 136 Foot long. It is a lofty Pile of Brick Building adorn'd with a Cupola. At the *North* End runs back a large Wing, which is a handsome Hall, answerable to which the *Chapel* is to be built; and there is a spacious *Piazza* on the *West* Side, from one Wing to the other. It is approached by a good Walk, and a grand Entrance by Steps, with good Courts and Gardens about it, with a good House and Apartments for the *Indian Master* and his Scholars, and Out-Houses; and a large Pasture enclosed like a Park with about 150 Acres of Land adjoining, for occasional Uses.

The Building is beautiful and commodious, being first modelled by Sir *Christopher Wren*, adapted to the Nature of the Country by the *Gentlemen* there; and since it was burnt down, it has been rebuilt, and nicely contrived, altered and adorned by the ingenious Direction of *Governor Spotswood*; and is not altogether unlike Chelsea Hospital.

This *Royal Foundation* was granted and established by *Charter*, by *King William and Queen Mary*, and endowed by them, with some thousand Acres of Land, with Duties upon Furs and Skins and a Penny a Pound for all Tobacco transported from *Virginia* and *Maryland*, to the other Plantations; to which have been made several additional Benefactions, as that handsome Establishment for Mr. Boyle, for the Education of *Indians*, with the many Contributions of the Country, especially a late one of 1000 £. to buy Negroes for the College Use and Service.

The Society is a Corporation established for a *President*, six *Masters or Professors*, with a hundred Scholars, more or less.

For some Causes that I can't account for, the Revenue is not improved as much as might be wished; neither is the College brought to that Method of Education and Advantage, as it might be; tho' 'tis hoped, that in a few years it will, like the Palm Tree, grow to the greater Perfection, under the Weighty Obstacles that load it.

The Salary of the President Mr. *James Blair*, has been lately ordered to be reduced from 150 to 100 £. *per Ann.*

The Salary of the Fellows (one of which I have been several Years), is 80 £. *Per Ann.* with 20 s. Entrance, and 20 s. a Year for Pupilage for each Scholar: The Payments are sometimes made in Current *Spanish Money*, and sometimes in *Sterling* Bills.

The Nature of the Country scarce yet admits of the Possibility of reducing the *Collegians* to the nice Methods of Life and Study observed in *Oxford* and *Cambridge*; tho' by Degrees they may copy from thence many useful Customs and Constitutions.

When the *College* shall be compleatly finished, and Scholarships founded, then is the Trust to be transferred from the *Trustees* to the *President and Masters*; but at present it is managed by a certain Number of Governors or Visitors, (one of which is chosen yearly Rector) appointed first by the Trustees, elected out of the Principal and worthiest Inhabitants.

These appoint a Person, to whom they grant several Privileges and Allowances to board and lodge the Masters and Scholars at an extraordinary cheap Rate.

This Office is at present performed in the neatest and most regular and plentiful Manner, by Mrs. *Mary Stith*, a Gentlewoman of great Worth and Discretion, in good Favour with the Gentry, and great Esteem and Respect with the common People.

Great Pity it is, but the noble Design of this College met with more Friends to encourage, and Benefactors to advance, its flourishing State.

One Happiness is, that it has always a *Chancellor* in *England*, chosen by the *Governors* of *Feoffees*; to whose Patronage and Direction it may have recourse upon emergent Occasions.

The last *Chancellor* was the late *Bishop of London*; and the present is his *Grace the Archbishop of Canterbury*.

The *Chancellor* continues in that office but seven Years; so that it may happen as soon as he has obtained a perfect Knowledge and Acquaintance with the Persons and Affairs belonging to the *College*, his Term is expired: Besides their Business in other momentous Affairs at

Home may divert them, and the Distance of the Country may prevent them from obtaining true Notions, and exact Accounts of the Nature of the *Colony* and the *College*; so that for these Reasons they can't do for it the Good, which they otherwise might: For their better Information, and for Direction of all, in promoting Religion and Learning in this Plantation, I have made Publick this Account of *it*, and *its* Inhabitants.

. . . .

The Royal Founders of *William* and *Mary* College, with Prospect of doing the greatest Good for the Colonies of *Virginia* and *Maryland*, conferred this princely Donation upon them; and were seconded with the ample Benefaction of the honourable Mr. *Boyle* and the Contributions of the Country. But this underwent the common Fate of most other charitable Gifts of this Kind, having met with several Difficulties to struggle with in its Infancy; but the most dangerous was, that it was as it were no sooner finished, but it was unfortunately and unaccountably consumed to Ashes. Yet observe the wonderful *Turns* of Fortune, and Power of Providence. This College, *Phoenix-like*, as the city of *London*, revived and improved out of its own Ruins. But though it has found such unexpected Success, and has proved of very great Service already; yet it is far short of such Perfection, as it might easily attain to by the united Power of the Persons concerned about this important Foundation.

For it is now a College without a Chapel, without a Scholarship, and without a Statute.

There is a Library without Books, comparatively speaking, and a President without a fix'd Salary till of late: A Burgess without certainty of Electors; and in fine, there have been disputes and Differences about these and the like Affairs of the College hitherto without End.

These Things greatly impede the Progress of Sciences and learned Arts, and discourage those that may be inclined to contribute their Assistance or Bounty towards the Good of the College.

Nevertheless the Difficulties of this Kind might be removed by some such Regulations as follow, *viz.*

Let none be permitted to teach School in any Parish, but such as shall be nominated by the Minister and Vestry, and licensed by the President of the College.

Let such Lads as have been taught to read and instructed in the Grounds of the *English* Language in those Schools, be admitted into the *Grammar* School at the College, if they pass Examination before the President and Masters; together with such Youth as shall be sent from *Maryland*, who have a Right to be educated at this College.

Provided always that the Number of Grammar Scholars shall never exceed one Hundred.

Let them be boarded and lodged in the Dormitory, as they are at present; or upon such Terms as may from Time to Time seem most proper to the President and Masters, or to the Governors, till a Transfer be obtained.

These Lads should be two Years under the Care of the Usher, and two more under the *Grammar* Master; and by them instructed in *Latin* and *Greek*, in such methods as the President and Masters shall direct.

And during these four Years, at certain appointed Times they should be taught to write as they now are in the Writing-School, or in such Methods as the President and Masters may judge better: There also should the Writing Master teach them the Grounds and Practice of Arithmetick, in order to qualify such for Business, as intend to make no farther Progress in Learning.

Out of the *Grammar* School should be yearly elected by the President and Masters (or Professors) five Scholars upon the Foundation, who should be allowed their Board, Education and Lodging in proper Apartments *gratis*; and should also be provided with cloaths and Gowns, &c. after the Charter-House Method.

These Scholars should continue three Years upon the Foundation; during which Time, at appointed *Terms* they should be instructed in Languages, in Religion, in Mathematicks, in Philosophy, and in History, by the five Masters or Professors appointed for that Purpose; who with the Grammar Master make up the Number appointed by the Charter.

Besides the Scholars, the Professors should for a certain Sum instruct such others as may be enter'd Commoners in the College out of the *Grammar* School, or from elsewhere, by the Approbation of the President and Masters, who should be obliged to wear Gowns, and be subject to the same Statutes and Rules as the Scholars; and as Commoners are in *Oxford*. These should maintain themselves, and have a particular Table, and Chambers for their Accommodation.

For to wait at the four high Tables hereafter mentioned, there should be elected by the President and Masters four Servitors, who should have their Education, and such Allowances, as the Servitors in Oxford.

Such Scholars, Commoners, and Servitors, as have behaved themselves well, and minded their Studies for three Years, and can pass proper Examination, and have performed certain Exercises, should have the Degree of Batchellor of Arts conferred upon them; should eat at a Table together, and be distinguished by a peculiar Habit; maintain themselves, be subject to certain Rules, and pursue proper Studies; being allowed the Use of the Library as well as the Masters, paying proper Fees upon their Admission for the Good of the Library.

Out of these Batchellors should be yearly elected by the Presidents and Masters, one Fellow to be allowed 20 £. for his Passage to England, and 20 £. *per Ann.* for three Years after his speedy Entrance and Continuance in some certain College in *Oxford* or *Cambridge*; after which he should commence Master of Arts; which Degree, with all others in our Universities, should be conferred in the same Manner in this College by the President and Masters.

Out of the Graduates above Batchellors should the Masters or Professors be chosen by the Election of the said Masters or Professors with the President; who also every seven Years should chose a new Chancellor, to whose Determination all Disputes and Differences should be referred.

And when the President's Place is vacant, it should be filled by such of the Masters as has belonged first to the College.

A *Testimonium* from this College should be of the same Use and Force as from others in our Universities.

If the present Fund be insufficient to defray the Expense, proper Improvement should be made of the Revenue, and Application made for additional Benefactions.

A Body of Statutes should be directly formed and established by the Visitors, President, and Masters; and a Transfer of the Trust should be then made.

Such an Establishment would encourage the bright Youth of *Virginia* to apply to their Studies, and in some Measure would compel them to improve themselves; whereas now being left to their own Liberty, they proceed but superficially, and generally commence *Man* before they have gone through the *Schools* in the College. Here too would be great Inducements for their Friends to advise and persuade them to go through with their Learning; when they are certain, that they will thus be regularly improved, and have Prospect of a cheap Education, and Hopes of the best Preferment in their Country in Church and State; and have equal (if not superior) Chance with others for Promotion abroad in the World; being bred compleat Gentlemen and good Christians, and qualified for the Study of the Gospel, Law, or Physick; and prepared for undertaking Trade, or any useful Projects and Inventions.

As for the Accomplishments of Musick, Dancing, and Fencing, they may be taught by such as the President and Masters shall appoint at such certain Times, as they shall fix for those Purposes.

'Till these Regulations (or the like) be made, Matters may be carried on as they are at present; only to me there seems an absolute Necessity now for a Professor of Divinity, in order to instruct the *Indians* and *English* Youth there in the Grounds of Religion, and read Lectures of Morality to the senior Lads, and to read Prayers and preach in the College as Chaplain: This I am certain is very much wanting, and what the present Income of the College with good Management will easily allow of; therefore I hope particular Notice will be taken hereof.

There is as yet no great Occasion for the Hall, so that it might be made a Chapel and Divinity School, for which Purpose it would serve nobly with little or no Alterations.

As there is lately built an Apartment for the *Indian* Boys and their Master, so likewise is there very great Occasion for a Quarter for the Negroes and inferior Servants belonging to the College; for these not only take up a great deal of Room and are noisy and nasty, but also have often made me and others apprehensive of the great Danger of being burnt with the College, thro' their Carelessness and Drowsiness.

Another thing prejudicial to the College, is the Liberty allowed the Scholars, and the negligent Observances of College Hours, and Opportunity they have of rambling Abroad.

To remedy this, there is wanting some contrivance to secure the Youth within the College at certain Hours; which has hitherto been in vain attempted, because of the many Servants lodged in the College, and the several Doors and Ways to get out of it.

Likewise the Privileges and Apartments of the Presidents and Masters, and House-Keeper, &c. ought to be fix'd and ascertain'd; for these being precarious and doubtful, upon this Account has arose much Difference and Ill-Will, to the great Scandal of the College, and Detriment of Learning.

Little additional Charge would put the Government of the College upon a much better Footing; whereas at present it scarcely merits the name of a College.

As for Election of a Burgess in Pursuance to a Clause in the Charter he ought to be chosen by the President and as many Masters as there shall actually be at any Time.

The Charter mentions six Masters or Professors, but does not specify the Professions; it directs to the making of Statutes and founding Scholarships, but the particulars are left to the Discretion of the Managers; and some such Establishment as this here mentioned may not be improper, especially if for greater Encouragement the Surveyors of each County were to be appointed by the President and Masters, out of such as have taken a Batchellor of Arts Degree there; and if also the Governor and Council were to elect a certain Number of Batchellors for Clerks into the Secretaries Office; out of which Clerks attending and writing there at certain Times, the County Clerks should be appointed by the Secretary.

The Office of the President would be to govern the College, be Treasurer, and Censor, and have a casting Vote in all Debates.

The six Professors or Masters would be

> Divinity, who should be Chaplain and Catechist
> Mathematicks.
> Philosophy.

one for
Languages
History.
Humanity, who should be *Grammar* Master.

The under Masters would be the Usher, the *Indian* Master, and the Writing Master.

The Town Masters must be such as occasion requires, for Fencing, Dancing and Musick.

There would be three *English* Fellows.

There would be fifteen Scholars, and a sufficient Number of School-Boys for a constant Supply.

Besides a Number of Batchellors and Masters of Arts, who would wait till they come in Fellows or Professors, or got to be made Surveyors or County Clerks.

For all this there might easily be contrived Room in the College, especially if a Hall was built in the Place intended for the Chapel.

As also would there be Room enough for the House-Keeper, Officers, and Servants; especially if a Quarter was built for the Negroes, &c.

The Tables might then be distinguished into four higher or four lower, *viz*.

The upper Table for the President and Masters.

The second for the Masters of Arts, &c.

The third for the Batchellors of Arts.

The fourth for the Scholars and Commoners.

The four lower Tables should be

The first for the House-Keeper, and the upper School Boys.

The second for the Usher, Writing Master, and the lower School-boys.

The third for the Servitors and College Officers.

And the last for the Indian Master and his Scholars.

This Regularity might easily be effected, and would prove not only decent and creditable, but also useful and advantageous to the Country and the College.

The Library is better furnished of late than formerly, by the kind gifts of several Gentlemen; but yet the Number of Books is but very small, and the sets upon each Branch of Learning are very imperfect, and not the best of the sort.

To remedy this Defect proper Application should be made to the Societies and to the superior Clergy in England, who would give at least what Duplicates they have upon such an useful Occasion; and what necessary Collection of Books cannot be obtain'd by begging, they may buy as soon as they shall be able to stock their Library; as a great help to which I believe considerable Contributions would be made by the Clergy Burgesses, and Gentry of the Country, if upon easy terms they were allowed the Use of the Library at certain Hours, at such Times as they shall be at *Williamsburg*, either for Pleasure or upon Business.

The Office of Librarian is given to Mr. *John Harris* the Usher, in order to make his Place more aggreeable to his Merit; and if the Gardener was made to execute the Office of Porter for his present Salary, it would be no great Hardship upon him, and would be an Ease to the College; and for the Benefit and Encouragement of the House-Keeper several small necessary Pensions and Privileges might be contrived more than what are at present allowed; so that it might be made well worth the while of a Person of Integrity, Knowledge, and Prudence, to undertake and carry on so troublesome an office.

The greater the Number of Collegians, the greater would be the Gain of the House-Keeper; so that when the College should be full and compleat as here directed and wished, the Collegians may be boarded upon easier Terms; boarded I say; because if any but the President dieted themselves, it would create Confusion; and if any belonging to the College but such Masters as have Families were permitted to eat elsewhere, it would not be worth any body's while to lay in Provision, when they could not tell what Number they must provide for.

As for the *English* College Customs of *Commons*, &c. it is thought as yet more adviseable to board in the College than to keep to those Methods, till the Country affords better Conveniences and Opportunities for so doing.

The *Indians* who are upon Mr. *Boyle's* Foundation have now a handsom Apartment for themselves and their Master, built near the College, which useful Contrivance ought to be carried on to the utmost Advantage in the real Education and Conversion of the Infidels; for hitherto but little Good has been done therein, though abundance of Money has been laid out, and a great many Endeavours have been used, and much Pains taken for that Purpose.

The young *Indians*, procured from the tributary or foreign Nations with much Difficulty, were formerly boarded and lodged in the Town; where abundance of them used to die, either thro' Sickness, change of Provision, and way of Life; or as some will have it, often for want of proper Necessaries and due Care taken with them. Those of them that have escaped well, and been taught to read and write, have for the most Part returned to their Home, some with and some without Baptism, where they follow their own savage Customs and heathenish Rites.

A few of them have lived as Servants among the English, or loitered and idled away their Time in Laziness and Mischief.

But 'tis great Pity that more Care is not taken about them, after they are dismissed from School.

They have admirable Capacities when their Humours and Tempers are perfectly understood; and if well taught, they might advance themselves and do great Good in the Service of Religion; whereas now they are rather taught to become worse than better by falling into the worst Practices of vile nominal Christians, which they add to their own *Indian* Manners and Notions.

To prevent this therefore, let there be chosen continually four Indian Servitors out of the *Indian* Schools, as the other four out of the *Grammar* School.

Let these be maintained in the Indian House, and wait upon the four lower Tables: Let them be instructed as the other Servitors, or as their Genius most aptly may require, but Particularly in Religion; and when they are found qualified let them be sent to England, or placed out to Captains of Ships or Trades, as the Mathematical Boys in *Christ-Hospital*, for a few Years; then let them return and be allowed a small Exhibition, and encouraged in their separate Callings and Occupations; and let them settle some among the *English*, and others return to their own Nations.

Undoubtedly many of them would become excellent artists and Proficients in Trade; and thus when Reason and Experience has convinced them of the Preference of our Religion and Manners, certainly they may not only save their own Souls; but also be extreamly instrumental in the Conversion of their barbarous Friends and Relations.

In proceeding thus, any that seem capable or inclinable to study Divinity, should by all Means be encouraged and forwarded in it, and sent over for a small Time to one of our Universities with an Allowance of Fellows; after which, if such were admitted into Orders, and then sent out Missionaries among their own Country-Folks, what great Good might we not expect from such, when thoroughly converted and instructed in Christianity, and made truly sensible of the Advantages of Religion, the deadly State of Infidelity, and the miserable Lives and Customs of the *Indians?*

In a Work of this Kind undoubtedly several good Christians would contribute their charitable Assistance; 'till which the present Fund should be applied in this Method, though the Managers should be obliged to reduce the Number of *Indian* Scholars upon this Account; since this was the main Intent of the Benefaction, and no other Method can well answer this Design; which may be evidenced by Experience both from the Colleges of *Virginia* and *New England* too, as I have been credibily informed from good Authors, as well as my own Experience.

By such Methods in Process of Time might the *Indian* Obstinacy be mollified, their seeming Dulness might be cleared from Rust; and the Gates of Heaven be opened for their Admission upon their Perfect Conversion to the Faith of Christ. In such glorious Designs as these neither should Humour, Interest, nor Prejudice divert any from their charitable Assistance therein, especially such as are concerned in Affairs of this Kind, and engaged by Duty to lend their best aid in *leading* the Infidels into the Pale of Christ's Church, and making them by mild and most gentle Measures to accompany his flock; since all the Force in the World would rather drive them from, than guide them, to the Congregation of the Faithful and Communion of Saints.

By some such prudent and mild Methods alone may they be made to live and die as true Christians, and not like the most savage Brutes, as they generally do.

Thus far as to the Education of the young Men in *Virginia,* and the instruction most proper for the Indians; and as for the Negroes each Owner ought to take Care that the Children born his Property, and all his intelligent adult Negroes be taught their Catechism and some short Prayers, be made to frequent the Church and be baptized, and hindered as much as may be from Swearing, Lying, Intemperance, Prophaness, and Stealing and Cheating.

Finally, as to the Education of Girls, it is great Pity but that good Boarding Schools were erected for them at *Williamsburgh* and other *Towns.*

4

The First Societies

13. ISAAC JOGUES, *NOVUM BELGIUM*, 1646*

Isaac Jogues (1607–46) was a missionary to the Huron Indians. While returning from an expedition to the Sioux, he was captured by a war party of Mohawks and carried to their grounds in central New York. His captors enslaved him, crippled his hands, and killed his companion. He was finally rescued by the Dutch and taken to New Amsterdam (1643), where he stayed with the Dutch Reformed minister Johannes Megapolensis (1603–70). Jogues's report to his Jesuit superiors marks him as an excellent observer; he described Dutch New York as already cosmopolitan, tolerant, and commercially active, though still rude and provincial in some aspects. Despite his former trials, Father Jogues returned to work with the Indians. He was tomahawked to death at Auriesville, New York, and became the martyr of New France.

New Holland—which the Dutch call, in Latin, Novum Belgium; in their own language, Nieuw Nederland; that is to say, New netherlands—is situated between Virginia and New England. The entrance to the River, which some call the River Nassau, or the great River of the North, to distinguish it from another which they call South River,—and [on] some charts, I believe, that I have recently seen, the River Maurice,—is in the latitude of 40 degrees, 30 minutes. Its channel is deep, and navigable by the largest ships, which go up to Manhattes Island, which is 7 leagues in circumference; thereon is a fort intended to serve as nucleus for a town to be built, and to be called New Amsterdam.

This fort, which is at the point of the island, about 5 or 6 leagues from the river's mouth, is called fort Amsterdam; it has 4 regular bastions,

* Reuben G. Thwaites, ed., *Jesuit Relations and Allied Documents* (Cleveland: Burrows Bros., 1896–1901), Vol. XXVIII, pp. 104–15.

provided with several pieces of artillery. All these bastions and the curtains were, in the year 1643, merely earthworks, most of which had quite given way, and through them the fort could be entered from all sides; there were no trenches. For the defense of this fort,—and of another which they had built, farther on, against the incursions of the savages, their enemies,—there were 60 soldiers. They were beginning to case the gates and the bastions with stone. In this fort there was a house of worship, built of stone, which was quite spacious; the house of the Governor,—whom they call the director General,—built quite neatly of brick; and the storehouses and soldiers' quarters.

There may be, on the Island of Manhate and in its environs, about 4 or five hundred men of various sects and nations,—the Director General told me that there were men of eighteen different languages; they are scattered here and there, up and down the stream, according as the beauty or convenience of the sites invited each one to settle. Some artisans, however, who work at their trades, are located under cover of the fort; while all the others are exposed to the incursions of the Savages, who, in the year 1643, when I was there, had actually killed about forty Hollanders, and burned many houses, and barns full of wheat.

The River, which is very straight, and flows directly from North to South, is at least a league wide before the Fort. The ships are at anchor in a bay which forms the other side of the island, and they can be defended by the Fort.

Shortly before I arrived there, 3 large ships of 300 tons had come to load wheat; two had received their lading, but the 3rd could not be laden, because the savages had burned a part of the grain. These ships had sailed from the West Indies, where the West india Company usually maintains seventeen war vessels.

There is no exercise of Religion except the Calvinist, and the orders declare that none but Calvinists be admitted; nevertheless, that point is not observed,—for besides the Calvinists, there are in this settlement Catholics, English Puritans, Lutherans, Anabaptists, whom they call Mnistes [Mennonites], etc.

When any one comes for the first time to dwell in the country, they furnish him horses, cows, etc., and give him provisions,—all which he repays when he is well settled; and, as for lands, at the end of ten years he gives the Company of the West indies a tenth of the produce that he harvests.

This country has for limits on the New England side a River which they call the Fresh River [Connecticut], which serves as boundary between them and the English; nevertheless, the English approach them very closely,—preferring to have lands among the Dutch, who require nothing from them, to depending upon English Milords, who exact rents and like to put on airs of being absolute. On the other side,—the Southern, toward Virginia,—it has for limits the River which they call South River [Delaware], on which there is also a Dutch settlement; but at its entrance the Swedes have another, extremely well equipped with cannon and people. It is believed that these Swedes are maintained by Amsterdam merchants, incensed because the Company of the west Indies monopolizes all the trade of these regions. It is toward this River that they have found, as is said, a gold mine.

. . . .

During fully 50 years the Dutch have frequented these regions. In the year 1615, the fort was begun; about 20 years ago, they began to make a settlement; and now there is already some little trade with Virginia and New England.

The first comers found lands quite suitable for use, cleared in former times by the savages, who tilled their fields there. Those who have come since have made clearings in the woods, which are commonly of oak; the lands are good. Deer hunting is abundant toward autumn. There are some dwellings built of stone: they make the lime with oyster shells, of which there are great heaps made in former times by the savages, who partly live by that fishery.

The climate there is very mild; as that region is situated at 40 and two-thirds degrees, there are plenty of European fruits, as apples, pears, Cherries. I arrived there in October, and even then I found many Peaches.

Ascending the River as far as the 43rd degree, you find the 2nd settlement, which the flow and Ebb of the tide reaches, but extends no further; ships of 100 and a hundred and twenty tons can land there.

There are two items in this settlement, which is called Renselaerswick,—as if one should say, "the settlement of Renselaers," who is a wealthy merchant of Amsterdam: first, a wretched little fort, named Fort orange,—built of logs, with 4 or 5 pieces of Breteuil cannon, and as many swivel guns,—which the Company of the West indies has reserved for itself, and which it maintains. This fort was formerly on an Island formed by the River; it is now on the mainland on the side of the Hiroquois, a little above the said Island. There is, secondly, a Colony sent thither by that Renselaers, who is its Patron. This colony is composed of about a hundred persons, who live in 25 or 30 houses built along the River, as each has found convenient. In the principal house is lodged the Patron's representative; the Minister has his own house apart, in which Preaching is held. There is also a sort of Bailiff, whom they call Seneschal, who has charge of Justice. All their houses are merely of boards, and are covered with thatch. There is as yet no masonry, except in the chimneys.

As the forests supply many stout pines, the people make boards by means of their mills, which they have for this purpose.

They have found some very suitable lands, which the savages had formerly prepared, on which they plant corn and oats, for their beer and for the horses, of which they have a great many. There are few lands fit to be tilled, as they are narrowed by hills, which are poor soil; that obliges them to separate from one another, and they already hold two or 3 leagues of territory.

Trade is free to every one, which enables the savages to obtain all things very cheaply: each of the Dutch outbidding his companion, and being satisfied, provided he can gain some little profit.

This settlement is not more than 20 leagues from the Agniehronons; there is access to them either by land or by water,—the River on which the Iroquois dwell falling into that which passes by the Dutch; but there are many shallow rapids, and a fall of a short half-league, past which the canoe must be carried.

There are several nations between the two Dutch settlements, which are 30 German leagues apart,—that is to say, 50 or 60 French leagues. The Wolves, whom the Iroquois call Agotsaganens, are the nearest to the settlement of Renselaerswick or to the fort of orange. Several years ago, there being a war between the Iroquois and the Wolves, the Dutch Joined these latter against the others; but, 4 having been taken and burned, peace was made. Later, some nations near the sea having slain some Dutch of the most remote settlement, the Dutch killed 150 savages,—not only men and women, but little children. The savages having, in various reprisals, killed 40 Dutch, burned many houses, and wrought damage reckoned, at the time when I was there, at 200,000 *ll*,—two hundred thousand livres,—troops were levied in New England. Accordingly, at the beginning of winter, the grass being short, and some snow on the ground, they gave the savages chase with six hundred men, two hundred being always on the march and one set continually relieving another. The result was, that, being shut up on a great Island, and unable to flee easily, because of the women and children, there were as many as sixteen hundred killed, including women and children. This compelled the remainder of the savages to make peace, which still continues. That occurred in 1643 and 1644.

From 3 Rivers, in
  New France,
    August 3, 1646.

14. JASPER DANCKAERTS, *JOURNAL OF A VOYAGE TO NEW YORK*, 1679–80*

Jasper Danckaerts (fl. 1679–83) traveled through New England and the Middle Colonies in 1680, seeking a genial place of settlement for his Labadist sect, a group of Calvinist mystics. His journal, in which he carefully noted down his impressions of people and places, presents a panoramic view and is an exceptionally good source for the social history of the seventeenth-century colonists. In the following selection he writes of New England in the days of Governor Edmund Andros. The economic and political distress of New England in this period prompted the Labadists finally to form a communal settlement at Bohemia Manor, in Cecil County, Maryland, where they attained a high degree of prosperity.

The Boston, Cambridge and the New England Scene, 1680

[July] 8*th, Monday*. We went accordingly, about eight o'clock in the morning, to Roxberry, which is three-quarters of an hour from the city, in order that we might get home early, inasmuch as our captain had informed us, he would come in the afternoon for our money, and in order that Mr. [The Rev. John] Eliot might not be gone from home. On arriving at his house, he was not there, and we therefore went to look around the village and the vicinity. We found it justly called *Rocksbury*, for it was very rocky, and had hills entirely of rocks. Returning to his house we spoke to him, and he received us politely. As he could speak neither Dutch nor French, and we spoke but little English, and were unable to express ourselves in it always, we managed, by means of Latin and English, to understand each other. He was seventy-seven years old [75], and had been forty-eight years in these parts. He had learned very well the language of the Indians, who lived about there. We asked him for an Indian Bible. He said in the late Indian war, all the Bibles and Testaments were carried away, and burnt or destroyed, so that he had not been able to save any for himself; but a new edition was in press, which he hoped would be much better than the first one, though that was not to be despised. We inquired whether any part of the old and new edition could be obtained by purchase, and whether there was any grammar of that language in English. Thereupon he went

---

* From *Journal of a Voyage to New York and a Tour in Several of the American Colonies . . .* , Henry C. Murphy, ed. (Brooklyn: Long Island Historical Society, 1867), pp. 382 *et passim*. See also "The Journal of Jasper Danckaerts, 1679–80" in Bartlett Burleigh James and J. Franklin Jameson, eds., *Original Narratives of Early American History* (New York: Scribner, 1913), pp. 264–76.

and brought us the Old Testaments, and also the New Testament, made up with some sheets of the new edition [of the New Testament], so that we had the Old and New Testaments complete. He also brought us two or three small specimens of the grammar. We asked him what we should pay him for them; but he desired nothing. We presented him our *Declaration* [of the Labadists] in Latin, and informed him about the persons and conditions of the church, whose declaration it was, and about Madame Schurman and others, with which he was delighted, and could not restrain himself from praising God the Lord that had raised up men, and reformers, and begun the reformation in Holland. He deplored the decline of the church in New England, and especially in Boston, so that he did not know what would be the final result. We inquired how it stood with the Indians, and whether any good fruit had followed his work. Yes, much, he said, if we meant true conversion of the heart; for they had in various countries, instances of conversion, as they called it, and had seen it amounted to nothing at all; that they must not endeavor, like scribes and pharisees, to make Jewish proselytes, but true Christians. He could thank God, he continued, and God be praised for it, there were Indians, whom he knew, who were truly converted of heart to God, and whose profession, was sincere. It seemed as if he were disposed to know us further, and we, therefore, said to him, if he had any desire to write to our people, he could use the names which stood on the title-page of the Declaration, and that we hoped to come and converse with him again. He accompanied us as far as the jurisdiction of Roxbury extended, where we parted from him.

9th, *Tuesday*. We started out to go to Cambridge, lying to the northeast of Boston, in order to see their college, and printing office. We left about six o'clock in the morning, and were set across the river at Charlestown. We followed a road which we supposed was the right one, but went full half an hour out of the way, and would have gone still further, had not a negro who met us, and of whom we inquired, disabused us of our mistake. We went back to the right road, which is a very pleasant one. We reached Cambridge, about eight o'clock. It is not a large village, and the houses stand very much apart. The college building is the most conspicuous among them. We went to it, expecting to see something curious, as it is the only college, or would-be academy of the Protestants in all America, but we found ourselves mistaken. In approaching the house, we neither heard nor saw anything mentionable; but, going to the other side of the building, we heard noise enough in an upper room to lead my comrade [Peter Sluytes] to suppose they were engaged in disputation. We entered, and went up stairs, when a person met us, and requested us to walk in, which we did. We found there, eight or ten young fellows, sitting around, smoking tobacco, with the smoke of which the room was so full, that you could hardly see; and the whole house smelt so strong of it that when I was going up stairs, I said, this is certainly a tavern. We excused ourselves, that we could speak English only a little, but understood Dutch or French, which they did not. However, we spoke as well as we could. We inquired how many professors there were, and they replied not one, that there was no money to support one. We asked how many students there were. They said at first, thirty, and then came down to twenty; I afterwards understood there are probably not ten. They could hardly speak a word of Latin [not one of them], so that my comrade could not converse with them. They took us to the library where there was nothing particular. We looked over it a little. They presented us with a glass of wine. This is all we ascertained there. The minister of the place goes there morning and evening to make prayer, and has charge over them; the students have tutors or masters. Our visit was soon over, and we left them to go and look at the land about there. We found the place beautifully situated on a large plain, more than eight miles square, with a fine stream in the middle of it, capable of bearing heavily laden vessels. As regards the fertility of the soil, we consider the poorest in New York superior to the best here. As we were tired, we took a mouthful to eat, and left. We passed by the printing office, but there was nobody in it; the paper sash however being broken, we looked in; and saw two presses with six or eight cases of type. There is not much work done there. Our printing office [at Wicuward, Holland] is well worth two of it, and even more. We went back to Charlestown, where, after waiting a little, we crossed over about three o'clock. We found our skipper, John Foy, at the house, and gave him our names, and the money for our passage, six pounds each. He wished to give us a bill of it, but we told him it was unnecessary, as we were people of good confidence. I spoke to my comrade, and we went out with him, and presented him with a glass of wine. His mate came to him there, who looked more like a merchant than a seaman, a young man and no sailor. We inquired how long our departure would be delayed, and, as we understood him, it would be the last of the coming week. That was annoying to us. Indeed, we have found the English the same everywhere, doing nothing but lying and cheating, when it but serves their interest. . . .

.   .   .   .

12th Friday. We went in the afternoon to Mr. John Taylor's, to ascertain whether he had any good wine, and to purchase some for our voyage, and also some brandy. On arriving at his house, we found him a little cool; indeed, not as he was formerly. We inquired for what we wanted, and he said he had good Madeira wine, but he believed he had no brandy, though he thought he could assist us in procuring it. We also inquired how we could obtain the history and laws of this place. At last it came out. He said we must be pleased to excuse him if he did not give us admission to his house; he durst not do it, in consequence of there being a certain evil report in the city concerning us; they had been to warn him not to have too much communication with us, if he wished to avoid censure; they said we certainly were Jesuits, who had come here for no good, for we were quiet and modest, and an entirely different sort of people from themselves; that we could speak several languages, were cunning and subtle of mind and judgment, had come there without carrying on any traffic or any other business, except only to see the place and country; that this seemed fabulous as it was unusual in these parts; certainly it could be for no good purpose. As regards the voyage to Europe, we could have made it as well from New York as from Boston, as opportunities were offered there. This suspicion seemed to have gained more strength because the fire at Boston over a year ago was caused by a Frenchman. Although he had been arrested, they could not prove it against him; but in the course of the investigation, they discovered he had been counterfeiting coin and had profited thereby, which was a crime as infamous as the other. He had no trade or profession; he was condemned; both of his ears were cut off; and he was ordered to leave the country. Mr. Taylor feared the more for himself, particularly because most all strangers were addressed to him, as we were, in consequence of his speaking several languages, French, some Dutch, Spanish, Portuguese, Italian, & c., and could aid them. There had also, some time ago, a Jesuit arrived here from Canada, who came to him disguised, in relation to which there was much murmuring, and they wished to punish this Jesuit, not because he was a Jesuit, but because he came in disguise, which is generally bad and especially for such as are the pests of the world, and are justly feared, which just hate we very unjustly [*sic*], but as the ordinary lot of God's children, had to share. We were compelled to speak French, because we could not speak English, and these people did not understand Dutch. There were some persons in New York who could speak nothing but French, and very little English. The French was common enough in these parts, but it seemed that we were different from them. Of all this, we disabused Mr. Taylor, assuring him we were as great enemies of that brood, as any persons could be, and were, on the contrary, good protestants or reformed, born and educated in that faith;

.   .   .   .

13th, *Saturday.* As we had promised Mr. Eliot, to call upon him again, we went to Roxbury this morning. We found him at home, but he excused himself that he had not much time, and had a great deal to do. He called his son, who was there, and who also appeared to be a minister, to speak with us; but we excused ourselves, and said we would not hinder him and would rather leave. However, several questions and reasons passed between us in relation to the Confession which we had given him, and which he praised highly, and in relation to the professors of it, both pastors and people, in regard to which we satisfied him; but the son, who was neither as good nor as learned as his father, had more disposition or inclination to ridicule and dispute, than to edify and be edified. We told him what was good for him, and we regretted we could not talk more particularly to him. But the father remarked that if the professors were truly what they declared in the Confession, he could not sufficiently thank God for what he had done. We assured him it was so, and took our leave. He requested us to stop and dine with them, but we excused ourselves.

14*th, Sunday.* We went to church, but heard a most miserable sermon by a young person, a candidate.

15*th Monday.* The burgesses drilled and exercised in the presence of the governor. There were eight companies on foot, and one on horseback, all which divided themselves into two troops or squadrons, and operated against each other in a sham battle, which was well performed. It took place on a large plain on the side of the city. It did not, however, terminate so well, but that a commander on horseback was wounded on the side of his face near the eye, by the shot of a fusil, as it is usually the case that some accident happens on such occasions. It was so in New York at the last parade, when two young men on horseback coming towards each other as hard as they could, to discharge their pistols, dashed against each other, and fell instantly with their horses. It was supposed they were both killed, and also their horses, for there were no signs of life in them; but they were bled immediately, and after two or three hours they began to recover, and in two days were able to go out again. One of the horses died. We went to see John Taylor, and paid him for the wine and brandy. He seemed to have more confidence in us. We gave him to read as further proofs, the letters which Mr. Ephraim Hermans and Mr. John Moll had written to us from the South River, both of whom he knew. He told us the reformed of Rochelle had sent some deputies to the colony of Boston and the independent church there to request the liberty to come over and live in a place near them, or among them, and in their country, which was granted them; and that they returned home three months ago.

16*th Tuesday.* We packed our goods in readiness to leave.

· · · ·

18*th Thursday.* We took leave of Mr. Taylor, thanking him for his attention and kindness, and presented him with a copy of our *Cantiques Sacrées*, for which he was thankful. We would cheerfully have given him the *Maximes* also, but our goods were packed on board the ship, and we could not get at them. He was now of a better mind and well satisfied, returning us our letters with thanks. While we were sitting at table this noon, it thundered very hard, whereupon one of the daughters of the woman of the house where we were staying commenced to scream and cry. We asked her if she were afraid of the thunder, upon which her mother inquired of us, if we were not. We said no, but the word had scarcely escaped our lips before there came a frightful clap, which seemed to cleave the heart from the body, and entirely changed our ideas. My comrade, Mr. Vorsman, turned as pale as a white sheet, and could hardly speak. I was fearful he had met with some mishap, but he recovered himself. It was said there had scarcely ever been heard there such thunder. One man was killed, and two others not far from being so. These three persons were running in a field, and two of them seeing and hearing the weather lay down flat on the ground under a tree; the third man played stout and brave, jeering at the others who called to him to come with them. Soon the lightning struck him dead to the earth, and separated the other two from each other. There was also a hard rock, not far from our lodgings, split through.

.   .   .   .

23d, Thursday. After some delay the captain came on board with the rest of the passengers, accompanied by many of their friends. Weighed anchor at three o'clock in the afternoon, it being almost low water, and set sail with a southwest and south southwest wind. In passing the fort we fired the *salvo*, which it answered; the pilot and the company then left us and we put to sea. But before going further to sea we must give a brief description of New England, and the city of Boston in particular.

When New Netherland was first discovered by the Hollanders, the evidence is that New England was not known; because the Dutch East India Company then sought a passage by the west, through which to sail to Japan and China; and if New England had been then discovered, they would not have sought a passage there, knowing it to be the main land; just as when New Netherland and New England did become known, such a passage was sought no longer through them, but farther to the north through Davis and Hudson straits. The Hollanders, when they discovered New Netherland, embraced under that name and title all the coast from Virginia or Cape *Hinloopen* eastwardly to Cape Cod, as it was then and there discovered by them and designated by Dutch names, as sufficiently appears by the charts. The English afterwards discovered New England and settled there. They increased so in consequence of the great liberties and favorable privileges which the king granted to the Independents, that they went to live not only west of Cape Cod and Rhode Island, but also on Long Island and other places, and even took possession of the whole of the Fresh River, which the Hollanders there were not able to prevent, in consequence of their small force in New Netherland, and the scanty population. The English went more readily to the west, because the land was much better there, and more accessible to vessels, and the climate was milder; and also because they could trade more conveniently with the Hollanders, and be supplied by them with provisions. New England is now described as extending from the Fresh River to Cape Cod and thence to Kennebec, comprising three provinces or colonies: Fresh River or Connecticut; Rhode Island and the other islands to Cape Cod; and Boston, which stretches from thence north. They are subject to no one, but acknowledge the king of England for their *honor* [lord], and therefore no ships enter unless they have English passports or commissions. They have free trade with all countries; but the return cargoes from there to Europe, go to England, except those which go *under the thumb* [secretly] to Holland. There is no toll or duty paid upon merchandise exported or imported, nor is there any impost or excise paid upon land. Each province chooses its own governor from the magistracy, and the magistrates are chosen from the principal inhabitants, merchants or planters. They are all *Independents* in matters of religion, if it can be called religion; many of them perhaps more for the purposes of enjoying the benefit of its privileges than for any regard to truth and godliness. I observed that while the English flag or color has a red ground with a small white field in the uppermost corner where there is a red cross, they have here dispensed with this cross in their colors, and preserved the rest. They baptize no children except those of the members of the congregation. All their religion consists in observing Sunday, by not working or going into the taverns on that day; but the houses are worse than the taverns. No stranger or traveller can therefore be entertained on a Sunday, which begins at sunset on Saturday, and continues until the same time on Sunday. At these two hours you see all their countenances change. Saturday evening the constable goes round into all the taverns of the city for the purpose of stopping all noise and debauchery, which frequently causes him to stop his search, before his search causes the debauchery to stop. There is a penalty for cursing and swearing, such as they please to impose, the witnesses thereof being at liberty to insist upon it. Nevertheless, you discover little difference between this and other places. Drinking and fighting occur there not less than elsewhere; and as to truth and true godliness, you must not expect more of them than of others. When we were there, four ministers' sons were learning the silversmith's trade.

The soil is not as fertile as in the west. Many persons leave there to go to the Delaware and New Jersey. They manure their lands with heads of fish. They gain their living mostly or very much by fish, which they salt and dry for selling; and by raising horses, oxen and cows, as well as hogs and sheep, which they sell alive, or slaughtered and salted, in the Caribbean Islands and other places. They are not as good farmers as the Hollanders about New York.

As to Boston particularly, it lies in latitude 42° 20′ on a very fine bay. The city is quite large, constituting about twelve companies. It has three churches, or meeting houses, as they call them. All the houses are made of thin, small cedar shingles, nailed against frames, and then filled in with brick and other stuff; and so are their churches. For this reason these towns are so liable to fires, as have already happened several times; and the wonder to me is, that the whole city has not been burnt down, so light and dry are the materials. There is a large dock in front of it constructed of wooden piers, where the large ships go to be careened and rigged; the smaller vessels all come up to the city. On the lefthand side across the river lies Charlestown, a considerable place, where there is some shipping. Upon the point of the bay, on the left hand, there is a block-house, along which a piece of water runs, called the Milk ditch. The whole place has been an island, but it is now joined to the main land by a low road to Roxbury. In front of the town there are many small islands, between which you pass in sailing in and out. On one of the middlemost stands the fort where the ships show their passports. At low tide the water in the channel between the islands is three and a half and four fathoms deep, in its shallowest part. You sail from the city southeasterly to the fort, by passing Governor's Island on the larboard, and having passed the fort, you keep close to the south, then southeast, and gradually more to the east to the sea. On reaching the sea we set our course due east, with the wind south-southeast, and made good progress.

15. EDWARD RANDOLPH, LETTER TO THE BOARD OF TRADE, 1699*

Edward Randolph (1632–1703) had a stormy and controversial political career as a servant of the Crown. He investigated Massachusetts Bay for the king in 1676, and incurred the wrath of the Puritan oligarchy because his reports led in large part to the recall of the charter and the establishment of the Dominion of New England. After the overthrow of the Dominion, in which he was secretary to Governor Andros, he secured the post of Surveyor General of Customs for North America, and in this capacity he describes proprietary South Carolina to the Board of Trade

* British Public Records Office, Records of the Board of Trade, Proprieties, Vol. XXV, pp. 448–59. See also Public Records of South Carolina, Microfilm, Vol. 4, South Carolina Archives Department.

and Plantations. Founded in 1670, South Carolina had already taken on many of the economic and social characteristics of the later royal colony, but in Randolph's time it was struggling with the lack of a marketable staple, the inefficiency of proprietary government, and the presence of enemies on its borders.

16 March, 1698/99

May it please yr Lordships,

After a dangerous voyage at Sea, I landed at Charles Town, in the Province of So. Carolina, & soon after my arrival, I administered the Oath to Mr. Jos. Blake, one of the Proprietors and Governor of this Province. But he is not allowed of by his Ma[jes]tys Order in Council to be Govr., the Act of Parlt. for preventing frauds being not taken notice of by the Proprietors.

There are but few settled Inhabitants in this Province, the Lords have taken up vast tracts of land for their own use, as in Colleton County and other places, where the land is most commodious for settlement, which prevents peopling the place, and makes them less capable to preserve themselves. As to their civil Governt., 'tis different from what I have met with in the other Proprieties. Their Militia is not above 1500 Soldiers White men, but have thro' the Province generally 4 Negroes to 1 White man, & not above 1100 families, English and French.

Their Chief Town is Charles Town, and the seat of Govt. in this Province, where the Governor, Council and Triennial Parliamt. set, & their Courts are holden, being above a league distance from the entrance to their harbour mouth, wch is barred, and not above 17 foot water at the highest tide, but very difficult to come in. The Harbour is called by the Spaniards, St. George; it lyes 75 leagues to the Northward of St. Augustine, belonging to the Spaniards. It is generally laid down in our English maps to be 2 deg., 45 min., within the southern bounds of this Province. In the year 1686, one hundred Spaniards, wth Negroes and Indians, landed at Edistoe, 50 miles to the southward of Charles Town, and broak open the house of Mr. Joseph Moreton, [Morton] then Governor of the Province, and carried away Mr. Bowell, his Brother-in-law, prisoner, who was found murdered 2 or 3 days after; they carried away all his money and plate, & 13 slaves, to the value of £1500 sterling, and their plunder to St. Augustine. Two of the Slaves made their escape from thence, & returned to their master. Some time after, Govr. Moreton sent to demand his slaves, but the Govr. of St. Augustine answered it was done without his orders, but to this day keeps them, and says he can't deliver them up wth out an ordr from the King of Spain. About the same time they robbed Mr. Grimball's House, the Sec. of the Province, whilst he attended the Council at Charles Town, & carried away to the value of over £1500 sterlg. They also fell upon a settlement of Scotchmen at Port Royal, where there was not above 25 men in health to oppose them. The Spaniards burnt down their houses, destroyed & carried away all that they had, because (as the Span[iar]ds pretended) they were settled upon their land, & had they at any time a superior force, they would also destroy this town built upon Ashley and Cooper Rivers. This whole Bay was called formerly St. George's, which they likewise lay claim to. The Inhabitants complained of the wrong done them by the Spaniards to the Lords Proprietors, & humbly prayed them (as I have been truly informed) to represent it to His Maty, but they not hearing from the Lord Proprs, fitted out two vessels with 400 stout men, well armed, and resolved to take St. Augustine. But Jas. Colleton came in that time from Barbadoes with a Commission to be Govr., and threatn'd to hang them if they proceeded, whereupon they went on shore very unwillingly. The Spaniards hearing the English were coming upon them for the damages, they left their Town and Castle, & fled into the woods to secure themselves. The truth is, as I have been credibly informed, there was a design on foot to carry on a Trade with the Spaniards.

I find the Inhabitants greatly alarmed upon the news that the French continue their resolution to make a settling at Messasipi River, from [which] they may come over land to the head of Ashley River wthout opposition, 'tis not yet known what care the Lords Proprs intend to take for their preservation. Some ingenious gentlemen of this Province (not of the Council) have lately told me the Deputies have talked of makg an Address to the Lords Proprs for relief, But 'tis apparent that all the time of this French War they never sent them one barrel of powder or a pound of lead to help them. They conclude they have no reason to depend upon them for assistance, and are resolved to forsake this Country betimes, if they find the French are settled at Meschasipi, or if upon the death of the King of Spain these Countries fall into the hands of the French, as inevitably they will (if not timely prevented), & return with their families to England or some other place where they may find safety and protection. It was one of the first questions asked by several of the Chief men at my arrival, whether His Maty will please to allow them half pay for 2 or 3 years at furthest, that afterwards they will maintain themselves and families (if they have any) in making Pitch & Tar & planting of Indian Corn. His Majesty will thereby have so many men seasoned to the Country ready for service upon all occasions, five such men will do more service by sea or land then 20 new raised men from home, they may be brought hither in the Virginia outward bound ships, 100 or 150 men in a year, till they are made up 1000, it will save the charge of transporting so many another time 2 or 3000 leagues at sea. I heard one of the Council (a great Indian Trader, and has been 600 miles up in the Country west from Charles Town) discourse that the only way to discover the Meschasipi is from this Province by land. He is willing to undertake it if His Maty will please to pay the charge wch will not be above £400 or £500 at most; he intends to take with him 50 white men of this Province and 100 Indians, who live 2 days journey east from the Meschasipi, and questions not but in 5 or 6 months time after he has His Maty's commands & instructions to find out the mouth of it and the true latitude thereof.

The great improvement made in this Province is wholly owing to the industry and labour of the Inhabitants. They have applied themselves to make such commodities as might increase the revenue of the Crown, as Cotton, Wool, Ginger, Indigo, & c. But finding them not to answer the end, they are set upon making Pitch, Tar and Turpentine, and planting rice, and can send over great quantityes yearly, if they had encouragement from England to make it, having about 5,000 Slaves to be employed in that service, upon occasion, but they have lost most of their vessels, which were but small, last war by the French, and some lately by the Spaniards, so that they are not able to send those Commodities to England for a market, neither are sailors here to be had to man their vessels.

I humbly propose that if His Maty will for a time suspend the Duties [of the Acts of Navigation] upon Commodities, & that upon rice also, it will encourage the Planter to fall vigilantly upon making Pitch and Tar, etc., wch the Lords Proprs ought to make their principal care to obtain from His Maty, being the only way to draw people to settle in their Province, a place of greatest encouragement to the English Navy in these parts of the world. Charles Town Bay is the safest port for all vessels coming thro' the gulf of Florida in distress, bound from the West Indies to the Northern Plantations; if they miss this place they may perish at sea for want of relief, & having beat upon the coast of New England, New York, or Virginia by a North West Wind in the Winter, be forced to go to Barbadoes if they miss this Bay, where no wind will damage them and all things to be had necessary to refitt them. My Lords, I did formerly present Your Lordships with proposals for supplying England with Pitch and Tar, Masts & all o[ther] Naval Stores from New England. I observed when I were at York in Septr. last, abundance of Tar brot. down Hudson's River to be sold at New York, as also Turpentine and Tar in great quantities from the Colony of Connecticut. I was told if they had encouragement they could load several Ships yearly for England. But since my arrival here I find I am come into the only place for such commodities upon the Continent of America; some persons have offered to deliver in Charlestown Bay upon their own account 1000 Barrels of Pitch and as much Tar, others greater quantities provided they were paid for it in Charles Town in Lyon [Dutch] Dollars passing here at 5s. pr piece, Tar at 8s. pr. Barrel, and very good Pitch at 12s. pr. Barrel, & much cheaper if it once became a trade. The reason for making those Commodities in this Province being 6 mos. longer than in Virginia and more Northern Plantations, a planter can make more tar in any one year here with 50 slaves than they can with double the number in those places, their slaves here living at very easy rates and with few clothes.

The inclosed* I received from M. [Peter] Girard, a French Protestant living in Carolina. I find them very industrious and good husbands, but are discouraged because some of them having been many years Inhabitants in this Province are denied the benefit of being Owners and Masters of Vessels, which other the Subjects of His Majesty's Plantations enjoy, besides many of them are made Denizons [i.e. naturalized]. If this Place were duly encouraged, it would be the most useful to the Crown of all the Plantations upon the continent of America. . . . The Spaniards now [in St. Augustine], the French, if ever they get it, will prove dangerous neighbours to this Province, a thing not considered nor provided against by the Lords Proprietors. I am going from hence to Bermuda, with His Matys Commissioners, to administer the Oath to the Govr. of that Island, with a Commission for the Judge and other Officers of the Court of Admiralty erected there, from whence I believe it necessary to hasten to the Bahamas Islands, where a Brigantine belonging to New England was carried in as a wreck. The Master and Sailors being pursued by some persons who had commission from Govr. [Nicholas] Webb, believing they were chased by Spaniards, forsook their Vessel and went on shore among the Natives to save their lives.

All which is humbly submitted by
Your Lordship's
Most humble Servant,
Ed. Randolph.

The want of a small Vessel to support the loss of the Frigate, which was appointed by the Lords Commissrs of the Admiralty to transplant me from one Plantation to another, makes me stay a great while

* [Enclosure]

14 March, 1698/99

The Number and quantity of the French Protestants, Refugees of the French Church of Charles Town, is	195
The quantity of the French Protestants of the French Church of Goes [Goose] Creek, is	31
The quantity of the French Protestants of the Eastern branch of Cooper River, is	101
The number and quantity of the French Protestants of the French Church of Santee River, is	111
Total of the French Protestants to this day in Carolina,	438

. . . .

at one place for a passage to another, which is uncertain, difficult and dangerous.

I have by the extreme of cold last Winter in Maryland and Pennsylvania, and by my tedious passage in the Winter time from New York to this place, got a great numbness in my right leg and foot. I am in hopes this warm climate will restore me to my health. I have formerly wrote to your Board and the Commissrs of H. M. Customs, the necescity of having a Vessel to transport me from one Plantation to another.

I humbly pray Your Lordships favour to direct that the little residence I am to make in these parts of the World, may be in this Province, and that a Vessel well manned may be sent me hither, which may answer all occasion, my intentions being not to lye idle, for when the Hurricane times come in these parts of the World, I can go securely to Virginia, Maryland and Pennsylvania and New England, without fear of being driven from those Plantations by North West Winds, and when they come I can pass from one Plantation to another without difficulty.

5

Literary Endeavors

16. MICHAEL WIGGLESWORTH, *THE DAY OF DOOM*, 1666*

Michael Wigglesworth (1631–1705), minister and poet, wrote to instruct the common Puritan in the Calvinist dogma of the depravity and possible doom of men. His poetry was widely read and even enjoyed by the Puritans. The Day of Doom *went into several editions, though it cannot really be considered good poetry. It had a simple appeal: it was childishly rhymed, carried biblical annotations for each verse, and was surrounded by an aura of religious sensationalism because of its vivid details of the last judgment. Wigglesworth's other works were equally grim. In* God's Controversy with New England, *Wigglesworth described the great drought of 1660 as God's punishment for man's sins, and in* Meat Out of the Eater, *he found comfort in the sorrow and affliction of mankind.*

(1)

Still was the night, Serene and Bright, when all Men sleeping lay;
Calm was the season, and carnal reason thought so 'twould last for ay.
Soul, take thine ease, let sorrow cease, much good thou hast in store:
This was their Song, their Cups among, the Evening before.

THE SECURITY OF THE WORLD BEFORE CHRISTS COMING TO JUDGMENT. LUK. 12: 19.

---

* Michael Wigglesworth, *The Day of Doom* (Cambridge: Samuel Green, 1666).

(2)

Wallowing in all kind of sin, vile wretches lay secure: MAT. 25: 5.
The best of men had scarcely then their Lamps kept
    in good ure.
Virgins unwise, who through disguise amongst the
    best were number'd
Had clos'd their eyes; yea, and the wise through sloth
    and frailty slumber'd

(3)

Like as of old, when Men grow bold Gods' threatnings   MAT. 24:
    to contemn,   37, 38.
Who stopt their Ear, and would not hear, when
    Mercy warned them:
But took their course, without remorse, till God began
    to powre
Destruction the World upon in a tempestuous showre.

(4)

They put away the evil day, And drown'd their care   1 THES. 5: 3.
    and fears,
Till drown'd were they, and swept away by vengeance
    unawares:
So at the last, whilst Men sleep fast in their security,
Surpriz'd they are in such a snare as cometh suddenly.

(5)

For at midnight brake forth a Light, which turn'd the   THE SUD-
    night to day,   DENNESS,
And speedily an hideous cry did all the world dismay.   MAJESTY,
Sinners awake, their hearts do ake, trembling their   & TERROR
    loynes surprizeth;   OF CHRIST'S
Amaz'd with fear, by what they hear, each one of   APPEARING.
    them ariseth.   MAT. 25: 6.
                                                        2 PET. 3. 10.

(6)

They rush from Beds with giddy heads, and to their   MAT. 24:
    windows run,   29, 30.
Viewing this light, which shines more bright then doth
    the Noon-day Sun.
Straightway appears (they see't with tears) the Son
    of God most dread;
Who with his Train comes on amain to Judge both
    Quick and Dead.

(7)

Before his face the Heav'ns gave place, and Skies are
    rent asunder,
With mighty voice, and hideous noise, more terrible
    than Thunder.
His brightness damps heav'ns glorious lamps and
    makes them hide their heads,
As if afraid and quite dismay'd, they quit their wonted
    steads.

2 PET. 3: 10.

(8)

Ye sons of men that durst contemn the Threatnings of
    Gods Word.
How cheer you now? Your hearts, I trow, are thrill'd
    as with a sword.
Now Atheist blind, whose brutish mind a God could
    never see,
Dost thou perceive, dost now believe that Christ thy
    Judge shall be?

(9)

Stout Courages, (whose hardiness could Death and
    Hell out-face)
Are you as bold now you behold your Judge draw
    near apace?
They cry, no, no: Alas! and wo! our Courage all is
    gone:
Our hardiness (fool hardiness) hath us undone, un-
    done.

(10)

No heart so bold, but now grows cold and almost dead
    with fear:
No eye so dry, but now can cry, and pour out many a
    tear.
Earths Potentates and pow'rful States, Captains and
    Men of Might
Are quite abasht, their courage dasht at this most
    dreadful sight.

REV. 6: 16.

(11)

Mean men lament, great men do rent their Robes, and
    tear their hair:
They do not spare their flesh to tear through horrible
    despair.

MAT. 24: 30.

All Kindreds wail: all hearts do fail: horror the world
　　doth fill
With weeping eyes, and loud out-cries, yet knows not
　　how to kill.

(12)

Some hide themselves in Caves and Delves, in places
　　under ground:
Some rashly leap into the Deap, to scape by being
　　drown'd:
Some to the Rocks (O sensless blocks!) and woody
　　Mountains run,
That there they might this fearful sight, and dreaded
　　Presence shun.

REV. 6: 15, 16.

(13)

In vain do they to Mountains say, Fall on us, and us
　　hide
From Judges ire, more hot than fire, for who may it
　　abide?
No hiding place can from his Face sinners at all
　　conceal,
Whose flaming Eyes hid things doth 'spy, and darkest
　　things reveal.

(14)

The Judge draws nigh, exalted high upon a lofty
　　Throne,
Amidst the throng of Angels strong, lo, Israel's Holy
　　One!
The excellence of whose presence and awful Majesty,
Amazeth Nature, and every Creature, doth more than
　　terrify.

MAT. 25: 31.

(15)

The Mountains smoak, the Hills are shook, the Earth
　　is rent and torn,
As if she should be clean dissolv'd, or from the Center
　　born.
The Sea doth roar, forsakes the shore, and shrinks
　　away for fear;
The wild Beasts flee into the Sea, so soon as he draws
　　near.

REV. 6: 14.

(16)

Whose Glory bright, whose wondrous might, whose
    Power Imperial,
So far surpass whatever was in Realms Terrestrial;
That tongues of men (nor Angels pen) cannot the
    same express,
And therefore I must pass it by, lest speaking should
    transgress.

(17)

Before his Throne a Trump is blown, Proclaiming th'
    Day of Doom:
Forthwith he cries, *Ye Dead arise, and unto Judgment*
    come.
No sooner said, but 'tis obey'd; Sepulchers open'd are:
Dead Bodies all rise at his call, and's mighty power
    declare.

1 THES. 4: 16.
RESURRECTION
OF THE DEAD.
JOHN 5:
28, 29.

(18)

Both Sea and Land, at his Command, their Dead at
    once surrender:
The Fire and Air constrained are also their dead to
    tender.
The mighty word of this great Lord links Body and
    Soul together
Both of the Just, and the unjust, to part no more for
    ever.

(19)

The same translates, from Mortal states to Immor-
    tality,
All that survive, and be alive, i' th' twinkling of an
    eye:
That so they may abide for ay to endless weal or woe;
Both the Renate and Reprobate are made to dy no
    more.

THE LIVING
CHANGED.
LUK. 20: 36.
1 COR. 15: 52.

(20)

His winged Hosts flie through all Coasts, together
    gathering
Both good and bad, both quick and dead, and all to
    Judgment bring.
Out of their holes those creeping Moles, that hid
    themselves for fear,

ALL BROUGHT
TO JUDGMENT.
MAT. 24: 31.

By force they take, and quickly make before the Judge
    appear.

(21)

Thus every one before the Throne of Christ the Judge
    is brought,
Both righteous and impious that good or ill had
    wrought.
A separation, and diff'ring station by Christ appointed
    is
(To sinners sad) 'twixt good and bad, 'twixt Heir of
    woe and bliss.

2 COR. 5: 10
THE SHEEP
SEPARATED
FROM THE
GOATS.
MAT. 25: 32.

(22)

At Christ's right hand the Sheep do stand, his holy
    Martyrs, who
For his dear Name suffering shame, calamity and woe.
Like Champions stood, and with their Blood their
    testimony sealed;
Whose innocence without offence, to Christ their
    Judge appealed.

WHO ARE
CHRIST'S
SHEEP.
MAT. 5:
10, 11.

(23)

Next unto whom there find a room all Christ's af-
    flicted ones,
Who being chastised, neither despised nor sank amidst
    their groans:
Who by the Rod were turn'd to God, and loved him
    the more,
Not murmuring nor quarrelling when they were
    chast'ned sore.

HEB. 12:
5, 6, 7.

(24)

Moreover, such as loved much, that had not such a
    tryal,
As might constrain to so great pain, and such deep
    self denyal:
Yet ready were the Cross to bear, when Christ them
    call'd thereto,
And did rejoyce to hear his voice, they'rd countred
    Sheep also.

LUKE 7:
41, 47.

(25)

Christ's Flock of Lambs there also stands, whose
    Faith was weak, yet true;

JOH. 21: 15.
MAT. 19: 14.

All sound Believers (Gospel receivers) whose Grace
    was small, but grew: JOH. 3: 3.
And them among an Infant throng of Babes, for whom
    Christ dy'd;
Whom for his own, by wayes unknown to men, he
    sanctify'd.

(26)

All stand before their Saviour in long white Robes,   REV. 6: 11.
    yclad,   PHIL. 3: 21.
Their countenance full of pleasance, appearing
    wondrous glad.
O glorious sight! Behold how bright dust heaps are
    made to shine,
Conformed so their Lord unto, whose Glory is Divine.

(27)

At Christ's left hand the Goats do stand, all whining   THE GOATS
    hypocrites,   DESCRIBED OR
Who for self-ends did seem Christ's friends, but   THE SEVERAL
    foster'd guileful sprites: SORTS OF
Who Sheep resembled, but they dissembled (their   REPROBATES
    hearts were not sincere)   ON THE LEFT
Who once did throng Christ's Lambs among, but now   HAND.
    must not come near.   MAT. 24: 51.

(28)

Apostates and Run-awayes, such as have Christ for-   LUK. 11:
    saken,   24, 26.
Of whom the Devil, with seven more evil, hath fresh   HEB. 6: 4, 5, 6.
    possession taken: HEB. 10: 29.
Sinners in grain, reserv'd to pain and torments most
    severe:
Because 'gainst light they sinn'd with spight, are also
    placed there.

(29)

There also stand a num'rous band, that no Profession   LUK. 12: 47.
    made   PROV. 1:
Of Godliness, nor to redress their wayes at all essay'd: 24, 26.
Who better knew, but (sinful Crew) Gospel and Law   JOH. 3: 19.
    despised;
Who all Christ's knocks withstood like blocks and
    would not be advised.

(30)

Moreover, there with them appear a number, number-
less
Of great and small, vile wretches all, that did Gods
Law transgress;
Idolaters, false worshippers, Prophaners of Gods
Name,
Who not at all thereon did call, or took in vain the
same.

GAL. 3: 10.
1 COR. 6: 9.
REV. 21: 8.

(31)

Blasphemers lewd, and Swearers shrewd, Scoffers at
Purity,
That hated God, contemn'd his Rod, and lov'd Secur-
ity;
Sabbath-polluters, Saints persecuters, Presumptuous
men and Proud,
Who never lov'd those that reprov'd; all stand amongst
this Crowd.

EXOD. 20:
7, 8.
2 THES. 1:
6, 8, 9.

(32)

Adulterers and Whoremongers were there, with all
unchast:
There Covetous, and Ravenous, that Riches got too
fast:
Who us'd vile ways themselves to raise t' Estates and
worldly wealth,
Oppression by, or Knavery, by force, or fraud, or
stealth.

HEB. 13: 4.
1 COR. 6: 10.

(33)

Moreover, there together were Children flagitious,
And Parents who did them undo by Nurture vicious.
False-witness-bearers, and self-forswearers, Murd'rers,
and Men of blood,
Witches, Inchanters, & Ale house-haunters, beyond
account there stood.

ZACH. 5: 3, 4.
GAL. 5: 19,
20, 21.

(34)

Their place there find all Heathen blink, that Natures
light abused,
Although they had no tydings glad of Gospel-grace re-
fused.
There stands all Nations and Generations of *Adam's*
Progeny,

ROM. 2: 13.

Whom Christ redeem'd not, who Christ esteem'd not
  through Infidelity.

(35)

Who no Peace-maker, no Undertaker, to shrow'd them   ACT. 4: 12.
  from Gods ire
Ever obtain'd; they must be pained with everlasting
  fire.
These num'rous bands wringing their hands, and
  weeping all stand there,
Filled with anguish, whose hearts do languish through
  self-tormenting fear.

(36)

Fast by them stand at Christ's left hand the Lion   1 COR. 6: 3.
  fierce and fell,
The Dragon bold, that Serpent old, that hurried Souls
  to Hell.
There also stand, under command, Legions of Sprights
  unclean,
And hellish Fiends, that are no friends to God, nor
  unto Men.

(37)

With dismal chains, and strongest reins, like Prisoners   JUDE 6
  of Hell,
They're held in place before Christ's face, till He their
  Doom shall tell.
These void of tears, but fill'd with fears, and dreadful
  expectation
Of endless pains, and scalding flames, stand waiting
  for Damnation.

17. ANNE BRADSTREET, *THE TENTH MUSE*, 1678[*]

Anne Dudley Bradstreet (c. 1612–72), wife of the Massachusetts Bay statesman, Simon Bradstreet, and daughter of Deputy Governor Joseph Dudley, was well educated in the best English tradition. A naturally gifted poet, she was a disciple and admirer of England's Spenser, Hall, and Ben Jonson. She was most influenced by the French Huguenot soldier and poet, Guillaume De Salluste Du Bartas, author of religious epics, which contrasted with the "paganistic" poetry current in his country. Mrs. Bradstreet's work, published in her collection, The Tenth Muse,

---

[*] Anne Dudley Bradstreet, *Several Poems* (Boston: John Foster, 1758), pp. 203–5.

was proudly endorsed by the Massachusetts fathers. Most of her poems deal with the land or Calvinistic dogma. Though some of her religious works are criticized as stilted, "Contemplations," which discusses the dilemma of how to love the world and God too, has received considerable acclaim.

Contemplations, 1678

1

Some time now past in the Autumnal tide,
When *Phoebus* wanted but one hour to bed,
The trees all richly clad, yet void of pride,
Were gilded o'rd by his rich golden head.
Their leaves & fruits seem'd painted, but was true
Of green, of red, of yellow, mixed hew,
Rapt were my Sences at this delectable view.

2

I wist not what to wish, yet fare thought I,
If So much excellence abide below;
How excellent is he that dwells on high?
Whose power and beauty by his works we know.
Sure he is goodness, wisdome glory, light,
That hath this underworld so richly dight:
More Heaven than Earth was here no winter & no night.

3

Then on a stately Oak I cast mine Eye,
Whose ruffling top the clouds seem'd to espire;
How long since thou wast in thine Infancy?
Thy strength, and stature, more thy years admire,
Hath hundred winters past since thou wast born?
Or thousand since thou brakest thy shell of horn.
If so, all these as nought, Eternity doth-scorn.

4

Then higher on the glistening Sun I gay'd,
Whose beams was shaded by the leavie Tree,
The more I look'd, the more I grew amaz'd,
And softly said, what glory's like to thee?
Soul of this world, this Universes Eye,
No wonder, some made thee a Deity:
Had I not better known, (alas) the same had I.

5

Thou as a Bridegroom from thy chamber rushes,
And as a strong man, joyes to run a race,
The morn doth usher thee, with smiles & blushes,
The Earth reflects her glances in thy face.
Birdes, insects, animals with vegative,
Thy heart from death and dulness doth revive:
And in the darksome womb of fruitful nature dive.

6

Thy swift annual, and diurnal Course,
Thy daily freight, and yearly oblique path,
Thy pleasing fervor, and thy scorching force,
All mortals here the feeling knowledge hath
Thy presence makes it day, thy absence night,
Quaternal Seasons caused by thy might:
Hail Creature, full of sweetness, beauty & delight.

7

Act thou so full of glory, that no Eye.
Hath strength, thy shining Rayes once to behold?
And is thy splendid Throne erect so high?
As to approach it, can no earthly mould.
How full of glory then must thy Creator be?
Who gave this bright light luster unto thee:
Admir'd, ador'd for ever, be that Majesty.

8

Silent alone, where none or saw or heard,
In pathless paths I lead my wandering feet,
My humble Eyes to lofty Skyes I rear'd
To sing some Song, my mazed Muse thought meet.
My great Creator I would magnifie,
That nature had, thus decked liberally:
But Ah, and Ah, again, my imbecility!

9

I heard the merry grashopper them Sing,
The black clad Cricket, bear a second part,
They kept one tune, and plaid on the same string,
Seeming to glory in their little Art.
Shall Creatures abject, thus their voices raise?
And in their kind resound their makers praise:
Whilst I as mute, can warble forth no higher layes.

10

When present times look back to Ages past,
And men in being fancy those are dead.
It makes things gone perpetually to last.
And calls back months and years that long since fled,
It makes a man more aged in conceit,
Then was *Methuselah,* or's grand-sire great:
While of their persons & their acts his mind doth treat.

11

Sometimes in *Eden* fair, he seems to be,
Sees glorious *Adam* there made Lord of all,
Fancyes the Apple, dangle on the Tree.
That turn'd his Sovereign to a naked thral.
Who like a miscreant's driven from that place,
To get his bread with pain, and sweat of face:
A penalty impos'd on his backsliding Race.

18. MARY WHITE ROWLANDSON, *THE SOVERAIGNTY AND GOODNESS OF GOD,* 1676*

Mary White Rowlandson (c. 1635–78) was the daughter of John White, the wealthiest of the proprietors of Lancaster, Massachusetts, and wife of Joseph Rowlandson, minister. Mrs. Rowlandson and her three children were captured by Indians during King Philip's War and held prisoner while her captors roamed western Massachusetts dodging English patrols. The youngest of her three children died of wounds and exposure. After she and her surviving family had suffered many hardships and privations, she was ransomed for twenty pounds and reunited with her family. In the Soveraignty and Goodness of God . . . Being A Narrative of the Captivity and Restoration of Mrs. Mary Rowlandson, *a seventeenth-century bestseller in England and America, she set down her experiences in vivid detail and "sinewy" style. However harrowing her trials, for Mrs. Rowlandson they were providential, and of her adversities she wrote, "as David . . . It is good for me that I have been afflicted."*

On the tenth of *February* came the Indians with great Numbers upon *Lancaster:* Their first coming was about Sun-rising; hearing the noise of some Guns, we looked out; several Houses were burning, and

---

* Mary White Rowlandson, *The Soveraignty and Goodness of God,* 2nd ed. (Boston: T. Fleet for Samuel Phillips, 1720), pp. 3–9, 11–19.

the Smoke ascending to Heaven. There were five persons taken in one House, the Father, and the Mother, and a suckling Child they knockt on the head; the other two they took and carried away alive. There were two others, who being out of their Garrison upon some Occasion, were set upon; one was knockt on the head, the other escaped. Another there was who running along was shot and wounded, and fell down; he begged of them his Life, promising them Money, (as they told me) but they would not hearken to him, but knockt him in head, stript him naked, and split open his Bowels. Another seeing many of the Indians about his Barn, ventured and went out, but was quickly shot down. There were three others belonging to the same Garrison who were killed; the *Indians* getting up upon the Roof of the Barn, had advantage to shoot down upon them over their Fortification. Thus these murtherous wretches went on burning and destroying before them.

At length they came & beset our own house, and quickly it was the dolefullest Day that ever mine eyes saw. The House stood upon the edge of a Hill; some of the *Indians* got behind the Hill, others into the Barn, and others behind any thing that would shelter them; from all which places they shot against the House, so that the Bullets seemed to fly like Hail; and quickly they wounded one man among us, then another, and then a third. About two hours (according to my Observation in that amazing time) they had been about the House before they prevailed to fire it, (which they did with Flax and Hemp which they brought out of the Barn, and there being no Defence about the House, only a Flankers at two opposite Corners, and one of them not finished) they fired it once, and one ventured out and quenched it, but they quickly fired it again, and that took. Now is that dreadful hour come, that I have often heard of (in the time of the War, as it was the Case of others) but now mine Eyes see it. Some in our House were fighting for their Lives, others wallowing in their Blood, the House on fire over our heads, and the bloody Heathen ready to knock us on the head if we stirred out. Now might we hear Mothers and Children crying out for themselves, and one another, *Lord what shall we do*! Then I took my Children (and one of my Sisters hers) to go forth and leave the House: but as soon as we came to the door, and appeared, the *Indians* shot so thick, that the bullets rattled against the House, as if one had taken an handful of Stones and threw them, so that we were forced to give back. We had six stout Dogs belonging to our Garrison, but none of them would stir, though another time, if an Indian had come to the Door, they were ready to fly upon him and tear him down. The Lord hereby would make us the more to acknowledge his Hand, and to see that our Help is always in him. But out we must go, the fire increasing, and coming along behind us, roaring, and the *Indians* gaping before us with their Guns, Spears, and Hatchets to devour us. No sooner were we out of the House, but my Brother-in-Law (being before Wounded in defending the House, in or near the Throat) fell down dead, whereat the *Indians* scornfully shouted, and halloed, and were presently upon him, stripping off his Cloaths. The Bullets flying thick, one went thorough my side, and the same (as would seem) thorough the Bowels and Hand of my poor Child in my Arms. One of my elder Sisters Children (named *William*) had then his Leg broke, which the *Indians* perceiving, they knockt him on head. Thus were we butchered by those merciless Heathen, standing amazed, with the Blood running down to our heels. My elder Sister being yet in the House, and seeing those wo[e]ful sights, the Infidels haling Mothers one way, and Children another, and some wallowing in their Blood: And her eldest Son telling her that her Son *William* was dead, and my self was wounded, she said, and *Lord, let me dye with them*: which was no sooner said, but she was struck with a Bullet, and fell down dead over the Threshold. I hope she is reaping the fruit of her good Labours, being faithful to the Service of God in her place. In her younger Years she lay under much trouble upon spiritual Accounts, till it pleased God to make that precious Scripture take hold of her Heart, 2 Cor. 12.9. *And he said unto me, My Grace is sufficient for thee.* More than twenty Years after, I have heard her tell how sweet and comfortable that place was to her. But to return; the *Indians* laid hold of us, pulling me one way, and the Children another, and said, *Come go along with us*: I told them they would kill me; they Answered, *If I were willing to go along with them, they would not hurt me.*

Oh! the doleful sight that was to behold at this House! Come, behold the Works of the Lord, what desolations he has made in the Earth. Of thirty seven Persons who were in this one House, none excaped either present Death, or a bitter Captivity, Save only one, who might say as he, *Job* 1. 15. *And I only am escaped alone to tell the News.* There were twelve killed, some shot, some stab'd with their Spears, some knock'd down with their Hatchets. When we are in Prosperity, Oh the little that we think of such dreadful Sights, to see our dear Friends and Relations lie bleeding out their Heartsblood upon the Ground. There was one who was chopt into the head with a Hatchet, and stript naked, & yet was crawling up and down. It is a solemn Sight to see so many christians lying in their Blood, some here and some there, like a company of Sheep torn by Wolves. All of them stript naked by a company of Hell-hounds, roaring, singing, ranting and insulting, as if they would have torn our very Hearts out; yet the Lord by his Almighty Power, preserved a number of us from Death, for there were twenty four of us taken alive and carried Captive.

I had often before this said, that if the *Indians* should come, I should chuse rather to be killed by them, than taken alive: but when it came to the tryal, my Mind changed; their glittering Weapons so daunted my Spirit, that I chose rather to go along with those (as I may say) ravenous Bears, than that moment to end my days. And that I may the better declare what happened to me during that grievous Captivity, I shall particularly speak of the several Removes we had up and down the Wilderness.

The First Remove

Now away we must go with those Barbarous Creatures, with our Bodies wounded and bleeding, and our Hearts no less than our Bodies. About a mile we went that night, up upon a hill within sight of the Town, where they intended to lodge. There was hard by a vacant House, (deserted by the *English* before, for fear of the *Indians*) I asked them whether I might not lodge in the House that night? to which they answered, What will you love *English-men* still? This was the dolefullest night that ever my eyes saw. Oh the roaring, and singing, and dancing, & yelling of those black creatures in the night, which *made* the place a lively resemblance of Hell: And as miserable was the waste that was there made, of Horses, Cattle, Sheep, Swine, Calves, Lambs, Roasting-Pigs, and Fowls, (which they had plundered in the Town) some Roasting, some lying & Burning, and some Boyling, to feed our merciless Enemies; who were joyful enough, though we were Disconsolate. To add to the dolefulness of the former Day, and the dismalness of the present Night, my thoughts ran upon my Losses and sad breaved Condition. All was gone, my Husband gone, (at least separated from me, he being in the *Bay*; and to add to my Grief, the *Indians* told me they would kill him as he came homeward) my Children gone, my Relations & Friends gone, our House and Home, and all our Comforts within Door and without, all was gone, (except my Life) and I knew not but the next Moment that might go too.

There remained nothing to me but one poor wounded Babe, and it seemed at present worse than Death, that it was in such a pitiful Condition, bespeaking Compassion, and I had no Refreshing for it, nor suitable things to Revive it. Little do many think, what is the Savageness and Bruitishness of this barbarous Enemy, even those that seem to profess more than others among them, when the *English* have fallen into their Hands.

Those seven that were killed at *Lancaster* the Summer before upon a Sabbath Day, and the One that was afterward killed upon a week Day, were slain and mangled in a barbarous manner, by one-ey'd *John*, and *Marlborough's* Praying *Indians*, [christianized Indians] which Capt. *Mosely* brought to *Boston*, as the *Indians* told me.

. . . .

The Third Remove

The Morning being come, they prepared to go on their way: one of the Indians got up upon a Horse, and they set me up behind him, with my poor sick Babe in my Lap. A very wearisome and tedious day I had of it; what with my own Wound, and my Child being so exceeding sick, and in a lamentable condition with her Wound, it may easily be judged what a poor feeble condition we were in, there being not the least crumb of Refreshing that came within either of our Mouths from *Wednesday* Night to *Saturday* Night, except only a little cold Water. This Day in the Afternoon, about an Hour by Sun, we came to the Place where they intended, *viz.* an *Indian* Town called *Wenimesset*, Northward of *Quabaug.* When we were come, Oh the number of *Pagans* (now merciless Enemies) that there came about me, that I may say as David, Psal. 27. 13. *I had fainted, unless I had believed,* &c. The next Day was the Sabbath: I then rememberd how careless I had been of God's holy Time: how many Sabbaths I had lost and mispent, & how evily I had walked in God's sight; which lay so close upon my Spirit, that it was easie for me to see how Righteous it was with God to cut off the thread of my Life, and cast me out of his presence for ever. Yet the Lord still shewed Mercy to me, and helped me; and as he wounded me with one Hand, so he healed me with the other. This Day there came to me one *Robert Pepper,* (a Man belonging to *Roxbury,*) who was taken at Capt. *Beers* his Fight; and had been now a considerable time with the *Indians*, and up with them almost as far as *Albany* to see King *Philip*, as he told me, and was now very lately come with them into these parts. Hearing I say, that I was in this Indian Town, he obtained leave to come and see me. He told me he himself was wounded in the Leg at Capt. *Beers* his Fight; and was not able sometime to go but as they carried him, and that he took Oak Leaves and laid to his Wound, and by the Blessing of God, he was able to Travel again. Then I took Oak Leaves and laid to my Side, and with the Blessing of God, it cured me also; yet before the Cure was wrought, I may say as it is in *Psal.* 38. 5, 6. *My Wounds Stink and are Corrupt, I am troubled, I am bowed down greatly, I go Mourning all the day long.* I sate much alone with my poor wounded Child in my Lap, which moaned Night and Day, having nothing to revive the Body, or chear the Spirits of her; but instead of that, one Indian would come and tell me one hour, your Master will knock your child on the head, and then a second, and then a third, your Master will quickly knock your Child on the head.

This was the Comfort I had from them; Miserable Comforters were they all. Thus nine Days I sate upon my Knees, with my Babe in my Lap, till my Flesh was raw again. My Child being even ready to depart this sorrowful *World*, they bid me carry it out to another Wigwam; (I suppose because they would not be troubled with such Spectacles) Wither I went with a very heavy Heart, and down I sate with the Picture of Death in my Lap. About two hours in the Night, my Sweet Babe like a Lamb departed this Life, on *Feb.* 18. 1675. it being about six Years and five Months old. It was nine Days from the first wounding, in this miserable Condition, without any Refreshing of one nature or other, except a little cold Water. I cannot but take notice, how at another time I could not bear to be in the room where any dead Person was, but now the case is changed; I must, and could lie down by my dead Babe all the Night after. I have thought since of the wonderful Goodness of God to me, in preserving me so in the use of my Reason and Senses, in that distressed time, that I did not use wicked and violent Means to end my own miserable Life. In the Morning, when they understood that my child was dead, they sent for me home to my Masters Wigwam: (By my Master in this Writing, must be understood *Quannopin*, who was a Saggamore, and married K. *Philip's* Sister; not that he first took me, but I was sold to him by a *Narraganset Indian*, who took me when I first came out of the Garrison) I went to take up my dead Child in my Arms to carry it with me, but they bid me let it alone: There was no resisting, but go I must and leave it. When I had been a while at my Masters Wigwam, I took the first opportunity I could get, to go look after my dead Child: When I came, I asked them what they had done with it? they told me it was upon the Hill; then they went and shewed me where it was, where I saw the Ground was newly digged, and where they told me they had buried it; there I left that Child in the Wilderness, and must commit it and my self also in this wilderness Condition, to him who is above all. God having taken away this dear Child, I went to see my Daughter *Mary*, who was at this same *Indian* Town, at a Wigwam not very far off, though we had little liberty or opportunity to see one another: She was about ten Years old, and taken from the Door at first by a Praying *Indian*, and afterward sold for a Gun. When I came in sight, she would fall a Weeping, at which they were provoked, and would not let me come near her, but bid me be gone; Which was a Heart cutting Word to me. I had one Child dead, another in the Wilderness, I knew not where, the third they would not let me come near to; *Me* (as he said) *have ye bereaved of my Children Joseph is not, and Simeon is not, and ye will take Benjamin also, all these things are against me.* I could not sit still in this Condition, but kept walking from one place to another. And as I was going along, my Heart was even overwhelmed with the thoughts of my Condition, and that I should have Children, and a Nation that I knew not ruled over them. Whereupon I earnestly intreated the Lord that he would consider my low Estate, &

shew me a Token for Good, and if it were his blessed Will, some sign and hope of some Relief. And indeed quickly the Lord answered, in some measure, my poor Prayer: For as I was going up and down mourning and lamenting my Condition, my Son came to me, and asked me how I did? I had not seen him before, since the destruction of the Town; and I knew not where he was, till I was informed by himself, that he was amongst a smaller parcel of *Indians*, whose place was about six Miles off, with tears in his eyes, he asked me whether his Sister *Sarah* was dead? and told me he had seen his Sister *Mary*; and prayed me, that I would not be troubled in reference to himself. The occasion of his coming to see me at this time was this: There was, as I said, about six Miles from us, a small Plantation of *Indians*, where it seems he had been during his Captivity; and at this time, there were some Forces of the *Indians* gathered out of our Company, and some also from them, (amongst whom was my Sons Master) to go to assault and burn *Medfield*: In this time of his Master's Absence, his Dame brought him to see me. I took this to be some gracious Answer to my earnest and unfeigned Desire. The next Day the *Indians* returned from *Medfield*: (all the Company, for those that belonged to the other smaller Company, came through the Town that now we were at) But before they came to us, Oh the outrageous Roaring and Hooping that there was! They began their din about a Mile before they came to us. By their Noise and Hooping they signified how many they had destroyed: (which was at that time twenty three) Those that were with us at home, were gathered together as soon as they heard the Hooping, and every time that the other went over their number, these at home gave a shout, that the very Earth rang again. And thus they continued till those that had been upon the Expedition were come up to the Saggamor's Wigwam; and then Oh the hideous Insulting and Triumphing that there was over some *English* Mens Scalps, that they had taken (as their manner is) and brought with them. I cannot but take notice of the wonderful Mercy of God to me in those Afflictions, in sending me a *Bible*: One of the *Indians* that came from *Medfield* Fight, and had brought some Plunder, came to me, and asked me if I would have a *Bible*, he had got one in his Basket, I was glad of it, and asked him if he thought the *Indians* would let me Read? he answered yes; so I took the *Bible*, and in that melancholy Time, it came into my Mind to Read first the 28th Chap. of *Deuteronomy*, which I did, and when I had read it, my dark Heart wrought on this manner, That there was no Mercy for me, that the Blessings were gone, and the Curses came in their room, and that I had lost my opportunity. But the Lord helped me still to go on reading, till I came to Chap. 30 the Seven first verses; where I found there was Mercy promised again, if we would return to him, by repentance; and though we were scattered from one end of the Earth to the other, yet the Lord would gather us together, and turn all those curses upon our Enemies. I do not desire to live to forget this Scripture, & what comfort it was to me.

Now the *Indians* began to talk of Removing from this place, some one way, and some another. There were now besides my self nine *English* Captives in this place, (all of them Children except one Woman) I got an opportunity to go and take my leave of them; they being to go one way, and I another. I asked them whether they were earnest with God for Deliverence, they all told me they did as they were able, and it was some Comfort to me, that the Lord stirred up Children to look to him. The Woman, *viz.* Goodwife *Jossin* told me, she should never see me again, and that she could find in her heart to run away: I desired her not to run away by any means, for we were near thirty Miles from any *English* Town, and she very big with Child, having but one Week to reckon; and another Child in her Arms two Years old, and bad Rivers there were to go over, and we were feeble with out poor and course Entertainment. I had my Bible with me, I pulled it out, and asked her whether she would Read; we opened the Bible, and lighted on *Psal.* 27. in which Psalm we especially took notice of that *verse, Wait on the Lord, be of good Courage, and he Shall Strengthen thine Heart, wait I say on the Lord.*

19. SAMUEL SEWALL, *DIARY*, 1676–85*

Samuel Sewall (1652–1730) came to New England with his parents at the age of nine. He was a student of divinity at Harvard, but became a Boston merchant and public servant. Of the several judges who presided over the witchcraft trials of Salem in 1692, he was the only one who admitted his grave errors in condemning innocent people; in 1697 he made a tearful public confession in the Old South Church. One of the country's earliest abolitionists, he published the antislavery tract, The Selling of Joseph, *in 1700. As a diarist he has been compared to his London contemporary, Samuel Pepys. The Sewall diary, sampled here, was never as erudite as Pepys', but does give a panoramic view of life in New England at the end of the seventeenth and the beginning of the eighteenth century.*

Saturday Even. Aug. 12, 1676, just as prayer ended Tim. Dwight sank down in a Swoun, and for a good space was as if he perceived not what was done to him: after, kicked and sprawled, knocking his hands and feet upon the floor like a distracted man. Was carried pickpack to bed by John Alcock, there his cloaths pulled off. In the night it seems he talked of ships, his master, father, and unckle Eliot. The Sabbath fol-

* *Collections of the Massachusetts Historical Society,* 5th series (Boston: Massachusetts Historical Society, 1878–79), Vol. V, pp. 15, 16, 69–70, 82–83, 86, 103–4, 112 *passim.*

lowing Father went to him, spake to him to know what ailed him, asked if he would be prayed for, and for what he would desire his friends to pray. He answered, for more sight of sin, and God's healing grace. I asked him, being alone with him, whether his troubles were from some outward cause or spiritual. He answered, spiritual. I asked him why then he could not tell it his master, as well as any other, since it is the honour of any man to see sin and be sorry for it. He gave no answer, as I remember. Asked him if he would goe to meeting. He said 'twas in vain for him; his day was out. I asked, what day: he answered, of Grace. I told him 'twas sin for any one to conclude themselves Reprobate, that this was all one. He said he would speak more, but could not, &c. Notwithstanding all this semblance (and much more than is written) of compunction for Sin, 'tis to be feared that his trouble arose from a maid whom he passionately loved: for that when Mr. Dwight and his master had agreed to let him goe to her, he eftsoons grew well.

Friday, Aug. 25. I spake to Tim of this, asked him whether his convictions were off. He answered, no. I told him how dangerous it was to make the convictions wrought by God's spirit a stakling horse to any other thing. Broke off, he being called away by Sam.

. . . .

July 8, 1677. New Meeting House *Mane*: In Sermon time there came in a female Quaker, in a Canvas Frock, her hair disshevelled and loose like a Periwigg, her face as black as ink, led by two other Quakers, and two other followed. It occasioned the greatest and most amazing uproar that I ever saw. Isaiah I. 12, 14.

. . . .

Apr. 14th 1685. A Ship arrives from New castle and brings News of the death of Charles the 2nd, and Proclamation of James the 2nd, King. Brought a couple of printed Proclamations relating to that affair. News came to us as we were busy opening the Nominations just before Dinner; it much startled the Governour and all of us. In the morn before I went the Governour said that a Ship master had been with him from Nevis, who told him Govr. Stapleton should say, we should have a new Governour before he got to Boston. Master dined with Magistrates and Commissioners at Capt. Wing's. Carried my wife to George Bairsto's yesterday, April 13th.—. Thorsday, April 16th, a Vessel arrives from London. Mr. Lord, commander, brings Orders to the several Colonies to proclaim the King. Mr. Blathwayt writes to Simon Bradstreet, Esq. superscribed For His Majestie's Service, advising that 't would be best for us early to doe it; and our Charter being vacated in Law and no Government settled here, was the reason we were not writt to: Copies and forms sent to us as to the other Colonies, but no mention of Governour and Company. Also another letter was writt to Simon Bradstreet, Wm. Stoughton, Jos. Dudley, Peter Bulkeley, Sam'l. Shrimpton, Richard Wharton, Esquires, to proclaim the King. Suppose this was done lest the Government should have neglected to do it. The Council agreed to proclaim the King before they knew of the Letter. Major Richards counted the Votes for Mr. Dudley, told them twice over, and still found them 666, and so 'twas entered and sent to the Towns.

Monday April 20th. The King is Proclaimed; 8 Companies, the Troop, and several Gentlemen on horseback assisting; three Volleys and then Cannon fired. This day a child falls upon a Knife which run through its cheek to the Throat, of which inward Wound it dies, and is buried on Wednesday. 'Tis one Gees child.—Thorsday, April 23, Mother Sewall comes by Water in Stephen Greenleaf to see us.

.   .   .   .

Wednesday, June 17th [1685] a Quaker or two goe to the Governour and ask leave to enclose the [common] Ground the Hanged Quakers are buried in under or near the Gallows, with Pales: Governour proposed it to the Council, who unanimously denied it as very inconvenient for persons so dead and buried in the place to have any Monument.

Thorsday, June 18. A Quaker comes to the Governour and speaks of a Message he had which was to shew the great Calamities of Fire and Sword that would suddenly come on New-England. Would fain have spoken in the Meetinghouse, but was prevented. Eliakim comes home this day, brings word that Capt. Henchman is coming away from Worcester with his Family.

Noyes this day of a French Pirat on the Coast, of 36 Guns.

Satterday, June 20th 1685. Voted. the 16th of July to be observed as a Fast.

Satterday, P.M. Carried my Wife to Dorchester to eat Cherries, Rasberries, chiefly to ride and take the Air: the Time my Wife and Mrs. Flint spent in the Orchard, I spent in Mr. Flint's Study, reading Calvin on the Psalms &c. 45. 68. 24.

Monday, July. 6th. I am taken with a Feverish Fit; yet go to Court in the Afternoon, the County Court, where was read Major Pynchon's Letter to the Council; which is that 5 Men came to one of the Houses of Westfield (I think) about midnight 28th June, knockt at the door, the Man bid him come in, so in they came all Armed with drawn Swords, and threatened to run the man and his wife through if they stirred: so plundered that House, and another in like manner: told they had 60 Men in their Company and that if they stirred out of door, they would kill them; so stayd in a great part of Monday, then when thought the Coast was clear told the Neighbors and some were sent to Search after them; at last found them: one of the 5 snapt and missed fire, another shot, then one of ours shot so as to shoot one of theirs dead: another of the 5 fought one of ours with his sword, till another of ours knockt him down. One or two that were taken are brought to Boston, one at least is escaped. Major Pynchon his Works will cost near an hundred Pounds.

An Indian was branded in Court and had a piece of his Ear cut off for Burglary.

.   .   .   .

Thorsday, Novr. 12. [1685] Mr. Moodey preaches from Isa. 57.1. Mr. Cobbet's Funeral Sermon; said also of Mr. Chauncy that he was a Man of Singular Worth. Said but 2 of the First Generation left.

After, the Ministers of this Town Come to the Court and complain against a Dancing Master who seeks to set up here and hath mixt Dances, and his time of Meeting is Lecture-Day; and 'tis reported he should say that by one Play he could teach more Divinity than Mr. Willard or the Old Testament. Mr. Moodey said 'twas not a time for N. E. to dance. Mr. Mather struck at the Root, speaking against mixt Dances.

.   .   .   .

Thorsday, Decr. 17th. [1685] . . . Mr. Francis Stepney, the Dancing Master, desired a Jury, so He and Mr. Shrimpton Bound in 50£ to Janr. Court. Said Stepney is ordered not to keep a Dancing School; if he does will be taken in contempt and be proceeded with accordingly. Mr. Shrimpton muttered, saying he took it as a great favour that the Court would take his Bond for 50£.

Friday Dec. 18. Begun in Course to read the New Testament, having ended the Revelation the night before.

Satterday Dec. 19. Mr. Willard Prayes with my little Henry, being very ill.

Sabbath-day, Dec. 20. Send Notes to Mr. Willard and Mr. Moodey to pray for my Child Henry.

Monday, about four in the Morn the faint and moaning noise of my child forces me up to pray for it.

21. Monday even Mr. Moodey calls. I get him to go up and Pray with my extream sick Son.

Tuesday Morn, Dec. 22. Child makes no noise save by a kind of snoaring as it breathed, and as it were slept.

Read the 16th of the first Chron. in the family. Having read to my Wife and Nurse out of John; the fourteenth Chapter fell now in course, which I read and went to Prayer: By that time had done, could hear little Breathing, and so about Sunrise, or little after, he fell asleep, I hope in Jesus, and that a Mansion was ready for him in the Father's

House. Died in Nurse Hill's Lap. Nurse Hill washes and layes him out: because our private Meeting hath a day of Prayer tomorrow, Thorsday Mr. Willard's Lecture, and the Child dying after Sunrise (wether cloudy), have determined to bury on Thorsday after Lecture. The Lord sanctify his Dispensation, and prepare me and mine for the coming of our Lord, in whatsoever way it be. Mr. Tho. Oakes our Physician for this Child. Read the 16th Chap. of the First Chronicles in the Family.

Thorsday, Decr. 24th 1685. We follow Little Henry to his Grave: Governour and Magistrates of the County here, 8 in all, beside my Self, Eight Ministers, and Several Persons of note. Mr. Phillips of Rowley here. I led Sam., then Cous. Savage led Mother, and Cousin Dumer led Cous. Quinsey's wife, he not well. Midwife Weeden and Nurse Hill carried the Corps by turns, and so by Men in its Chestnut Coffin 'twas set into a Grave (The Tomb full of water) between 4 and 5. At Lecture the 21. Psalm was Sung from 8*th* to the end. The Lord humble me kindly in respect of all my Enmity against Him, and let his breaking my Image in my Son be a means of it. Considerable snow this night.

Dec. 25. Friday. Carts come to Town and Shops open as is usual. Some somehow observe the day; but are vexed I believe that the Body of the People profane it, and blessed be God no Authority yet to compell them to keep it. A great Snow fell last night so this day and night very cold.

20. EBENEZER COOK, *THE SOT-WEED FACTOR—A SATYR,* 1708*

Little is known about the satirist Ebenezer Cook (fl. 1693–1730). Evidently he voyaged to Maryland to become a tobacco planters' factor —or middleman—and there voiced his displeasure with the natives as rude, uncultured, and boorish.

It is uncertain whether Cook settled in the province or was merely a visiting Englishman who, like the later observer Charles Dickens, returned home with a dim view of American refinements and manners. There was an Ebenezer Cook residing in St. Mary's City in 1693. The December 17, 1728, issue of the Maryland Gazette *published an elegy on Nicholas Lowe, of no mean poetical achievement, signed E. C. "Laureat." As Lowe had been a member of Lord Baltimore's Council, the possibility exists that the author was Cook, and that he had been appointed laureate by his Lordship. In 1730, another poem, "Sot-Weed Redivivus" was published in the* Maryland Gazette *signed "E. C. Gent" The "Sot-Weed Factor" is an excellent satire of life in the Chesapeake*

* *Early Maryland Poetry: The Works of Ebenezer Cook. Gent: Laureat of Maryland . . .* Bernard C. Steiner, ed., Maryland Historical Society Fund Publication, No. 36 (Baltimore: Maryland Historical Society, 1900), pp. 11–21.

region—irreverent and earthy, especially compared to contemporary Puritan poetry.

THE SOT-WEED FACTOR; OR, A VOYAGE TO MARYLAND, &C.

Condemn'd by Fate to way-ward Curse,
Of Friends unkind, and empty Purse;
Plagues worse than fill'd *Pandora's* Box,
I took my leave of *Albion's* Rocks:
With heavy Heart, coucern'd that I
Was fore'd my Native Soil to fly,
And the *Old World* must bid good-buy.
But Heav'n ordain'd it should be so.
And to repine is vain we know:
Freighted with Fools, from *Plymouth* sound,
To *Mary-Land* our Ship was bound,
Where we arriv'd in dreadful Pain,
Shock'd by the Terrours of the Main;
For full three Months, our wavering Boat,
Did thro' the surley Ocean float,
And furious Storms and threat'ning Blasts,
Both tore our Sails and sprung our Masts:
Wearied, yet pleas'd, we did escape
Such Ills, we anchor'd at the *Cape*;
But weighing soon, we plough'd the *Bay*,
To Cove it in *Piscato-way*,
Intending there to open Store,
I put myself and Goods a-shore:
Where soon repair'd a numerous Crew,
In Shirts and Drawers of *Scotch-cloth* Blue.
With neither Stockings, Hat, nor Shooe.
These *Sot-weed* Planters Crowd the Shoar,
In Hue as tawny as a Moor:
Figures so strange, no God design'd,
To be a part of Humane Kind:
But wanton Nature, void of Rest,
Moulded the brittle Clay in Jest.
At last a Fancy very odd
Took me, this was the Land of *Nod*;
Planted at first, when Vagrant *Cain*,
His Brother had unjustly slain:

Then conscious of the Crime he'd done,
From Vengeance dire, he hither run;
And in a Hut supinely dwelt,
The first in *Furs* and *Sot-weed* dealt.
And ever since his Time, the Place,
Has harbour'd a detested Race;
Who when they cou'd not live at Home,
For Refuge to these Worlds did roam;
In hopes by Flight they might prevent,
The Devil and his fell intent;
Obtain from Tripple Tree repreive,
And Heav'n and Hell alike deceive:

The Planter

Encountring soon the smoaky Seat,
The Planter old did thus me greet:
"Whether you come from Gaol or Colledge,
"You're welcome to my certain Knowledge;
"And if you please all Night to stay,
"My Son shall put you in the way.
Which offer I most kindly took,
And for a Seat did round me look;
When presently amongst the rest,
He plac'd his unknown *English* Guest,
Who found them drinking for a whet,
A Cask of Syder on the Fret,
Till Supper came upon the Table,
On which I fed whilst I was able.
So after hearty Entertainment,
Of Drink and Victuals without Payment;
For Planters Tables, you must know,
Are free for all that come and go.
While Pon and Milk, with Mush well stoar'd,
In wooden Dishes grac'd the Board;
With Homine and Syder-pap,
(Which scarce a hungry Dog wou'd lap)
Well stuff'd with Fat, from Bacon fry'd,
Or with *Molossus* dulcify'd.
Then out our Landlord pulls a Pouch,
As greasy as the Leather Couch
On which he sat, and straight begun,
To load with Weed his *Indian* Gun;

In length, scarce longer than ones Finger,
Or that for which the Ladies linger.
His Pipe smoak'd out with aweful Grace,
With aspect grave and solemn pace;
The reverend Sire walks to a Chest,
Of all his Furniture the best,
Closely confin'd within a Room,
Which seldom felt the weight of Broom;
From thence he lugs a Cag of Rum,
And nodding to me, thus begun:
I find, says he, you don't much care,
For this our *Indian* Country Fare;
But let me tell you, Friend of mine,
You may be glad of it in time,
Tho' now your Stamach is so fine;
And if within this Land you stay,
You'll find it true what I do say.
This said, the Rundlet up he threw,
And bending backwards strongly drew:
I pluck'd as stoutly for my part,
Altho' it made me sick at Heart,
And got so soon into my Head
I scarce cou'd find my way to Bed;

The Maid Servant

Where I was instantly convey'd
By one who pass'd for Chamber-Maid;
Tho' by her loose and sluttish Dress,
She rather seem'd a *Bedlam-Bess*:
Curious to know from whence she came,
I prest her to declare her Name.
She Blushing, seem'd to hide her Eyes,
And thus in Civil Terms replies;
["]In better Times, e'er to this Land,
I was unhappily Trapann'd;
Perchance as well I did appear,
As any Lord or Lady here,
Not then a Slave for twice two Year.
My Cloaths were fashionably new,
Nor were my Shifts of Linnen Blue;
But things are changed now at the Hoe,
I daily work, and Bare-foot go,

In weeding Corn or feeding Swine,
I spend my melancholy Time.
Kidnap'd and Fool'd, I hether fled,
To shun a hated Nuptial Bed,
And to my cost already find,
Worse Plagues than those I left behind.["]
Whate'er the Wanderer did profess,
Good-faith I cou'd not choose but guess
The Cause which brought her to this place,
Was supping e'er the Priest said Grace.

. . . .

Court Days

Scarce had we finish'd serious Story,
But I espy'd the Town before me,
And roaring Planters on the ground,
Drinking of Healths in Circle round:
Dismounting Steed with friendly Guide,
Our Horses to a Tree we ty'd,
And forwards pass'd amongst the Rout,
To chuse convenient *Quarters* out:
But being none were to be found,
We sat like others on the ground
Carousing Punch in open Air
Till Cryer did the Court declare;
The planting Rabble being met,
Their Drunken Worships likewise set:
Cryer proclaims that Noise shou'd cease,
And streight the Lawyers broke the Peace:
Wrangling for Plaintiff and Defendant,
I thought they ne'er would make an end on't:
With nonsense stuff and false quotations,
With brazen Lyes and Allegations;
And in the splitting of the Cause,
They us'd such Motions with their Paws,
As shew'd their Zeal was strongly bent,
In Blows to end the Argument.
A reverend Judge, who to the shame
Of all the Bench, cou'd write his Name:
At Petty-fogger took offence,
And wonder'd at his Impudence.
My Neighbour *Dash* with scorn replies,

And in the Face of Justice flies;
The Bench in fury streight divide,
And Scribbles take, or Judges side;
The Jury, Lawyers, and their Clyents,
Contending, fight like earth-born Gyants:
But Sheriff wily lay perdue,
Hoping Indictments wou'd ensue,
And when _____
A Hat or Wig fell in the way,
He seiz'd them for the *Queen* as stray:
The Court adjourn'd in usual manner,
In Battle Blood, and fractious Clamour;
I thought it proper to provide,
A Lodging for myself and Guide,
So to our Inn we march'd away,
Which at a little distance lay;
Where all things were in such Confusion,
I thought the World at its conclusion:
A Herd of Planters on the ground,
O'er-whelm'd with Punch, dead drunk we found:
Others were fighting and contending,
Some burnt their Cloaths to save the Mending.
A few whose Heads by frequent use,
Could better bare the potent Juice,
Gravely debated State Affairs.
Whilst I most nimbly trip'd up Stairs;
Leaving my Friend discoursing oddly,
And mixing things Prophane and Godly:
Just then beginning to be Drunk,
As from the Company I slunk,
To every Room and Nook I crept,
In hopes I might have somewhere slept;
But all the Bedding was possest
By one or other drunken Guest:
But after looking long about,
I found an antient Corn-loft out,
Glad that I might in quiet sleep,
And there my bones unfractur'd keep.
I lay'd me down secure from Fray,
And soundly snoar'd till break of Day;
When waking fresh I sat upright,
And found my Shoes were vanish'd quite;
Hat, Wig, and Stockings, all were fled
From this extended *Indian* Bed:

Business, Justice, and Departure

How I might sell my *British* Ware,
That with my Freight I might comply,
Did on my Charter party lie;
To this intent, with Guide before,
I tript it to the Eastern Shoar;
While riding near a Sandy Bay,
I met a *Quaker, Yea* and *Nay*;
A Pious Conscientious Rogue,
As e'er woar Bonnet or a Grogue,
Who neither Swore nor kept his Word,
But cheated in the Fear of God;
And when his Debts he would not pay,
By Light within he ran away.
With this sly Zealot soon I struck
A Bargain for my *English* Truck,
Agreeing for ten thousand weight,
Of *Sot-weed* good and fit for freight,
Broad *Oronooko* bright and sound,
The growth and product of his ground;
In Cask that should contain compleat,
Five hundred of Tobacco neat.
The Contract thus betwixt us made,
Not well acquainted with the Trade,
My Goods I trusted to the Cheat,
Whose crop was then aboard the Fleet;
And going to receive my own,
I found the Bird was newly flown:
Cursing this execrable Slave,
This damn'd pretended Godly Knave;
On due Revenge and Justice bent,
I instantly to Counsel went,
Unto an ambodexter *Quack*,
Who learnedly had got the knack
Of giving Glisters, making Pills,
Of filling Bonds, and forging Wills;
And with a stock of Impudence,
Supply'd his want of Wit and Sense;
With Looks demure, amazing People,
No wiser than a Daw in Steeple;
My Anger flushing in my Face,
I stated the pre[c]eeding Case:
And of my Money was so lavish,

That he'd have poyson'd half the Parish,
And hang'd his Father on a Tree,
For such another tempting Fee;
Smiling, said he, the Cause is clear,
I'll manage him you need not fear;
The Case is judg'd, good Sir, but look
In *Galen*, No _____ in my Lord *Cook*,
I vow to God I was mistook:
I'll take out a Provincial Writ,
And Trounce him for his Knavish Wit;
Upon my Life we'll win the Cause,
With all the ease I cure the *Yaws*:
Resolv'd to plague the holy Brother,
I set one Rogue to catch another;
To try the Cause then fully bent,
Up to *Annapolis* I went,
A City Situate on a Plain,
Where scarce a House will keep out Rain;
The Buildings fram'd with Cyprus rare,
Resembles much our *Southwark* Fair:
But Stranger here will scarcely meet
With Market-place, Exchange, or Street;
And if the Truth I may report,
'Tis not so large as *Tottenham Court*.
St. *Mary's* once was in repute,
Now here the Judges try the Suit,
And Lawyers twice a Year dispute.
As oft the Bench most gravely meet,
Some to get Drunk, and some to eat
A swinging share of Country Treat.
But as for Justice right or wrong,
Not one amongst the numerous throng,
Knows what they mean, or has the Heart,
To give his Verdict on a Stranger's part:
Now Court being call'd by beat of Drum,
The Judges left their Punch and Rum,
When Pettifogger Doctor draws,
His Paper forth, and opens Cause:
And least I shou'd the better get,
Brib'd *Quack* supprest his Knavish Wit.
So Maid upon the downy Field,
Pretends a Force, and Fights to yield:
The Byast Court without delay,
Adjudg'd my Debt in Country Pay;

In Pipe staves, Corn, or Flesh of Boar,
Rare Cargo for the *English* Shoar;
Raging with Grief, full speed I ran,
To joyn the Fleet at *Kicketan*;
Embarqu'd and waiting for a Wind,
I left this dreadful Curse behind.

    May Canniballs transported o'er the Sea
Prey on these Slaves, as they have done on me;
May never Merchant's, trading Sails explore
This Cruel, this Inhospitable Shoar;
But left abandon'd by the World to starve,
May they sustain the Fate they well deserve:
May they turn Savage, or as *Indians* Wild,
From Trade, Converse, and Happiness exil'd;
Recreant to Heaven, may they adore the Sun,
And into Pagan Superstitions run
For Vengence ripe ⸻⸻
May Wrath Divine then lay those Regions wast
Where no Man's Faithful, nor a Woman Chast.

FINIS.

6

Political Thought

21. *JOURNAL OF JOHN WINTHROP, 1639–45**

John Winthrop (1588–1649), Squire of Groton, Suffolk, was the most influential political figure in early New England. Educated at Cambridge, and trained in law at the Inner Temple, he led the Massachusetts Bay Puritans in settling Boston in 1630, and several times was elected governor of the powerful colony. His Journal, from which the following is drawn, is one of the most important sources for the history of early America. The two selections exemplify the Puritans' economic and political philosophy.

The first, which examines the concept of the "just price," is a comment on government's role in the business affairs of the community. The second is a reply to the General Court which had criticized Winthrop's assistance of French Catholic troops in the wars against the Indians.

Liberty, Authority and Government and Business Morality in Business 1639

Mo. 9 (*November*). At a general court holden at Boston, great complaint was made of the oppression used in the country in sale of foreign commodities; and Mr. Robert Keaine, who kept a shop in Boston, was notoriously above others observed and complained of; and being convented, he was charged with many particulars; in some, for taking above six pence in the shilling profit; in some above eightpence, and in some small things, above two for one; and being hereof convict, (as appears by the records,) he was fined £200, which came thus to pass: The deputies considered, apart, of his fine, and set it at £200, the

* *John Winthrop's Journal, History of New England,* James K. Hosmer, ed. (New York: Scribner, 1908), Vol. I, pp. 315–18; Vol. II, pp. 237–39.

magistrates agreed but to £100. So, the court being divided, at length it was agreed, that his fine should be £200, but he should pay but £100, and the other should be respited to the further consideration of the next general court. By this means the magistrates and deputies were brought to an accord, which otherwise had not been likely, and so much trouble might have grown, and the offender escaped censure. For the cry of the country was so great against oppression, and some of the elders and magistrates had declared such detestation of the corrupt practice of this man (which was the more observable because he was wealthy and sold dearer than most other tradesmen, and for that he was of ill report for the like covetous practice in England, that incensed the deputies very much against him). And sure the course was very evil, especial circumstances considered: 1. He being an ancient professor of the gospel: 2. A man of eminent parts: 3. Wealthy, and having but one child: 4. Having come over for conscience's sake, and for the advancement of the gospel here: 5. Having been formerly dealt with and admonished, both by private friends and also by some of the magistrates and elders, and having promised reformation; being a member of a church and commonwealth now in their infancy, and under the curious observation of all churches and civil states in the world. These added much aggravation to his sin in the judgment of all men of understanding. Yet most of the magistrates (though they discerned of the offence clothed with all these circumstances) would have been more moderate in their censure: 1. Because there was no law in force to limit or direct men in point of profit in their trade. 2. Because it is the common practice, in all countries, for men to make use of advantages for raising the prices of their commodities. 3. Because (though he were chiefly aimed at, yet) he was not alone in this fault. 4. Because all men through the country, in sale of cattle, corn, labor, etc., were guilty of the like excess in prices. 5. Because a certain rule could not be found out for an equal rate between buyer and seller, though much labor had been bestowed on it, and divers laws had been made, which, upon experience, were repealed, as being neither safe nor equal. Lastly, and especially, because the law of God appoints no other punishment but double restitution; and, in some cases, as where the offender freely confesseth, and brings his offering, only half added to the principal. After the court had censured him, the church of Boston called him also in question, where (as before he had done in this court) he did, with tears, acknowledge and bewail his covetous and corrupt heart, yet making some excuse for many of the particulars, which were charged upon him, as partly by pretense of ignorance of the true prices of some wares, and chiefly by being misled by some false principles, as 1. That, if a man lost in one commodity, he might help himself in the price of another. 2. That if, through want of skill or other occasion his commodity cost him more than the price of the market in England, he might then sell it for more than the price of the market in New England, etc. These things gave occasion to Mr. Cotton, in his public exercise the next lecture day, to lay open the error of such false principles, and to give some rules of direction in the case.

Some false principles were these:—

1. That a man might sell as dear as he can, and buy as cheap as he can.

2. If a man lose by casualty of sea, etc. in some of his commodities, he may raise the price of the rest.

3. That he may sell as he bought, though he paid too dear, etc., and though the commodity be fallen, etc.

4. That, as a man may take the advantage of his own skill or ability, so he may of another's ignorance or necessity.

5. Where one gives time for repayment, he is to take like recompense of one as of another.

The rules for trading were these:—

1. A man may not sell above the current price, i.e., such a price as is usual in the time and place, and as another (who knows the worth of the commodity) would give for it, if he had occasion to use it; as that is called current money, which every man will take, etc.

2. When a man loseth in his commodity for want of skill, etc., he must look at it as his own fault or cross, and therefore must not lay it upon another.

3. Where a man loseth by casualty of the sea, or, etc., it is a loss cast upon himself by providence, and he may not ease himself of it by casting it upon another; for so a man should seem to provide against all providences, etc., that he should never lose; but where there is a scarcity of the commodity, there men may raise the price; for now it is a hand of God upon the commodity, and not the person.

4. A man may not ask any more for his commodity than his selling price, as Ephron to Abraham, the land is worth thus much.

The cause being debated by the church, some were earnest to have him excommunicated; but the most thought an admonition would be sufficient. Mr. Cotton opened the causes which required excommunication, out of that in 1 Cor. 5.11. The point now in question was, whether these actions did declare him to be such a covetous person, etc. Upon which he showed, that it is neither the habit of covetousness, (which is in every man in some degree,) nor simply the act, that declares a man to be such, but when it appears, that a man sins against his conscience, or the very light of nature, and when it appears in a man's whole conversation. But Mr. Keaine did not appear to be such, but rather upon an error in his judgment, being led by false principles; and, beside, he is otherwise liberal, as in his hospitality, and in church communion, etc. So, in the end, the church consented to an admonition.

The Just Bounds of Liberty 1645

I suppose something may be expected from me, [Winthrop] upon this charge that is befallen me, which moves me to speak now to you; yet I intend not to intermeddle in the proceedings of the [General] court, or with any of the persons concerned therein. Only I bless God, that I see an issue of this troublesome business. I also acknowledge the justice of the court, and, for mine own part, I am well satisfied, I was publicly charged, and I am publicly and legally acquitted, which is all I did expect or desire. And though this be sufficient for my justification before men, yet not so before the God, who hath seen so much amiss in my dispensations (and even in this affair) as calls me to be humble. For to be publicly and criminally charged in this court, is matter of humiliation, (and I desire to make a right use of it,) notwithstanding I be thus acquitted. If her father had spit in her face, (saith the Lord concerning Miriam,) should she not have been ashamed seven days? Shame had lien upon her, whatever the occasion had been. I am unwilling to stay you from your urgent affairs, yet give me leave (upon this special occasion) to speak a little more to this assembly. It may be of some good use, to inform and rectify the judgments of some of the people, and may prevent such distempers as have arisen amongst us. The great questions that have troubled the country, are about the authority of the magistrates and the liberty of the people. It is yourselves who have called us to this office, and being called by you, we have our authority from God, in way of an ordinance, such as hath the image of God eminently stamped upon it, the contempt and violation whereof hath been vindicated with examples of divine vengeance. I entreat you to consider, that when you choose magistrates, you take them from among yourselves, men subject to like passions as you are. Therefore when you see infirmities in us, you should reflect upon your own, and that would make you bear the more with us, and not be severe censurers of the failings of your magistrates, when you have continual experience of the like infirmities in yourselves and others. We account him a good servant, who breaks not his covenant. The covenant between you and us is the oath you have taken of us, which is to this purpose, that we shall govern you and judge your causes by the rules of God's laws and our own, according to our best skill. When you agree with a workman to build you a ship or house, etc., he undertakes as well for his skill as for his faithfulness, for it is his profession, and you pay him for both. But when you call one to be a magistrate, he doth not profess nor undertake to have sufficient skill for that office, nor can you furnish him with gifts, etc., therefore you must run the hazard of his skill and ability. But if he fail in faithfulness, which by his oath he is bound unto, that he must answer for. If it fall out that the case be clear to common apprehension, and the rule clear also, if he transgress here, the error is not in the skill, but in the evil of the will: it must be required of him. But if the case be doubtful, or the rule doubtful, to men of such understanding and parts as your magistrates are, if your magistrates should err here, yourselves must bear it.

For the other point concerning liberty, I observe a great mistake in the country about that. There is a twofold liberty, natural (I mean as our nature is now corrupt) and civil or federal. The first is common to man with beasts and other creatures. By this, man, as he stands in relation to man simply, hath liberty to do what he lists; it is a liberty to evil as well as to good. This liberty is incompatible and inconsistent with authority, and cannot endure the least restraint of the most just authority. The exercise and maintaining of this liberty makes men grow more evil, and in time to be worse than brute beast: omnes sumus licentia deteriores. This is that great enemy of truth and peace, that wild beast, which all the ordinances of God are bent against, to restrain and subdue it. The other kind of liberty I call civil or federal, it may also be termed moral, in reference to the covenant between God and man, in the moral law, and the politic covenants and constitutions, amongst men themselves. This liberty is the proper end and object of authority, and cannot subsist without it; and it is a liberty to that only which is good, just, and honest. This liberty you are to stand for, with the hazard (not only of your goods, but) of your lives, if need be. Whatsoever crosseth this, is not authority, but a distemper thereof. This liberty is maintained and exercised in a way of subjection to authority; it is of the same kind of liberty wherewith Christ hath made us free. The woman's own choice makes such a man her husband; yet being so chosen, he is her lord, and she is to be subject to him, yet in a way of liberty, not of bondage; and a true wife accounts her subjection her honor and freedom, and would not think her condition safe and free, but in her subjection to her husband's authority. Such is the liberty of the church under the authority of Christ, her king and husband; his yoke is so easy and sweet to her as a brides's ornaments; and if through forwardness or wantonness, etc., she shake it off, at any time, she is at no rest in her spirit, until she take it up again; and whether her lord smiles upon her, and embraceth her in his arms, or whether he frowns, or rebukes, or smites her, she apprehends the sweetness of his love in all, and is refreshed, supported, and instructed by every such dispensation of his authority over her. On the other side, ye know who they are that complain of this yoke and say, let us break their bands, etc., we will not have this man to rule over us. Even so, brethren, it will be between you and your magistrates. If you stand for your natural corrupt liberties, and will do what is good in your own eyes, you will not endure the least weight of authority, but will murmur, and oppose, and be always striving to shake off that yoke; but if you will be satisfied to enjoy such civil and lawful liberties, such as Christ allows you, then will you quietly and cheerfully submit unto that authority which is set over you, in all the administrations of it, for your good. Wherein, if we fail at any time, we hope we shall be willing (by God's assistance) to hearken to good advice from any of you, or in any other way of God; so shall your liberties be preserved, in upholding the honor and power of authority amongst you.

22. ROGER WILLIAMS, *THE BLOUDY TENET OF PERSECUTION FOR CAUSE OF CONSCIENCE,* 1644*

Roger Williams (1604?–83), founder of Rhode Island, was the "first rebel" against the theocratic establishment of Massachusetts Bay. As minister of the Salem congregation, he reiterated the position he had taken earlier in England which emphasized the "Libertys of the Church" from governmental interference. Writing while Europe was in the throes of war and Anglican contended against Puritan in England, he charged that religious doctrine enforced by the state was the cause of the "bloudy" wars of religion abroad and unscriptural and unlawful persecution at home. His political philosophy, like Calvin's, was drawn from the scriptures. He states in the preface to his book that he will use "Pregnant Scriptures and Arguments throughout the Works proposed against the Doctrine of Persecution *for Cause of Conscience."*

1644

Deare Truth, I have two sad Complaints:

First, the most sober of thy Witnesses, that dare to plead thy Cause, how are they charged to be mine Enemies, contentious, turbulent, seditious?

Secondly, Thine Enemies, though they speake and raile against thee, though they outragiously pursue, imprison, banish, kill thy faithfull Witnesses, yet how is all vermillion'd ore for Justice 'gainst the Hereticks? Yea, if they kindle coales, and blow the flames of devouring Warres, that leave neither Spirituall nor Civill State, but burns up Branch and Root, yet how doe all pretend an holy War? He that kills,

---

* From *The Bloudy Tenent of Persecution for Cause of Conscience* . . . (London [?], [N.P.], 1644), pp. a2, 16–19, 216–19, 226–29. See also "The Bloudy Tenet of Persecution," in Samuel L. Caldwell, ed., *The Complete Writings of Roger Williams* (New York: Russell and Russell, 1963), Vol. III, pp. 58–62, 376–80, 392–97. Italics, Williams' marginal commentary, and most of the biblical citations have been deleted here.

and hee that's killed, they both cry out, It is for God, and for their conscience.

Tis true, nor one nor other seldome dare to plead the mighty Prince Christ Jesus for their Authour, yet both (both Protestant and Papist) pretend they have spoke with Moses and the Prophets, who all, say they (before Christ came) allowed such holy persecutions, holy Warres against the enemies of holy Church.

Truth. Deare Peace (to ease thy first complaint) tis true, thy dearest Sons, most like their mother, Peace-keeping, Peacemaking Sons of God, have borne and still must beare the blurs of troublers of Israel, and turners of the World upside downe. And tis true againe, what Solomon once spake: The beginning of strife is as when one letteth out Water, therefore (saith he) leave off contention before it be medled with. This Caveat should keepe the bankes and sluces firme and strong, that strife, like a breach of waters, breake not upon the sons of men.

Yet strife must be distinguished: It is necessary or unnecessary, godly or ungodly, Christian or unchristian, &c. It is unnecessary, unlawfull, dishonourable, ungodly, unchristian, in most cases in the world, for there is a possibility of keeping sweet Peace in most cases, and if it be possible, it is the expresse command of God that Peace be kept.

Againe, it is necessary, honourable, godly, &c. with civill and earthly weapons to defend the innocent, and to rescue the oppressed from the violent pawes and jaws of oppressing persecuting Nimrods.

It is as necessary, yea more honourable, godly, and Christian, to fight the fight of faith, with religious and spirituall Artillery, and to contend earnestly for the faith of Jesus, once delivered to the Saints against all opposers, and the gates of earth and hell, men or devils, yea against Paul himselfe, or an Angell from heaven, if he bring any other faith or doctrine.

Peace. With the clashing of such Armes am I never wakened. Speake once againe (deare Truth) to my second complaint of bloody persecution, and devouring wars, marching under the colours of upright Justice, and holy Zeale. &c.

Truth. Mine eares have long beene filled with a threefold dolefull Outcry.

First, of one hundred forty foure thousand Virgins forc'd and ravisht by Emperours, Kings, and Governours to their beds of worship and Religion, set up (like Absaloms) on high in their severall States and Countries.

Secondly, the cry of those precious soules under the Altar, the soules of such as have beene persecuted and slaine for the testimony and witnesse of Jesus, whose bloud hath beene spilt like water upon the earth, and that because they have held fast the truth and witnesse of

Jesus, against the worship of the States and Times, compelling to an uniformity of State Religion.

These cries of murthered Virgins who can sit still and heare? Who can but rune with zeale inflamed to prevent the deflowering of chaste soules, and spilling of the bloud of the innocent? Humanity stirs up and prompts the Sonnes of men to draw materiall sword for a Virgins chastity and life, against a ravishing murtherer? And Piety and Christianity must needs awaken the Sons of God to draw the Spirituall sword (the word of God) to preserve the chastity and life of Spirituall Virgins, who abhorre the spirituall defilements of false worship.

Thirdly, the cry of the whole earth, made drunke with the bloud of its inhabitants, slaughtering each other in their blinded zeale, for Conscience, for Religion, against the Catholickes, against the Lutherans, &c.

· · · ·

What fearfull cries within these twenty years of hundred thousands men, women, children, fathers, mothers, husbands, wives, brethren, sisters, old and young, high, and low, plundred, ravished, slaughtered, murthered, famished? And hence these cries, that men fling away the spirituall sword and spirituall artillery (in spirituall and religious causes) and rather trust for the suppressing of each others God, Conscience, and Religion (as they suppose) to an arme of flesh, and sword of steele?

Truth. Sweet Peace, what hast thou there?

Peace. Arguments against persecution for cause of Conscience.

Truth. And what there?

Peace. An Answer to such Arguments, contrarily maintaining such persecution for cause of Conscience.

Truth. These Arguments against such persecution, and the Answer pleading for it, written (as Love hopes) from godly intentions, hearts, and hands, yet in a marvellous different stile and manner. The Arguments against persecution in milke, the Answer for it (as I may say) in bloud.

The Authour of these Arguments (against persecution) (as I have beene informed) being committed by some then in power, close prisoner to Newgate, for the witnesse of some truths of Jesus, and having not the use of Pen and Inke, wrote these Arguments in Milke, in sheets of Paper, brought to him by the Woman his Keeper, from a friend in London, as the stopples of his milk bottle.

In such Paper written with Milk nothing will appeare, but the way of reading it by fire being knowne to this friend who received the Papers, he transcribed and kept together the Papers, although the Author himselfe could not correct, nor view what himselfe had written.

It was in milke, tending to soule nourishment, even for Babes and Sucklings in Christ.

It was in milke, spiritually white, pure and innocent, like those white horses of the Word of truth and meeknesse, and the white Linnen or Armour of righteousnesse, in the Arm of Jesus.

It was in milke, soft, meeke, peacable and gentle, tending both to the peace of soules, and the peace of States and Kingdomes.

Peace. The Answer (though I hope out of milkie pure intentions) is returned in bloud: bloudy & slaughterous conclusions; bloudy to the souls of all men, forc'd to the Religion and Worship which every civil State or Common-weale agrees on, and compells all subjects to in a dissembled uniformitie.

Bloudy to the bodies, first of the holy witnesses of Christ Jesus, who testifie against such invented worships.

Secondly, of the Nations and Peoples slaughtering each other for their severall respective Religions and Consciences.

. . . .

Peace. Passe on (holy Truth) to that similitude whereby they illustrate that Negative Assertion: "The Prince in the Ship (say they) is governour over the bodies of all in the Ship, but he hath no power to governe the Ship or the Mariners in the Actions of it: If the Pilot manifestly erre in his Action, the Prince may reprove him, (and so say they may and passenger) if hee offend against the life or goods of any, the Prince may in due time and place punish him, which no private person may.

Truth. Although (deare Peace) wee both agree that civill powers may not injoyne such devices, no nor inforce on any Gods Institutions, since Christ Jesus his comming: Yet for further illustration I shall propose some Quaeries concerning the civill Magistrates passing in the ship of the Church, wherein Christ Jesus hath appointed his Ministers and Officers as Governours and Pilots, &c.

If in a ship at Sea, wherein the Governour or Pilot of a ship undertakes to carry the ship to such a Port, the civill Magistrate (suppose a King or Emperour) shall command the Master such and such a course, to steere upon such or such a point, which the Master knowes is not their course, and which if they steere he shall never bring the Ship to that Port or harbour: What shall the Master doe? Surely all men will say, the Master of the Ship or Pilot is to present Reasons and Arguments from his Mariners Art (if the Prince bee capable of them) or else in humble and submissive manner to perswade the Prince not to interrupt them in their course and duty properly belonging to them, to wit, governing of the ship, steering of the course, &c.

If the Master of the Ship command the Mariners thus and thus, in cunning the ship, managing the helme, trimming the saile, and the Prince command the Mariners a different or contrary course, who is to be obeyed?

It is confest that the Mariners may lawfully disobey the Prince, and obey the governour of the ship in the actions of the ship.

Thirdly, what if the Prince have as much skill (which is rare) as the Pilot himselfe? I conceive it will be answered, that the Master of the ship and Pilot, in what concernes the ship, are chiefe and above (in respect of their office) the Prince himselfe, and their commands ought to be attended by all the Mariners: unlesse it bee in manifest errour, wherein is granted any passenger may reprove the Pilot.

Fourthly, I aske if the Prince and his Attendants be unskilfull in the ships affaires, whether every Sayler and Mariner, the youngest and lowest, be not (so farre as concernes the ship) to be preferred before the Princes followers, and the Prince himselfe? and their counsell and advice more to be attended to, and their service more to bee desired and respected, and the Prince to bee requested to stand by and let the businesse alone in their hands.

Fifthly, in case a wilfull King and his Attendants, out of opinion of their skill, or wilfulnesse or passion, would so steere the course, trim sayle, &c. as that in the judgement of the Master and Seamen the ship and lives shall bee indangered: whether (in case humble perswasions prevaile not) ought not the Ships company to refuse to act in such a course, yea and (in case power be in their hands) resist and suppresse these dangerous practices of the Prince and his followers, and so save the ship?

Lastly, suppose the Master out of base feare and cowardise, or covetous desire of reward, shall yeeld to gratifie the minde of the Prince, contrary to the rules of Art and Experience, &c. and the ship come in danger, and perish, and the Prince with it: if the Master get to shore, whether may he not be justly questioned, yea and suffer as guilty of the Princes death, and those that perished with him: These cases are cleare, wherein according to this similitude, the Prince ought not to governe and rule the actions of the ship, but such whose office and charge and skill it is.

The result of all is this: The Church of Christ is the Ship, wherein the Prince (if a member, for otherwise the case is altred) is a passenger. In this ship the Officers and Governours, such as are appointed by the Lord Jesus, they are the chiefe, and (in those respects) above the Prince himselfe, and are to bee obeyed and submitted to in their works and administrations, even before the Prince himselfe.

In this respect every Christian in the Church, man or woman (if of more knowledge and grace of Christ) ought to be of higher esteeme (concerning Religion and Christianity) then all the Princes in the world, who have either none or lesse grace and knowledge of Christ: although in civill things all civill reverence, honour and obedience ought to be yeelded by all men.

Therefore, if in matters of Religion the King command what is contrary to Christ's rule (though according to his perswasion and conscience) who sees not that (according to the similitude) he ought not to be obeyed? yea, and (in case) boldly with spirituall force and power he ought to be resisted: and if any Officer of the Church of Christ shall out of basenesse yeeld to the command of the Prince, to the danger of the Church, and soules committed to his charge, the soules that perish (notwithstanding the Princes command) shall be laid to his charge.

If so then, I rejoyne thus: How agree these truths of this similitude with those former positions, viz. that the Civill Magistrate is keeper of both Tables, That he is to see the Church doe her duty, That he ought to establish the true Religion, suppresse and punish the false, and so consequently must discerne, judge and determine what the true gathering and governing of the Church is; what the dutie of every Minister of Christ is; what the true Ordinances are, and what the true Administrations of them; and where men faile, correct, punish, and reforme by the Civill Sword: I desire it may be answered in the feare and presence of him whose eyes are as a flame of fire, if this be not (according to the similitude, though contrary to their scope in proposing of it) to be Governour of the Ship of the Church, to see the Master, Pilot and Mariners do their duty, in setting the course, steering the ship, trimming the sailes, keeping the watch, &c. and where they faile, to punish them; and therefore by undeniable consequences, to judge and determine what their duties are, when they doe right, and when they doe wrong: and this not only in manifest Errour, their ordinary course and practice.

The similitude of a Physitian obeying the Prince in the Body politick; but prescribing to the Prince concerning the Princes body, wherein the Prince (unlesse the Physitian manifestly erre) is to be obedient to the Physitian, and not to be Judge of the Physitian in his Art, but to be ruled and judged (as touching the state of his body) by the Physitian: I say this similitude and many others suiting with the former of a ship, might be alleadged to prove the distinction of the Civill and Spirituall estate, and that according to the rule of the Lord Jesus in the Gospel, the Civill Magistrate is only to attend the Calling of the Civill Magistracie, concerning the bodies and goods of the Subjects, and is himselfe (if a member of the Church and within) subject to the power of the Lord Jesus therein, as any member of the Church is, 1 Cor. 5.

.   .   .   .

Truth. I May well compare this passage to a double picture; on the first part or side of it a most faire and beautifull countenance of the pure and holy word of God: on the later side or part, a most sowre and uncomely deformed looke of a meere humane invention. Concerning the former, they prove the true and unquestionable power and priviledge of the Churches of Christ to assemble and practice all the holy Ordinances of God, without or against the consent of the Magistrate.

Their Arguments from Christs and the Angels voyce, from the Apostles and Churches practice, I desire may take deepe impression written by the point of a diamond, the finger of Gods spirit, in all hearts whom it may concerne.

This Libertie of the Churches of Christ he inlargeth and amplifieth so far, that he calls it an usurpation of some Magistrates to determine the time and place of Worship: and say, that rather the Churches should be left to their inoffensive libertie.

Upon which Grant I must renew my former Quaerie, Whether this be not to walke in contradictions, to hold with light, yet walke in darknes? for

How can they say the Magistrate is appointed by God and Christ the Guardian of the Christian Church and Worship, bound to set up the true Church, Ministrie and Ordinances, to see the Church doe her duty, that is, to force her to it by the Civill sword: bound to suppresse the false Church, Ministrie and Ordinances, and therefore consequently, to judge and determine which is the true Church, which is the false, and what is the duty of the Church officers and members of it, and what not: and yet (say they) the Churches must assemble, and practice all Ordinances, without his consent, yea against it: Yea and he hath not so much power as to judge what is a convenient time and place for the Churches to assemble in; which if he should doe, he should be an usurper, and should abridge the Church of her inoffensive libertie.

As if the Master or Governour of a Ship had power to judge who were true and fit officers, mariners, &c. for the managing of the Ship, and were bound to see them each performe his duty, and to force them thereunto, and yet he should be an usurper if hee should abridge them of meeting and managing the vessel at their pleasure, when they please, and how they please, without and against his consent: Certainly if a Physitian have power to judge the disease of his patient, and what course of Physicke he must use, can he bee counted an usurper unlesse the patient might take what physicke himselfe pleased, day or night, summer or winter, at home in his chamber, or abroad in the aire?

Secondly, by their grant in this passage that Gods people may thus assemble and practice ordinances without and against the consent of the Magistrate I infer, then also may they become a Church, constitute and gather without or against the consent of the Magistrate:

Therefore may the Messengers of Christ preach and baptise, that is, make disciples and wash them into the true profession of Christianity according to the commission, though the Magistrate determine and publickly declare, such Ministers, such baptismes, such Churches to be hereticall.

Thirdly, it may here be questioned what power is now given to the Civill Magistrate in Church Matters and Spirituall affairs.

If it be answered that although Gods people may doe thus against the Magistrates consent, yet others may not.

I answer (as before) who sees not herein partiality to themselves: Gods people must enjoy their Liberty of Conscience, and not be forced; but all the Subjects in a Kingdome or Monarchie, or the whole world beside, must be compelled by the power of the Civill Sword to assemble thus and thus.

Secondly, I demand who shall judge whether they are Gods people or no, for they say whether the Magistrate consent or consent not, that is judge so or not, they ought to goe on in the Ordinance *renuente Magistratu?*

How agrees this with their former and general assertion, that the Civill Magistrate must set up the Christian Church and Worship, therefore by their owne grant he must judge the godly themselves, he must discerne who are fit matter for the House of God, living stones, and what unfit matter, trash and rubbish?

Those worthy men, the Authours of these positions, and others of their judgement have cause to examine their soules with feare and trembling in the presence of God upon this intergatory, viz. whether or no this be not the bottome and root of the matter: If they could have the same supply of maintenance without the helpe of the Civill Sword, or were perswaded to live upon the voluntary contribution of poore Saints, or their owne labour, as the Lord Jesus and his first Messengers did: I say, if this lay not in the bottom, whether or no they could not be willingly shut of the Civill power, and left only to their inoffensive liberties?

I could also put a sad Quaerie to the consciences of some, viz. what should be the reason why in their native Country where the magistrate consented not, they forbore to practice such Ordinances as now they doe and intended to doe, so soone as they got into another place where they might set up Magistrates of their owne, and a Civill Sword, &c. How much is it to be feared that in case their Magistracie should alter, or their persons be cast under a Magistracie prohibiting their practice, whether they would then maintaine their separate meetings without and against the consent of the Magistrate, *renuente Magistratu?*

Lastly, it may be questioned how it comes to passe that in pleading for the Churches liberty more now under the Christian Magistrate, since the Christians tooke that liberty in dangerours times under the Heathen, why he quotes to prove such liberty, Pharaohs hindring the Israelites from worship, Ezra 7.23 Artaxerxes his feare of wrath upon the Realme?

Are not all their hopes and arguments built upon the Christian Magistrate, whom (say they) the first Christians wanted, and yet do they scare the Christian Magistrate (whom they account the governour of the Church) with Pharaoh and Artaxerxes that knew not god, expecting that the Christian Magistrate should act and command no more in God worship then they?

But what can those instances of Pharaohs evill in hindring the Israelites worshipping of God, and Artaxerxes giving liberty to Israel to Worship God, and build the Temple, what can they prove but a duty in all Princes and Civill Magistrates to take off the yoake of bondage, which commonly they lay on the necks of the soules of their subjects in matters of Conscience and Religion?

23. WILLIAM PENN, *THE EXCELLENT PRIVILEGES OF LIBERTY AND PROPERTY*, 1687[*]

While the New Englanders argued over the definition, role, and nature of governmental authority, William Penn simply stated what he believed were the rights of Englishmen. He wrote the following preface to an edition containing the Magna Carta and other fundamental laws of England for Europeans whom he offered asylum and political liberty in Pennsylvania. The statements in his tract, all the more profound because of their simplicity and practicality, reflect both his experiences as a colonizer and much of the liberal political thought of his time, as advanced by Locke, Harrington, and Sydney.

It may reasonably be supposed that we shall find in this part of the world, many men, both old and young, that are strangers, in a great measure, to the true understanding of that inestimable inheritance that every Free-born Subject of England is heir unto by Birth-right, I mean that unparalleled privilege of Liberty and Property, beyond all the Nations in the world beside; and it is to be wished that all men did rightly understand their own happiness therein; in pursuance of which I do here present thee with that ancient Garland, the Fundamental Laws of England, bedecked with many precious privileges of Liberty and Property, by which every man that is a Subject of the Crown of England, may understand what is his right, and how to preserve it from unjust and unreasonable men: whereby appears the eminent care, wisdom and

[*] William Penn, *The Excellent Privileges of Liberty and Property*, Reprint (Philadelphia: Philobiblon Club, 1897), pp. 3–12. Italics deleted here.

industry of our progenitors in providing for themselves and posterity so good a fortress that is able to repel the lust, pride and power of the Noble, as well as ignorance of the Ignoble; it being that excellent and discreet balance that gives every man his even proportion, which cannot be taken from him, nor be dispossessed of his life, liberty or estate, but by the trial and judgment of twelve of his equals, or Law of the Land, upon the penalty of the bitter curses of the whole people; so great was the zeal of our predecessors for the preservation of these Fundamental Liberties (contained in these Charters) from encroachment, that they employed all their policy and religious obligations to secure them entire and inviolable, albeit the contrary hath often been endeavoured, yet Providence hitherto hath preserved them as a blessing to the English Subjects.

The chief end of the publication hereof is for the information and understanding (what is their native right and inheritance) of such who may not have leisure from their Plantations to read large volumes; and beside, I know this Country is not furnished with Law-Books, and this being the root from whence all our wholesome English Laws spring, and indeed the line by which they must be squared, I have ventured to make it public, hoping it may be of use and service to many Freemen, Planters and Inhabitants in this Country, to whom it is sent and recommended, wishing it may raise up noble resolutions in all the Freeholders in these new Colonies, not to give away any thing of Liberty and Property that at present they do, (or of right as loyal English Subjects, ought to) enjoy, but take up the good example of our ancestors, and understand, that it is easy to part with or give away great privileges, but hard to be gained, if once lost. And therefore all depends upon our prudent care and actings to preserve and lay sure foundations for ourselves and the posterity of our loins.

Philopolites.

.   .   .   .

In France, and other nations, the mere will of the Prince is Law, his word takes off any man's head, imposeth taxes, or seizes any man's estate, when, how and as often as he lists; and if one be accused, or but so much as suspected of any crime, he may either presently execute him, or banish, or imprison him at pleasure; or if he will be so gracious as to proceed by form of their laws, if any two villains will but swear against the poor party, his life is gone; nay, if there be no witness, yet he may be put on the rack, the tortures whereof make many an innocent person confess himself guilty, and then, with seeming justice, is executed. But,

In England the Law is both the measure and the bound of every Subject's duty and allegiance, each man having a fixed Fundamental Right born with him, as to freedom of his person and property in his estate, which he cannot be deprived of, but either by his consent, or some crime, for which the law has imposed such a penalty or forfeiture. For (1) all our kings take a solemn oath at their Coronation to observe and cause the laws to be kept: (2) all our Judges take an oath wherein among other points they swear, to do equal Law and Right to all the King's Subjects, rich and poor, and not to delay any person of Common Right for the Letters of the King, or of any other Person, or for any other cause: Therefore saith Fortescue, (who was first Chief Justice, and afterwards Lord Chancellor to King Henry the Sixth) in his Book *De Laudibus Legum Angliae*, cap. 9, *Non potest Res Angliae*, etc. The King of England cannot alter nor change the laws of his realm at his pleasure; For why, he governeth his people by power not only royal, but also politic; for he can neither change laws without the consent of his Subjects, nor yet charge them with impositions against their wills. With which accords Bracton, a learned Judge and Law-Author, in the Reign of King Henry the Third, saying, *Rex in Regno suo superiores habet Deum et Legem*; i.e., The King in his Realm hath two superiors, God and the Law; for he is under the directive, though not coercive Power of the Law.

Tis true, the Law itself affirms, the King can do no wrong, which proceeds not only from a presumption, that so excellent a Person will do none, but also because he acts nothing but by Ministers, which (from the lowest to the highest) are answerable for their doings; so that if a King in passion should command A. to kill B. without process of law, A. may yet be prosecuted by Indictment or upon an Appeal (where no royal pardon is allowable) and must for the same be executed, such command notwithstanding.

This original happy Fame of Government is truly and properly called an Englishman's Liberty, a Privilege not exempt from the law, but to be freed in person and estate from arbitrary violence and oppression. A greater inheritance (saith Judge Coke) is derived to every one of us from our laws than from our parents. For without the former, what would the latter signify? And this Birth-right of Englishmen shines most conspicuously in two things:

1. Parliaments.
2. Juries.

By the First the Subject has a share by his chosen Representatives in the Legislative (or law-making) Power; for no new laws bind the people of England, but such as are by common consent agreed on in that great Council.

By the Second, he has a share in the executive part of the law, no causes being tried, nor any man adjudged to lose life, member or estate, but upon the verdict of his Peers or Equals his neighbours, and of his own condition: These two grand pillars of English liberty, are the Fundamental Vital Privileges, whereby we have been and are preserved more free and happy than any other people in the world, and (we Trust) shall ever continue so: For whoever shall design to impair, pervert or undermine either of them, do strike at the very Constitution of our Government, and ought to be prosecuted and punished with the utmost zeal and rigour. To cut down the banks and let in the sea, or to poison all the springs and rivers in the kingdom, could not be a greater mischief; for this would only affect the present age, but the other will ruin and enslave all our posterity.

.   .   .   .

24. THE NEW YORKERS' BILL OF RIGHTS, 1691*

Few colonies suffered more from mismanagement than New York. Saddled with authoritarian, inefficient, and often dishonest government from the days of the Dutch Directors through the rule of the Duke of York, the people finally exploded in revolt in 1689. Their rebellion, precipitated by the overthrow of James II in England and led by the German immigrant Jacob Leisler, devolved into a confusing conflict of commoner against aristocrat, Protestant versus Catholic, and local against imperial interests. Leisler was later executed by his enemies. The ascendancy of William III brought the promise of stability through representative government and the disorder came to an end. The new Crown granted a royal charter and permitted an assembly of freemen which promptly fashioned a Bill of Rights reflecting the English model. The New York document, presented below, became the basis of that province's political development. But it also summarizes the political goals of most seventeenth-century colonists.

Forasmuch as the Representatives of this their Majesties Province of New York now Convened in Generall Assembly are deeply sensible of their Majesties most gracious Favour in restoring to them the undoubted Rights and Priviledges of English-men by declaring their Royal Will and Pleasure in their Letters Patents to his Excellency . . . *That he should with the advice and consent of their Council from Time to Time as need shall require to summon and call generall Assemblies of the Inhabitants being Free-holders according to usage* of their Majesties other Plantations in America. And that this most excellent constitution so necessary and so much Esteemed by our Ancestors may ever continue

---

* *Laws and Acts of the General Assembly . . . of New York* (New York: William Bradford, 1694), pp. 15–19.

unto their Majesties Subjects within this Province of New-York. The Representatives . . . humbly pray that the Rights, Priviledges, Liberties, and Franchises, according to the Lawes and statutes of their Majesties Realm of England may be confirmed unto their Majesties most Dutifull and Loyal Subjects . . . of New York by Authority of this General Assembly . . . and it is hereby enacted and declared by the Authority of the same, That the supream Legislative power and authorite under their Majesties . . . shall forever be and reside in A Governour in Chief and Council appointed by their Majesties . . . ; and the People by their Representatives met and Convened in Generall Assembly. That the Exercice and Administration of the Government over the said Province shall, persuant to Their Majesties Letters Patents be in the said Governour in Chief and Councill, with whose advice and Consent or with at least five of them, he is to rule and Govern the same, according to the Lawes thereof, and for any defect therein, according to the Laws of *England* and not otherwise. That in Case the Governour in Chief should Dye, or be Absent out of this Province, and that there be noe person within the said Province commissionated by their Majesties . . . to be Governour or Commander in Chief, That then the Council for the time being, or so many of them as are in the said Province, do take upon them the administration of the government and the Execution of the Laws thereof, and Powers and Authorities belonging to the Governour in Chief and Council; the first in Nomination in which Council is to preside untill the said Governour shall return and arrive in the said Province again or the pleasure of their Majesties . . . be further known.

That for the good Government and Rule of their Majesties Subjects, a Session of a Generall Assembly be held in this Province once every Year. That every Free-holder within this Province and Free-man in any Corporation shall have his free Choice and Vote in the Electing of the Representatives, without any manner of constraint or Imposition; And that in all Elections the Majority of votes shall carry it.

And by Free-holders is to be understood every one who shall have forty Shillings *per annum* in Free-hold.

That the Persons to be elected to Sit as Representatives in the General Assembly from time to time, for the several Cities, Towns, Counties, Shires, Divisions or Mannors of this Providence . . . shall be according to the proportion and number hereafter expressed. . . .

An as many more as their Majesties . . . shall think fit to establish.

That all persons Chosen and Assembled in manner aforesaid, or the major part of them shall be deemed and accounted the Representatives of this Province in General Assembly.

That the Representatives . . . may appoint their own Times of meeting during their Sessions, and may adjourn their house from time to time, as to them shall seem meet and convenient.

That the said representatives as aforesaid Convened are the sole Judges of the Qualifications of their own Members, and likewise of all Undu[e] Elections, and may from time to time purge their House as they shall see occasion.

That no Member of the Generall Assembly or their Servants, during the Time of their Sessions, and whilst they shall be going to and returning from the said Assembly shall be arrested, sued, Imprisoned or any way molested or troubled nor be compelled to make answer to any Suit, Bill, Plaint, Declaration, or otherwise, cases of High-Treason and Fellony only excepted.

That all Bills agreed upon by the . . . Representatives or the Major part of them shall be presented unto the Governour and the Councill for their approbation and consent. All and every which said Bills, so approved of and consented to by the Governor and the Council, shall be esteemed and accounted the Laws of this Province. Which said Lawes shall continue and remain in force untill they be disallowed by their Majesties . . . or expire by their own Limitation.

That in All Cases of Death or absence of any of the said Representatives, the Governour for the time being, shall issue out A Writ of Summons . . . *Willing and requiring the Free-holders . . . to elect others in their places and stead.*

That no Free-man shall be taken and Imprisoned or be deprived of his Free-hold, or Liberty or free Customs, or Out-Lawed, or Exiled or any other wayes destroyed; nor shall be passed upon, adjudged or condemned, but by the lawfull Judgment of his Peers, and by the Law of this Province.

Justice nor Right shall be neither Sold Denied or Delayed to any Person within this Province.

That no Aid, Tax, Tolliage or Custom, Loan, Benevolence, Gift, Excise, Duty or Imposition whatsoever shall be laid assessed, imposed, levied or required of or on any of their Majesties Subjects within this Province &c. or their Estates upon any manner or Colour or Pretence whatsoever, but by the Act and Consent of the Governor and Council and Representatives of the People in Generall Assembly met and Convened.

That no Man of what Estate or Condition soever, shall be put out of his Lands, Tenements, nor taken, nor imprisoned nor disinherited nor banished nor any ways destroyed or molested without first being brought to Answer by due Course of Law.

That a Free-man shall not be Amerced for a small Fault, but after the manner of his Fault, And for a great fault after the greatness thereof, saving to him his Free-hold and A Husband-man, saving to him his Wainage; and A Merchant, saveing to him his Merchandize; and none of the said Amercements shall be Assessed, but by the Oath of Twelve Honest and Lawfull men of the Vicinage. Provided, the faults and Misdemeaners be not in Contempt of Courts of Judicature. All tryals shall be by the verdict of Twelve Men, and as near as may be Peers or Equals of the Neighbourhood of the place where the fact shall arise or grow: whether the same be by Indictments, Declaration, Information or otherwayes against the person or defendant. That in all Cases Capital or Criminal there shall be a grand Inquest, who shall first present the Offence; and then Twelve Good Men of the Neighbourhood, to try the offender, who after his plea to the Indictment shall be allowed his reasonable Challenges.

That in all Cases whatsoever, Bayle by sufficient Sureties shall be allowed and taken, unless for Treason or Fellony plainly and specially expressed and mentioned in the Warrant of Committment and that the Fellony be such as is restrained from bayle by the Law of *England.*

That no Free-man shall be compelled to receive any souldiers or Marriners, except Inholders, and other Houses of publick Entertainment, who are to quarter for ready Money into his House, and there suffer them to sojourn against their Wills; provided it be not in time of actual War within this Province.

That no Commission for proceeding by Martial Law, against any of their Majesties Subjects within this Province, &c. shall issue forth to any Person or Persons whatsoever, least by Colour of them any of his Majesties Subjects be destroyed or put to Death, except all such Officers and Souldiers that are in Garrison, and pay during the time of actual War.

That all the Lands within this Province shall be esteemed and accounted Lands of Free-hold, and Inheritance in free and Common Soccage, according to the tenor of *East-Greenwich* in their Majesties Realm of *England.* . . .

That no Person or Persons which profess Faith in God by Jesus Christ his only Son, shall at any time be any way molested, punished, disturbed, disquieted or called in question for any Difference in Opinion, or matter of Religious Concernment, who do not under that pretence disturb the Civil Peace of the Province &c. And that all and every such Person or persons may from time to time, and at all times hereafter, freely and fully enjoy his or their Opinion, Persuasions, Judgements in matters of Conscience and Religion, throughout all this Province and freely meet at Convenient Places within this Province, and there Worship according to their respective Perswasions, without being hindred or molested, they behaving themselves peaceably, quietly, modestly and Religiously, and not useing this Liberty to Licentiousness, nor to the Civill Injury or outward Disturbance of others. Allways provided that nothing herein mentioned or Contained shall extend to give Liberty for any persons of the *Romish Religion* to exercise their manner of Worship, contrary to the Laws and Statutes of their Majesties Kingdom of *England.*

Selected Bibliography: The Seventeenth Century

ADAMS, James Truslow. *The Founding of New England: History of New England.* Vol. I. Boston: Atlantic Monthly Press, 1921.*

ANDREWS, Charles McLean. *The Colonial Period of American History.* 4 Vols. New Haven: Yale University Press, 1934–38.*

————. *Colonial Self-Government.* New York: Harper & Brothers, 1904.

————. *The Fathers of New England.* Vol. VI of *Chronicles of America Series.* New Haven: Yale University Press, 1919.

BAILYN, Bernard. *The New England Merchants in the Seventeenth Century.* Cambridge: Harvard University Press, 1955.*

BARNES, Viola Florence. *The Dominion of New England.* New York: Frederick Ungar Publishing Co., 1960.

BEATTY, Edward Corbyn Obert. *William Penn as a Social Philosopher.* New York: Columbia University Press, 1939.

BLACKER, Irwin R. (ed.) *Hakluyt's Voyages.* New York: The Viking Press, Inc., 1965.*

BLAIR, James, HARTWELL, Henry and CHILTON, Edward. *The Present State of Virginia and the College.* Edited by Hunter Dickenson Farish. Williamsburg, Va.: Colonial Williamsburg, Inc., 1940.

BRIDENBAUGH, Carl. *Cities in the Wilderness.* 2nd ed. New York: Alfred A. Knopf, Inc., 1955.*

BRUCE, Philip Alexander. *Economic History of Virginia in the Seventeenth Century.* 2 Vols. New York: Peter Smith Publisher, 1935.

————. *Institutional History of Virginia in the Seventeenth Century.* 2 Vols. New York: G. P. Putnam's Sons, 1910.*

————. *Social Life of Virginia in the Seventeenth Century.* Richmond: Whittet & Shepherdson, 1907.

COVEY, Cyclone. *The Gentle Radical: A Biography of Roger Williams.* New York: The Macmillan Company, 1966.

CRAVEN, Wesley Frank. *The Southern Colonies in the Seventeenth Century.* Baton Rouge: Louisiana State University Press, 1949.

ELLIS, John Harvard. *The Works of Anne Bradstreet.* New York: Peter Smith Publisher, 1932.

FLICK, Alexander C. (ed.) *History of the State of New York.* Vol 1, *Wigwam and Bowerie.* 2nd ed. New York: Columbia University Press, 1961.

HALL, Michael Garibaldi. *Edward Randolph and the American Colonies, 1676–1703.* Chapel Hill: University of The North Carolina Press for the Institute of Early American History and Culture, 1960.

————, LEDER, Lawrence H., and KAMMEN, Michael G. *Glorious Revolution* *in America*. Chapel Hill: The University of North Carolina Press for the Institute of Early American History and Culture, 1964.*

History of the College of William and Mary from Its Foundation in 1660 to 1874. Richmond: J. W. Randolph & English, 1874.

JAMESON, J. Franklin. (ed.) *Original Narratives of Early American History*. 13 Vols. New York: Charles Scribner's Sons, 1906–17.

JONES, Howard Mumford. *The Literature of Virginia in the Seventeenth Century: Memoirs of the Academy of Arts and Sciences*. Vol. XIX, Part II. Boston: A.A.A.S., 1946.

KESSLER, Henry H., and RACHLIS, Eugene. *Peter Stuyvesant and His New York*. New York: Random House, Inc., 1959.

LEWIS, Paul. *The Great Rogue: A Biography of Captain John Smith*. New York: David McKay Company, Inc., 1966.

MCCRADY, Edward. *South Carolina under the Proprietary Government, 1670–1719*. New York: The Macmillan Company, 1901.

MILLER, Perry. *The New England Mind: The Seventeenth Century*. New York: The Macmillan Company, 1939.*

————. *Roger Williams, His Contribution to the American Tradition*. Indianapolis: The Bobbs-Merrill Company, Inc., 1953.*

MORGAN, Edmund S. *The Puritan Dilemma*. Boston: Little, Brown and Company, 1958.*

MORISON, Samuel Eliot. *Builders of the Bay Colony*. Boston: Houghton Mifflin Company, 1930.*

————. *The Intellectual Life of Colonial New England*. New York: New York University Press, 1956.*

————. (ed.) *Of Plymouth Plantation 1620–1647 by William Bradford*. New York: Alfred A. Knopf, Inc., 1952.

————. *Three Centuries of Harvard, 1636–1936*. Cambridge: Harvard University Press, 1942.

MORTON, Richard L. *Colonial Virginia*. Vol. I, *The Tidewater Period*. Chapel Hill: The University of North Carolina Press for the Virginia Historical Society, 1960.

NOTESTEIN, Wallace. *The English People on the Eve of Colonization*. Vol. II of *The New American Nation Series*. New York: Harper & Row, Publishers, 1954.*

NYE, Russell B. *This Almost Chosen People: Essays in the History of American Ideas*. East Lansing: The Michigan State University Press, 1966.

OSGOOD, Herbert L. *The American Colonies in the Seventeenth Century*. 3 Vols. New York: Columbia University Press, 1930.

PARRINGTON, Vernon Louis. *The Colonial Mind: Main Currents in American Thought*. New York: Harcourt, Brace & World, Inc., 1927.*

PEARES, Cathrine Owens. *William Penn: A Biography*. Philadelphia: J. B. Lippincott Company, 1957.

PIERCY, Josephine K. *Anne Bradstreet*. New York: Twayne Publishers, 1965.*

————. *Studies in Literary Types in Seventeenth Century America*. New Haven: Yale University Press, 1939.

REICH, Jerome R. *Leisler's Rebellion: A Study of Democracy in New York, 1664–1720*. Chicago: The University of Chicago Press, 1953.

RUTMAN, Darrett B. *Winthrop's Boston: Portrait of a Puritan Town, 1630–1649.* Chapel Hill: The University of North Carolina Press for the Institute of Early American History and Culture, 1965.

SCHNEIDER, Herbert W. *The Puritan Mind.* New York: Henry Holt and Company, Inc., 1930.*

SIMPSON, Alan. "How Democratic Was Roger Williams," *William and Mary Quarterly,* 3rd ser., XIII (January, 1956), pp. 53–67.

SIRMANS, M. Eugene. *Colonial South Carolina: A Political History, 1663–1763.* Chapel Hill: The University of North Carolina Press for the Institute of Early American History and Culture, 1966.

SMITH, James Morton, ed. *Seventeenth Century America: Essays in Colonial America.* Chapel Hill: The University of North Carolina Press for the Institute of Early American History and Culture. 1959.

TRENT, William Peterfield, and others (eds.) *Cambridge History of American Literature.* Vol. I. New York: The Macmillan Company, 1946.

TYLER, Moses Coit. *A History of American Literature.* Vol. I. New York: G. P. Putnam's Sons, 1879.

VAUGHAN, Alden T. *New England Frontier 1620–1675.* New York: Little, Brown and Company, 1965.*

WARD, Harry M. *The United Colonies of New England: 1643–90.* New York: The Vintage Press, Inc., 1961.

WASHBURN, Wilcomb E. *The Governor and the Rebel.* Chapel Hill: The University of North Carolina Press for the Institute of Early American History and Culture, 1957.*

WEEDEN, William Babcock. *Economic and Social History of New England.* 2 Vols. Boston: Houghton Mifflin Company, 1890.

WERTENBAKER, Thomas Jefferson. *The First Americans, 1607–1690.* New York: The Macmillan Company, 1927.

———. *The Puritan Oligarchy.* New York: Charles Scribner's Sons, 1947.*

———. *The Shaping of Colonial Virginia: Patrician and Plebian in Virginia; The Planters of Colonial Virginia; and Virginia under the Stuarts.* New York: Russell and Russell, 1958.

WINSLOW, Ola Elizabeth. *Master Roger Williams.* New York: The Macmillan Company, 1957.

———. *Samuel Sewell of Boston.* New York: The Macmillan Company, 1964.

ZIFF, Larzer. *The Career of John Cotton Puritanism and the American Experience.* Princeton: Princeton University Press, 1962.

* Denotes availability in a paperbound edition. See the monthly *Paperbound Books in Print*, New York: R. R. Bowker Co., 1955–   , for dates and publishers.

TWO

Provincial Society
1713–63

INTRODUCTION

In 1743, Benjamin Franklin surveyed provincial society and concluded that "the first drudgery" of settling new colonies had ended, and in every colony there were now men of wealth and leisure free "to cultivate the finer arts and improve the common stock of knowledge."

Science had ushered in a new age. The discoveries of the English mathematician and physicist Isaac Newton implied that the world was governed by natural laws, not by the capricious acts of the Creator, and his Principia *and* Optics *challenged men to find these immutable principles ruling the universe. Franklin wrote that the pursuit of science and knowledge should contribute toward the "benefit of mankind in general." Consult "the Book of Nature" rather than the Scriptures he advised Americans.*

The hypothesis of a mechanistic world, rapidly gaining acceptance in America, produced varying reactions. Philosophers and theologians found a godless materialism inherent in such a concept and countered powerfully. They attacked materialistic intellectuals by explaining the nature of the universe in terms of platonic idealism. They either inspired common people to an enthusiastic, irrational fervor for a benevolent God or frightened them by depicting His pervasive power and possible vengeance against men.

In provincial writings on history, economics, business, planting, politics, and literature, there is a general absence of philosophical abstraction or theory. Authors mirrored the substantially practical attitudes of provincial Americans who were preoccupied with the problems of governing themselves locally; improving and expanding agriculture, commerce, and wealth; absorbing new immigrants from the Germanies, Scotland, and Northern Ireland; and pushing their frontiers ever westward.

1

Science

25. JOHN WINTHROP, *LECTURES ON COMETS*, 1759[*]

John Winthrop (1714–79), Hollis Professor of Science at Harvard College, was among colonial America's first Newtonian scientists. Primarily a mathematician, he introduced new discoveries to his students and wrote for the Boston newspapers explaining natural phenomena to the general public. He showed that the hitherto mysterious movements of the planets or the fearful quakes of the earth were not the machinations of a capricious God to punish mankind, but the result of natural laws which man should discover, observe, and understand. Winthrop was greatly respected by fellow philosophers; for his work in astronomy, he was elected a member of the Royal Society of London and several of his papers were published in its Philosophical Transactions.

A variety of opinions hath been entertained, as to the nature and place of [comets]. Some have looked upon them to be worlds on fire; (Which seems to be the idea conveyed by our vulgar term blazing stars.) and some, nothing more than lucid meteors: and while many have confined them within the narrow limits of our atmosphere, others have raised them up to the fixed stars. So widely do men differ, when instead of searching into the nature of things, they indulge their own imaginations.

It was an ancient doctrine of some Pythagorean philosophers; that the Comets are a peculiar kind of wandering stars; that they are to be

[*] John Winthrop, *Lectures on Comets. Read in the Chapel at Harvard College . . . in April 1759 on the Occasion of the Comet which Appeared in that Month* (Boston: W. Wells & T. B. Wait & Co. 1811), pp. 4–9, 14–15.

reckoned among the permanent bodies of the universe; that they move in their proper orbits, completing their courses in stated times: but that they are visible only in a small part of their orbit, and return not again till after a long period of years; being too remote, during the greatest part of their revolution, to be discerned by us. But the Peripatetic scheme afterward prevailing, the philosophers of that sect, who held that the heavens are absolutely immutable and incapable of generations and corruptions, regarded the Comets not as standing works of nature, but as new productions which quickly perish; and maintained them to be only a kind of meteors formed out of the exhalations of our atmosphere, and much below the moon; being apprehensive that, if they were placed higher, their appearing and disappearing so uncertainly would divest the heavenly region of that privilege of immutability which they had assigned it. In this they were confirmed by another notion they had taken up, that the planets were carried round in their courses by solid crystal orbs; through which, to be sure, the Comets could not penetrate. Thus does one error lead to another. And by the way, the prevalance of this opinion has had an ill effect, and has been the true reason why this most curious part of astromony, which relates to Comets, lay uncultivated for so many ages; the philosophers, who had imbibed such notions, thinking it to no purpose to describe with accuracy the irregular motions of such vanishing vapors. Had the ancients observed the paths of Comets among the fixed stars with the same care as they did those of the planets, the astronomy of Comets had, in all probability, by this time been brought to almost the same perfection with that of the planets. But as the opinion, that the Comets were meteors and below the moon, obtained for many ages almost universally, and was the only one publicly taught till the time of Tycho Brahe, an eminent astronomer of the sixteenth century, it has hence come to pass, that we have nothing certain transmitted to us, of the motion of any Comet, till within these last 200 years; those which appeared before, having not been described by astronomers, but only mentioned by historians as prodigies, or omens of dreadful calamities. But Tycho, having carefully observed a remarkable Comet, found by repeated trials, that it was not subject to a diurnal parallax; for it appeared at the same time in the same place among the fixed stars, to two observers at the distance of several hundred miles from each other. This observation at once overthrew the doctrine of the schools, and placed the Comet far above the moon. The astronomers, who came after Tycho, having diligently watched the Comets which appeared in their days, have found that the diurnal parallax of all of them is either wholly imperceptible, or extremely small;—a demonstration, that Comets cannot be aerial meteors, but ought to be ranked amongst the heavenly bodies. Indeed, their partaking of the apparent diurnal motion of the

heavens might have taught those philosophers better, and was a sufficient indication that Comets are not appendages of the earth.

As the want or smallness of a diurnal parallax has raised Comets
above the moon, so from their being subjects to an annual parallax it is
certain that they are not among the fixed stars, but descend into the
region of the planets. Though they are at too great a distance to have
their apparent place altered by being viewed from different parts of the
earth, yet they come near enough to have it altered by being viewed from
different parts of our annual orbit. Accordingly, their apparent motion is
sensibly affected by the annual motion of the earth, in the same manner
as that of the planets. The real motion of all the planets round the sun
is constantly direct, or from west to east; and not very unequal in the
several parts of their orbits; and would appear to be so, if viewed from
the sun, which is fixed in the centre of their orbits; but their apparent
motion, as viewed from the earth, which moves the same way as they
do, is very various. Sometimes they are seen to go swifter, sometimes
slower, with a direct motion; then to be retrograde, going the contrary
way, or from east to west; and between these opposite motions, they
appear for a little while stationary, or without any motion at all. These
appearances depend on the motion of the earth, as that happens to
conspire with, or be contrary to, and to be swifter or slower than, the
real motion of the planets. And for the same reason must the apparent
motion of Comets be changed, if they move within the planetary orbs.
Those, whose real motion is direct, will appear stationary and retrograde,
or at least much slower, in nearly the same aspects with the sun, as the
planets appear so; but those, whose real motion is retrograde (for such
is the motion of some Comets) will, in the same aspects, appear stationary and direct. And conversely, since this is the case in fact; since the
visible motion of Comets is altered, as the earth's annual motion would
require on the supposition of their coming into the region of the planets,
it follows, that they do come into the region of the planets. Thus, by the
way, the Comets supply us with a new proof, that the earth revolves
round the sun; for without supposing this revolution, their motions cannot be reduced to any sort of regularity. So far indeed are Comets from
being among the fixed stars, that it appears from their annual parallax,
that they are seldom seen till they come within the orb of Jupiter.
(Newtoni Principia, p. 480) and that they frequently descend below the
orbs of Mars and the inferior planets.

Some astronomers, who had rightly placed Comets in the region of
the planets, have been mistaken in their thoughts on the constitution of
these bodies. It has been supposed, that Comets were formed by the coali-
tion of some subtle exhalations from the planets; and that they were, with
regard to the sun, of the same nature as what are called shooting stars,

with regard to the earth. But this opinion is overthrown by what Sir Issac Newton has observed (Princip. p. 508) of the remarkable Comet which appeared in the year 1680. The earth is above 160 times farther from the sun, than that Comet was in its perihelion. Now the heat of the sun at the Comet in its perihelion was above 26000 times greater than it is at the earth. But the heat of boiling water is about three times as great as that which dry earth contracts from the summer sun; and so the heat at the Comet was about 9000 times greater than that of boiling water. And the heat of red-hot iron Sir Isaac conjectures to be about three or four times greater than that of boiling water; wherefore the heat, which dry earth on the Comet in its perihelion might contract from the rays of the sun, was about 2000 times greater than that of red-hot iron. But by so intense an heat as this, all volatile matter must presently have been consumed and dissipated; and the Comet, which could endure this most violent heat, certainly did not consist of vapors or exhalation of any kind.

·   ·   ·   ·

Indeed, the opinions concerning Comets, which formerly passed current with many, were suspected by others. Thus Seneca the philosopher, dissatisfied with the doctrine of his time relating to them, and unable to substitute a better, foretold, that "in future ages, some man would demonstrate in what parts of the heavens the Comets wander, why they depart so far from the other wandering stars, and what sort of bodies they are." (Seneca Natural. Quaest. Lib. vii. Cap xxvi.) The prediction has been fulfilled in the present age; and this man was Sir Isaac Newton. After many centuries elapsed, with little insight gained into the true constitution of these bodies, and none at all into their real motions, this great genius arose, and with a strength of mind peculiar to himself (I had almost said, more than human)

> *Pursu'd the Comets where they farthest run,*
> *And brought them back obsequious, to the sun,*

as Pope has happily expressed it. Formed to penetrate into the most abstruse recesses of nature, he traced these unknown travellers through every step of their long journey, delineated the particular tour they make, and shewed by what secret influence they are determined to revisit our planetary regions, after an absence of scores, or rather centuries of years.

26. DAVID RITTENHOUSE, *DESCRIPTION OF A NEW ORRERY*, 1770[*]

David Rittenhouse (1732–96), a clock and instrument maker of Pennsylvania, was regarded by his contemporaries as a genius in mathematics. Thomas Jefferson, upon viewing his orrery (planetarium), said that he had imitated his Creator more "than any man who had lived from the creation to this day." Rittenhouse constructed his instrument at the College of Philadelphia. Others like it soon followed at the College of New Jersey and elsewhere, and new institutions of higher learning strained resources to obtain their own orreries and maintain prestige in training students in the Newtonian science.

The Machine is intended to have three faces, standing perpendicular to the horizon; that in the front to be four square, made of sheet-brass, curiously polished, silvered, and painted in proper places, and otherwise ornamented. From the centre arises an axis, to support a gilded brass ball, intended to represent the Sun. Round this ball move others, made of brass or ivory, to represent the Planets: They are to move in elliptical orbits, having the central ball in one focus; and their motions to be sometimes swifter, and sometimes slower, as nearly according to the true law of an equable description of areas as is possible, without too great a complication of wheel-work. The orbit of each Planet is likewise to be properly inclined to those of the others; and their Aphelia and Nodes justly placed; and their velocities so accurately adjusted, as not to differ sensibly from the tables of Astronomy in some thousands of years.

For the greater beauty of the instrument, the balls representing the planets are to be of a considerable bigness; but so contrived, that they may be taken off at pleasure, and others, much smaller, and fitter for some purposes, put in their places.

When the Machine is put in motion, by the turning of a winch, there are three indexes which point out the hour of the day, the day of the month, and the year (according to the Julian account), answering to that situation of the heavenly bodies which is then represented; and so continually, for a period of 5000 years, either forward or backward.

In order to know the true situation of a Planet at any particular time, the small set of balls are to be put each on its respective axis; then the winch to be turned round until each index points to the given time. Then a small telescope, made for the purpose, is to be applied to the central ball; and directing it to the planet, its longitude and inclination

[*] William Barton, *Memoirs of the Life of David Rittenhouse* . . . (Philadelphia: for William Parker, 1813), pp. 198–202.

will be seen on a large brass circle, silvered, and properly graduated, representing the zodiac, and having a motion of one degree in seventy-two years, agreeable to the precession of the equinoxes. So, likewise, by applying the telescope to the ball representing the earth, and directing it to any planet—then will both the longitude and latitude of that planet be pointed out (by an index and graduated circle), as seen from the earth.

The two lesser faces are four feet in height, and two feet three inches in breadth. One of them will exhibit all the appearances of Jupiter and his Satellites—their eclipses, transits, and inclinations; likewise, all the appearances of Saturn, with his ring and satellites. And the other will represent all the phaenomena of the moon, particularly, the exact time, quantity, and duration of her eclipses—and those of the sun, occasioned by her interposition; with a most curious contrivance for exhibiting the appearance of a solar eclipse, at any particular place on the earth: likewise, the true place of the moon in the signs, with her latitude, and the place of her apogee in the nodes, the sun's declination, equation of time &c. It must be understood, that all these motions are to correspond exactly, with the celestial motions; and not to differ several degrees from the truth, in a few revolutions, as is common in Orreries.

If it shall be thought proper, the whole is to be adapted to, and kept in motion by, a strong pendulum clock; nevertheless, at liberty to be turned by the winch, and adjusted to any time, past or future.

N.B. The diurnal motions of such planets as have been discovered to revolve on their own axes, are likewise to be properly represented; both with regard to the Times, and the situation of their Poles.

27. WILLIAM BARTRAM, *TRAVELS THROUGH NORTH AND SOUTH CAROLINA, GEORGIA, AND EAST AND WEST FLORIDA*, c. 1773[*]

William Bartram (1739–1823), like his father John Bartram (1699–1777), was a botanist. The virgin land of the New World fostered numerous distinguished naturalists—among them Mark Catesby, whose drawings and descriptions of wild life are classic, Alexander Garden, Thomas Jefferson, and Cadwallader Colden. Probably the most distinguished was William Bartram, a dedicated and modern scientist who worked in the field and kept a botanical garden in Philadelphia in which to experiment with his collections. The first excerpt from his Travels *contains acute observations of the culture of the Indians, into whose*

[*] William Bartram, *Travels Through North and South Carolina, Georgia, and East and West Florida* (Philadelphia: James and Johnson, 1791), pp. 467–68, 494–500.

country he ventured on his extended journeys. His interpretation of the Indian as the natural man was in keeping with the current social philosophy of John Locke and Jean Jacques Rousseau.

OF [the Indian's] GOVERNMENT AND CIVIL SOCIETY

The constitution or system of their [The Cherokee Indians'] police is simply natural, and as little complicated as that which is supposed to direct or rule the approved economy of the ant and the bee and seems to be nothing more than the simple dictates of natural reason, plain to every one, yet recommended to them by their wise and virtuous elders as divine, because necessary for securing mutual happiness: equally binding and effectual, as being proposed and assented to in the general combination: every one's conscience being a sufficient conviction (the golden rule, do as you would be done by) instantly presents to view, and produces a society of peace and love, which in effect better maintains human happiness, than the most complicated system of modern politics, or sumptuary laws, enforced by coercive means: for here the people are all on an equality, as to the possession and enjoyments of the common necessaries and conveniences of life, for luxuries and superfluities they have none.

This natural constitution is simply subordinate; and the supreme, sovereign or executive power resides in a council of elderly chiefs, warriors and others, respectable for wisdom, valour and virtue.

At the head of this venerable senate, presides their mico or king, which signifies a magistrate or chief ruler: the governors of Carolina, Georgia, &c. are called mico; and the king of England is called Antapala-mico-clucco, (Clucco signifies great or excellent.) that is, the great king, over or beyond the great water.

The king, although he is acknowledged to be the first and greatest man in the town or tribe, and honoured with every due and rational mark of love and esteem, and when presiding in council, with a humility and homage as reverent as that paid to the most despotic monarch in Europe or the East, and when absent, his seat is not filled by any other person, yet he is not dreaded; and when out of the council, he associates with the people as a common man, converses with them, and they with him, in perfect ease and familiarity.

The mico or king, though elective, yet his advancement to that supreme dignity must be understood in a very different light from the elective monarchs of the old world, where the progress to magistracy is generally effected by schism and the influence of friends gained by craft, bribery, and often by more violent efforts; and after the throne is obtained, by measures little better than usurpation, he must be protected and supported there, by the same base means that carried him thither.

But here behold the majesty of the Muscogulge mico! he does not either publicly or privately beg of the people to place him in a situation to command and rule them: no, his appearance is altogether mysterious; as a beneficent deity he rises king over them, as the sun rises to bless the earth!

No one will tell you how or when he became their king; but he is universally acknowledged to be the greatest person among them, and he is loved, esteemed and reverenced, although he associates, eats, drinks, and dances with them in common as another man; his dress is the same, and a stranger could not distinguish the king's habitation from that of any other citizen, by any sort of splendour or magnificence; yet he perceives they act as though their mico beheld them, himself invisible. In a word, their mico seems to them the representative of Providence or the Great Spirit, whom they acknowledge to preside over and influence their councils and public proceedings. He personally presides daily in their councils, either at the rotunda or public square: and even here his voice in regard to business in hand, is regarded no more than any other chief's or senator's, no farther than his advice, as being the best and wisest man of the tribe, and not by virtue of regal prerogative. But whether their ultimate decisions require unanimity, or only a majority of voices, I am uncertain; but probably where there is a majority, the minority voluntarily accede.

The most active part the mico takes is in the civil government of the town or tribe: here he has the power and prerogative of calling a council, to deliberate on peace and war, or all public concerns, as inquiring into, and deciding upon complaints and differences; but he has not the least shadow of exclusive executive power. He is complimented with the first visits of strangers, giving audience to ambassadors, with presents, and he has also the disposal of the public granary.

The next man in order of dignity and power, is the great war chief: he represents and exercises the dignity of the mico, in his absence, in council; his voice is of the greatest weight, in military affairs; his power and authority are entirely independent of the mico, though when a mico goes on an expedition, he heads the army, and is there the war chief. There are many of these war chiefs in a town or tribe, who are captains or leaders of military parties; they are elderly men, who in their youthful days have distinguished themselves in war by valour, subtilty and intrepidity; and these veteran chiefs, in a great degree, constitute their truly dignified and venerable senates.

There is in every town or tribe a high priest, usually called by the white people jugglers, or conjurers, besides several juniors or graduates. But the ancient high priest or seer, presides in spiritual affairs, and is a person of consequence; he maintains and exercises great influence in the state, particularly in military affairs; the senate never determine on an expedition against their enemy without his counsel and assistance. These people generally believe that their seer has communion with powerful invisible spirits, who they suppose have a share in the rule and government of human affairs, as well as the elements; that he can predict the result of an expedition; and his influence is so great, that they have been known frequently to stop, and turn back an army, when within a day's journey of their enemy, after a march of several hundred miles; and indeed their predictions have surprized many people. They foretell rain or drought, and pretend to bring rain at pleasure, cure diseases, and exercise witchcraft, invoke or expel evil spirits, and even assume the power of directing thunder and lightning.

These Indians are by no means idolaters, unless their puffing the tobacco smoke towards the sun, and rejoicing at the appearance of the new moon, may be termed so. (I have observed the young fellows very merry and jocose, at the appearance of the new moon, saying how ashamed she looks under the veil, since sleeping with sun these two or three nights, she is ashamed to show her face.) So far from idolatry are they, that they have no images amongst them, nor any religious rite or ceremony that I could perceive; but adore the Great Spirit, the giver and taker away of the breath of life, with the most profound and respectful homage. They believe in a future state, where the spirit exists, which they call the world of spirits, where they enjoy different degrees of tranquillity or comfort, agreeably to their life spent here: a person who in his life has been an industrious hunter, provided well for his family, an intrepid and active warrior, just, upright, and done all the good he could, will, they say, in the world of spirits, live in a warm, pleasant country, where are expansive, green, flowery savannas and high forests, watered with rivers of pure waters, replenished with deer, and every species of game; a serene, unclouded and peaceful sky; in short, where there is fulness of pleasure uninterrupted.

They have many accounts of trances and visions of their people, who have been supposed to be dead, but afterwards reviving, have related their visions, which tend to enforce the practice of virtue and the moral duties.

Before I went amongst the Indians, I had often heard it reported, that these people, when their parents, through extreme old age, become decrepit and helpless, in compassion for their miseries, send them to the other world, by a stroke of the tomahawk or bullet. Such a degree of depravity and species of impiety, always appeared to me so incredibly inhuman and horrid, that it was with the utmost difficulty I assumed resolution sufficient to inquire into it.

The [Indian] traders assured me that they knew no instance of such barbarism; but that there had been instances of the communities performing such a deed at the earnest request of the victim.

When I was at Mucclasse town, early one morning, at the invitation of the chief trader, we repaired to the public square, taking with us some presents for the Indian chiefs. On our arrival we took our seats in a circle of venerable men, round a fire in the centre of the area: other citizens were continually coming in, and amongst them I was struck with awe and veneration at the appearance of a very aged man: his hair, what little he had, was as white as snow; he was conducted by three young men, one having hold of each arm, and the third behind to steady him. On his approach the whole circle saluted him, "welcome," and made way for him: he looked as smiling and cheerful as youth, yet stoneblind by extreme old age: he was the most ancient chief of the town, and they all seemed to reverence him. Soon after the old man had seated himself, I distributed my presents, giving him a very fine handkerchief and a twist of choice tobacco, which passed through the hands of an elderly chief who sat next him, telling him it was a present from one of their white brothers, lately arrived in the nation from Charleston: he received the present with a smile, and thanked me, returning the favour immediately with his own stone pipe and cat skin of tobacco: and then complimented me with a long oration, the purport of which was the value he set on the friendship of the Carolinians. He said, that when he was a young man they had no iron hatchets, pots, hoes, knives, razors nor guns, that they then made use of their own stone axes, clay pots, flint knives, bows and arrows; and that he was the first man who brought the white people's goods into his town, which he did on his back from Charleston, five hundred miles on foot, for they had no horses then amongst them.

The trader then related to me an anecdote concerning this ancient patriarch, which occurred not long before.

One morning after his attendants had led him to the council fire, before seating himself, he addressed himself to the people after this manner—

"You yet love me; what can I do now to merit your regard? nothing; I am good for nothing; I cannot see to shoot the buck or hunt up the sturdy bear; I know I am but a burthen to you; I have lived long enough; now let my spirit go; I want to see the warriors of my youth in the country of spirits: (bareing his breast) here is the hatchet, take it and strike." They answered with one united voice, "We will not; we cannot; we want you here."

Botanical Observations

After my return from the Creek nation, I employed myself during the spring and fore part of summer, in revisiting the several districts in

Georgia and the East borders of Florida, where I had noted the most curious subjects; collecting them together, and shipping them off to England. In the course of these excursions and researches, I had the opportunity of observing the new flowering shrub, resembling the Gordonia, in perfect bloom, as well as bearing ripe fruit. (On first observing the fructifications and habit of this tree, I was inclined to believe it a species of Gordonia, but afterwards, upon stricter examination, and comparing its flowers and fruit with those of the Gordonia Lafianthus, I presently found striking characteristics abundantly sufficient to separate it from that genus, and to establish it the head of a new tribe, which we have honoured with the name of the illustrious Dr. Benjamin Franklin. Franklinia Alatamaha.) It is a flowering tree, of the first order for beauty and fragrance of blossoms: the tree grows fifteen or twenty feet high, branching alternately; the leaves are oblong, broadest towards their extremities, and terminate with an acute point, which is generally a little reflexed; they are lightly serrated, attenuate downwards, and sessile, or have very short petioles; they are placed in alternate order, and towards the extremities of the twigs are crowded together, but stand more sparsedly below; the flowers are very large, expand themselves perfectly, are of a snow white colour, and ornamented with a crown or tassel of gold coloured refulgent staminae in their centre, the inferior petal or segment of the corolla is hollow, formed like a cap or helmet, and entirely includes the other four, until the moment of expansion; its exterior surface is covered with a short silky hair; the borders of the petals are crisped or plicated: these large white flowers stand single and sessile in the bosom of the leaves, and being near together towards the extremities of the twigs, and usually many expanded at the same time, make a gay appearance: the fruit is a large, round, dry, woody apple or pericarp, opening at each end oppositely by five alternate fissures, containing ten cells, each replete with dry woody cuneiform seed. This very curious tree was first taken notice of about ten or twelve years ago, at this place, when I attended my father (John Bartram) on a botanical excursion; but, it being then late in the autumn, we could form no opinion to what class or tribe it belonged.

We never saw it grow in any other place, nor have I ever since seen it growing wild, in all my travels, from Pennsylvania to Point Coupé, on the banks of the Mississippi, which must be allowed a very singular and unaccountable circumstance; at this place there are two or three acres of ground where it grows plentifully.

The other new, singular and beautiful shrub, (I gave it the name Bignonia bracteata, extrempore.) now here in full bloom, I never saw grow but at two other places in all my travels, and there very sparingly, except in East Florida, in the neighbourhood of the sea-coast.

28. BENJAMIN FRANKLIN, LETTERS ON ELECTRICITY, 1749, 1752*

In his time Benjamin Franklin (1706–90), printer, businessman, politician, patriot, and statesman, was as highly esteemed as Newton. He was one of the first contributors to the newly developing subject of electronics. His discoveries had a profound effect on the thought of his period. He harnessed lightning, one of nature's most fearsome and destructive forces, thereby inviting men to discover and perhaps control universal laws for their benefit. Franklin's curiosity took him further in this field than was generally known. New discoveries of Musschenbrook and Kleist, such as the Leyden Jar, in 1745–6, led him to experiment with making and storing electricity and to theorize on the nature of electrical current. Like Bartram, Franklin used the modern scientific methods of experiment and observation, from which he drew conclusions that he communicated to men of science throughout the world.

Electrical Current

.   .   .

To Peter Collinson   [Philadelphia] April 29, 1749
    18. Upon this [experiment with electrically charged phials] we made what we called an *electrical battery*, consisting of eleven panes of large sash-glass, arm'd with thin leaden plates, pasted on each side, placed vertically, and supported at two inches distance on silk cords, with thick hooks of leaden wire, one from each side, standing upright, distant from each other, and convenient communications of wire and chain, from the giving side of one pane, to the receiving side of the other; that so the whole might be charged together, and with the same labour as one single pane, and another contrivance to bring the giving sides, after charging, in contact with one long wire, and the receivers with another, which two long wires would give the force of all the plates of glass at once through the body of any animal forming the circle with them. The plates may also be discharged separately, or any number together that is required. But this machine is not much used, as not perfectly answering our intention with regard to the ease of charging for the reason given, Sec. 10. We made also, of large glass panes, magical pictures, and self-moving animated wheels, presently to be described.

    * Benjamin Smyth, *The Writings of Benjamin Franklin* (New York: Macmillan, 1907), Vol. II, pp. 402–11; Vol. III, pp. 99–100. See also the recent *The Papers of Benjamin Franklin*, Leonard W. Laboree *et. al,* ed. (New Haven: Yale University Press, 1959–   ), Vol. III, pp. 357–65; Vol. IV, pp. 366–67.

19. I perceive by the ingenious Mr. *Watson's* last book, lately received, that Dr. *Bevis* had used, before we had, panes of glass to give a shock; though, till that book came to hand, I thought to have communicated it to you as a novelty. The excuse for mentioning it here is, that we tried the experiment differently, drew different consequences from it (for Mr. Watson still seems to think the fire *accumulated on the non-electric* that is in contact with the glass, p. 72) and, as far as we hitherto know, have carried it further.

20. The magical picture is made thus. Having a large netzotinto with a frame and glass, suppose of the KING, (God preserve him) take out the print, and cut a panel out of it near two inches distant from the frame all round. If the cut is through the picture, it is not the worse. With thin paste, or gum-water, fix the border that is cut off on the inside the glass, pressing it smooth and close; then fill up the vacancy by gilding the glass well with leaf-gold, or brass. Gild likewise the inner edge of the back of the frame all round, except the top part, and form a communication between that gilding and the gilding behind the glass: then put in the board, and that side is finished. Turn up the glass, and gild the foreside exactly over the back gilding, and when it is dry, cover it by pasting on the pannel of the picture that hath been cut out, observing to bring the correspondent parts of the border and picture together, by which the picture will appear of a piece, as at first, only part is behind the glass, and part before. Hold the picture horizontally by the top, and place a little moveable gilt crown on the king's head. If now the picture be moderately electrified, and another person take hold of the frame with one hand, so that his fingers touch its inside gilding, and with the other hand endeavour to take off the crown, he will receive a terrible blow, and fail in the attempt. If the picture were highly charged, the consequences might perhaps be as fatal as that of high treason, for when the spark is taken through a quire of paper laid on the picture by means of a wire communication, it makes a fair hole through every sheet, that is through forty-eight leaves, though a quire of paper is thought good armour against the push of a sword, or even against a pistol bullet, and the crack is exceeding loud. The operator, who holds the picture by the upper end, where the inside of the frame is not gilt, to prevent its falling, feels nothing of the shock, and may touch the face of the picture without danger, which he pretends is a test of his loyalty. If a ring of persons take the shock among them, the experiment is called *The Conspirators*.

21. On the principle, that hooks of bottles, differently charged, will attract and repel differently, is made an electrical wheel, that turns with considerable strength. A small upright shaft of wood passes at right angles through a thin round board, of about twelve inches diameter, and turns on a sharp point of iron, fixed in the lower end, while a strong wire

in the upper end, passing through a small hole in a thin brass plate, keeps the shaft truly vertical. About thirty *radii* of equal length, made of sash-glass, cut in narrow strips, issue horizontally from the circumference of the board, the end most distant from the circumference of the board, the end most distant from the center being about four inches apart. On the end of every one, a brass thimble is fixed. If now the wire of a bottle electrified in the common way, be brought near the circumference of this wheel, it will attract the nearest thimble, and so put the wheel in motion; that thimble, in passing by, receives a spark, and thereby being electrified is repelled, and so driven forwards; while a second being attracted, approaches the wire, receives a spark, and is driven after the first, and so on till the wheel has gone once round, when the thimbles before electrified approaching the wire, instead of being attracted as they were at first, are repelled, and the motion presently ceases. But if another bottle, which had been charged through the coating, be placed near the same wheel, its wire will attract the thimble repelled by the first, and thereby double the force that carries the wheel round; and not only taking out the fire that had been communicated to the thimbles by the first bottle, but even robbing them of their natural quantity, instead of being repelled when they come again towards the first bottle, they are more strongly attracted, so that the wheel mends its pace, till it goes with great rapidity, twelve or fifteen rounds in a minute, and with such strength, as that the weight of one hundred *Spanish* dollars, with which we once loaded it, did not seem in the least to retard its motion. This is called an electrical jack; and if a large fowl were spitted on the upright shaft, it would be carried round before a fire with a motion fit for roasting.

    22. But this wheel, like those driven by wind, water, or weights, moves by a foreign force, to wit, that of the bottles. The self-moving wheel, though constructed on the same principles, appears more surprising. 'Tis made of a thin round plate of window-glass, seventeen inches diameter, well gilt on both sides, all but two inches next the edge. Two small hemispheres of wood are then fixed with cement to the middle of the upper and under sides, centrally opposite, and in each of them a thick strong wire eight or ten inches long, which together make the axis of the wheel. It turns horizontally on a point at the lower end of its axis, which rests on a bit of brass cemented within a glass salt-cellar. The upper end of its axis passes through a hole in a thick brass plate cemented to a long strong piece of glass, which keeps it six or eight inches distant from any non-electric, and has a small ball of wax or metal on its top, to keep in the fire. In a circle on the table which supports the wheel, are fixed twelve small pillars of glass, at about four inches distance, with a thimble on the top of each. On the edge of the wheel is a small leaden bullet, communicating by a wire with the gilding

of the *upper* surface of the wheel; and about six inches from it is another bullet communicating in like manner with the *under* surface. When the wheel is to be charged by the upper surface, a communication must be made from the under surface to the table. When it is well charged, it begins to move; the bullet nearest to a pillar moves towards the thimble on that pillar, and passing by, electrifies it, and then pushes itself from it; the succeeding bullet, which communicates with the other surface of the glass, more strongly attracts that thimble, on account of its being before electrified by the other bullet; and thus the wheel increases its motion till it comes to such a height that the resistance of the air regulates it. It will go half an hour, and make one minute with another twenty turns in a minute, which is six hundred turns in the whole; the bullet of the upper surface giving in each turn twelve sparks, to the thimbles, which makes seven thousand two hundred sparks; and the bullet of the under surface receiving as many from the thimbles; those bullets moving in the time near two thousand five hundred feet. The thimbles are well fixed, and in so exact a circle, that the bullets may pass within a very small distance of each of them. If, instead of two bullets you put eight, four communicating with the upper surface, and four with the under surface, placed alternately; which eight, at about six inches distance, completes the circumference, the force and swiftness will be greatly increased, the wheel making fifty turns in a minute; but then it will not continue moving so long. These wheels may be applied, perhaps, to the ringing of chimes, and moving of light-made orreries.

23. A small wire bent circularly, with a loop at each end; let one end rest against the under surface of the wheel, and bring the other end near the upper surface, it will give a terrible crack, and the force will be discharged.

24. Every spark in that manner drawn from the surface of the wheel, makes a round hole in the gilding, tearing off a part of it in coming out; which shews that the fire is not accumulated on the gilding, but is in the glass itself.

25. The gilding being varnished over with turpentine varnish, the varnish, though dry and hard, is burnt by the sparks drawn through it, and gives a strong smell and visible smoke. And when the spark is drawn through paper, all round the hole made by it, the paper will be blacked by the smoke, which sometimes penetrates several of the leaves. Part of the gilding torn off, is also found forcible driven into the hole made in the paper by the stroke.

26. It is amazing to observe in how small a portion of glass a great electrical force may lie. A thin glass bubble, about an inch diameter, weighing only six grains, being half filled with water, partly gilt on the outside, and furnish'd with a wire hook, gives, when electrified, as great a shock as a man can well bear. As the glass is thickest near the

orifice, I suppose the lower half, which being filt was electrified and gave the shock, did not exceed two grains; for it appeared, when broke, much thinner than the upper half. If one of these thin bottles be electrified by the coating, and the spark taken out through the gilding, it will break the glass inwards, at the same time that it breaks the gilding outwards.

27. And allowing that there is no more electrical fire in a bottle after charging than before, how great must be the quantity in this small portion of glass! It seems as if it were of its very substance and essence. Perhaps if that due quantity of electrical fire so obstinately retained by glass, could be separated from it, it would no longer be glass; it might lose its transparency, or its brittleness, or its elasticity. Experiments may possible be invented hereafter to discover this.

28. We were surprised at the account given in Mr. Watson's book, of a shock communicated through a great space of dry ground, and suspect there must be some metaline quality in the gravel of that ground; having found that simple dry earth, rammed in a glass tube, open at both ends, and a wire hook inserted in the earth at each end, the earth and wires making part of a circuit, would not conduct the least perceptible shock, and indeed when one wire was electrified, the other hardly shewed any signs of its being in connection with it. Even a thoroughly wet packbread sometimes fails of conducting a shock, though it otherwise conducts Electricity very well. A dry cake of ice, or an icicle, held between two in a circle, likewise prevents the shock, which one would not expect, as water conducts it so perfectly well. Gilding on a new hook, though at first it conducts the shock extremely well, yet fails after ten or a dozen experiments, though it appears otherwise in all respects the same which we cannot account for.

29. There is one experiment more which surprizes us, and is not hitherto satisfactorily accounted for; it is this: Place an iron shot on a glass stand, and let a ball of damp cork, suspended by a silk thread, hang in contact with the shot. Take a bottle in each hand, one that is electrified through the hook, the other through the coating: Apply the giving wire to the shot, which will electrify it *positively*, and the cork shall be repelled: then apply the requiring wire, which will take out the spark given by the other; when the cork will return to the shot: Apply the same again, and take out another spark, so will the shot be electrified *negatively*, and the cork in that case shall be repelled equally as before. Then apply the giving wire to the shot, and give the spark it wanted, so will the cork return: Give it another, which will be an addition to its natural quantity, so will the cork be repelled again: And so may the experiment be repeated as long as there is any charge in the bottles. Which shews, that bodies having less than the common quantity of Electricity, repel each other, as well as those that have more.

Chagrined a little that we have been hitherto able to produce nothing in this way of use to mankind; and the hot weather coming on, when electrical experiments are not so agreeable, it is proposed to put an end to them for this season, somewhat humorously, in a party of pleasure on the banks of *Skuylkil*. Spirits, at the same time, are to be fired by a spark sent from side to side through the river, without any other conductor than the water; and experiment which we some time since performed, to the amazement of many. A turkey is to be killed for our dinner by the *electrical shock*, and roasted by the *electrical jack*, before a fire kindled by the electrified bottle: when the healths of all the famous electricians in *England, Holland, France*, and *Germany* are to be drank in *electrified bumpers*, under the discharge of guns from the *electrical battery*.

The Kite Experiment

To Peter Collinson

[Philadelphia] October 19, 1752

Sir,

As frequent mention is made in public papers from *Europe* of the success of the *Philadelphia* experiment for drawing the electric fire from clouds by means of pointed rods of iron erected on high buildings, etc., it may be agreeable to the curious to be informed that the same experiment has succeeded in *Philadelphia*, though made in a different and more easy manner, which is as follows:

Make a small cross of two light strips of cedar, the arms so long as to reach to the four corners of a large thin silk handkerchief when extended, tie the corners of the handkerchief to the extremities of the cross, so you have the body of a kite; which, being properly accommodated with a tail, loop, and string, will rise in the air, like those made of paper; but this being of silk, is fitter to bear the wet and wind of a thunder gust without tearing. To the top of the upright stick of the cross is to be fixed a very sharp-pointed wire, rising a foot or more above the wood. To the end of the twine, next the hand, is to be tied a silk ribbon, and where the silk and twine join, a key may be fastened. This kite is to be raised when a thunder-gust appears to be coming on, and the person who holds the string must stand within a door or window or under some cover, so that the silk ribbon may not be wet; and care must be taken that the twine does not touch the frame of the door or window. As soon as any of the thunderclouds come over the kite, the pointed wire will draw the electric fire from them, and the kite, with all the twine, will be electrified, and the loose filaments of the twine will stand out every way, and be attracted by an approaching finger. And when the rain has wet the kite and twine, so that it can conduct the electric fire freely, you will find it stream out plentifully from the key on the approach of your knuckle. At this key the phial may be charged; and from electric fire thus obtained, spirits may be kindled, and all the other electric experiments be performed, which are usually done by the help of a rubbed glass globe or tube, and thereby the sameness of the electric matter with that of lightning completely demonstrated. . . .

2

Philosophy

29. CADWALLADER COLDEN, OBSERVATIONS OF AN EXPERIMENT WITH YEAST, c. 1750*

Cadwallader Colden (1688–1776), conservative governor of New York during the Stamp Act crisis and historian of the Iroquois nation, experimented in botany, medicine, physics, and mathematics. He was one of the foremost American students of Newtonian science. In his treatise on this subject, An Explication of the Causes of Action in Matter *(1747), mentioned in the document below, he attempted to explain the forces causing gravitation. But this work was never accepted in America; his friend and fellow scientist, Benjamin Franklin, stated he could not understand it perhaps because Colden was more concerned with philosophy than scientific method. Indeed, the work was assessed at the University of Edinburgh and in German universities as a philosophical study, and with good reason because Colden went beyond contemporary investigators, became deeply speculative, and seemed to be in the process of formulating a philosophy of science. The following conclusions, reached after an experiment with fermentation, indicate that he was searching for a life substance found intrinsically in matter. In deference to the influential philosopher and theologian Samuel Johnson, Colden admitted that God might possibly be identified with this intrinsic matter.*

· · · ·

Tho I say, that Fermentation is the Principle of Animal and Vegetable life, I am far from thinking it to be a primary & simple power of any one thing. It is truely the perpetual effect of the complicated Ac-

---

* Cadwallader Colden MSS, New York Historical Society. [The italics are mine—Editor's Note]

161

tions of the Primary Material & Intellectual powers, combined in particular Animal & Vegetable Systems, which continue their combined Actions, so long as that particular system subsists. This, I think, may be affirmed as a Principle of Animal & Vegetable life, without being able to explain in what manner the primary powers produce this Fermentation: in the same manner as Sir Isaac Newton has, with so much success, affirmed Gravitation in explaining the phoenomena of the Solar System, tho he allows Gravitation to be only a perpetual effect of unknown causes. It certainly is the effect of the combined Actions of the primary powers.

  53 *To discover the Primary powers, which produce all the Phoenomena in nature, has been the principal object of inquiry to Philosophers in all ages. To have hopes of succeeding, after the most sagaceous have failed, appears extremely vain; but to cut off all hopes of success, must be injurious to the acquiring of knowledge, & absolutely deprive the Philosopher of his greatest pleasure. Such hope may not be vain, when it is considered, that the greatest discoveries have been made by a sagaceous observation of the most obvious phoenomena. Much time has been spent in curious & elaborate experiments, to discover the Elementary principles of matter, which perhaps may be more easily discovered, by a proper reflexion on the phoenomena or effects of the primary powers which we cannot avoid when our eyes are open & while we make the common use of our senses.* For instance, the most obvious appearances, which occur every where & at all times, show, that Matter or body has a power of resisting all change in its present state, whether it be in motion or at rest, & by supposing it to be deprived of this power, every Idea we have of it is lost. On the other hand Motion, or a perpetual change of its present state, is every where as obvious. It is impossible to conceive that Motion can arise from a power which resists all change of its present state. Some other Being must therefore have the power of moving. Again consider the Phoenomena of Light every where likewise as obvious, & that we loose every conception we have of it, by supposing it to be at rest, & that every effect produced by it must cease, it seems a natural conclusion that motion is essential to Light & that Light is the Principle of Motion: consequently that it is a Being essentially different from Matter or Body. Numerous obvious phoenomena confirm this. The rays of Light mutually pervade or penetrate each other, without the least resistance or deviation in their course. A small quantity of Light fills a large Space, viz the quantity of Light emitted by a candle in a single moment, & a large quantity may be contained in a small space as in the focus of a large Corning glass where they mutually penetrate & pass without the least resistence & pass in straight lines. The gravitation of bodies to the Earth is a phoenomenon no less obvious. There must therefore be some Medium, something between the Earth & all other bodies, perpetually acting, by which all bodies are attracted or impelled

to the Earth. Nothing can act where it is not, either at the greatest or least distance. We have no method of discovering any simple or primary power otherwise than by the effects which it produces: and if, by going over all the effects or phoenomena of that power, we can reduce them all to the effect of one simple action, we may conclude, that the power of producing this action is the peculiar power of that medium or thing by which bodies are mutually attracted or impelled towards each other, especially if we clearly perceive that this action or the effects of it cannot be produced by any other known power. Now, after going over all the phoenomena of the mutual attraction of bodies analitically, I conclude, that there is some Medium or Being universally diffused between all bodies, & in the interstices between the parts of all bodies, that the Peculiar property or Power, of this Medium is to receive the Action of the resisting power of bodies & of the moveing power of Light in every point of that Medium, & to react the same from every point of the Medium with the same force that the several points of the Medium receive it. If from this power of Reaction the mutual apparent attraction of bodies can be clearly demonstrated, I conclude, that such a Medium or Being does really exist. It is besides my present purpose to explain this more particularly. It has been attempted several years since in a small Treatise entituled *The Principles of Action in Matter.* I have often, since the publication of that Treatise, reflected on the subject of it. I have discovered nothing in the phoenomena to contradict those Principles, & numerous phoenomena to confirm them.

54   On the whole, I am strongly possessed with an opinion, that all the phoenomena in Nature can be deduced from three distinct & essentially different powers or Beings. The Resisting power in Matter, the Moving power in Light, & the Reacting power of the Universal Medium. That the Phoenomena of every System, the great Solar System, & the Small Systems of Animals & Vegetables may be deduced from the combined actions of these three simple powers, under the direction of an Intelligent Being. What pleasure must a philosophic Mind receive, in deducing such innumerable phoenomena, from so few & such simple powers, obvious to every conception, when prejudices are removed.

55   The primary Powers cannot be complicated, they are simple & single in each power; but several beings, all having the same simple power, may each have it in a different degree. It is observed that different rays of light have different degrees of refrangibility essential to them, and as motion is essential to light, without which we can have no conception of it, we may suppose that different rays have different degrees of velocity essential to them, & if from this difference of velocity alone, all the phoenomena of Light & Colours can be deduced, all doubt of the Truth of this must be removed. In like manner, if, from the different phoenomena of the Resisting power, it appear, that different parts

of Matter have different degrees of resistence essential to them, we must conclude that it is really so; for we have no means of discovering the different powers in nature, otherwise than from their effects. From an attentive reflexion on the Phoenomena it will appear, that the Universal Medium of Reaction is absolutely simple, every part of it has the same degree of power in reacting the actions of the Moveing & Resisting powers. The Property or Virtue, of any composition of Matter or particular thing are the effects of the peculiar complication of the primary powers in that thing.

30. SAMUEL JOHNSON, *ELEMENTA PHILOSOPHICA*, 1752*

Samuel Johnson (1696–1772), born in Connecticut, was graduated from Yale and appointed minister to the Congregational church at West Haven. Despite his puritanical upbringing and training, he discarded Congregationalism, finding its basic scholastic and Calvinistic approaches inadequate. In 1772, he took orders in the Anglican church and was greatly influenced in religion and philosophy by Bishop George Berkeley's neoplatonism. Following Berkeleian thought, he wrote the first philosophy textbook in America, Elementa Philosophica, *in which he combatted the growing rationalism of his time. He argued that perception is not gained by experience alone, as the disciples of John Locke believed, but that ideas are implanted by God, and all the world is but a reflection of His mind.*

Of the Mind in General, Its Objects and Operations

.   .   .

The word mind or spirit, in general, signifies any intelligent active being, which notion we take from what we are conscious of in ourselves, who know that we have within us a principle of conscious perception, intelligence, activity, and self-exertion; or rather, that each of us is a conscious, preceptive, intelligent, active, and self-exerting being; and by reasoning and analogy from ourselves we apply it to all other minds or intelligences besides, or superior to us; and (removing all limitations and imperfections) we apply it even to that *Great Supreme Intelligence,* who is the universal parent of all created spirits, and (as far as our words and conceptions can go) may be defined, *an infinite Mind or Spirit,* or *a Being infinitely intelligent and active.* But by the human mind, we mean that principle of sense, intelligence and free activity, which we

* Samuel Johnson, *Elementa Philosophica* . . . (Philadelphia: Benjamin Franklin and D. Hall, 1752), pp. 2–8.

feel within ourselves, or rather feel ourselves to be, furnished with those objects and powers, and under those confinements and limitations, under which it hath pleased our great Creator to place us in this present state.

We are, at present, spirits or minds connected with gross, tangible bodies, in such manner, that as our bodies can perceive and act nothing but by our minds, so, on the other hand, our minds perceive and act by means of our bodily organs. Such is the present law of our nature, which I conceive to be no other than a meer arbitrary constitution or establishment of Him that hath made us to be what we are. And accordingly I apprehend that the union between our souls and bodies, during our present state, consists in nothing else but this law of our nature, which is the will and perpetual fiat of that infinite Parent Mind, who made, and holds our souls in life, and in whom we live, and move, and have our being, viz. that our bodies should be thus acted by our minds, and that our minds should thus perceive and act by the organs of our bodies, and under such limitations as in fact we find ourselves to be attended with.

The immediate object of these perceptions and actions we call *Ideas*; as this word has been commonly defined and used by the moderns, with whom it signifies any immediate object of the mind in thinking, whether sensible or intellectual, and so is, in effect, synonymous with the word *Thought*, which comprehends both. Plato, indeed, by the word *Idea*, understood the original exemplar of things, whether sensible or intellectual, in the eternal Mind, conformable to which all things exist; or the abstract essences of things, as being originals or Archetypes in that infinite Intellect, of which our ideas or conceptions are a kind of copies. But perhaps, for the more distinct understanding ourselves upon this subject, it may be best to confine the word *Idea* to the immediate objects of sense and imagination, which was the original meaning of it; and to use the word *Notion* or *Conception*, to signify the objects of consciousness and pure intellect, tho' both of them may be expressed by the general term *Thought*; for these are so entirely, and *toto Caelo* different and distinct one from the other, that it may be apt to breed confusion in our thoughts and language, to use the same word promiscuously for them both; tho' we are indeed generally obliged to substitute sensible images and the words annexed to them, to represent things purely intellectual; such, for instance, *Spirit, Reflect, Conceive, Discourse*, and the like.

Our minds may be said to be created meer *tabulae rasae*, i.e., they have no notices of any objects of any kind properly created in them, or created with them: Yet I apprehend that in all the notices they have of any kind of objects, they have an immediate dependence upon the Deity, as really as they depend upon Him for their existence; i.e., they are no more authors to themselves of the objects of their perceptions, or the light by which they perceive them, than of the power of perceiving itself; but that they perceive them by a perpetual intercourse with that great Parent Mind, to whose incessant agency they are entirely passive, both in all the perceptions of sense, and in all that intellectual light by which they perceive the objects of the pure intellect. Notwithstanding which, it is plain from experience, that in consequence of these perceptions they are entirely at liberty to act, and all their actions flow from a principle of self-exertion. But in order the better to understand these things, I must more particularly define these terms. And as all the notices we have in our minds derive to them originally from (or rather by means of) these two fountains, *Sense* and *Consciousness*, it is necessary to begin with them.

By *Sense*, we mean, those perceptions we have of objects *ab extra*, or by means of the several organs of the bodies. Thus, by *Feeling* or touch, we perceive an endless variety of tangible, resistance, extension, figure, motion, hard, soft, heat, cold, &c. By *Sight* we perceive light and colours, with all their endlessly various modifications, red, blue, green, &c. By *Hearing*, we perceive sounds: by *Tasting*, sapors: by *Smelling*, odors, &c. These are called *Simple Ideas*. And of these sorted out into a vast variety of fixed combinations, or *Compound Ideas*, distinct from each other, and in which they are always found to coexist, consists every sort and individual *Body* in nature, such as we call man, horse, tree, stone, apple, cherry, &c. And of all these various distinct combinations or compounds, connected together in such a manner as to contribute one most beautiful, useful and harmonious whole, consist what we call Universal Nature, or one entire sensible or natural world.

In the perception of these ideas or objects of sense, we find our minds are merely passive, it not being in our power (supposing our organs rightly disposed and situated) whether we will see light and colors, hear sounds, &c. We are not causes to ourselves of these perceptions, nor can they be produced in our minds without a cause; or (which is the same thing) by any imagined unintelligible, inert, or unactive cause (which is a contradiction in terms) from whence it is demonstration that they must derive to us from an Almighty, intelligent active Cause, exhibiting them to us, impressing our minds with them, or producing them in us; and consequently (as I intimated) it must be by a perpetual intercourse of our minds with the Deity, the great Author of our beings, or by His perpetual influence or activity upon them that they are possessed of all these objects of sense, and the light by which we perceive them.

These ideas or objects of sense are commonly supposed to be pictures or representations of things without us, and indeed external to any mind, even that of the Deity himself, and the truth or reality of them is conceived to consist in their being exact pictures of things or objects without us, which are supposed to be the real things. But as it is impossible for us to know what is without our minds, and consequently, what those supposed originals are, and whether these ideas of ours are just resemblances of them or not; I am afraid this notion of them will lead us into an inextricable scepticism. I am therefore apt to think that these ideas or immediate objects of sense, are the real things, at least all that we are concerned with, I mean, of the sensible kind; and that the reality of them consists in their stability and consistence, or their being, in a stable manner, exhibited to our minds, or produced in them, and in a steady connection with each other, conformable to certain fixed laws of nature, which the great *Father of Spirits* hath established to Himself, according to which He constantly operates and affects our minds, and from which He will not vary, unless upon extraordinary occasions, as in the case of miracles.

Thus, for example, there is a fixed stable connection between *things tangible* and *things visible*, or the immediate objects of *Touch* and *Sight*, depending as I conceive, immediately upon the permanent, most wise and Almighty *Will* and *Fiat* of the great Creator and Pre-server of the world. By which, neither can it be meant, that visible objects are pictures of tangible objects (which yet is all the sense that can be made of our ideas of sense being images of real things without us) for they are entirely different and distinct things; as different as the sound *Triangle*, and the figure signified by it; so different, that a man born blind, and made to see, could have no more notion that a visible globe hath any connection with a tangible globe, by mere sight, without being taught, than a Frenchman that should come into England, and hear the word *Man*, could imagine, without being taught, that it signified the same thing with the word *Homme*, in his language. All that can be meant by it, therefore, is, that, as *tangible things* are the things immediately capable of producing or rather, being attended with sensible pleasure or pain in us, according to the present laws of our nature, on account of which they are conceived of as being properly the *real Things*; so the immediate *objects of sight* or *visible things*, are always, by the same stable law, of our nature, connected with them, and ever correspondent and proportioned to them; *visible extension, figure, motion*, &c., with those of the *tangible kind*, which go by the same names; and so in the compounds or combinations of them; the visible man, horse, tree, stone, &c. with those of the tangible kind, signified by the same names. (*See* Bishop Berkeley's *Theories of Vision, Principles of Human Knowledge, and Three Dialogues.*)

Not that it is to be doubted but that there are *Archetypes* of these sensible ideas existing, external to our minds; but then they must exist in some other mind, and be ideas also as well as ours; because an idea can resemble nothing but an idea; and an idea ever implies in the very nature of it, relation to a mind perceiving it, or in which it exists. But then those archetypes or originals, and the manner of their existence in that eternal mind, must be entirely different from that of their existence in our minds; as different, as the manner of His existence is from that of ours: in Him they must exist, as in original Intellect; in us, only as faint copies; such as he thinks fit to communicate to us, according to such laws and limitations as he hath established, and such as are sufficient to all the purposes relating to our well-being, in which only we are concerned. Our ideas, therefore, can no otherwise be said to be images or copies of the archetypes in the eternal Mind, than as our souls are said to be images of Him. . . .

31. JONATHAN EDWARDS, CAUSATION AND THE NATURE OF TRUE VIRTUE, 1754–58*

Jonathan Edwards (1703–58), minister, Calvinistic theologian, and philosopher, was formally educated at Yale, where he taught for a year. He was appointed assistant minister at Northampton Church, Massachusetts, where he joined his liberal grandfather, Samuel Stoddard. Edwards' staunchly Calvinistic views of predestination led to his dismissal in 1750. His next seven years, spent as an Indian missionary and minister to the church at Stockbridge, Connecticut, were his most fruitful, and his labors and writings earned him the presidency of the College of New Jersey (Princeton) in 1757, shortly before his death.

Edwards is often regarded as wishing to return to the earliest New England Puritanism, but his formal theology and philosophy placed him in his own times. In the first essay, taken from Treatise on the Freedom of the Will, *he assaults the age of science, reason, and materialism with its own weapons: the writings of Locke and Newton. He shows that a First Cause is exemplified in the natural order of the universe. In* The Nature of True Virtue *he foreshadows the Transcendentalists of the next century. According to Edwards, true virtue is singular, without reward, and is equated with beauty, because it is a part of universal benevolence. Edwards, like Johnson, was a neoplatonist, but far more original and subtle.*

Whether any Event Whatsoever, and Volition in Particular, can come to pass without a Cause of its Existence

Before I enter on any argument on this subject, I would explain how I would be understood, when I use the word *Cause* in this dis-

* Jonathan Edwards, *Works* (Worcester, Mass.: Isaiah Thomas, 1808–9), Vol. II, pp. 397–404; Vol. V, pp. 53–60.

course: since, for want of a better word, I shall have occasion to use it in a sense which is more extensive, than that in which it is sometimes used. The word is often used in so restrained a sense as to signify only that which has a *positive efficiency* or influence *to produce* a thing, or bring it to pass. But there are many things which have no such positive productive influence; which yet are Causes in that respect, that they have truly the nature of a ground or reason why some things are, rather than otherwise. Thus the absence of the sun in the night, is not the Cause of the falling of the dew at that time, in the same manner as its beams are the Cause of the ascending of the vapours in the day-time; and its withdrawment in the winter, is not in the same manner the Cause of the freezing of the waters, as its approach in the spring is the cause of the thawing. But yet the withdrawment or absence of the sun is an antecedent, with which these effects in the night and winter are connected, and on which they depend; and is one thing that belongs to the ground and reason why they come to pass at that time, rather than at other times; though the absense of the sun is nothing positive, nor has any positive influence.

It may be further observed, that when I speak of *connection of Causes and Effects*, I have respect to *moral* Causes, as well as those that are called *natural* in distinction from them. Moral Causes may be Causes in as proper a sense, as any causes whatsoever; may have as real an influence and may as truly be the ground and reason of an Event's coming to pass.

Therefore I sometimes use the word Cause, in this enquiry, to signify an *antecedent*, either natural or moral, positive or negative, on which an Event, either a thing, or the manner and circumstance of a thing, so depends, that it is the ground and reason, either in whole, or in part, why it is, rather than not; or why it is as it is, rather than otherwise; or, in other words, any antecedent with which a consequent Event is so connected, that it truly belongs to the reason why the proposition which affirms that Event, is true; whether it has any positive influence, or not. And in an agreeableness to this, I sometimes use the word effect for consequence of another thing, which is perhaps rather an occasion than a Cause, most properly speaking.

I am the more careful to explain my meaning, that I may cut off occasion, from any that might seek occasion to cavil and object against some things which I may say concerning the dependence of all things which come to pass, on some cause, and their connection with their Cause.

Having thus explained what I mean by Cause. I assert that nothing ever comes to pass without a Cause. What is self-existent must be from eternity, and must be unchangeable: but as to all things that *begin to be*, they are not self-existent, and therefore must have some foundation of their existence without themselves. That whatsoever begins to be, which before was not, must have a Cause why it then begins to exist, seems to be the first dictate of the common and natural sense which God has implanted in the minds of all mankind, and the main foundation of all our reasonings about the existence of things, past, present, or to come.

And this dictate of common sense equally respects substances and modes, or things and the manner and circumstance of things. Thus, if we see a body which has hitherto been at rest, start out of a state of rest, and begin to move, we do as naturally and necessarily suppose there is some Cause or reason of this new mode of existence, as of the existence of a body itself which had hitherto moved in a certain direction, should suddenly change the direction of its motion; or if it should put off its old figure, and take a new one; or change its colour: the beginning of these new modes is a new Event, and the mind of mankind necessarily supposes that there is some Cause or reason of them.

If this grand principle of common sense be taken away, all arguing from effects to Causes ceases, and so all knowledge of any existence, besides what we have by the most direct and immediate intuition. Particularly all our proof of the being of God ceases: we argue His being from our being, and the being of other things, which we are sensible once were not, but have begun to be; and from the being of the world, with all its constituent parts, and the manner of their existence; all which we see plainly are not necessary in their own nature, and so not self-existent, and therefore must have a Cause. But if things, not in themselves necessary, may begin to be without a Cause, all this arguing is vain.

Indeed, I will not affirm, that there is in the nature of things no foundation for the knowledge of the Being of God without any evidence of it from His works. I do suppose there is a great absurdity, in the nature of things simply considered, in supposing that there should be no God, or in denying Being in general, and supposing an eternal, absolute, universal nothing: and therefore that here would be foundation of intuitive evidence that it cannot be, and that eternal infinite most perfect Being must be; if we had strength and comprehension of mind sufficient, to have a clear idea of general and universal Being, or, which is the same thing, of the infinite, eternal, most perfect Divine Nature and Essence. But then we should not properly come to the knowledge of the Being of God by arguing; but our evidence would be intuitive: we should see it, as we see other things that are necessary in themselves, the contraries of which are in their own nature absurd and contradictory; as we see that twice two is four; and as we see that a circle has no angles. If we had as clear an idea of universal, infinite entity, as we have of these other things, I suppose we should most intuitively see the absurdity of supposing such Being not to be; should immediately see there is no room for the question, whether it is possible that Being, in the most general abstracted notion of it, should not be. But we have the strength and extent of mind, to know this certainly in this intuitive independent manner: but the way that mankind comes to the knowledge of the Being of God, is that which the apostle speaks of, (Rom. i: 20.) *"The invisible things of Him, from the creation of the world, are clearly seen; being understood by the things that are made; even his eternal Power and Godhead."* We first ascend, and prove *a posteriori*, or from effects, that there must be an eternal Cause; and then *secondly*, prove by argumentation, not intuition, that this Being must be necessarily existent; and then *thirdly*, from the proved necessity of his existence, we may descend, and prove many of his perfections *a priori*.

But if once this grand principle of common sense be given up, that *What is not necessary in itself, must have a Cause*; and we begin to maintain, that things may come into existence, and begin to be, which heretofore have not been of themselves, without a cause; all our means of ascending in our arguing from the creature to the Creator, and all our evidence of the Being of God, is cut off at one blow. In this case, we cannot prove that there is a God, either from the Being of the World, and the creatures in it, or from the manner of their being, their order, beauty and use. For if things may come into existence without any cause at all, then they doubtless may without any Cause answerable to the effect. Our minds do alike naturally suppose and determine both these things; namely, that what begins to be has a Cause, and also that it has a Cause proportionable and agreeable to the effect. The same principle which leads us to determine, that there cannot be any thing coming to pass without a Cause, leads us to determine that there cannot be more in the effect than in the Cause.

Yea, if once it should be allowed, that things may come to pass without a Cause, we should not only have no proof of the being of God, but we should be without evidence of the existence of any thing whatsoever, but our own immediately present ideas and consciousness. For we have no way to prove any thing else, but by arguing from effects to Causes: from the ideas now immediately in view; from sensations now excited in us, we infer the existence of things without us, as the causes of these sensations: and from the existence of these things, we argue other things, which they depend on, as effects on Causes. We infer the past existence of ourselves, or any thing else, by memory; only as we argue, that the ideas, which are now in our minds, are the consequences of past ideas and sensations. We immediately perceive nothing else but the ideas which are this moment extant in our minds. We perceive or know other things only *by means* of these, as necessarily connected with others, and dependent on them. But if things may be without Causes, all this necessary connection and dependence is dissolved, and so all means of our knowledge is gone. If there be no absurdity or difficulty in supposing one thing to start out of non-existence, into being, of itself without a Cause; then there is no absurdity or difficulty in supposing the same of millions of millions. For nothing, or no difficulty multiplied, still is nothing, or no difficulty: nothing multiplied by nothing, doesn't increase the sum.

And indeed, according to the hypothesis I am opposing, of the acts of the will coming to pass without a Cause, it is the case in fact, that millions of millions of Events are continually coming into existence *contingently*, without any Cause or reason why they do so, all over the world, every day and hour, through all ages. So it is in constant succession, in every moral agent. This contingency, this efficient nothing, this effectual No-Cause, is always ready at hand, to produce this sort of effects, as long as the agent exists, and as, often as he has occasion.

If it were so, that things only of one kind, *viz.* acts of the will, seemed to come to pass of themselves: but those of this sort in general came into being thus; and it were an event that was continual, and that happened in a course, wherever were capable subjects of such events; this very thing would demonstrate that there was some Cause of them, which made such a difference between this Event and others, and that they did not really happen contingently. For contingence, is blind, and does not pick and choose for particular sort of Events. Nothing has no choice. This No-Cause, which causes no existence, cannot cause the existence which comes to pass, to be of one particular sort only, distinguished from all others. Thus, that only one sort of matter drops out of the heavens, even water, and that this comes so often, so constantly and plentifully, all over the world, in all ages, shows that there is some Cause or Reason of the falling of water out of heavens; and that something besides mere contingence has a hand in the matter.

If we should suppose Non-entity to be about to bring forth; and things were coming into existence, without any Cause or Antecedent, on which the existence, or kind, or manner of existence depends; or which could at all determine whether the things should be; stones, or stars, or beasts, or angels, or human bodies, or souls, or only some new motion or figure in natural bodies, or some new sensations in animals, or new ideas in the human understanding, or new volitions in the will; or any thing else of all the infinite number of possibles; then certainly it would not be expected, although many millions of millions of things are coming into existence in this manner, all over the face of the earth, that they should all be only of one particular kind, and that it should be thus in all ages, and that this sort of existence should never fail to come to pass where there is room for them, or a subject capable of them and that constantly, whenever there is occasion for them.

If any should imagine, there is something in the sort of Event that renders it possible for it to come into existence without a Cause, and should say, that the free acts of the will are existences of an exceeding different nature from other things; by reason of which they may come into existence without any previous ground or reason of it, though other things cannot; if they make this objection in good earnest, it would be an evidence of their strangely forgetting themselves: for they would be giving an account of some ground of the existence of a thing, when at the same time they would maintain there is no ground of its existence. Therefore I would observe, that the particular nature of existence, be it never so diverse from others, can lay no foundation for that thing's coming into existence without a Cause; because to suppose this, would be to suppose the particular nature of existence; and so a thing which makes way for existence, with such a circumstance, namely, without a cause or reason of existence. But that which in any respect makes way for a thing's coming into being, or for any manner or circumstance of its first existence, must be prior to the existence. The distinguished nature of the effect, which is something belonging to the effect, cannot have influence backward, to act before it is. The peculiar nature of that thing called volition, can do nothing, can have no influence, while it is not. And afterwards it is too late for its influence: for then the thing has made sure of existence already, without its help.

So that it is indeed as repugnant to reason, to suppose that an act of the will should come into existence without a cause, as to suppose the human soul, or an angel, or the globe of the earth, or the whole universe, should come into existence without a cause. And if once we allow, that such a sort of effect as a Volition may come to pass without a Cause, how do we know but that many other sorts of effects may do so too? It is not the particular kind of effect that makes the absurdity of supposing it has being without a Cause, but something which is common to all things that ever begin to be, *viz*, that they are not self-sufficient, or necessary in the nature of things.

A Dissertation Concerning the Nature of True Virtue

．　．　．　．

True virtue most essentially consists in benevolence to being in general. Or perhaps, to speak more accurately, it is that consent, propensity and union of heart to being in general, which is immediately exercised in a general good will.

The things before observed respecting the nature of true virtue, naturally lead us to such a notion of it. If it has its seat in the heart, and is the general goodness and beauty of the disposition and its exercise, in the most comprehensive view, considered with regard to its universal tendency, and as related to every thing with which it stands connected; what can it consist in, but a consent and good will to being in general? Beauty does not consist in discord and dissent, but in consent and agreement. And if every intelligent being is some way related to being in general, and is a part of the universal system of existence; and so stands in connection with the whole; what can its general and true beauty be, but its union and consent with the great whole?

If any such thing can be supposed as an union of heart to some particular being, disposing it to benevolence to a private circle or system of beings, which are but a small part of the whole; not implying a tendency to an union with the great system, and not at all inconsistent with enmity towards being in general, this I suppose not to be of the nature of true virtue; although it may in some respects be good, and may appear beautiful in a confined and contracted view of things. But of this more afterwards.

It is abundantly plain by the holy scriptures, and generally allowed, not only by christian divines, but by the more considerable Deists, that virtue most essentially consists in love. And I suppose it is owned by the most considerable writers, to consist in general love of benevolence, or kind affection: though it seems to me the meaning of some in this affair is not sufficiently explained; which perhaps occasions some error or confusion in discourses on this subject.

When I say true virtue consists in *love to being in general*, I shall not be likely to be understood, that no one act of the mind or exercise of love is of the nature of true virtue, but what has being in general, or the great system of universal existence, for its *direct* and *immediate* object: so that no exercise of love, or kind affection to any one particular being, that is but a small part of this whole, has any thing of the nature of true virtue. But that the nature of true virtue consists in a *disposition* to benevolence towards being in general; though from such a disposition may arise exercises of love to *particular* beings, as objects are presented and occasions arise. No wonder that he who is of a *generally* benevolent disposition, should be more disposed than another to have his heart moved with benevolent affection to *particular* persons, with whom he is acquainted and conversant, and from whom arise the greatest and most frequent *occasions* for exciting his benevolent temper. But my meaning is, that no affections towards particular persons or beings are of the nature of true virtue, but such as arise from a generally benevolent temper, or from that habit or frame of mind, wherein consists a disposition to love being in general.

And perhaps it is needless for me to give notice to my readers, that when I speak of an intelligent being having a heart united and benevolently disposed to being in general, I thereby mean *intelligent* being in general. Not inanimate things, or beings that have no perception or will; which are not properly capable objects of benevolence.

Love is commonly distinguished into love of benevolence, and love of complacence. Love of *benevolence* is that affection or propensity of the heart to any being, which causes it to incline to its well-being, or disposes it to desire and take pleasure in its happiness. And if I mistake not, it is agreeable to the common opinion, that beauty in the object is not always the ground of this propensity; but that there may be a disposition to the welfare of those that are not *considered* as beautiful, unless mere existence be accounted a beauty. And benevolence or goodness in the divine Being is generally supposed, not only to be prior to the beauty of many of its objects, but to their existence; so as to be the ground both of their existence and their beauty, rather than the foundation of God's benevolence; as it is supposed that it is God's goodness which moved him to give them both being and beauty. So that if all virtue primarily consists in that affection of heart to being, which is exercised in benevolence, or an inclination to its good, then God's virtue is so extended as to include a propensity not only to being actually existing, and actually beautiful, but to possible being, so as to include him to give a being beauty and happiness.

What is commonly called love of *complacence*, presupposed beauty. For it is no other than delight in beauty; or complacence in the person or being beloved for his beauty. If virtue be the beauty of an intelligent being, and virtue consists in love, then it is a plain inconsistence, to suppose that virtue primarily consists in any love to its object for its beauty; either in a love of complacence, which is delight in a being for his beauty, or in a love of benevolence, that has the beauty of its object for its foundation. For that would be to suppose, that the beauty of intelligent beings primarily consists in love to beauty; or that their virtue first of all consists in their love to virtue. Which is an inconsistence, and a going in a circle. Because it makes virtue, or beauty of mind, the foundation or first motive of that love wherein virtue originally consists, or wherein the very first virtue consists; or, it supposes the first virtue to be the consequence and effect of virtue. Which makes the first virtue both the ground and the consequence, both cause and effect of itself. Doubtless virtue primarily consists in something else besides any effect or consequence of virtue. If virtue consists primarily in love to virtue, then virtue, the thing loved, is the love of virtue: so that virtue must consist in the love of the love of virtue—and so on *in infinitum*. For there is no end of going back in a circle. We never come to any beginning or foundation; it is without beginning and hangs on nothing. Therefore, if the essence of *virtue*, or *beauty* of mind, lies in love, or a disposition to live, it must primarily consist in something *different* both from complacence, which is a delight in beauty, and also from any benevolence that has the beauty of its object for its foundation. Because it is absurd to say, that virtue is primarily and first of all the consequence of itself; which makes virtue primarily prior to itself.

Nor can virtue consist in *gratitude*; or one being's benevolence to another for his benevolence to him. Because this implies the same inconsistence. For it supposes a benevolence prior to gratitude, which is the cause of gratitude. Therefore there is room left for no other conclusion, than that the primary object of virtuous love is being, simply considered; of that true virtue primarily consists, not in love to any particular beings, because of their virtue or beauty, nor in gratitude, because they love us; but in a propensity and union of heart to being simply considered; exciting *absolute* benevolence, if I may so call it, to being in general. I say true virtue *primarily* consists in this. For I am far from asserting, that there is no true virtue in any other love than this absolute benevolence. But I would express what appears to me to be the truth on this subject, in the following particulars.

The *first* object of a virtuous benevolence is *being*, simply considered; and if being, *simply* considered, be its object, then being *in general* is its object; and what it has an ultimate propensity to is the *highest good* of being in general. And it will seek the good of every *individual* being unless it be conceived as not consistent with the highest good of being in general. In which case the good of a particular being, or some beings, may be given up for the sake of the highest good of being in general. And particularly, if there be any being statedly and irreclaimably opposite, and an enemy to being in general, then consent and adherence to being in general will induce the truly virtuous heart to forsake that enemy, and to oppose it.

Further, if being, simply considered, be the first object of a truly virtuous benevolence, then that object who has *most* of being, or has the greatest share of existence, *other things being equal*, so far as such a being is exhibited to our faculties, will have the *greatest* share of the propensity and benevolent affections of the heart. I say "other things being equal," especially because there is a *secondary* object of virtuous benevolence, that I shall take notice of presently, which must be considered as the ground or motive to a purely virtuous benevolence. Pure benevolence in its *first* exercise is nothing else but being's uniting consent, or propensity to being; and inclining to the general highest good, and to each being, whose welfare is consistent with the highest general good, in proportion to the degree of existence, understand, "other things being equal."

The second object of a virtuous propensity of heart is *benevolent* being. A secondary ground of pure benevolence is virtuous benevolence itself in its object. When any one under the influence of general benevolence sees another being possessed of the like general benevolence, this attaches his heart to him, and draws forth greater love to him, than merely his having existence: because so far as the being beloved has love being in general, so far his own being is, as it were, enlarged; extends to, and in some sort comprehends being in general: and therefore, he that is governed by love to being in general, must of necessity have complacence in him, and the greater degree of benevolence to him, as it were out of gratitude to him for his love to general existence, that his own heart is extended and united to, and so looks on its interest as its own. It is because his heart is thus united to being in general, that he looks on a benevolent propensity to being in general, wherever he sees it, as the beauty of the being in whom it is; an excellency that renders him worthy of esteem, complacence, and the greater good-will. But several things may be noted more particularly concerning this *secondary* ground of a truly virtuous love.

1. That loving a being on *this* ground necessarily arises from pure benevolence to being in general, and comes to the same thing. For he that has a simple and pure good will to general existence, must love that temper in others, that agrees and conspires with itself. A spirit of consent to being must agree with consent to being. That which truly and sincerely seeks the good of others, must approve of, and love that which joins with him in seeking the good of others.

2. This secondary ground of virtuous love is the thing wherein true moral or spiritual *beauty* primarily consists. Yea, spiritual beauty consists wholly in this, and in the various qualities and exercises of the mind which proceed from it, and the external actions which proceed from these internal qualities and exercises. And in these things consists all true *virtue*, viz. in this love of being, and the qualities and acts which arise from it.

3. As all spiritual beauty lies in these virtuous principles and acts, so it is primarily *on this account* they are beautiful, viz. that they imply *consent* and *union* with being in *general*. This is the primary and most essential beauty of every thing that can justly be called by the name of virtue, or is any moral excellency in the eye of one that has a perfect view of things. I say, "the *primary* and most *essential* beauty," because there is a secondary and inferior sort of beauty, . . .

4. This spiritual beauty, which is but a *secondary* ground of virtuous benevolence, is the ground not only of benevolence, but *complacence*, and is the *primary* ground of the latter; that is, when the complacence is truly virtuous. Love to us in particular and kindness received may be a secondary ground: but this is the primary objective foundation of it.

5. It must be noted, that the *degree* of the *amiableness* of true

virtue primarily consisting in consent, and a benevolent propensity of heart to being in general, is not in the *simple* proportion of the degree of benevolent affection seen, but in a proportion *compounded* of the greatness of the benevolent being, or the degree of *being* and the degree of *benevolence.* One that loves being in general, will necessarily value good will to being in general, wherever he sees it. But if he sees the same benevolence in *two* beings, he will value it *more* in two, than in one only. Because it is a greater thing, more favorable to being in general, to have two beings to favour it, than only one of them. For there is more being that favours being: both together having more being than one alone. So if one being be as great as two, has as much existence as both together, and has the same degree of general benevolence, it is more favorable to being in general, than if there were general benevolence in a being that had but half that share of existence. As a large quantity of gold, with the same quality, is more valuable than a small quantity of the same metal.

6. It is impossible that any one should truly *relish* this beauty, consisting in general benevolence, who has *not* that temper himself. I have observed, that if any being is possessed of such a temper, he will unavoidably be pleased with the same temper in another. And it may in like manner be demonstrated, that it is such a spirit, and nothing else, which will relish such a spirit. For if a being destitute of benevolence, should love benevolence to being in general, it would prize and seek that for which it had no value. For how should one love and value a *disposition* to a thing, or a *tendency* to *promote* it, and for that very reason, when the *thing* itself is what he is regardless of, and has no value for, nor desires to have promoted.

32. JOHN WITHERSPOON, LECTURES ON MORAL PHILOSOPHY, c. 1769*

John Witherspoon (1723–94) signer of the Declaration of Independence, teacher, and clergyman, was educated at the University of Edinburgh. Before emigrating to America he earned fame as a vigorous proponent of old Presbyterianism against those who would moderate its Calvinistic doctrines. In 1768, he accepted the presidency of the College of New Jersey, where his lectures on moral philosophy gained a wide audience and popularity. Witherspoon's ideas took firm root in his new country, for his practical common sense constituted an acceptable middle ground between materialism and idealism. The industrious Witherspoon

* John Witherspoon, *Lectures on Moral Philosophy and Eloquence*, 3rd ed. (Philadelphia: William W. Woodward, 1810), pp. 12–15, 17–19.

was also responsible for reviving an apathetic Presbyterianism in the Middle Colonies, and he played an active political role in his adopted state and the Continental Congress in the fight for independence.

A Consideration of Man

CONSIDERING man as an individual, we discover the most obvious and remarkable circumstances of his nature, that he is a compound of body and spirit. . . .

The body and spirit have a great reciprocal influence upon one another. The body on the temper and disposition of the soul, and the soul on the state and habit of the body. The body is properly the minister of the soul, the means of conveying perceptions to it, but nothing without it.

It is needless to enlarge upon the structure of the body: this is sufficiently known to all, except we descend to anatomical exactness, and then, like all the other parts of nature, it shows the infinite wisdom of the Creator. With regard to morals, the influence of the body in a certain view may be very great in enslaving men to appetite, and yet there does not seem any such connexion with morals as to require a particular description. I think there is little reason to doubt that there are great and essential differences between man and man, as to the spirit and its proper powers; but it seems plain that such are the laws of union between the body and spirit, that many faculties are weakened and some rendered altogether incapable of exercise, merely by an alteration of the state of the body. Memory is frequently lost and judgement weakened by old age and disease. Sometimes, by a confusion of the brain in a fall, the judgement is wholly disordered. The instinctive appetites of hunger, and thirst, seem to reside directly in the body, and the soul to have little more than a passive perception. Some passions, particularly fear and rage, seem also to have their seat in the body, immediately producing a certain modification of the blood and spirits. This indeed is perhaps the case in some degree with all passions whenever they are indulged; they give modification to the blood and spirits, which make them easily rekindled; but there are none which do so instantaneously arise from the body, and prevent deliberation, will and choice, as these now named. To consider the evil passions to which we are liable, we may say those that depend most upon the body, are fear, anger, voluptuousness; and those that depend least upon it, are ambition, envy, covetousness.

The faculties of the mind are commonly divided into these three kinds, the understanding, the will, and the affections; though perhaps it is proper to observe, that these are not three qualities wholly distinct, as if they were three different beings, but different ways of exerting the same simple principle. It is the soul or mind that understands, wills, or is affected with pleasure and pain. The understanding seems to have truth for its object, the discovering things as they really are in themselves, and in their relations one to another. It has been disputed whether good be in any degree the object of the understanding. On the one hand it seems as if truth, and that only, belonged to the understanding; because we can easily suppose persons of equal intellectual powers and opposite moral characters. Nay, we can suppose malignity joined to a high degree of understanding, and virtue or true goodness to a much lower. On the other hand, the choice made by the will seems to have the judgement or deliberation of the understanding as its foundation. How can this be, it will be said, if the understanding has nothing to do with good or evil? A considerable opposition of sentiments among philosophers has arisen from this question. [Some] make understanding or reason the immediate principle of virtue. [O]thers, make affection the principle of it. Perhaps neither the one nor the other is wholly right. Probably both are necessary.

The connection between truth and goodness, between the understanding and the heart, is a subject of great moment, but also of great difficulty. I think we may say with certainty, that infinite perfection, intellectual and moral, are united and inseparable in the Supreme Being. There is not however in inferior natures an exact proportion between the one and the other; yet I apprehend that truth naturally and necessarily promotes goodness, and falsehood the contrary; but as the influence is reciprocal, malignity of disposition, even with the greatest natural powers, blinds the understanding, and prevents the perception of truth itself.

.   .   .   .

There are but two ways in which we come to the knowledge of things, *viz.* 1st, Sensation, 2d, Reflection.

The first of these must be divided again into two parts, external and internal.

External arises from the immediate impression of objects from without. The external senses in number are five; seeing, hearing, feeling, tasting, and smelling.

In these are observable the impression itself, or the sensation we feel, and the supposition inseparable from it, that it is produced by an external object. *That our senses are to be trusted in the information they give us* [editor's italics] seems to me a first principle, because they are the foundation of all our reasonings. The few exceptions of accidental irregularity in the senses can found no just objection to this, as there are so many plain and obvious ways of discovering and correcting it.

The reality of the material system, I think, may be easily established, except upon such principles as are subversive of all *certainty*, and *lead to universal scepticism*; and persons who would maintain such principles do not deserve to be reasoned with, because they do not pretend to communicate knowledge, *but to take all knowledge from us.* [Editor's Italics.]

The Immaterialists say, that we are conscious of nothing but the impression or feeling of our own mind; but they do not observe that the impression itself implies and supposes something external that communicates it, and cannot be separated from that supposition. Sometimes such reasoners tell us, that we cannot shew the substance separate from its sensible qualities; no more can any man shew me a sensible quality separate from a particular subject. If any man will shew me whitness, without shewing me anything that is white, or roundness, with out anything that is round, I will shew him the substance without either colour or shape.

Immaterialism takes away the distinction between truth and falsehood. [Editor's Italics.] I have an idea of a house or tree in a certain place, and I call this true, that is, I am of opinion there is really a house or tree in that place. Again, I form an idea of a house or tree, as what may be in that place; I ask what is the difference, if after all, you tell me, there is neither tree, house nor place any where existing. An advocate for that system says, that truth consists in the liveliness of the idea, than which nothing can be more manifestly false. I can form as distinct an idea of any thing that is not, as any thing that is, when it is absent from my sight. I have a much more lively idea of Jupiter and Juno, and many of their actions, from Homer and Virgil, though I do not believe that any of them ever existed, than I have of many things that I know happened within these few months.

The truth is, the immaterial system is a wild and ridiculous attempt to unsettle the principles of common sense by metaphysical reasoning, which can hardly produce any thing but contempt in the generality of persons who hear it, and which, I verily believe, never produced conviction even on the persons who pretend to espouse it.

3

Religion and Revivalism

33. S.P.G., INSTRUCTIONS FOR THE CLERGY EMPLOYED BY THE SOCIETY FOR THE PROPAGATION OF THE GOSPEL IN FOREIGN PARTS, 1706*

With no resident American bishop, and with few English clergymen willing to leave their remunerative and comfortable places for the New World, colonial Anglicanism tended increasingly toward secularism. To buttress the faith, the Society for the Propagation of the Gospel in Foreign Parts was established in 1701. From that year until after the Revolution, when it was forced to withdraw from America, the Society made valiant efforts spiritually to aid Anglicans. Many able ministers were sent to America, with half their salaries paid by the Society which studiously oversaw its missionaries.

This selection contains instructions to clergymen who were leaving England for their colonial cures.

Upon their Admission by the Society

I. THAT, from the Time of their Admission, they lodge not in an Publick House; but at some Bookseller's, or in other private and reputable Families, till they shall be otherwise accommodated by the Society.

II. That till they can have a convenient Passage, they employ their Time usefully, in Reading, Prayers, and Preaching, as they have Opportunity; in hearing others Read and Preach; or in such Studies as may tend to fit them for their Employment.

* From *A Collection of Papers Printed by Order of the Society*, pp. 10–16; see also C. F. Pascoe, *Two Hundred Years of the S.P.G. . . . 1701–1900*, vol. II, pp. 837–40.

III. That they constantly attend the Standing Committee of this Society, at the St. *Paul's* Chapter-House, and observe their Directions.

IV. That before their Departure, they wait upon his Grace the Lord Archbishop of *Canterbury*, their Metropolitan, and upon the Lord Bishop of *London*, their Diocesan, to receive their Paternal Benediction and Instructions.

Upon their going on Board the Ship designed for their Passage

I. THAT they demean themselves not only inoffensively and prudently, but so, as to become remarkable Examples of Piety and Virtue to the Ship's Company.

II. That whether they be Chaplains in the Ships, or only Passengers, they endeavor to prevail with the Captain or Commander, to have Morning and Evening Prayer said daily; as also Preaching and catechizing every Lord's Day.

III. That throughout their passage they Instruct, Exhort, Admonish, and Reprove, as they have Occasion and Opportunity, with such Seriousness and Prudence, as may gain them Reputation and Authority.

Upon their Arrival in the Country whither they shall be sent. First, with respect to themselves

I. THAT they always keep in their View the great Design of their Undertaking, viz. To promote the Glory of Almighty God, and the Salvation of Men, by Propagating the Gospel of our Lord and Saviour.

II. That they often consider the Qualifications requisite for those who would effectually promote this Design, viz. A sound Knowledge and hearty Belief of the Christian Religion; an Apostolical Zeal, tempered with Prudence, Humility, Meekness and Patience; a fervent Charity towards the Souls of Men; and finally, that Temperance, Fortitude, and Constancy, which become good Soldiers of Jesus Christ.

III. That in order to the obtaining and preserving the said Qualifications, they do very frequently in their Retirements offer up fervent Prayers to Almighty God for his Direction and Assistance; converse much with the Holy Scriptures; seriously reflect upon their Ordination Vows; and consider the Account which they are to render to the Great Shepherd and Bishop of our Souls at the last Day.

IV. That they acquaint themselves thoroughly with the Doctrine of the Church of *England*, as contained in the Articles and Homilies; its Worship and Discipline, and Rules for Behaviour of the Clergy, as contained in the Liturgy and Canons; and that they approve themselves accordingly, as genuine Missionaries from this Church.

V. That they endeavour to make themselves Masters in those Controversies, which are necessary to be understood, in order to the Preserving their Flock from the Attempts of such Gainsayers, as are mixt among them.

VI. That in their outward Behaviour they be circumspect and unblameable, giving no Offence either in Word or Deed; that their ordinary Discourse be grave and edifying; their Apparel decent, and proper for Clergymen; and that in their whole Conversation they be Instances and Patterns of the Christian Life.

VII. That they do not board in, or frequent Publick-Houses, or lodge in Families of evil Fame; that they wholly abstain from Gaming, and all such Pastimes; and converse not familiarly with lewd or prophane Persons, otherwise than to order to reprove, admonish, and reclaim them.

VIII. That in whatsoever Family they shall lodge, they persuade them to join with them in daily Prayer Morning and Evening.

IX. That they be not nice about Meats or Drinks, nor immoderately careful about their Entertainment in the Places where they shall sojourn; but contented with what Health requires, and the Place easily affords.

X. That as they be Frugal, in Opposition to Luxury, so they avoid all Appearance of Covetousness, and recommend themselves, according to their Abilities, by the prudent Exercise of Liberality and Charity.

XI. That they take special Care to give no offence to the Civil Government, by intermeddling in Affairs not relating to their own Calling and Function.

XII. That avoiding all Names of Distinction, they endeavour to preserve a Christian Agreement and Union one with another, as a Body of Brethren of one and the same Church, united under the Superior Episcopal Order, and all engaged in the same great Design of Propagating the Gospel; and to this End, keeping up a Brotherly Correspondence, by meeting together at certain Times, as shall be most convenient, for mutual Advice and Assistance.

Secondly, with respect to their Parochial Cure

I. THAT they conscientiously observe the Rules of our Liturgy, in the Performance of all the Offices of their Ministry.

II. That besides the stated Service appointed for Sundays and Holydays, they do, as far as they shall find it practicable, publickly read the daily Morning and Evening Service, and decline no fair Opportunity of Preaching to such as may be occasionally met together from remote and distant Parts.

III. That they perform every Part of Divine Service with that Seriousness and Decency, that may recommend their Ministrations to their Flock, and excite a Spirit of Devotion in them.

IV. That the chief Subjects of their Sermons be the great Fundamental Principles of Christianity, and the Duties of a sober, righteous, and godly Life, as resulting from those Principles.

V. That they particularly preach against those Vices, which they Shall observe to be most predominant in the Places of their Residence.

VI. That they carefully instruct the People concerning the Nature and Use of the Sacraments of Baptism and the Lord's Supper, as the peculiar Institutions of Christ, Pledges of Communion with Him, and Means of deriving Grace from Him.

VII. That they duly consider the Qualifications of those adult Persons to whom they administer Baptism; and of those likewise whom they admit to the Lord's Supper; according to the Directions of the Rubricks in our Liturgy.

VIII. That they take special Care to lay a good Foundation for all their other Ministrations, by Catechizing those under their Care, whether Children, or other ignorant Persons, explaining the Catechism to them in the most easie and familiar Manner.

IX. That in their instructing *Heathens* and *Infidels*, they begin with the Principles of Natural Religion, appealing to their Reason and Conscience; and thence proceed to shew them the Necessity of Revelation, and the Certainty of that contained in the Holy Scriptures, by the plain and most obvious Arguments.

X. That they frequently visit their respective Parishioners; those of our own Communion, to keep them steady in the Profession and Practice of Religion, as taught in the Church of *England*; those that oppose us, or dissent from us, to convince and reclaim them with a Spirit of Meekness and Gentleness.

XI. That those, whose Parishes shall be of large Extent, shall, as they have opportunity and Convenience, officiate in the several Parts thereof, so that all the Inhabitants may by Turns partake of their Ministrations; and that such as shall be appointed to officiate in several Places shall reside sometimes at one, sometimes at another of those Places, as the Necessities of the People shall require.

XII. That they shall, to the best of their Judgments, distribute those small Tracts given by the Society for that Purpose, amongst such of their Parishioners as shall want them most, and appear likely to make the best Use of them; and that such useful Books, of which they have not a sufficient Number to give, they be ready to lend to those who will be most careful in reading and restoring them.

XIII. That they encourage the setting up of Schools for the teaching of Children; and particularly by the Widows of such Clergymen as shall die in those Countries, if they be found capable of that Employment.

XIV. That each of them keep a Register of his Parishioners Names, Profession of Religion, Baptism, & according to the Scheme annexed, No. I for his own Satisfaction, and the Benefit of the People.

Thirdly, with respect to the Society

I. That each of them keep a constant and regular Correspondence with the Society, by their Secretary.

II. That they send every six Months an Account of the State of their respective Parishes. . . .

III. That they communicate what shall be done at the Meetings of the Clergy, when settled, and whatsoever else may concern the Society.

34. JOHN WOOLMAN, *JOURNAL*, 1756*

John Woolman (1720–72) was a merchant of Burlington, New Jersey, and an influential member of the Society of Friends. By the mid-eighteenth century the Friends had drifted away from the spirituality of Fox and Penn and accumulated property and slaves at the expense of the "Inner plantation"—the spirit—endangering the continuance of the sect as it was originally constituted. A model Quaker, Woolman forsook wealth and "persuaded" against worldliness and slavery. He visited and influenced Friends throughout the Middle Colonies and even as far south as North Carolina. A revival of the old tenets resulted, chiefly because of "preachers" like Woolman, and the Quakers turned once again toward the cultivation of the "Inner plantation." A strong antislavery movement also began, given impetus by Woolman's tract, Some Considerations on the Keeping of Negroes *(1754).*

Pietism, War and Slavery
CHAPTER III
1749–56

About this time, believing it good for me to settle, and thinking seriously about a companion, my heart was turned to the Lord with desires that he would give me wisdom to proceed therein agreeably to his will, and he was pleased to give me a well-inclined damsel, Sarah Ellis, to whom I was married the 18th of eighth month, 1749.

* *The Works of John Woolman*, 2d ed. (Philadelphia: Joseph Cruckshank, 1775), pp. 32–49.

In the fall of the year 1750 died my father, Samuel Woolman, of a fever, aged about sixty years. In his lifetime he manifested much care for us his children, that in our youth we might learn to fear the Lord; and often endeavored to imprint in our minds the true principles of virtue, and particularly to cherish in us a spirit of tenderness, not only towards poor people, but also towards all creatures of which we had the command.

After my return from Carolina in 1746, I made some observations on keeping slaves, which some time before his decease I showed to him; he perused the manuscript, proposed a few alterations, and appeared well satisfied that I found a concern on that account. In his last sickness, as I was watching with him one night, he being so far spent that there was no expectation of his recovery, though he had the perfect use of his understanding, he asked me concerning the manuscript, and whether I expected soon to proceed to take the advice of friends in publishing it? After some further conversation thereon, he said, "I have all along been deeply affected with the oppression of the poor negroes; and now, at last, my concern for them is as great as ever."

By his direction I had written his will in a time of health, and that night he desired me to read it to him, which I did; and he said it was agreeable to his mind. He then made mention of his end, which he believed was near; and signified that though he was sensible of many imperfections in the course of his life, yet his experience of the power of truth, and of the love and goodness of God from time to time, even till now, was such that he had no doubt that on leaving this life he should enter into one more happy.

The next day his sister Elizabeth came to see him, and told him of the decease of their sister Anne, who died a few days before; he then said, "I reckon Sister Anne was free to leave this world?" Elizabeth said she was. He then said, "I also am free to leave it;" and being in great weakness of body said, "I hope I shall shortly go to rest." He continued in a weighty frame of mind, and was sensible till near the last.

Second of ninth month, 1751.—Feeling drawings in my mind to visit Friends at the Great Meadows, in the upper part of West Jersey, with the unity of our Monthly Meeting, I went there, and had some searching laborious exercise amongst Friends in those parts, and found inward peace therein.

Ninth month, 1753.—In company with my well-esteemed friend, John Sykes, and with the unity of Friends, I travelled about two weeks, visiting Friends in Buck's County. We labored in the love of the gospel, according to the measure received; and through the mercies of Him who is strength to the poor who trust in him, we found satisfaction in our visit. In the next winter, way opening to visit Friends' families within the compass of our Monthly Meeting, partly by the labors of two Friends from Pennsylvania, I joined in some part of the work, having had a desire some time that it might go forward amongst us.

About this time, a person at some distance lying sick, his brother came to me to write his will. I knew he had slaves, and, asking his brother, was told he intended to leave them as slaves to his children. As writing is a profitable employ, and as offending sober people was disagreeable to my inclination, I was straitened in my mind; but as I looked to the Lord, he inclined my heart to his testimony. I told the man that I believed the practice of continuing slavery to this people was not right, and that I had a scruple in my mind against doing writings of that kind; that though many in our Society kept them as slaves, still I was not easy to be concerned in it, and desired to be excused from going to write the will. I spake to him in the fear of the Lord, and he made no reply to what I said, but went away; he also had some concerns in the practice, and I thought he was displeased with me. In this case I had fresh confirmation that acting contrary to present outward interest, from a motive of Divine love and in regard to truth and righteousness, and thereby incurring the resentments of people, opens the way to a treasure better than silver, and to a friendship exceeding the friendship of men.

The manuscript before mentioned having laid by me several years, the publication of it rested weightily upon me, and this year I offered it to the revisal of my friends, who, having examined and made some small alterations in it, directed a number of copies thereof to be published and dispersed amongst members of our Society. [*Some Considerations on the Keeping of Negroes,* 1754]

In the year 1754 I found my mind drawn to join in a visit to Friends' families belonging to Chesterfield Monthly Meeting, and having the approbation of our own, I went to their Monthly Meeting in order to confer with Friends, and see if way opened for it. I had conference with some of their members, the proposal having been opened before in their meeting, and one Friend agreed to join with me as a companion for a beginning; but when meeting was ended, I felt great distress of mind, and doubted what way to take, or whether to go home and wait for greater clearness. I kept my distress secret, and going with a friend to his house, my desires were to the great Shepherd for his heavenly instruction. In the morning I felt easy to proceed on the visit, though very low in my mind. As mine eye was turned to the Lord, waiting in families in deep reverence before him, he was pleased graciously to afford help, so that we had many comfortable opportunities, and it appeared as a fresh visitation to some young people. I spent several weeks this winter in the service, part of which time was employed near home. And again in the following winter I was several weeks in the same service; some part of the time at Shrewsbury, in company with my beloved friend, John Sykes; and I have cause humbly to acknowledge that through the goodness of the Lord our hearts were at times enlarged in his love, and strength was given to go through the trials which, in the course of our visit, attended us.

From a disagreement between the powers of England and France, it was now a time of trouble on this continent, and an epistle to Friends went forth from our general spring meeting, which I thought good to give a place in this Journal.

An Epistle from our general Spring Meeting of ministers and elders for Pennsylvania and New Jersey, held at Philadelphia, from the 29th of the third month to the 1st of the fourth month inclusive, 1755.

"To Friends on the Continent of America:—

Dear Friends, In an humble sense of Divine goodness, and the gracious continuation of God's love to his people, we tenderly salute you, and are at this time therein engaged in mind, that all of us who profess the truth, as held forth and published by our worthy predecessors in this latter age of the world, may keep near to that Life which is the light of men, and be strengthened to hold fast the profession of our faith without wavering, that our trust may not be in man, but in the Lord alone, who ruleth in the army of heaven and in the kingdoms of men, before whom the earth is "as the dust of the balance, and her inhabitants as grasshoppers." (Isa. XI. 22.)

Being convinced that the gracious design of the Almighty in sending his Son into the world was to repair the breach made by disobedience, to finish sin and transgression, that his kingdom might come, and his will be done on earth as it is in heaven, we have found it to be our duty to cease from those national contests which are productive of misery and bloodshed, and submit our cause to him, the Most High, whose tender love to his children exceeds the most warm affections of natural parents, and who hath promised to his seed throughout the earth, as to one individual, "I will never leave thee, nor forsake thee." (Heb. xiii. 5.) And we, through the gracious dealings of the Lord our God, have had experience of that work which is carried on, not be earthly might, nor by power, but by my Spirit, saith the Lord of Hosts." (Zech. iv. 6.) By which operation that spiritual kingdom is set up, which is to subdue and break in pieces all kingdoms that oppose it, and shall stand forever. In a deep sense thereof, and of the safety, stability, and peace that are in it, we are desirous that all who profess the truth may be inwardly acquainted with it, and thereby be qualified to conduct ourselves in all parts of our life as becomes our peaceable profession; and we trust as there is a faithful continuance to depend wholly upon the almighty arm, from one generation to another, the peaceable kingdom will gradually be extended "from sea to sea, and from the river to the ends of the earth" (Zech. ix. 10), to the completion of those prophecies already begun, that "nation shall not lift up a sword against nation, nor learn war any more." (Isa. ii. 4. Micah iv. 3.)

And, dearly beloved friends, seeing that we have these promises, and believe that God is beginning to fulfil them, let us constantly endeavor to have our minds sufficiently disentangled from the surfeiting cares of this life, and redeemed from the love of the world, that no earthly possessions nor enjoyments may bias our judgments, or turn us from that resignation and entire trust in God to which his blessing is most surely annexed; then may we say, "Our Redeemer is mighty, he will plead our cause for us." (Jer. 1, 34.) And if, for the further promoting of his most gracious purposes in the earth, he should give us to taste of that bitter cup of which his faithful ones have often partaken, O that we might be rightly prepared to receive it!

And now, dear friends, with respect to the commotions and stirrings of the powers of the earth at this time near us, we are desirous that none of us may be moved thereat, but repose ourselves in the munition of that rock which all these shakings shall not move, even in the knowledge and feeling of the eternal power of God, keeping us subjectly given up to his heavenly will, and feeling it daily to mortify that which remains in any of us which is of this world; for the worldly part in any is the changeable part, and that is up and down, full and empty, joyful and sorrowful, as things go well or ill in this world. For as the truth is but one, and many are made partakers of its spirit, so the world is but one, and many are made partakers of the spirit of it; and so many as do partake of it, so many will be straitened and perplexed with it. But they who are single to the truth, waiting daily to feel the life and virtue of it in their hearts, shall rejoice in the midst of adversity, and have to experience with the prophet, that, "although the fig-tree shall not blossom, neither shall fruit be in the vines; the labor of the olive shall fail, and the fields shall yield no meat; the flock shall be cut off from the fold, and there shall be no herd in the stalls; yet will they rejoice in the Lord, and joy in the God of their salvation." (Hab. iii. 17, 18.)

If, contrary to this, we profess the truth, and, not living under the power and influence of it, are producing fruits disagreeable to the purity thereof, and trust to the strength of man to support ourselves, our confidence therein will be vain. For he who removed the hedge from his vineyard, and gave it to be trodden under foot by reason of the wild grapes it produced (Isa. v. 6), remains unchangeable; and if, for the chastisement of wickedness and the further promoting of his own glory, he doth arise, even, to shake terribly the earth; who then may oppose him, and prosper!

We remain, in the love of the gospel, your friends and brethren."
(Signed by fourteen Friends)

Scrupling to do writings relative to keeping slaves has been a means of sundry small trials to me, in which I have so evidently felt my own will set aside that I think it good to mention a few of them. Tradesmen and retailers of goods, who depend on their business for a living, are naturally inclined to keep the good-will of their customers; nor is it a pleasant thing for young men to be under any necessity to question the judgment or honesty of elderly men, and more especially of such as have a fair reputation. Deep-rooted customs, though wrong, are not easily altered; but it is the duty of all to be firm in that which they certainly know is right for them. A charitable, benevolent man, well acquainted with a negro, may, I believe, under some circumstances, keep him in his family as a servant, on no other motives than the negro's good; but man, as man, knows not what shall be after him, nor hath he any assurance that his children will attain to that perfection in wisdom and goodness necessary rightly to exercise such power; hence it is clear to me, that I ought not to be the scribe where wills are drawn in which some children are made absolute masters over others during life.

About this time an ancient man of good esteem in the neighborhood came to my house to get his will written. He had young negroes, and I asked him privately how he purposed to dispose of them. He told me; I then said, "I cannot write thy will without breaking my own peace," and respectfully gave him my reasons for it. He signified that he had a choice that I should have written it, but as I could not, consistently with my conscience, he did not desire it, and so he got it written by some other person. A few years after, there being great alterations in his family, he came again to get me to write his will. His negroes were yet young, and his son, to whom he intended to give them, was, since he first spoke to me, from a libertine become a sober young man, and he supposed that I would have been free on that account to write it. We had much friendly talk on the subject, and then deferred it. A few days after he came again and directed their freedom, and I then wrote his will.

Near the time that the last-mentioned Friend first spoke to me, a neighbor received a bad bruise in his body and sent for me to bleed him, which having done, he desired me to write his will. I took notes, and amongst other things he told me to which of his children he gave his young negro. I considered the pain and distress he was in, and knew not how it would end, so I wrote his will, save only that part concerning his slave, and carrying it to his bedside read it to him. I then told him in a friendly way that I could not write any instruments by which my fellow-creatures were made slaves, without bringing trouble on my own mind. I let him know that I charged nothing for what I had done, and desired to be excused from doing the other part in the way he proposed. We then had a serious conference on the subject; at length, he agreeing to set her free, I finished his will.

Having found drawings in my mind to visit Friends on Long Island, after obtaining a certificate from our Monthly Meeting, I set off 12th of fifth month, 1756. When I reached the island, I lodged the first night at the house of my dear friend, Richard Hallett. The next day being the first of the week, I was at the meeting in New Town, in which we experienced the renewed manifestations of the love of Jesus Christ to the comfort of the honest-hearted. I went that night to Flushing, and the next day I and my beloved friend, Matthew Franklin, crossed the ferry at White Stone; were at three meetings on the main, and then returned to the island, where I spent the remainder of the week in visiting meetings. The Lord, I believe, hath a people in those parts who are honestly inclined to serve him; but many I fear, are too much clogged with the things of this life, and do not come forward bearing the cross in such faithfulness as he calls for.

My mind was deeply engaged in this visit, both in public and private, and at several places where I was, on observing that they had slaves, I found myself under a necessity, in a friendly way, to labor with them on that subject; expressing, as way opened, the inconsistency of that practice with the purity of the Christian religion, and the ill effects of it manifested amongst us.

The latter end of the week their Yearly Meeting began; at which were our friends, John Scarborough, Jane Hoskins, and Susannah Brown, from Pennsylvania. The public meetings were large, and measurably favored with Divine goodness. The exercise of my mind at this meeting was chiefly on account of those who were considered as the foremost rank in the Society; and in a meeting of ministers and elders way opened for me to express in some measure what lay upon me; and when Friends were met for transacting the affairs of the church, having sat awhile silent, I felt a weight on my mind, and stood up; and through the gracious regard of our Heavenly Father strength was given fully to clear myself of a burden which for some days had been increasing upon me.

Through the humbling dispensations of Divine Providence, men are sometimes fitted for his service. The messages of the prophet Jeremiah were so disagreeable to the people, and so adverse to the spirit they lived in, that he became the object of their reproach, and in the weakness of nature he thought of desisting from his prophetic office; but saith he, "His word was in my heart as a burning fire shut up in my bones; and I was weary with forbearing, and could not stay." I saw at this time that if I was honest in declaring that which truth opened in me, I could not please all men; and I labored to be content in the way of my duty, however disagreeable to my own inclination. After this I went homeward, taking Woodbridge and Plainfield in my way, in both which meetings the pure influence of Divine love was manifested, in an humbling sense whereof I went home. I had been out about twenty-four days, and rode about three hundred and sixteen miles.

While I was out on this journey my heart was much affected with a sense of the state of the churches in our southern provinces; and believing the Lord was calling me to some further labor amongst them, I was bowed in reverence before him, with fervent desires that I might find strength to resign myself to his heavenly will.

Until this year, 1756, I continued to retail goods, besides following my trade as a tailor; about which time I grew uneasy on account of my business growing too cumbersome. I had begun with selling trimmings for garments, and from thence proceeded to sell cloths and linens; and at length, having got a considerable shop of goods, my trade increased every year, and the way to large business appeared open, but I felt a stop in my mind.

Through the mercies of the Almighty, I had, in a good degree, learned to be content with a plain way of living. I had but a small family; and, on serious consideration, believed truth did not require me to engage much in cumbering affairs. It had been my general practice to buy and sell things really useful. Things that served chiefly to please the vain mind in people, I was not easy to trade in; seldom did it; and whenever I did I found it weakened me as a Christian.

The increase of business became my burden; for though my natural inclination was toward merchandise, yet I believed truth required me to live more free from outward cumbers; and there was now a strife in my mind between the two. In this exercise my prayers were put up to the Lord, who graciously heard me, and gave me a heart resigned to his holy will. Then I lessened my outward business, and, as I had opportunity, told my customers of my intentions, that they might consider what shop to turn to; and in a while I wholly laid down merchandise, and followed my trade as a tailor by myself, having no apprentice. I also had a nursery of apple-trees, in which I employed some of my time in hoeing, grafting, trimming, and inoculating. In merchandise it is the custom where I lived to sell chiefly on credit, and poor people often get in debt; when payment is expected, not having wherewith to pay, their creditors often sue for it at law. Having frequently observed occurrences of this kind, I found it good for me to advise poor people to take such goods as were most useful, and not costly.

In the time of trading I had an opportunity of seeing that the too liberal use of spirituous liquors and the custom of wearing too costly apparel led some people into great inconveniences; and that these two things appear to be often connected with each other. But not attending to that use of things which is consistent with universal righteousness, there is an increase of labor which extends beyond what our Heavenly Father intends for us. And by great labor, and often by much sweating, there is even among such as are not drunkards a craving of liquors to revive the spirits; that partly by the luxurious drinking of some, and partly by the drinking of others (led to it through immoderate labor), very great quantities of rum are every year expended in our colonies; the greater part of which we should have no need of, did we steadily attend to pure wisdom.

When men take pleasure in feeling their minds elevated with strong drink, and so indulge their appetitie as to disorder their understandings, neglect their duty as members of a family or civil society, and cast off all regard to religion, their case is much to be pitied. And where those whose lives are for the most part regular, and whose examples have a strong influence on the minds of others, adhere to some customs which powerfully draw to the use of more strong liquor than pure wisdom allows; this also as it hinders the spreading of the spirit of meekness, and strengthens the hands of the more excessive drinkers, is a case to be lamented.

Every degree of luxury hath some connection with evil; and if those who profess to be disciples of Christ, and are looked upon as leaders of the people, have that mind in them which was also in Christ, and so stand separate from every wrong way, it is a means of help to the weaker. As I have sometimes been much spent in the heat and I have taken spirits to revive me, I have found by experience, that in such circumstances the mind is not so calm, nor so fitly disposed for Divine meditation, as when all such extremes are avoided. I have felt an increasing care to attend to that Holy Spirit which sets right bounds to our desires, and leads those who faithfully follow it to apply all the gifts of Divine Providence to the purposes for which they were intended. Did those who have the care of great estates attend with singleness of heart to this heavenly Instructor, which so opens and enlarges the mind as to cause men to love their neighbors as themselves, they would have wisdom given them to manage their concerns, without employing some people in providing the luxuries of life, or others in laboring too hard; but for want of steadily regarding this principle of Divine love, a selfish spirit takes place in the minds of people, which is attended with darkness and manifold confusions in the world.

Though trading in things useful is an honest employ, yet through the great number of superfluities which are bought and sold, and through the corruption of the times, they who apply to merchandise for a living have great need to be well experienced in that precept which the Prophet Jeremiah laid down for his scribe: "Seekest thou great things for thyself? seek them not."

In the winter this year I was engaged with friends in visiting families, and through the goodness of the Lord we oftentimes experienced his heart-tendering presence amongst us.

35. NICHOLAS LUDWIG VON ZINZENDORF, PASTORAL LETTER CONCERNING THE WORK OF THE MORAVIANS, 1742*

Count Nicholas Ludwig von Zinzendorf (1700–60) of Saxony was a leader of the evangelical sect, the Unitas Fratrum, or Moravians, who came to Savannah, Georgia, in 1735, and founded communities along the frontiers of North Carolina (the present Winston-Salem) and in Bethlehem, Pennsylvania. By 1775, there were nearly 2,500 Moravians in America. They believed in religious communalism and were noted for their missionary zeal among the Indians, to whom they preached their doctrine of love and brotherhood. It was their evangelical method which John and Charles Wesley and Francis Asbury adopted and used effectively on the settlers of the West and even in the more staid Eastern regions.

Narrative of A Journey to Shecomeco, in August of 1742

Communicated to the Brethren in Europe in a letter written by Zinzendorf, on his way to Wyoming [Valley, Pennsylvania], dated

Shamokin, The Feast of Angels (Michaelmas),
Saturday, Sept. 29, 1742

Servants of the Precious Lamb,

I will proceed to communicate to you as much more as I can of my second journey, and something of the one in which I am now engaged. I keep no diary, and have no gift for narrative, and these are the reasons why I have failed to keep the dear Brethren at Bethlehem informed of my movements. You are indebted soley to this day of rest and leisure for the following outpourings of my heart in reference to persons and things, which I would otherwise not have committed to paper. As I remarked before, I have no faculty to relate, being inclined to forget and to repeat. I am also without my Secretary. You will, therefore, excuse imperfections, and allow the Brethren Spangenberg and Herman to select what they think proper for communication. Blessed are those who can read church intelligence aright!

* *Memorials of the Moravian Church*, William C. Reichel, ed. (Philadelphia: Lippencott, 1870), Vol. I, 47–57.

Aug. 10. We set out from Bethlehem.

Aug. 11. Crossed the Blue Mountain, en route for Sopus. [on Hudson, 80 miles north of New York] The road tried our horses severely. We were however, in a tranquil frame of mind. Anton Seyffert and Benigna [Zinzendorf's oldest daughter] were the principal persons in the company. In the evening we reached the bank of the Delaware, and came to Mr. De Pui's, who is a large landholder, and wealthy. While at his house, he had some Indians arrested for robbing his orchard.

Aug. 12 (*Sunday*). His son escorted us to the church, and, in course of conversation, put a number of indifferent and idle questions on religious subjects. My inability to answer him gratified rather than chagrined me, and was, I thought, altogether an advantage on my side.

We dismounted at the church, and were compelled to listen to two sermons, which wearied us.

In the morning the heat had been overpowering. In order to avoid being drawn into religious controversy, I went into the woods and read Josephus. The Dominie came to me and annoyed me with questions and remarks. Although my curt manner provoked him, it served to bring him to reflection, and he sought to propitiate me afterwards by riding with us for several hours. He is the well-known Caspar, [minister] from Zurich, a well-meaning man, I must confess,—one of the so-called "Convictionists" without much conviction, however, and yet efficient for good in his denomination.

Aug. 13. As we rode along, we were joined by a man who complained of the burden of his sins, and who inquired of me what to do to be saved. From his remarks, during the conversation, I failed to discover any solid grounds, in his religious experience, on which to erect an abiding super-structure.

On passing a house, a female stepped out, spoke to us, and, after the interchange of a few words, asked us to dismount, adding that her son, she knew, would be pleased to converse with us. We were unable to gratify her wish, as we had purposed passing the Minnisinks, and through half of the wilderness beyond, and there was a journey of *thirty* miles before us. When we reached the house that stands in the heart of it, night had already set in, and it was dark as pitch.

Aug. 14. Set out early in the morning; rode through the remainder of the wilderness, and reached Mombach and Marbletown. [between Port Jervis and Kingston, New York] We were much annoyed by ill-natured questions that were put to us, at a house at which we dismounted. Rode on through Hurley [in Ulster County] to Sopus. Here we met Sr. Anna and Christian Frohlich [the confectioner] and his wife. I dispatched Christian to the Delawares, to be with them at their festival, and retained Mary.

In the afternoon, we resumed our journey, crossed the North River, and halted for the night. The people here regarded us as saints.

Aug. 15. At noon we reached Bro. Jacob Maul's, in Rhinebeck. Having rested, we set out for Shecomeco, [Dutchess County, New York] and, after riding through an almost impenetrable swamp, came to our journey's end at 1 o'clock in the morning of the 16th.

Bro. Rauch lodged us in his hut for the night, and on the 17th we occupied the house that had been built for us. I was delighted with it; it was a perfect palace of bark, and furnished with a table and writing materials for my special convenience. My seat was on the ground. Here we lodged eight days, and, although it rained almost continuously, and we underwent numerous internal conflicts, our dear Indians had clear sky overhead, and rejoiced us each day anew. They are Mohicans, a confessedly worthless tribe of Indians.

The Maquas, who belong to the Six Nations of the Iroquois, are their neighbors, and the acknowledged head of that great Confederacy, although their passion for strong drink, by making them hopelessly indolent, has rendered them unworthy of the distinction. They are one division of the Indians with whom I ratified a covenant at Tulpehocken, [August 3, 1742] whither I had turned at the close of my journey into the Indian country, drawn by an irresistible power, which I followed in strong faith, although I knew neither why nor wherefore.

The Mohicans, although naturally fierce and vindictive, and given to excessive drinking, are tender-hearted, and susceptible of good impressions. When our pale-faced Bro. Rauch first came among them, they regarded him as a fool, and threatened his life. But after his recital of the Saviour's sufferings had made a powerful impression upon the most abandoned of their number (an impression which allowed him peace neither day nor night, until he experienced the preciousness of grace), the work of the Lord proceeded, and others were moved.

All the machinations of his mother-in-law, who sought to perplex him, were unsuccessful, although they proved effectual in causing his wife and daughter to vacillate. This brand snatched from the fire, is no longer Tschoop, but *John*, and is an esteemed teacher among his people. Abraham, Isaac, and Jacob, who, you recollect, were baptized at Oley, were appointed to offices in the mission—Abraham elder, Jacob exhorter, and Isaac sexton.

The four are in all respects incomparable Indians, and men of God. When met in conference on affairs of the mission, they deliberated in a manner which astonished us. I confess that at times I felt pity for these poor people, whose imperfect language is inadequate for the expression of their new experiences, and of their views and wishes, as assistants in the Saviour's work. Our language is divine in comparison with theirs, and yet how unsatisfactorily can we give utterance to the emotions and aspirations of our hearts!

The result of our deliberations while at Shecomeco, was the adoption of the following resolutions, viz.:

1. To mark out a new plan of operations for Bro. Rauch.

2. To preach the gospel to the whites of the neighborhood, and gather a congregation from them.

3. To organize our Mohicans into a congregation.

4. To contract a marriage between Jeannette Rau and Bro. Mack, to which union we have her father's consent.

5. To visit Conrad Weisser.

6. To employ Benigna and Jeanette in the Indian mission.

7. To baptize twelve Indians.

8. To appoint native assistants in the infant congregation here.

9. To take with us on our return to Bethlehem, Gabriel, Nanhan, and Abraham's son. Techtanoah, John's daughter, will not accompany us, as she is entertaining an offer of marriage.

10. To explore Albany and New England.

11. To confer with Abraham, Isaac, Jacob, and John, on our method of laboring among the heathen, and on its object, which is not the indiscriminate acquisition of large numbers, but the admission into the congregation of souls that have been renewed to life in Christ.

12. To commend the awakened Indians here to the blessing of the Lamb, and to inform them of the course we design to pursue in their case.

13. To consider the propriety of admitting a son and a second daughter of John Rau into our communion, and of appointing them to labor among the class of Indians just named.

14. To take a public farewell.

I shall never forget my stay here, and when we parted, it was with sadness and regret, though with mutual assurances of the tenderest love.

36. DEVEREAUX JARRATT, REVIVALISM IN VIRGINIA, 1763–76*

Devereaux Jarratt (1733–1801) of Virginia was one of the first Anglican evangelists. A teacher early in life and later a Presbyterian minister, he converted to Anglicanism in 1763 and was ordained by the Bishop of London. Differing in approach from established Anglicanism, Jarratt anticipated Wesley in emphasizing rebirth and repentance, a typical theme of the Great Awakening preachers. His forceful sermons

* *Journal of the Rev. Francis Asbury* . . . (New York: N. Bangs and T. Mason, 1821), Vol. I, pp. 157–63.

did much to convert the people of the back country of Virginia and North Carolina. When Methodism was formed, Jarratt chose to remain in the Anglican fold, although he addressed one Methodist conference in 1782 in its own fiery manner. His work received wide acclaim from the Methodists and particularly from John Wesley who regarded Jarratt as a "proper preacher."

Jarratt's "Brief Narrative of the Revival of Religion in Virginia" was part of a letter to Bishop Francis Asbury, and can be found in Asbury's Journal, *dated December 19, 1776. In it he describes his pastoral activities.*

Devereaux Jarratt was also noteworthy for his Thoughts . . . in Divinity *(1791) which was later published as the autobiography,* The Life of Devereaux Jarratt. *In 1793–94, he published* Sermons on Various and Important Subjects in Practical Divinity.

Brief Narrative of the Revival of Religion in Virginia

Thursday, 19. Received a narrative of the work of God in Virginia, written by Mr. J. to be sent to Mr. Wesley. The Lord has been displaying the power of his grace in a marvellous manner, through many parts of Virginia. An extract of the narrative is here subjoined.

Dear Sir,—You were pleased, when in Virginia, to desire a narrative of of the work of God in these parts. I shall give you matter of fact, in a plain, artless dress; relating only what I have myself seen and heard, and what I have received from men on whose judgment and veracity I can fully depend.

That you may have a full view of the whole, I shall go back as far as my first settlement in this parish. August 29, 1763, I was chosen rector of B[ath], in the county of D[inwiddie], in Virginia. Ignorance of the things of God, profaneness, and irreligion, then prevailed among all ranks and degrees. So that I doubt if even the form of godliness was to be found in any one family of this large and populous parish. I was a stranger to the people: my doctrines were quite new to them; and were neither preached nor believed by any other clergyman, so far as I could learn, throughout the province.

My first work was, to explain the depravity of our nature; our fall in Adam, and all the evils consequent theron; the impossibility of being delivered from them by anything which we could do, and the necessity of a living faith, in order to our obtaining help from God. While I continued to insist upon these truths, and on the absolute necessity of being born again, no small outcry was raised against this way, as well as against him that taught it. But by the help of God, I continued to witness the same both to small and great.

The common people, however, frequented the church more constantly, and in larger numbers than usual. Some were affected at times, so as to drop a tear. But still, for a year or more, I perceived no lasting effect, only a few were not altogether so profane as before. I could discover no heartfelt convictions of sin, no deep or lasting impression of their lost estate. Indeed I have reason to believe that some have been a good deal alarmed at times. But they were shy of speaking to me (thinking it would be presumption) till their convictions wore off.

But in the year 1765, the power of God was more sensibly felt by a few. These were constrained to apply to me, and inquire, "What they must do to be saved?" And now I began to preach abroad, as well as in private houses; and to meet little companies in the evenings, and converse freely on divine things. I believe some were this year converted to God, and thenceforth the work of God slowly went on.

The next year I became acquainted with Mr. M'R., rector of a neighbouring parish; and we joined hand in hand in the great work. He laboured much therein; and not in vain. A remarkable power attended his preaching, and many were truly converted to God, not only in his parish, but in other parts where he was called to labour.

In the years 1770 and 1771, we had a more considerable outpouring of the Spirit, at a place in my parish called White-Oak. It was here first I formed the people into a society, that they might assist and strengthen each other. The good effects of this were soon apparent. Convictions were deep and lasting: and not only knowledge, but faith, and love, and holiness continually increased.

In the year 1772, the revival was more considerable, and extended itself in some places, for fifty or sixty miles round. It increased still more in the following year, and several sinners were truly converted to God. In spring, 1774, it was more remarkable than ever. The word preached was attended with such energy, that many were pierced to the heart. Tears fell plentifully from the eyes of the hearers, and some were constrained to cry out. A goodly number were gathered in this year, both in my parish and in many of the neighbouring counties. I formed several societies out of those which were convinced or converted; and I found it a happy means of building up those that had believed, and preventing the rest from losing their convictions.

In the counties of Sussex and Brunswick, the work from the year 1773, was chiefly carried on by the labours of the people called Methodists. The first of them who appeared in these parts was Mr. R. W., who, you know, was a plain, artless, indefatigable preacher of the gospel: he was greatly blessed in detecting the hypocrite, razing false foundations and stirring believers up to press after a present salvation from the remains of sin. He came to my house in the month of March, in the year 1773. The next year others of his brethren came, who gathered many societies both in this neighbourhood, and in other places, as far as North Carolina. They now began to ride the circuit, and to take care of the societies already formed, which was rendered a happy means, both of deepening and spreading the work of God.

I earnestly recommended it to my societies, to pray much for the prosperity of Sion, and for a larger outpouring of the Spirit of God. They did so; and not in vain. We have had a time of refreshing indeed: a revival of religion, as great as perhaps ever was known, in country places, in so short a time. It began in the latter end of the year 1775: but was more considerable in January, 1776, the beginning of the present year. It broke out nearly at the same time, at three places, not far from each other. Two of these places are in my parish; the other in Amelia county —which had for many years been notorious for carelessness, profanenes, and immoralities of all kinds. Gaming, swearing, drunkenness, and the like, were their delight, while things sacred were their scorn and contempt. However, some time last year one of my parish (now a local preacher) appointed some meetings among them, and after a while induced a small number to join in society. And though few, if any of them were then believers, yet this was a means of preparing the way of the Lord.

As there were few converts in my parish the last year, I was sensible a change of preachers was wanting. This has often revived the work of God: and so it did at the present time. Last December one of the Methodist preachers, Mr. S., preached several times at the three places above mentioned. He confirmed the doctrine I had long preached; and to many of them not in vain. And while their ears were opened by novelty, God set his word home upon their hearts. Many sinners were powerfully convinced, and mercy! mercy! was their cry. In January, the news of convictions and conversions was common; and the people of God were inspired with new life and vigour by the happiness of others. But in a little time they were made thoroughly sensible that they themselves stood in need of a deeper work in their hearts than they had yet experienced. And while those were panting and groaning for pardon, these were entreating God, with strong cries and tears, to save them from the remains of inbred sin, to "sanctify them throughout, in spirit, soul, and body;" so to "circumcise their hearts," that they might "love God with all their hearts," and serve him with all their strength.

During this whole winter, the Spirit of the Lord was poured out in a manner we had not seen before. In almost every assembly might be seen signal instances of divine power, more especially in the meetings of the classes. Here many old stout-hearted sinners felt the force of truth, and their eyes were open to discover their guilt and danger. The shaking among the dry bones was increased from week to week: nay, sometimes ten or twelve have been deeply convinced of sin in one day. Some of these were in great distress, and when they were questioned concerning the state of their souls, were scarce able to make any reply but by weeping and falling on their knees, before all the class, and earnestly soliciting the prayers of God's people. And from time to time he has answered these petitions, set the captives at liberty, and enabled them to praise a pardoning God in the midst of his people. Numbers of old and gray-headed, of middle-aged persons, of youth, yea, of little children, were the subjects of the work. Several of the latter we have seen painfully concerned for the wickedness of their lives, and the corruption of their nature. We have instances of this sort from eight or nine years old. Some of these children are exceedingly happy in the love of God—and they speak of the whole process of the work of God, of their convictions, the time when, and the manner how, they obtained deliverance—with such clearness as might convince an atheist that this is nothing else but the great power of God.

Many in these parts who had long neglected the means of grace now flocked to hear, not only me and the travelling preachers, but also the exhorters and leaders. And the Lord showed he is not confined to man; for whether there was preaching or not, his power was still sensible among the people. And at their meetings for prayer, some have been in such distress that they have continued therein for five or six hours. And it has been found that these prayer meetings were singularly useful in promoting the work of God.

The outpouring of the Spirit which began here, soon extended itself, more or less, through most of the circuit, which is regularly attended by the travelling preachers, and which takes in a circumference of between four and five hundred miles. And the work went on, with a pleasing progress, till the begining of May, when they held a quarterly meeting at B.'s chapel, in my parish. This stands at the lower line of the parish, thirty miles from W.'s chapel, at the upper line of it, where the work began. At this meeting, one might truly say, the windows of heaven were opened, and the rain of Divine influence poured down for more than forty days. The work now became more deep than ever, extended wider, and was swifter in its operations. Many were savingly converted to God, and in a very short time, not only in my parish, but through several parts of Brunswick, Sussex, Prince George, Lunenburg, Mecklenburg, and Amelia counties.

The second day of the quarterly meeting a love-feast was held. As soon as it began the power of the Lord came down on the assembly like a rushing mighty wind; and it seemed as if the whole house was filled with the presence of God. A flame kindled and ran from heart to heart. Many were deeply convinced of sin; many mourners were filled with consolation; and many believers were so overwhelmed with love, that they could not doubt but God had enabled them to love him with *all* their heart.

When the love-feast was ended, the doors were opened. Many who had stayed without then came in; and beholding the anguish of some, and the rejoicing of others, were filled with astonishment, and not long after with trembling apprehensions of their own danger. Several of them prostrating themselves before God, cried aloud for mercy. And the convictions which then began in many, have terminated in a happy and lasting change.

The multitudes that attended on this occasion, returning home all alive to God, spread the flame through their respective neighbourhoods, which ran from family to family: so that within four weeks, several hundreds found the peace of God. And scarce any conversation was to be heard throughout the circuit, but concerning the things of God: either the complaining of the prisoners, groaning under the spirit of bondage unto fear; or the rejoicing of those whom the Spirit of adoption taught to cry, "Abba, Father." The unhappy disputes between England and her colonies, which just before had engrossed all our conversation, seemed now in most companies to be forgot, while things of far greater importance lay so near the heart. I have gone into many, and not small companies, wherein there did not appear to be one careless soul; and the far greater part seemed perfectly happy in a clear sense of the love of God.

One of the doctrines, as you know, which we particularly insist upon, is that of a present salvation; a salvation not only from the guilt and power, but also from the root of sin; a cleansing from all filthiness of flesh and spirit, that we may perfect holiness in the fear of God; a going on to perfection, which we sometimes define by loving God with all our hearts. Several who had believed were deeply sensible of their want of this. I have seen both men and women, who had long been happy in a sense of God's pardoning love, as much convicted on account of the remains of sin in their hearts, and as much distressed for a total deliverance from them, as ever I saw any for justification. Their whole cry was:—

> O that I now the rest might know—
> Believe, and enter in;
> Now, Saviour, now the power bestow,
> And let me cease from sin!

And I have been present when they believed that God answered this prayer, and bestowed this blessing upon them. I have conversed with them several times since, and have found them thoroughly devoted to God. They all testify, that they have received the gift instantaneously, and by simple faith. We have sundry witnesses of this perfect love who are above all suspicion. I have known the men and their communication for many years, and have ever found them zealous for the cause of God —men of sense and integrity, patterns of piety and humility; whose testimony therefore may be depended on.

It has been frequently observed, that there never was any remarkable revival of religion, but some degree of enthusiasm was mingled with it—some wildfire mixed with the sacred flame. It may be doubted whether this is not unavoidable in the nature of things. And notwithstanding all the care we have taken, this work has not been quite free from it; but it never rose to any considerable height, neither was of long continuance. In some meetings there has not been that decency and order observed which I could have wished. Some of our assemblies resembled the congregation of the Jews at laying the foundation of the second temple in the days of Ezra—some wept for grief; others shouted for joy; so that it was hard to distinguish one from the other. So it was here: the mourning and distress were so blended with the voice of joy and gladness, that it was hard to distinguish the one from the other, till the voice of joy prevailed—the people shouting with a great shout, so that it might be heard afar off. . . .

4

History and Literature

37. ROBERT BEVERLEY, *HISTORY AND PRESENT STATE OF VIRGINIA*, 1705–22*

Robert Beverley (1673–1722) of Middlesex County, Virginia, was the brother-in-law of the powerful, aristocratic William Byrd of Westover. Beverly held various political offices in the Old Dominion and was elected a member of the House of Burgesses between 1699 and 1706. Called to London on a matter of litigation in 1703, he chanced to read John Oldmixon's manuscript of the British Empire in America. *Beverley was so critical of the author's misinformation about Virginia that he wrote his* History and Present State of Virginia, *the first edition of which appeared in 1705. Because of its scope, insights into provincial government, and excellent style, it was an immediate success and has been popular ever since.*

On Bacon's Rebellion, 1676

The Occasion of this Rebellion is not easie to be discover'd: But 'tis certain there were many Things that concurr'd towards it. For it cannot be imagined, that upon the Instigation of two or three Traders only, who aim'd at a Monoply of the *Indian* Trade, as some pretend to say, the whole Country would have fallen into so much Distraction; in which People did not only hazard their Necks by Rebellion: But endeavor'd to ruin a Governor [William Berkeley], whom they all entirely

* Robert Beverley, *The History and Present State of Virginia, In Four Parts*, 2nd ed. (London: B. and S. Tooke, 1722), pp. 74–84. [The enumeration of paragraphs in the original are here deleted. Editor's note.] See also Robert Beverley, *The History and Present State of Virginia, In Four Parts*, Louis B. Wright, ed. (Chapel Hill: University of North Carolina Press Institute of Early American History and Culture, 1947), pp. 74ff.

loved, and had unaminously chosen; a Gentleman who had devoted his whole Life and Estate to the Service of the Country; and against whom in thirty five Years Experience, there had never been one single complaint. Neither can it be supposed, that upon so slight Grounds, they would make choice of a Leader they hardly knew, to oppose a Gentleman, that had been so long, and so deservedly the Darling of the People. So that in all Probability there was something else in the Wind, without which the Body of the Country had never been engaged in that Insurrection.

Four Things may be reckon'd to have been the main Ingredients towards this intestine Commotion, *viz.* First, the extream low Price of Tobacco, and the ill Usage of the Planters in the Exchange of Goods for it, which the Country, with all their earnest Endeavours, could not remedy. Secondly, the splitting the Colony into Proprieties, contrary to the original Charters; and the extravagant Taxes they were forced to undergo, to relieve themselve from those Grants. Thirdly, The heavy Restraints and Burdens laid upon their Trade by Act of Parliament in *England.* Fourthly, The Disturbance given by the *Indians.* Of all which I beg Leave to speak in their Order.

First, Of the low Price of Tobacco, and the Disappointment of all Sort of Remedy, I have spoken sufficiently before. Secondly, Of splitting the Country into Proprieties.

King *Charles* the Second, to gratifie some Nobles about him, made Two great Grants out of that Country. These Grants were not of the uncultivated Wood-Land only, but also of Plantations, which for many Years had been seated and improv'd, under the Encouragement of several Charters granted by his Royal Ancestors to that Colony. Those Grants were distinguished by the Names of the Northern and Southern Grants of *Virginia*, and the same Men were concern'd in both. They were kept dormant some Years after they were made, and in the Year 1674 begun to be put in Execution. As soon as ever the Country came to know this, they remonstrated against them; and the Assembly drew up an humble Address to his Majesty, complaining of the said Grants, as derogatory to the previous Charters and Privileges granted to that Colony, by his Majesty and his Royal Progenitors. They sent to *England* Mr. Secretary [Thomas] *Ludwell* and Colonel [Daniel] *Park*, as their Agents to address the King to vacate those Grants. And the better to defray that Charge, they laid a Tax of Fifty Pounds of Tobacco *per* Poll, for Two Years together, over and above all other Taxes, which was an excessive Burden. They likewise laid Amercements of seventy, fifty, or thirty Pounds of Tobacco on every cause tried throughout the Country. Besides all this, they applied the Balance, remaining due upon Account of the two Shilling *per* Hogshead, and Fort Duties, to this Use. Which Taxes and Amercements fell heaviest on the poor People, the Effect of whose Labour wou'd not cloath their Wives and Children. This made them desperately uneasie, especially when, after a whole Year's Patience under all these Pressures, they had no Encouragement from their Agents in *England*, to hope for Remedy; nor any Certainty when they should be eased of those heavy Impositions.

Thirdly, Upon the Back of all these Misfortunes came out the Act of 25 *Car.* II. for better securing the Plantation Trade. By this Act several Duties were laid on the Trade from one Plantation to another. This was a new Hardship, and the rather, because the Revenue arising by this Act, was not applied to the Use of the Plantation wherein it was raised: But given clear away; nay, in that Country it seem'd to be of no other Use, but to burden the Trade or to create a good Income to the Officers; for the Collector had Half, the Comptroller a Quarter, and the remaining Quarter was subdivided into Salaries, till it was lost.

By the same Act also very great Duties were laid on the Fisheries of the Plantations, if manufactured by the *English* Inhabitants there; while the People of *England* by *English* Men, and in English built Ships, yet it was held to a considerable Duty, more than the Inhabitants of *England* paid.

These were the Afflictions that Country labour'd under, when the fourth Accident happen'd, *viz.* The Disturbance offer'd by the *Indians* to the Frontiers.

This was occasion'd, First, By the *Indians* on the Head of the Bay. Secondly, By the *Indians* on their own Frontiers.

First, The *Indians* at the Head of the Bay drove a constant Trade with the *Dutch* in *Monadas*, now call'd New-York; and, to carry on this, they used to come and return every Year by their Frontiers of *Virginia*, to purchase Skins and Furs of the *Indians* to the Southward. This Trade was carried on peaceably while the *Dutch* held *Monadas*; and the *Indians* used to call on the *English*, in Virginia on their return, to whom they would sell Part of their Furs, and with the rest go on to *Monadas*. But after the *English* came to possess that Place, and understood the Advantages the Virginians made by the Trade of their *Indians*, they inspired them with such a Hatred to the Inhabitants of *Virginia*, that, instead of coming peaceably to trade with them, as they had done for several Years before, they afterwards never came, but only to commit Robberies and Murders upon the People.

Secondly, The *Indians* upon their own Frontiers were likewise inspir'd with ill Thoughts of 'em. For their *Indian* Merchants had lost a considerable Branch of their Trade they knew not how; and apprehended the Consequences of Sir *William Berkeley's* intended Discoveries (espoused by the Assembly), might take away the remaining Part of their Profit. This made them very troublesome to the Neighbour *Indians*; who on their part, observing an unusual Uneasiness in the *English*, and being terrified by their rough Usage, immediately suspected some wicked Design against their Lives, and so fled to their remoter Habitations. This confirm'd the English in the Belief, that they had been the Murderers, till at last they provoked them to be so in Earnest.

This Addition of Mischief to Minds already full of Discontent, made People ready to vent all their Resentment against the poor *Indians*. There was nothing to be got by Tobacco; neither could they turn any other Manufacture to Advantage; so that most of the poorer Sort were willing to quit their unprofitable Employments, and go Voluntiers against the *Indians*.

At first they flock'd together tumultuously, running in Troops from one Plantation to another without a Head; till at last the seditious Humor of Colonel *Nath*[aniel] *Bacon*, led him to be of the Party. This Gentleman had been brought up at one of the Inns of Court in *England*, and had a moderate Fortune. He was young, bold, active, of an inviting Aspect, and powerful Elocution. In a Word, he was every way qualified to head a giddy and unthinking Multitude. Before he had been Three Years in the Country, he was, for his extraordinary Qualifications, made one of the Council, and in great Honour and Esteem among the People. For this Reason he no sooner gave Countenance to this riotous Mob, but they all presently fix'd their Eyes upon him for their General, and accordingly made their Addresses to him. As soon as he found this, he harangued them publickly. He aggravated the Indian Mischiefs, complaining, that they were occasion'd for Want of a due Regulation of their Trade. He recounted particularly the other Grievances and Pressures they lay under; and pretended, that he accepted of their Command with no other Intention, but to do them and the Country Service, in which he was willing to encounter the greatest Difficulties and Dangers. He farther assured them, he would never lay down his Arms, till he had revenged their Sufferings upon the *Indians*, and redress'd all their other Grievances.

By these Insinuations he wrought his Men into so perfect a Unanimity, that they were one and all at his Devotion. He took care to exasperate them to the utmost, by representing all their Misfortunes. After he had begun to muster them, he dispatch'd a Messenger to the Governour, by whom he aggravated the Mischiefs done by the *Indians*, and desired a Commission of General to go out against them. This Gentleman was in so great Esteem at that time with the Council, that the Governour did not think fit to give him a flat Refusal: But sent him Word, he would consult the Council, and return him a further Answer.

In the mean time, *Bacon* was expeditious in his Preparations, and having all Things in Readiness, began his March, depending on the Authority the People had given him. He would not lose so much Time, as to stay for his Commission; but dispatched several Messengers to the Governour to hasten it. On the other Hand, the Governour, instead of a Commission, sent positive Orders to him to disperse his Men, and come down in Person to him, upon Pain of being declared a Rebel.

This unexpected Order, was a great Surprize to *Bacon*, and not a little Trouble to his Men. However, he was resolved to prosecute his first Intentions, depending upon his Strength, and Interest with the People. Nevertheless, he intended to wait upon the Governour, but not altogether defenceless. Pursuant to this Resolution, he took about forty of his Men down with him in a Sloop to *James-Town* where the Governour was with his Council.

Matters did not succeed there to Mr. *Bacon's* Satisfaction: wherefore he express'd himself a little too freely. For which being suspended from the Council, he went away again in a Huff with his Sloop and Followers. The Governour fill'd a Long-Boat with Men, and pursued the Sloop so close, that Colonel *Bacon* removed into his Boat to make more Haste. But the Governour had sent up by Land to the Ships at *Sandy-Point*, where he was stopp'd, and sent down again. Upon his Return he was kindly received by the Governour, who, knowing he had gone a Step beyond his Instructions in having suspended him, was glad to admit him again of the Council; after which he hoped all Things might be pacified.

Notwithstanding this, Col. *Bacon* still insisted upon a Commission to be General of the Voluntiers, and to go out against the *Indians*; from which the Governour endeavour'd to dissuade him, but to no Purpose, because he had some secret Project in View. He had the Luck to be countenanced in his Importunities, by the News of fresh Murder and Robberies committed by the *Indians*. However, not being able to accomplish his Ends by fair Means, he stole privately out of Town; and having put himself at the Head of Six Hundred Voluntiers, marched directly to *James-Town*, where the Assembly was then sitting. He presented himself before the House wherein they sat. He urged to them his Preparations; and alledged, that if the Commission had not been delay'd so long, the War against the Indians might have been finish'd.

The Governour resented this insolent Usage worst of all, and now obstinately refused to grant him any thing, offering his naked Breast against the presented Arms of his Followers. But the Assembly, fearing the fatal Consequence of provoking a discontented Multitude ready arm'd, who had the Governour, Council and Assembly entirely in their Power, address'd the Governour to grant *Bacon* his Request. They prepar'd themselves the Commission, constituting him General of the Forces of *Virginia*, and brought it to the Governour to be sign'd.

With much Reluctancy the Governour sign'd it, and thereby put the Power of War and Peace into *Bacon's* Hands. Upon this he march'd away immediately, having gain'd his End, which was in effect a Power to secure a Monopoly of the *Indian* Trade to himself and his Friends.

As soon as General Bacon had march'd to such a convenient Distance from *James-Town*, that the Assembly thought they might deliberate with Safety, the Governour, by their Advice, issued a Proclamation of Rebellion against him, commanding his Followers to surrender him, and forthwith disperse themselves. Not contented with this, he likewise gave Orders at the same time, for raising the Militia of the Country against him.

The People being much exasperated, and General *Bacon* by his Address and Eloquence having gain'd an absolute Dominion over their Hearts, they unanimously resolved, that not a Hair of his Head should be touch'd, much less that they shou'd surrender him as a Rebel. Therefore, they kept to their Arms, and instead of proceeding against the *Indians*, they march'd back to *James-Town*; directing their Fury against such of their Friends and Countrymen, as should dare to oppose them.

The Governour seeing this, fled over the Bay to *Accomack*, whither he hoped the Infection of *Bacon's* Conspiracy had not reach'd. But there, instead of that People's receiving him with open Arms, in Remembrance of the former Services he had done them; they began to make Terms with him for Redress of their Grievances, and for the Ease and Liberty of Trade against the Acts of Parliament. Thus Sir *William* who had been almost the Idol of the People, was, by reason of their Calamity and Jealousy, abandon'd by all, except some few, who went over to him from the Western Shore in Sloops and Boat; among which one Major *Robert Beverley* was the most active and successful Commander; So that it was some time before he could make head against *Bacon*: But he left him to range thro' the Country at Discretion.

General *Bacon* at first held a Convention of such of the chief Gentlemen of the Country, as would come to him, especially of those about *Middle-Plantation* [Williamsburg], who were near at Hand. At this Convention they made a Declaration to justify his unlawful Proceedings; and obliged People to take an Oath of Obedience to him as their General. Then, by their Advice, on Pretence of the Governour's Abdication, he call'd an Assembly, by Writs sign'd by himself, and four others of the Council.

The Oath was word for Word as follows.

Whereas the Country hath raised an Army against our common Enemy the Indians, *and the same under the Command of General* Bacon, *being upon the Point to march forth against the said common Enemy, hath been diverted, and necessitated to move to the Suppressing of Forces, by evil disposed Persons raised against the said General* Bacon, *purposely to foment and stir up Civil War among us, to the Ruine of this his Majesty's Country. And,*

Whereas it is notoriously manifest, that Sir William Berkeley, Knight, Governour of the Country, assisted, counselled and abetted by those evil disposed Persons aforesaid, hath not only commanded, fomented and stirr'd up the People to the said Civil War; but failing therein, hath withdrawn himself, to the great Astonishment of the People, and the Unsettlement of the Country. And, Whereas the said Army, raised by the Country for the Causes aforesaid, remain full of Dissatisfaction in the Middle of the Country, expecting Attempts from the said Governour and the evil Counsellors aforesaid. And since no proper Means have been found out for the Settlement of the Distractions, and preventing the horrid Outrages and Murders daily committed in many Places of the Country by the barbarous Enemy; It hath been thought fit by the said General, to call unto him all such sober and discreet Gentlemen, as the present Circumstances of the Country will admit, to the Middle-Plantation, to consult and advise of reestablishing the Peace of the Country. So we the said Gentlemen, being this 3d of August, 1676, accordingly met, do advise, resolve, declare and conclude, and for our selves do swear in manner following.

First, That we will at all Times join with the said General Bacon, and his Army, against the common Enemy in all Points whatsoever.

Secondly, That whereas certain Persons have lately contrived and design'd the Raising Forces against the said General, and the Army under his Command, thereby to beget a Civil War; We will endeavour the Discovery and Apprehending of all and every of those evil disposed Persons, and them secure, untill further Order from the General.

Thirdly, And whereas it is credibly reported, that the Governour hath inform'd the King's Majesty, that the said General, and the People of the Country in Arms under his Command, their Aiders and Abettors, are Rebellious, and removed from their Allegiance; and that upon such like Information, he the said Governour hath advised and petition'd the King to send Forces to reduce them; We do further declare and believe in our Consciences, That it consists with the Welfare of this Country, and with our Allegiance to his most Sacred Majesty, that we the Inhabitants of Virginia, to the utmost of our Power, do oppose and suppress all Forces whatsoever of that Nature, until such time as the King be fully inform'd of the State of the Case, by such Person or Persons, as shall be sent from the said Nathaniel Bacon, in the Behalf of the People; and the Determination thereof be remitted hither. And we do swear, That we will him the said General, and the Army under his Command, aid and assist accordingly.

By this Time the Governor had got together a small Party to side with him. These he furnished with Sloops, Arms and Ammunition, under command of Major Robert Beverley, in order to cross the Bay, and oppose the Malecontents. By this Means there happen'd some Skirmishes, in which several were Kill'd, and others taken Prisoners. Thus they were going on by a Civil War to destroy one another, and lay waste their Infant Country; when it pleased God, after some Months Confusion, to put an End to their Misfortunes, as well as to *Bacon's* Designs, by his natural Death.

He died at Dr. *Green's* [rather Major Thomas Pate's], in *Glouces-ter* County: But where he was bury'd was never yet discover'd; tho afterward there was great Enquiry made, with Design to expose his Bones to publick Infamy.

In the mean while, those Disorders occasion'd a general Neglect of Husbandry, and a great Destruction of the Stocks; so that People had a dreadful Prospect of Want and Famine. But the Malecontents being thus disunited by the Loss of their General, in whom they all confided, they began to squabble among themselves; and every Man's Business was how to make the best Terms he could for himself.

Lieutenant-General *Ingram* (whose true Name was *Johnson*) and Major-General *Walklate* surrender'd on Condition of Pardon for them-selves and their Followers; tho' they were both forced to submit to an Incapacity of bearing Office in that Country for the future.

Peace being thus restored, Sir *William Berkeley* return'd to his former Seat of Government, and every Man to his several Habitation.

38. WILLIAM BYRD, *SECRET HISTORY OF THE DIVIDING LINE*, 1729[*]

William Byrd (1674–1744) of Westover, Virginia, was the ideal cavalier gentlemen: of good inheritance, a wealthy planter and slave owner (constantly improving his estate), learned and worldly but not un-godly. Active in Virginia and imperial politics, he passed nearly as much time in sophisticated English salons as in provincial drawing rooms. In 1729, he led an expedition to fix the boundary between North Carolina and Virginia. Of these adventures he wrote two histories: one an unembellished report of the expedition; the other, below, a satire, whose earthiness has entertained and amused readers since it was passed about in manuscript form among Byrd's friends. One author-ity on American literature rightly called Byrd's histories "unique in our colonial age" and hails his work as "without question, one of the most delightful of the literary legacies which that age has handed down to ours."

April

1. We prepar'd for a March very early, & then I discharg'd a long Score with my Landlord, & a Short one with his Daughter Rachel for

[*] William K. Boyd, ed., *William Byrd's Histories of the Dividing Line betwixt Virginia and North Carolina* (Raleigh: North Carolina State Department of Archives and History, 1929), pp. 105, 107, 109, 111, 113, 115, 123. Printed by permission of the publishers. For a modern recent edition of this and some other Byrd works see *The Prose Works of William Byrd of Westover: Narrative of a Colonial Virginian,* Louis B. Wright, ed. (Cambridge: Belknap Press, 1966).

some Smiles that were to be paid for in Kisses. We took leave in form of the whole Family, & in 8 Miles reach't Richard Parkers, where we found Young Astrolabe & some of our Men. Here we refresh't ourselves with what a Neat Landlady cou'd provide, & Christen'd 2 of her Children, but did not discharge our reckoning that way. Then we proceeded by Somerton Chappel (which was left 2 Miles in Virginia) as far as the Plantation of William Speight, that was cut in Two by the Line, taking his Tobacco House into Carolina. Here we took up our Quarters & fared the better for a Side of fat Mutton sent us by Captain Baker. Our Lodging was exceedingly Airy, the Wind having a free circulation quite thro' our Bed-Chamber, yet we were so hardy as to take no Cold, tho' the Frost was Sharp enough to endanger the Fruit. Meanwell entertain'd the Carolina Commissioners with several Romantick Passages of his Life, with Relation to his Amours, which is a Subject he is as fond of, as a Hero to talk of Battles he never fought.

2. This Morning early Capt Baker came to make us a Visit, & explain'd to us the Reason of the present of Mutton which he sent us Yesterday. It seems the Plantation where he lives is taken into Virginia which without good Friends might prejudice him in his Surveyor's Place of Nansimond County. But we promised to employ our Interest in his Favour. We made the best of our way to Chowan River, crossing the Line several times. About a Mile before we came to that River, we crost Somerton Creek. We found our Surveyors at a little Cottage on the Banks of Chowan over against the Mouth of Nottoway River. They told us that our Line cut Black-Water River, about half a Mile to the Northward of that Place but in Obedience to his Majesty's Order in that Case, we directed them to continue the Line from the Middle of the Mouth of Nottoway River. According the Surveyors post Cowan there, & carry'd the Line over a miry Swamp more than half a mile thro', as far as an Indian Old-Field.

In the meantime our Horses & Baggage were ferry'd over the River, a little lower, to the same Field, where we pitch't our Tent, promising ourselves a comfortable Repose: but our Evil Genius came at Night & interrupted all our Joys. Firebrand arriv'd with his most humble Servant Shoebrush, tho' to make them less unwelcome, they brought a present from Mr. Oshields, of 12 Bottles of Wine, & as many of Strong Beer. But to say the Truth we had rather have drunk Water the whole Journey to have been fairly quit of such disagreeable Company.

Our Surveyor found by an Observation made this Night, that the Variation was no more than 2° .30″ Westerly, according to which we determined to proceed in the rest of our Work towards the Mountains. Three of the Meherin Indians came hither to see us from the Place where they now live about 7 Miles down the River, they being lately removed from the Mouth of Meherin. They were frighten'd away from thence by the late Massacre committed upon 14 of their Nation by the Catawbas. They are now reduced to a small Number and are the less to be pity'd because they have always been suspected to be very dishonest & treacherous to the English.

3. We sent away the Surveyors about 9 a Clock & follow'd them at ten. By the way Firebrand & Shoebrush having spy'd a House that promised good Chear filed off to it, & took it in Dudgeon that we wou'd not follow their Vagarys. We thought it our Duty to attend the Business in hand, & follow the Surveyors. These we overtook about Noon, after passing several Miry Branches, where I had like to have Stuck fast. However this only gave me an Opportunity to shew my Horsemanship, as the fair spoken Plausible told me. After passing several Dirty Places & uneven Grounds, we arriv'd about Sun Set on the Banks of Meherin, which we found 13¼ Miles from the mouth of Notoway River. The County of Isle of Wight begins about 3 miles to the East of this River, parted from Nansimond by a dividing Line only. We pitch't our Tent, & flatter'd ourselves we shou'd be secure from the disturber of our Peace one Night more, but we were mistaken for the Stragglers came to us after it was dark with some Danger to their Necks, because the Low Grounds near the River were full of Cypress Snaggs as dangerous as so many Cheveaux de Frise. But this deliverance from Danger was not enough to make Firebrand good Humour'd, because we had not been so kind as to rejoice at it.

4. Here we call'd a Council of War, whether we shou'd proceed any farther this season, and we carry'd it by a Majority of votes to run the Line only about 2 Miles beyond this place. Firebrand voted for going on a little longer, tho' he was glad it was carry'd against him. However he thought it gave him an Air of Industry to vote against leaving off so soon, but the Snakes began to be in great Vigour which was an unanswerable Argument for it.

The River was hardly fordable & the Banks very Steep, which made it difficult for our Baggage Horses to pass over it. But thank God we got all well on the other Side without any Damage. We went to a House just by the River-Side, belonging to a Man, who learnedly call'd himself Carolus Anderson, where we christen'd his child. Then we proceeded to Mr Kinchin's a Man of Figure in these parts, & his Wife a much better Figure than he. They both did their utmost to entertain us & our People in the best Manner. We pitch't our Tent in the Orchard, where the Blossoms of the Apple Trees mended the Air very much. There Meanwell & I lay; but Firebrand & his Flatterers stuck close to the House. The Surveyors crost this River 3 times with the Line in the Distance of 2½ Miles, & left off about half a Mile to the Northward of this Place.

5. Our Surveyors made an Elegant Plat of our Line, from Cora-tuck Inlet to the Place where they left off, containing the Distance of 73 Miles & 13 Polls. Of this exact Copys were made, & being carefully examin'd were both Sign'd by the Commissioners of each Colony. This Plat was chiefly made by Astrolabe, but one of the Copys was taken by Plausible; but Orion was content with a Copy which the Parson took for him. However he deliver'd me the minutes which he had kept of our Proceedings by Order of the Commissioners. The poor Chaplain was the common Butt at which all our Company aim'd their profane Wit, & gave him the Title of Dear Pipp, because instead of a Prick't Line, he had been so maidenly as to call it a Pipp't Line. I left the Company in good time, taking as little pleasure in their low Wit, as in their low liquor which was Rum Punch. Here we discharg'd 6 of the Men, that were near their own Habitations.

6. We paid our Scores, settled our Accounts, & took leave of our Carolina Friends. Firebrand went about 6 Miles with us as far as one Corkers, where we had the grief to part with that sweet temper'd Gentleman, & the Burr that stuck with him Orion. In about ten Miles we reach't a Musterfield near Mr Kindred's House, where Capt Gerald was exercising his Company. There were Girls enough come to see this Martial Appearance to form another Company, & Beauty's enough among them to make Officers of. Here we call'd & Christen'd 2 Children, and offered to marry as many of the Wenches as had got Sweethearts, but they were not ripe for Execution. Then we proceeded ten Miles farther to Bolton's Ferry, where we past Nottoway River at Mr Symonds's Quarter. From hence we intended to proceed to Nottaway Town to satisfy the Curiosity of some of our Company, but loseing our Way we wander'd to Richard Parkers Plantation, where we had formerly met with very kind Entertainment. Our Eyes were entertain'd as well as our Stomachs by the Charms of pretty Sally the Eldest Daughter of the Family.

7. This being Sunday we had a Sermon to which very few of the Neighbours resorted, because they wanted timely Notice. However some good Christians came & amongst them Molly Izzard the smartest Damsel in these Parts. Meanwell made this Girle very Vain by saying sweet things to her, but Sally was more engaging, whose wholesome Flesh & Blood, neither had nor needed any Ornament. Nevertheless in the After-noon we cou'd find in our Hearts to change these fair Beauty's for the Copper Colour'd Ones of Nottaway Towne. Thither we went having given Notice by a Runner that we were coming, that the Indians might be at home to entertain us. Our Landlord shew'd us the way, and the Scouts had no sooner spy'd us, but they gave Notice of our Approach, to the whole Town, by perpetual Whoops & Crys, which to a Stranger sound very dismal. This call'd their great Men to the Fort, where we

alighted, & were conducted to the best Cabins. All the Furniture of those Appartments was Hurdles cover'd with clean Mats. The Young Men had painted themselves in a Hideous Manner, not for Beauty, but Terrour, & in that Equipage entertain'd us with some of their War Dances. The Ladies had put on all their Ornaments to charm us, but the whole Winter's Dirt was so crusted on their Skins, that it requir'd a strong appetite to accost them. Whatever we were, Our Men were not quite so nice, but were hunting after them all Night. But tho' Meanwell might perhaps want Inclinations to these sad-colour'd Ladys, yet curiousity made him try the difference between them & other Women, to the dis-obligation of his Ruffles, which betray'd what he had been doing. Instead of being entertain'd by these Indians, we entertain'd them with Bacon & Rum, which they accepted of very kindly, the Ladys as well as the Men. They offer'd us no Bedfellows, according to the good Indian fashion, which we had reason to take unkindly. Only the Queen of Weynoke told Steddy that her Daughter had been at his Service if She had not been too Young. Some Indian Men were lurking all Night about our Cabin, with the felonious intent to pilfer what they cou'd lay their hands upon, & their Dogs slunk into us in the Night, & eat up what remain'd of our Provisions.

8. When we were drest, Meanwell & I visited most of the Prin-cesses at their own Appartments, but the Smoke was so great there, the Fire being made in the middle of the Cabbins, that we were not able to see their Charms. Prince James' Princess sent my Wife a fine Basket of her own making, with the Expectation of receiving from her some present of ten times its Value. An Indian Present like those made to Princess, is only a Liberality put out to Interest, & a bribe placed to the greatest Advantage. I cou'd discern by some of our Gentlemen's Linnen, discolour'd by the Soil of the Indian Ladys, that they had been con-vincing themselves in the point of their having no furr. About Ten we march't out of the Town, some of the Indians giving us a Volley of small Arms at our departure. We drank our Chocolate at one Jones's about 4 Miles from the Town, & then proceeded over Black-Water Bridge to Colo Henry Harrisons, where we were very handsomely entertain'd, & congratulated one another upon our Return into Christendome.

9. We scrubb'd off our Indian dirt, & refresht our selves with clean Linnen. After a plentifull Breakfast, we took our Leave, & set our Faces towards Westover. By the way we met Boller Cocke & his Lady, who told me my Family was well, Heaven be prais'd; When we came to the New Church near Warren's Mill, Steddy drew up his Men, & harangued them in the following Manner. "Friends & Fellow Travellers, It is a great Satisfaction to me, that after so many difficultys & Fatigues, you are return'd in safety to the place where I first Join'd you. I am much oblidg'd to you for the great readiness & Vigour you have shew'd

in the business we went about, & I must do you all, the Justice to declare, that you have not only done your Duty but also done it with
Cheerfullness & Affection. . . ."

39. WILLIAM SMITH, *HISTORY OF NEW YORK*, 1757*

*William Smith (1728–93) was a conservative leader in the early
phases of the Revolution who, disgusted with the radical changes in the
old order, turned Tory in 1780 and fled to England in 1783.*

*Born in New York and educated at Yale, he was a lawyer by
profession, and a student of history, the classics, and Newtonian mathematics by predilection. A brilliant man, he turned out a book of literary
criticism at the age of sixteen, and between 1751 and 1753 he collaborated with William Livingston and John Morin Scott to produce essays for* The Independent Reflector. *This New York magazine was one of
three published in the colonies, and the most successful because of the
controversial articles it contained, one of which Smith extensively quotes
below.*

*As history, Smith's work is marred by his personal yet pun-
gently amusing barbs aimed at historical figures and contemporary
enemies, one of whom described him as "a most profound dissembler . . .
a noted flatterer, [and] a great sycophant." Contemporary historians have
noted that "more sympathetic observers were impressed with his charm,
grace, and urbanity." The narrative of his* History of New York *is chiefly
political; although he did not ignore social history, he undervalued it,
and in the following relegated it to an appendix which ironically is
acclaimed by present-day historians.*

Chapter II.
Of the Inhabitants

This province is not so populous as some may have imagined.
Scarce a third part of it is under Cultivation. The colony of *Connecticut*,
which is vastly inferior to this in its extent, contains, according to a
late authentic enquiry, above 133,000 inhabitants, and has a militia of
27,000 Men; but the militia of New-York, according to the general estimate, does not exceed 18,000. The whole number of souls is computed
at 100,000.

Many have been the discouragements to the Settlement of this
Colony. The *French* and *Indian* Irruptions, to which we have always

* William Smith, *History of New York* (London: Thomas Wilcox, 1757), pp.
207–12.

been exposed, have driven many families into *New-Jersey*. At home, the *British* acts for the Transportation of felons, have brought all the *American* colonies into Discredit with the industrious and honest Poor, both in the Kingdoms of *Great-Britain* and *Ireland*. The mischievious tendency of those laws was shown in a late paper, which it may not be improper to lay before the reader.

(The Independent Reflector)

It is too well known that, in Pursuance of divers Acts of parliament, great numbers of Fellows who have forfeited their Lives to the Public, for the most atrocious crimes, are annually transported from home to these plantations. Very surprising one would think, that thieves, burglars, pickpockets, and Cutpurses, and a Herd of the most flagitious Banditti upon earth, should be sent as agreeable Companions to us! That the supreme Legislature did intend a Transportation to *America*, for a Punishment of these Villains, I verily believe: but so great is the Mistake, that confident I am, they are thereby, on the contrary, highly rewarded. For what, in God's Name, can be more agreeable to a penurious wretch, driven, through necessity, to seek a Livelihood by breaking of Houses, and robbing upon the King's Highway, than to be saved from the Halter, redeemed from the stench of a gaol and transported, Passage free, into a Country, where, being unknown, no Man can reproach him with his Crimes; where Labour is high, a little of which will maintain him; and where all his Expenses will be moderate and low. There is scarce a thief in *England*, that would not rather be transported than hanged. Life in any Condition, but that of extreme Misery, will be preferred to Death. As long, therefore, as there remains this wide Door of Escape, the Number of Thieves and Robbers at Home will perpetually multiply, and their Depredations be incessantly reiterated.

But the acts were intended, *for the better peopling the Colonies*. And will Thieves and Murderers be conducive to that End? What Advantage can we reap from a Colony of unrestrainable Renegadoes? will they exalt the Glory of the Crown? or rather, will not the Dignity of the most illustrious Monarch in the World be sullied by a Province of subjects so lawless, detestable, and ignominious? Can Agriculture be promoted, when the *wild Boar of the Forest breaks down our Hedges and pulls up our Vines*? Will trade flourish, or Manufactures be encouraged, where Property is made the Spoil of such who are too idle to work, and wicked enough to murder and steal?

. . . . *But the Colonies must be peopled*. Agreed: and will the Transportation Acts ever have that Tendency? No; they work the contrary Way, and counteract their own Design. We want People 'tis true, but not Villains, ready at any Time, encouraged by impunity, and habituated upon the slightest occasions, to cut a Man's Throat for a small part of his Property. The Delights of such Company is a noble Inducement, indeed, to the honest Poor, to convey themselves into a strange country. Amidst all our Plenty, they will have enough to exercise their Virtues, and stand in no Need of the Association of such as will prey upon their Property, and gorge themselves with the Blood of the

Adventurers. They came over in Search of Happiness; rather than starve will live any where, and would be glad to be excused from so afflicting an Antepart of the Torments of Hell. In Reality, Sir, these very Laws, though otherwise designed, have turned out, in the End, the most effectual Expedients that the Art of Man could have contrived, to prevent the Settlement of these remote Parts of the King's Dominions. They have actually taken away almost every Encouragement to so laudable a Design. I appeal to Facts. The Body of the *English* are struck with Terror at the Thought of coming over to us, not because they have a vast Ocean to cross, or leave behind them their Friends; or that the Country is new and uncultivated: but from the shocking Ideas, the Mind must necessarily form, of the Company of inhuman Savages, and the more terrible Herd of exiled Malefactors. There are Thousands of honest Men, labouring in *Europe*, at four pence a Day, starving in spite of all their Efforts, a dead Weight to the respective Parishes to which they belong; who, without any other Qualifications than common Sense, Health, and Strength, might accumulate Estates among us, as many have done already. These, and not the others, are the Men that should be sent over for the *better peopling the Plantations. Great-Britain* and *Ireland*, in their present Circumstances, are overstocked with them; and he who would immortalize himself, for a *Lover of Mankind*, should concert a scheme for the transportation of the industriously honest abroad, and the immediate Punishment of Rogues and Plunderers at Home. The pale-faced, half-clad, meagre, and starved skeletons, that are seen in every Village of those Kingdoms, call loudly for the Patroit's generous Aid. The Plantations too, would thank him for his Assistance, in obtaining the Repeal of those Laws which, though otherwise intended by the Legislature, have so unhappily proved injurious to his own Country, and ruinous to us. . . .

The Bigotry and Tyranny of some of our Governors, together with the great Extent of their Grants, may also be considered among the Discouragements against the full Settlement of the Province. Most of these Gentlemen coming over with no other View than to raise their own Fortunes, issued extravagant Patents, charged with small Quit-Rents, to such as were able to serve them in the Assembly; and these Patentees, being generally Men of Estates, have rated their Lands so exorbitantly high, that very few poor Persons could either purchase or lease them. Add to all these, that the *New-England* planters have always been disaffected to the *Dutch*; nor was there, after the Surrender, any foreign Accession from the *Netherlands*. The Province being thus poorly inhabited, the Price of Labour became so enormously enhanced, that we have been constrained to import Negroes from *Africa*, who are employed in all Kinds of Servitude and Trades.

English is the most prevailing Language amongst us, but not a little corrupted by the *Dutch* Dialect, which is still so much used in some Counties, that the Sheriffs find it difficult to obtain Persons, sufficiently acquainted with the English Tongue, to serve as Jurors in the Courts of Law.

The Manners of the People differ as well as their Language. In *Suffolk* and *Queen's* County, the first settlers of which were either Natives of *England*, or the immediate Descendants of such as begun the Plantations in the Eastern Colonies, their Customs are similar to those prevailing in the *English* Counties from whence they originally sprang. In the City of *New York*, through our Intercourse with the *Europeans*, we follow the *London* Fashions; though, by the Time we adopt them, they become disused in *England*. Our Affluence, during the late War, introduced a Degree of Luxury in Tables, Dress, and Furniture, with which we were before unacquainted. But still we are not so gay a People as our Neighbours in *Boston*, and several of the Southern Colonies. The *Dutch* counties, in some Measure, follow the Example of *New-York*, but still retain many Modes peculiar to the *Hollanders*.

The city of *New-York* consists principally of Merchants, Shopkeepers, and Tradesmen, who sustain the Reputation of honest, punctual, and fair Dealers. With Respect to Riches, there is not so great an Inequality amongst us as is common in *Boston* and some other Places. Every Man of Industry and Integrity has it in his Power to live well, and many are the Instances of Persons who came here distressed by their Poverty, who now enjoy easy and plentiful Fortunes.

New-York is one of the most social Places on the Continent. The Men collect themselves into weekly Evening Clubs. The Ladies, in Winter, are frequently entertained either at Concerts of Music or Assemblies, and make a very good Appearance. They are comely and dress well, and scarce any of them have distorted Shapes. Tinctured with a *Dutch* education, they manage their Families with becoming Parsimony, good Providence, and singular Neatness. The Practice of extravagant Gaming, common to the fashionable Part of the fair Sex, in some Places, is a Vice with which my Countrywomen cannot justly be charged. There is nothing they so generally neglect as Reading, and indeed all the Arts for the Improvement of the Mind, in which, I confess, we have set them the Example. They are modest, temperate, and charitable; naturally sprightly, sensible, and good-humoured; and, by the Helps of a more elevated Education, would possess all the Accomplishments desirable in the Sex. Our Schools are in the lowest Order, the Instructors want Instruction; and, through a long shameful Neglect of all the Arts and Sciences, our common Speech is extremely corrupt, and the Evidences of a bad Taste, both as to Thought and Language, are visible in all our Proceedings, public and private.

The People, both in Town and Country, are sober, industrious, and hospitable, though intent upon Gain. The richer Sort keep very plentiful Tables, abounding with great Varieties of Flesh, Fish, Fowl, and all Kinds of Vegetables. The common Drinks are Beer, Cider, weak

Punch, and *Madeira* Wine. For Dessert, we have Fruits in vast Plenty, of different Kinds and various Species.

Gentlemen of Estates rarely reside in the Country, and hence few or no Experiments have yet been made in Agriculture. The farms being large, our Husbandmen, for that Reason, have little Recourse to Art for manuring and improving their lands; but it is said, that Nature has furnished us with sufficient Helps, whenever Necessity calls us to use them. It is much owing to the Disproportion between the Number of our Inhabitants, and the vast Tracts remaining still to be settled, that we have not, as yet, entered upon scarce any other Manufactures than such as are indispensably necessary for our Home Convenience. Felt-making, which is perhaps the most natural of any we could fall upon, was begun some Years ago, and Hats were exported to the *West-Indies* with great Success, till lately prohibited by an Act of Parliament.

The Inhabitants of this Colony are in general healthy and robust, taller but shorter lived than *Europeans*, and, both with Respect to their Minds and Bodies, arrive sooner to an Age of Maturity. Breathing a serene, dry Air, they are more sprightly in their natural Tempers than the People of *England*, and hence Instances of Suicide are here very uncommon. The History of our Diseases belongs to a Profession with which I am very little acquainted. Few Physicians amongst us are eminent for their Skill. Quacks abound like Locusts in *Egypt*, and too many have recommended themselves to a full Practice and profitable Subsistence. This is the less to be wondered at, as the Profession is under no Kind of Regulation. Loud as the Call is, to our Shame be it remembered, we have no Law to protect the Lives of the King's Subjects from the Malpractice of Pretenders. Any Man at his Pleasure sets up for Physician, Apothecary, and Chirurgeon. No Candidates are either examined or licensed, or even sworn to fair Practice. . . .

40. BENJAMIN FRANKLIN, ON STYLE AND THE WAY TO WEALTH, 1757[*]

Americans of the mid-eighteenth century had neither the patience nor the time to read the citation-laden and latinized prose of their fathers. Benjamin Franklin, as essayist and newspaper editor, trained himself in the new rhetoric by reading and emulating the informal gossipy pieces of Addison and Steele in the London Spectator. *The resulting "plaine*

[*] Jared Sparks, ed., From "Poor Richard's Almanack" in *The Works of Benjamin Franklin* (Boston: Hilliard Gray and Company, 1840), Vol. II, p. 553; Benjamin Smyth, *The Writings of Benjamin Franklin* (New York: Macmillan, 1907), Vol. III, pp. 407–11.

style" and homely advice and wit of his Poor Richard's Almanack *gained him wide acceptance among the colonists.*

On Style

How shall we judge of the goodness of a writing? Or what qualities should a writing have to be good and perfect in its kind?

Answer. To be good, it ought to have a tendency to benefit the reader, by improving his virtue or his knowledge. But, not regarding the intention of the author, the method should be just; that is, it should proceed regularly from things known to things unknown, distinctly and clearly without confusion. The words used should be the most expressive that the language affords, provided that they are the most generally understood. Nothing should be expressed in two words that can be as well expressed in one; that is, no synonymes should be used, or very rarely, but the whole should be as short as possible, consistent with clearness. The words should be so placed as to be agreeable to the ear in reading; summarily, it should be *smooth, clear,* and *short.* For the contrary qualities are displeasing.

But, taking the query otherwise, an ill man may write an ill thing well; that is, having an ill design, he may use the properest style and arguments (considering who are to be readers) to attain his ends. In this sense, that is best wrote, which is best adapted for obtaining the end of the writer.

The Way to Wealth
Preface to Poor Richard Improved: 1757

COURTEOUS READER

I have heard that nothing gives an Author so great Pleasure, as to find his Works respectfully quoted by other learned Authors. This Pleasure I have seldom enjoyed; for tho' I have been, if I may say it without Vanity, an *eminent Author* of Almanacks annually now a full Quarter of a Century, my Brother Authors in the same Way, for what Reason I know not, have ever been very sparing in the Applauses, and no other Author has taken the least Notice of me, so that did not my Writings produce me some solid *Pudding*, the great Deficiency of *Praise* would have quite discouraged me.

I concluded at length, that the People were the best Judges of my Merit; for they buy my Works; and besides, in my Rambles, where I am not personally known, I have frequently heard one or other of my Adages repeated, with *as Poor Richard says*, at the End on 't; this gave me some Satisfaction, as it showed not only that my Instructions were regarded, but discovered likewise some Respect for my Authority; and I own, that to encourage the Practice of remembering and repeating those wise Sentences, I have sometimes *quoted myself* with great Gravity.

Judge, then how much I must have been gratified by an Incident I am going to relate to you. I stopt my Horse lately where a great Number of People were collected at a Vendue of Merchant Goods. The Hour of Sale not being come, they were conversing on the Badness of the Times and one of the Company call'd to a plain clean old Man, with white Locks, 'Pray, Father Abraham, what think you of the Times? Won't these heavy Taxes quite ruin the Country? How shall we be ever able to pay them? What would you advise us to?' Father *Abraham* stood up, and reply'd, 'If you'd have my Advice, I'll give it you in short for *A Word to the Wise is enough*, and *many Words won't fill a Bushel*, as *Poor Richard* says. They join'd in desiring him to speak his Mind, and gathering round him, he proceeded as follows;

'Friends,' says he, and Neighbours, 'the Taxes are indeed very heavy, and if those laid on by the Government were the only Ones we had to pay, we might more easily discharge them; but we have many others, and much more grievous to some of us. We are taxed twice as much by our *Idleness*, three times as much by our *Pride*, and four times as much by our *Folly*; and from these Taxes the Commissioners cannot ease or deliver us by allowing an Abatement. However let us hearken to good Advice, and something may be done for us; *God helps them that help themselves*, as *Poor Richard* says, in his Almanack of 1733.

It would be thought a hard Government that should tax its People one-tenth Part of their *Time*, to be employed in its Service. But *Idleness* taxes many of us much more, if we reckon all that is spent in absolute *Sloth*, or doing of nothing, with that which is spent in idle Employments or Amusements, that amount to nothing. *Sloth*, by bringing on Diseases, absolutely shortens Life. *Sloth, like Rust, consumes faster than Labour wears; while the used Key is always bright*, as *Poor Richard* says. *But dost thou love Life, then do not squander Time, for that's the stuff Life is made of*, as *Poor Richard* says. How much more than is necessary do we spend in sleep, forgetting that *The sleeping Fox catches no Poultry*, and that *There will be sleeping enough in the Grave*, as *Poor Richard* says.

If *Time be of all Things the most precious, wasting Time must be*, as *Poor Richard* says, *The greatest Prodigality*; since, as he elsewhere tells us, *Lost Time is never found again; and what we call Time enough, always proves little enough*: Let us then up and be doing, and doing to the Purpose; so by Diligence shall we do more with less Perplexity. *Sloth makes all Things difficult, but Industry all easy*, as *Poor Richard* says; and *He that riseth late must trot all Day, and shall scarce overtake his Business at Night*; while *Laziness travels so slowly, that Poverty soon overtakes him,* as we read in *Poor Richard,* who adds, *Drive thy Business, let not that drive thee;* and *Early to Bed, and early to rise, makes a Man healthy, wealthy, and wise.*

So what signifies *wishing* and *hoping* for better Times. We may make these Times better, if we bestir ourselves. *Industry need not wish,* as *Poor Richard* says, *and he that lives upon Hope will die fasting. There are no Gains without Pains; then Help Hands, for I have no Lands,* or if I have, they are smartly taxed. And, as *Poor Richard* likewise observes, *He that hath a Trade hath an Estate; and he that hath a Calling, hath an Office of Profit and Honour*; but then the *Trade* must be worked at, and the *Calling* well followed, or neither the *Estate* nor the *Office* will enable us to pay our Taxes. If we are industrious, we shall never starve; for as *Poor Richard* says, *At the working Man's House Hunger looks in, but dares not enter.* Nor will the Bailiff or the Constable enter, for *Industry pays Debts, while Despair encreaseth them,* says *Poor Richard.* What though you have found no Treasure, nor has any rich Relation left you a Legacy, *Diligence is the Mother of Goodluck* as *Poor Richard* says *and God gives all Things to Industry. Then plough deep, while Sluggards sleep, and you shall have Corn to sell and to keep,* says *Poor Dick.* Work while it is called To-day, for you know not how much you may be hindered To-morrow, which makes *Poor Richard* say, *One today is worth two To-morrows,* and farther, *Have you somewhat to do Tomorrow, do it Today.* If you were a Servant, would you not be ashamed that a good Master should catch you idle? Are you then your own Master, *be ashamed to catch yourself idle,* as *Poor Dick* says. When there is so much to be done for yourself, your Family, your Country, and your gracious King, be up by Peep of Day; *Let not the Sun look down and say, Inglorious here he lies.* Handle your Tools without Mittens; remember that *The Cat in Gloves catches no Mice,* as *Poor Richard* says. 'Tis true there is much to be done, and perhaps you are weak-handed, but stick to it steadily; and you will see great Effects, for *Constant Dropping wears away Stones,* and by *Diligence and Patience the Mouse ate in two the Cable;* and *Little Strokes fell great Oaks,* as *Poor Richard* says in his Almanack, the Year I cannot just now remember.

5

Economic Theory and Practice

41. BENJAMIN FRANKLIN, *A MODEST ENQUIRY INTO THE NATURE AND NECESSITY OF A PAPER CURRENCY*, 1729[*]

Industrious colonial America produced no true economic theorist. Yet Franklin's essay calling for an issue of paper money—always in short supply in the colonies—hints of Adam Smith and the Classical School of economists. In this piece, he does not invoke doctrines of free trade or seek the destruction of mercantilism, but he does emphasize the productivity and value of labor. Clearly, he disagrees with the mercantilists about the importance of the accumulation of precious metals and a favorable balance of trade.

There is a certain proportionate Quantity of Money requisite to carry on the Trade of a Country freely and currently; More than which would be of no Advantage in Trade, and Less, if much less, exceedingly deterimental to it.

This leads us to the following general Considerations.

First. *A great Want of Money, in any Trading Country, occasions Interest to be at a very high Rate.* And here it may be observed, that it is impossible by any Laws to restrain Men from giving and receiving exorbitant Interest, where Money is suitably scarce: For he that wants Money will find out Ways to give 10 *per cent*, when he cannot have it for less, altho' the Law forbids to take more than 6 *per cent*. Now the Interest of Money being high is prejudicial to a Country several Ways: It makes Land bear a low Price, because few Men will lay out their

[*] Smyth, *op. cit.*, Vol. II, 133–155. See also Benjamin Franklin, *A Modest Enquiry into the Nature and Necessity of a Paper Currency* . . . (Philadelphia: New Printing Office, 1729).

Money in Land, when they can make a much greater Profit by lending it
out upon Interest. And much less will Men be inclined to venture their
Money at Sea, when they can, without Risque or Hazard, have a great
and certain Profit by keeping it at home; thus Trade is discouraged. And
if in two Neighbouring Countries the Traders of one, by Reason of a
greater Plenty of Money, can borrow it to trade with at a lower Rate
than the Traders of the other, they will infallibly have the Advantage,
and get the greatest Part of that Trade into their own Hands; For he
that trades with Money he hath borrowed at 8 or 10 *per cent*, cannot hold
Market with him that borrows his money at 6 or 4. On the contrary, *a
plentiful Currency will occasion Interest to be low*: And this will be an
Inducement to many to lay out their money in Lands, rather than put it
out to Use, by which means Land will begin to rise in Value and bear
a better Price. And at the same Time it will tend to enliven Trade exceedingly, because People will find more Profit in employing their Money
that Way than in Usury; and many that understand Business very well,
but have not a Stock sufficient of their own, will be encouraged to borrow Money to trade with, when they can have it at moderate Interest.

Secondly. *Want of Money in a Country reduces the Price of that
Part of its Produce which is used in Trade*: Because, Trade being discouraged by it as above, there is a much less Demand for that Produce.
And this is another Reason why Land in such a Case will be low, especially where the Staple Commodity of the Country is the immediate
Produce of the Land; because, that Produce being low, fewer people find
an Advantage in Husbandry, or the Improvement of Land. On the
contrary, *a Plentiful Currency will occasion the Trading Produce to bear
a good Price*; because, Trade being encouraged and advanced by it, there
will be a much greater Demand for that Produce; which will be a great
Encouragement of Husbandry and Tillage, and consequently make Land
more valuable, for that many People would apply themselves to Husbandry, who probably might otherwise have sought some more profitable
Employment.

As we have already experienced how much the Increase of our
Currency, by what Paper Money has been made, has encouraged our
Trade, particularly to instance only in one Article, *Ship-Building*, it may
not be amiss to observe under this Head, what a great Advantage it
must be to us as a Trading Country, that has Workmen and all the
Materials proper for that Business within itself, to have Ship-Building
as much as possible advanced: for every Ship, that is built here for the
English Merchants, gains the Province her clear Value in Gold and
Silver, which must otherwise have been sent Home for Returns in her
Stead; and likewise, every Ship, built in and belonging to the Province,
not only saves the Province her first Cost, but all the Freight, Wages, and
Provisions she ever makes or requires as long as she lasts; provided Care

is taken to make This her *Pay-Port*, and that she always takes Provisions with her for the whole Voyage, which may easily be done. And how considerable an Article this is yearly in our Favour, every one, the least acquainted with mercantile Affairs, just needs be sensible; for, if we could not Build ourselves, we must either purchase so many Vessels as we want from other Countries, or else Hire them to carry our Produce to Market, which would be more expensive than Purchasing, and on many other Accounts exceedingly to our Loss. Now as Trade in general will decline where there is not a plentiful Currency, so Ship-Building must certainly of Consequence decline where Trade is declining.

Thirdly. *Want of Money in a Country discourages Labouring and Handicrafts Men (which are the chief Strength and Support of a People) from coming to settle in it, and induces many that were settled to leave the Country, and seek Entertainment and Employment in other Places, where they can be better paid.* For what can be more disheartning to an industrious labouring Man than this, that, after he hath earned his Bread with the Sweat of his Brows, he must spend as much Time, and have near as much Fatigue in getting it, as he had to earn it? *And nothing makes more bad Paymasters than a general Scarcity of Money.* And here again is a Third Reason for Land's bearing a low Price in such a Country, because Land always increases in Value in Proportion with the Increase of the People settling on it, there being so many more Buyers; and its Value will infallibly be diminished, if the Number of its Inhabitants diminish. On the contrary, *a Plentiful Currency will encourage great Numbers of labouring and Handicrafts Men to come and Settle in the Country*, by the same Reason that a Want of it will discourage and drive them out. Now the more Inhabitants, the greater Demand for Land (as is said above), upon which it must necessarily rise in Value, and bear a better Price. The same may be said of the Value of House-Rent, which will be advanced for the same Reasons; and, by the Increase of Trade and Riches, People will be enabled to pay greater Rents. Now the value of House-Rent rising, and Interest becoming low, many that in a Scarcity of Money practiced Usuary, will probably be more inclined to Building; which will likewise sensibly enliven Business in any Place; it being an Advantage not only to *Brickmakers, Bricklayers, Masons, Carpenters, Joiners, Glaziers*, and several other Trades immediately employed by Building, but likewise to *Farmers, Brewers, Bakers, Taylors, Shoemakers, Shopkeepers*, and, in short, to every one that they lay their Money out with.

Fourthly. *Want of Money in such a Country as ours, occasions a Greater Consumption of English and European Goods, in Proportion to the Number of the People, than there would otherwise be.* Because Merchants and Traders, by whom abundance of Artificers and labouring Men are employed, finding their other Affairs require what Money they can get into their hands, oblige those who work for them to take one half or perhaps two-thirds Goods in Pay. By this Means a greater Quantity of Goods are disposed of, and to a greater Value; because Working-Men and their Families are thereby induced to be more profuse and extravagant in fine Apparel and the like, than they would be if they were obliged to pay ready Money for such Things after they had earn'd and received it, or if such Goods were not imposed upon them, of which they can make no other Use. For such People cannot send the Goods they are paid with to a Foreign Market, without losing considerably by having them sold for less than they stand 'em in here; neither can they easily dispose of them at Home, because their Neighbours are generally supplied in the same Manner. But how unreasonable would it be, if some of those very Men who *have been a Means* of thus forcing People into unnecessary Expense, should be the first and most earnest in accusing them of *Pride and Prodigality.* Now, tho' this extraordinary Consumption of Foreign Commodities may be a Profit to particular Men, yet the Country in general grows poorer by it apace. On the contrary, As *a plentiful Currency will occasion a less consumption of European Goods, in proportion to the Number of the People,* so it will be a means of making the Balance of our Trade more equal than it now is, if it does not give it in our Favour; because our own Produce will be encouraged at the same Time. And it is to be observed, that, tho' less Foreign Commodities are consumed in Proportion to the Number of People, yet this will be no Disadvantage to the Merchant, because the Number of People increasing, will occasion an increasing Demand of more Foreign Goods in the Whole.

The foregoing Paragraphs being well considered, we shall naturally be led to draw the following Conclusions with Regard to what Persons will probably be for or against Emitting a large Additional Sum of Paper Bills in this Province.

1. Since Men will always be powerfully influenced in their Opinions and Actions by what appears to be their particular Interest: Therefore all those, who, wanting Courage to venture in Trade, now practise Lending Money on Security for exorbitant Interest, which, in a Scarcity of Money will be done, notwithstanding the Law, I say all such will probably be against a large Addition to our present Stock of Paper Money; because a plentiful Currency will lower Interest, and make it common to lend on less Security.

2. All those who are Possessors of large Sums of Money, and are

disposed to purchase Land, which is attended with a great and sure Advantage in a growing Country as this is; I say, the Interest of all such Men will encline them to oppose a large Addition to our Money. Because their Wealth is now continually increasing by the large Interest they receive, which will enable them (if they can keep Land from rising) to purchase More some time hence than they can at present; and in the mean time all Trade being discouraged, not only those who borrow of them, but the Common People in general will be impoverished, and consequently obliged to sell More Land for less Money than they will do at present. And yet, after such Men are possessed of as much Land as they can purchase, it will then be their Interest to have Money made plentiful, because that will immediately make Land rise in Value in *their* Hands. Now it ought not to be wonder'd at, if People from the Knowledge of a Man's Interest do sometimes make a true Guess at his Designs; for *Interest*, they say, *will not Lie.*

3. Lawyers, and others concerned in Court Business, will probably many of them be against a plentiful Currency; because People in that Case will have less Occasion to run in Debt, and consequently less Occasion to go to Law and Sue one another for their Debts. Tho' I know some even among these Gentlemen, that regard the Publick Good before their own apparent private Interest.

4. All those who are any way Dependants on such Persons as are above mentioned, whether as holding Offices, as Tenants, or as Debtors, must at least *appear* to be against a large Addition; because, if they do not, they must sensibly feel their present Interest hurt. And besides these, there are, doubtless, many wellmeaning Gentlemen and Others, who, without any immediate private Interest of their own in View, are against making such an Addition, thro' an Opinion they may have of the Honesty and sound Judgement of some of their Friends that oppose it (perhaps for the Ends aforesaid), without having given it any thorough Consideration themselves. And thus it is no Wonder if there is a *powerful* Party on that Side.

On the other Hand, those who are Lovers of Trade, and delight to see Manufactures encouraged, will be for having a large Addition to our Currency: For they very well know, that People will have little Heart to advance Money in Trade, when what they can get is scarce sufficient to purchase Necessaries, and supply their Families with Provisions. Much less will they lay it out in advancing new Manufactures; nor is it possible new Manufactures should turn to any Account, where there is not Money to pay the Workmen, who are discouraged by being paid in Goods, because it is a great Disadvantage to them.

Again. Those, who are truly for the Proprietor's Interest (and have no separate Views of their own that are predominant), will be heartily for a large Addition: Because, as I have shewn above, Plenty of Money will for several Reasons make Land rise in Value exceedingly: And I appeal to those immediately concerned for the Proprietor in the Sale of his Lands, whether Land has not risen very much since the first Emission of what Paper Currency we now have, and even by its Means. Now we all know the Proprietary has great Quantities to sell.

And since a Plentiful Currency will be so great a Cause of advancing this Province in Trade and Riches, and increasing the Number of its People; which, tho' it will not sensibly lessen the Inhabitants of *Great Britain*, will occasion a much greater Vent and Demand for their Commodities here; and allowing that the Crown is the more powerful for its Subjects increasing in Wealth and Number, I cannot think it the Interest of *England* to oppose us in making as great a Sum of Paper Money here, as we, who are the best Judges of our own Necessities, find convenient. And if I were not sensible that the Gentlemen of Trade in *England*, to whom we have already parted with our Silver and Gold, are misinformed of our Circumstances, and therefore endeavour to have our Currency stinted to what it now is, I should think the Government at Home had some Reasons for discouraging and impoverishing this Province, which we are not acquainted with.

It remains now that we enquire, *Whether a large Addition to our Paper Currency will not make it sink in Value very much*. And here it will be requisite that we first form just Notions of the Nature and Value of Money in general.

As Providence has so ordered it, that not only different Countries, but even different Parts of the same Country, have their peculiar most suitable Productions; and likewise that different Men have Geniuses adapted to Variety of different Arts and Manufactures, Therefore Commerce, or the Exchange of one Commodity or Manufacture for another, is highly convenient and beneficial to Mankind. As for Instance, A may be skilful in the Art of Making Cloth, and B understand the raising of Corn; A wants Corn, and B Cloth; upon which they make an Exchange with each other for as much as each has Occasion, to the mutual Advantage and Satisfaction of both.

But as it would be very tedious, if there were no other Way of general Dealing, but by an immediate Exchange of Commodities; because a Man that had Corn to dispose of, and wanted Cloth for it, might perhaps, in his Search for a Chapman to deal with, meet with twenty People that had Cloth to dispose of, but wanted no Corn; and with twenty others that wanted his Corn, but had no Cloth to suit him with; to remedy such Inconveniences, and facilitate Exchange, Men have invented MONEY, properly called a *Medium of Exchange*, because through or by its Means Labour is exchanged for Labour, or one Commodity for another. And whatever particular Thing Men have agreed to make this

Medium of, whether Gold, Silver, Copper, or Tobacco, it is, to those who possess it (if they want any Thing), that very Thing which they want, because it will immediately procure it for them. It is Cloth to him that wants Cloth, and Corn to those that want Corn; and so of all other Necessaries, it *is* whatsoever it will procure. Thus he who had Corn to dispose of, and wanted to purchase Cloth with it, might sell his Corn, for its Value in this general Medium, to one who wanted Corn but had no Cloth; and with this Medium he might purchase Cloth of him that wanted no Corn, but perhaps some other Thing, as Iron it may be, which this medium will immediately procure, and so he may be said to have exchanged his Cloth for Iron; and thus the general Exchange is soon performed, to the Satisfaction of all Parties, with abundance of Facility.

For many Ages, those Parts of the World which are engaged in Commerce, have fixed upon Gold and Silver as the chief and most proper Materials for this Medium; they being in themselves valuable Metals for their Fineness, Beauty, and Scarcity. By these, particularly by Silver, it has been usual to value all Things else. But as Silver itself is of no certain permanent Value, being worth more or less according to its Scarcity or Plenty, therefore it seems requisite to fix upon Something else, more proper to be made a *Measure of Values*, and this I take to be *Labour*.

By Labour may the Value of Silver be measured as well as other Things. As, Suppose one Man employed to raise Corn, while another is digging and refining Silver; at the Year's End, or at any other Period of Time, the compleat Produce of Corn, and that of Silver, are the natural Price of each other; and if one be twenty Bushels, and the other twenty Ounces, then an Ounce of that Silver is worth the Labour of raising a Bushel of that Corn. Now if by the Discovery of some nearer, more easy or plentiful Mines, a man may get Forty Ounces of Silver as easily as formerly he did Twenty, and the same Labour is still required to raise Twenty Bushels of Corn, then Two Ounces of Silver will be worth no more than the same Labour of raising one Bushel of Corn, and that Bushel of Corn will be as cheap at two Ounces, as it was before at one, *coeteris paribus*.

Thus the Riches of a Country are to be valued by the Quantity of Labour its Inhabitants are able to purchase, and not by the Quantity of Silver and Gold they possess; which will purchase more or less Labour, and therefore is more or less valuable, as is said before, according to its Scarcity or Plenty. . . .

42. JOHN RUTHERFURD, *IMPORTANCE OF THE COLONIES TO GREAT BRITAIN*, 1761*

John Rutherfurd (1735–82), of Rocky Point and Wilmington, North Carolina, was one of His Majesty's Customs Collectors and a prominent merchant and officeholder. In 1761, when Great Britain was on the verge of triumph over France and Spain and had nearly completed acquisition of an empire greater than Rome's, men on both sides of the Atlantic turned their minds toward the political and economic reorganization of the Empire.

Rutherfurd was a mercantilist who believed this system should benefit the colonies. Parliament, he contended, should not merely regulate but subsidize necessary products which could be produced in America (for example hemp), thereby improving imperial commerce and reducing the need to import items from foreign states. Such a policy would bring mutual prosperity to the colonies and England.

It must be allowed that this nation cannot subsist as a maritime power without importing materials for manufactures, such as hemp, flax, silk, cotton, pot-ashes, various sorts of dying stuffs, bar iron &c. and that hitherto, in order to obtain such articles in sufficient quantities to supply our manufactures it has cost this nation vast sums yearly in ready money to foreigners, for what is now generally known may be had from our colonies on the continent of North America, on the giving proper encouragement to British merchants to import them.

That for the future, being the growers as well as manufacturers of these valuable articles of commerce within ourselves, we may thereby be enabled not only to save the vast sums that we now yearly pay to foreigners, but also to extend our trade and commerce.

The late czar of Muscovy, who believed that we must have our hemp from him, made a monopoly of it; which, as we are under a necessity of having, ought (in the event of quarrelling with the Russians) to put us on all imaginable care and study how to provide so necessary an article independent of them, lest we should happen to labour under the same necessity as in 1703, for pitch, tar, and turpentine, when the government of Sweden absolutely refused to let us have them for our ready money, otherwise than in their bottoms, at their own prices, and in such quantities as they pleased; . . . This behaviour of the Swedish tar company so raised upon us the price of naval stores, as reduced us to

* John Rutherfurd, "The Importance of the Colonies to Great Britain, 1761" in William K. Boyd, ed., *Some Eighteenth Century Tracts Concerning North Carolina* (Raleigh: North Carolina State Department of Archives and History, 1927), pp. 110–15. Reprinted by permission of the publisher.

the greatest distress, and induced the British Parliament to grant bounties on naval stores imported from our own colonies, which has been the means of lowering the price thereof to less than one third of what we formerly paid the Swedes.

The remembrance of such conduct in the Swedes (now leagued with the French and Russians) ought to put us on our guard against a like necessity, which, if it should happen would be of infinite prejudice to us.

By the 3d and 4th Ann, cap. 18. sect. 8. a bounty was granted on naval stores, including hemp, from the first of January 1705 to the first of January 1714; by the 12th Ann, cap. 9. the same was continued to the first of January 1725; and by the 8th Geo. I. cap. 12. sect. 1. the bounty of 6l. per ton on hemp was only continued till the first of January 1741, when the bounty on hemp expired.

As little hemp was imported when the above acts of Parliament were in force for granting a bounty on the importation thereof from the colonies, many imagine that little or none would be imported, should the Parliament again grant a bounty to encourage the importation thereof from the colonies.

The granting a bounty on naval stores has already had its full effect with regard to pitch, tar, and turpentine; and there seems no reason to doubt, but that the renewal of the bounty on the importation of hemp would have the same advantage result from it: for though no great quantities of hemp were exported between 1705 and 1741, yet it must be considered, that many of the colonies were then in their infancy, and others fully employed in cultivating more valuable branches of commerce, such as tobacco, rice, pitch, tar, and turpentine; but since that time the people in our colonies are greatly increased, and in a fair way of making more tobacco (their principal staple) than can be found vent for; and it is well known that some years since the province of South Carolina made as much rice as could be found sale for, and with the other colonies are now in a fair way of making a sufficient quantity of indigo.

When it is considered the many difficulties those who on their first settling in America must have laboured under, to provide themselves with the conveniences of life, it will not be so much wondered at that they should hitherto have been so backward in cultivating hemp, when even at this time in Britain very few are acquainted with the best manner of preparing it for manufactures.

There are gentlemen now in London, who remember to have seen a quantity of hemp imported from Virginia, which by direction from the Lords of the Admiralty was tried in the King's yards, and found to be as good as any from Russia, or even from Egypt: and since that hemp must be imported, it will certainly be more advantageous to the State to pay money to our own merchants for importing it in our own ships from the colonies, than to pay ready money to strangers for it.

It has been computed, that in the year 1759 about 25,000 tons of hemp were imported from Russia, which (including the duty at the Sound, with the charges) stood the British merchant on board his ship about 18£ per ton, the amount of which is 450,000£. sterling, which is much more than the amount of all the manufactures they receive from Great Britain. It has been reckoned for some years past, that we have not paid less to Russia than 500,000£. sterling in ready money for so much balance in their favour; this may fairly be charged to the article of hemp, which in our present situation as a maritime power, we must have, cost what it will.

In peaceable times the freight of hemp from the Baltic is from 40s. to 45s. per ton, and used to be sold from 18£. to 22£. per ton; in war time freight from thence is from 65s. to 70s. per ton, and now sold from 24£. to 28£. per ton; Does not this look as if they had already risen in their demands upon us? The medium price in peaceable times used to be 20£. the medium price is now 26£. 6£. per ton is too much to be allowed only for the difference betwixt freight and insurance in peace and in war.

The interest of the money now annually paid for hemp, at 5 per cent, will amount to 22,500£. which for six years, being the time humbly proposed to allow 8£. per ton bounty on the importation thereof from the colonies, will amount to 135,000£. and in that time may be supposed to have taken effect.

It is presumed no true lover of his country will think this paying too dear for inducing the people in the colonies to go upon such a product for merchandize, as at present brings into Russia from Britain, and all others trading with them, above one million yearly; and which would not only have the good effect of saving ready money to the nation, and increase a greater demand of manufactures for the colonies, but would also increase our strength as a maritime power.

Upon the conclusion of this war [French and Indian, 1754–1763], if Canada and those fine countries at the back of our settlements could be ceded to us, there will indeed be room enough to settle vast multitudes of industrious people (which are the real and true strength of a nation); on proper encouragement they without doubt in time may be able to supply us with all the materials for manufactures so much wanted in Britain, and which yearly cost us vast sums; viz. hemp, flax, silk, cotton, and bar iron; and when we are possessed of such countries from whence we can draw such materials (more valuable in the hands of industrious people than mines of gold and silver) we may then indeed be said to be independent of the world in point of trade.

It has been objected, that in the case of our retaining Canada,

&c. the Americans would then be at leisure to manufacture for them-selves, and throw off their dependence on their mother country. .

In answer; This is an object at too great a distance to be dreaded, and cannot be so easily done as some may imagine, who have not thoroughly considered the connections that must and ought to subsist betwixt Great Britain and her colonies; and how much all of them are independent and jealous of each other; and that where interest of money is high and lands cheap (as it is in general in America) labour will always be dear: and further we can be certain, that so long as the American planter can find vent for the produce of his lands to enable him to purchase British manufactures, it will never occur to him to manu-facture, because in every respect it would be contrary to his interest.

It has also been objected, that the settling such vast tracts of land would drain Great Britain of its inhabitants, if we are obliged to keep force and garisons there to guard against the incroachments of the French, &c. this would cost both men and treasure; but if no other forts are necessary than to keep the Indians in awe, so far from draining us of our inhabitants, it would be the means of employing more manu-facturers in Britain than have heretofore been employed in any one period of time.

It cannot be supposed that any persons in Britain in full employ-ment will leave their native country to endure hardships, in order to make a settlement in America; such as are not fully or usefully employed must either go abroad or starve; such, in England, are useless members of society; if they go abroad to America, whether they are employed by others or for themselves, they in some sort become useful, insomuch as they help to consume the manufactures of their native country at an advanced price; and he must be very worthless indeed, who cannot in that country afford to buy himself clothes; for there is little danger of starving where all sorts of provisions are so cheap, where there are so few people in proportion to the extent thereof. And it is apprehended that nothing will now contribute to the employing great numbers of manufacturers in England than people in America, which way soever they get there, if they are employed in cultivating and sending to Britain such beforementioned valuable materials for manufactures; all which un-doubtedly are to be had in America, and for which in return they will gladly take those very materials and others manufactured in Britain.

It is not believed that trade in Britain is upon the decline, but seems rather of late to have greatly increased; which without doubt must be a good deal owing to the great advantages gained over the French: it is however certain, that paper money was never more used in England than at this time, and that we have been much drained of our specie; how this has come to pass is an inquiry of national importance.

The assisting the king of Prussia and supplying our armies in

Germany could not alone have this effect; neither can it be owing to money paid amongst ourselves for the fitting out of fleets or armies, or for what is sent to America, which would soon return and circulate amongst us again: it cannot be said to be owing to the state leeches, the stock-jobbers, or the Dutch having so many millions in our funds; for so long as we continue to give higher interest than in Holland, they will not withdraw their money. It must therefore be owing to some other cause that we are so much drained of our specie; and which, in order to find out, it will be necessary to take a general view of the state of our trade with all the world, which will enable us to form some judgment of these affairs: and the better to know what trade is beneficial and what hurtful to the State, in order to regulate the laws, that the nation may be gainers, and not losers, by their foreign trade, it will not be improper to begin with premising some general maxims of trade, which, though the system of policy of foreign nations with whom we trade may change, and occasion our different conduct towards them, yet the fundamental principles of trade will be always the same.

1. That the trade of a country which contributes most to the employment and subsistence of our people is the most valuable.
2. That the trade which lessens most the subsistence of our people is most detrimental to the nation.
3. That we are most enriched by those countries which pay us the greatest sums upon the balance, and most impoverished by those who carry off the greatest balance from us.
4. That the exchange is what will generally in all countries decide where the balance lies.
5. That we ought to take less of the produce and manufactures of other nations, as they decline in the importation of ours; and more of the produce of those countries which increase in their imports of our produce and manufactures.
6. That every country which takes off our finished manufactures, and returns us unwrought materials to be manufactured here, contributes so far to the employment and subsistence of our manufacturing those materials.

43. THE PLANTATION, THE PLANTER, AND HIS SLAVES: GEORGE WASHINGTON AND RICHARD CORBIN, 1759*

George Washington (1732–99) was one of the wealthiest planters and largest landholders in the colonies. When his military and public

* "Washington to Robert Cary & Co." in John C. Fitzpatrick, ed., *The Writings of George Washington* (Washington: Government Printing Office, 1931–44), Vol. II, pp. 319–21. "Corbin to James Semple," in U. B. Phillips, ed., *Docu-*

career permitted, he was typical of the busy Southern planter whose economic interests extended beyond the boundaries of the province in which he resided. He carried on a frequent and necessary correspondence with English mercantile houses, such as Robert Cary's of London, which sold vital manufactured good, tools, slave clothes, and a myriad of luxury items so that the colonists could live in the manner of the squirearchy of England. Washington's letter, below, also speaks of his recent marriage to Martha Custis and of her dowry which increased his landholdings. It was not only through hard work and attention to detail that the planter accumulated wealth—the judicious uniting of families helped too.

Richard Corbin (1708–90) presents another aspect of plantation management. He owned several plantations and, like Washington, endeavored to make them self-sufficient economic units. The importation of manufactured goods was expensive and kept the planter indebted to his English factors. But the greater reason for his indebtedness was the importation and use of expensive Negro slaves, in lieu of even more costly white laborers. Corbin's instructions to his agent James Semple emphasize careful management of slaves on whom much of the southern colonial economy depended.

To Robert Cary & Company, Merchants, London

Williamsburg, May 1, 1759.

Gentln. The Inclos'd is the Ministers Certificate of my Marriage with Mrs. Martha Custis, properly as I am told, Authenticated, You will therefore for the future please to address all your Letters which relate to the Affairs of the late Danl. Parke Custis Esqr. to me, as by Marriage I am entitled to a third part of that Estate, and Invested likewise with the care of the other two thirds by a Decree of our Genl. Court which I obtain'd in order to strengthen the Power I before had in consequence of my Wifes Administration.

I have many Letters of yours in my possession unanswered but at present this serves only to advise you of the above Change and at the same time to acquaint you that I shall continue to make you the same Consignments of Tobo. [tobacco] as usual, and will endeavour to encrease it in proportion as I find myself and the Estate benefitted thereby.

The Scarcity of the last years Crop, and the high prices of Tobo. consequent thereupon wou'd in any other Case, have induc'd me to sell the Estates Crop (which indeed is only 16 Hdhs.) in the Country but for a present, and I hope small advantage only I did not care to break the

Chain of Corrispondance that had so long subsisted, and therefore have, according to your desire, given Captn. Talman an offer of the whole.

On the otherside is an Invoice of some Goods which I beg of you to send me by the first Ship bound either to Potomack or Rappahannock, as I am in immediate want of them. Let them be Insur'd, and in case of Accident reshipp'd witht. Delay; direct for me at Mount Vernon Po-tomack River Virginia; the former is the name of my Seat the other of the River on which 'tis Situated. I am, &c.

Invoice of Sundry Goods to be ship'd by Robt. Cary, Esq., and Company for the use of George Washington—Viz:

May, 1759.

1 Tester Bedstead 7½ feet pitch, with fashionable bleu or bleu and White Curtains to suit a Room lind w't the Ireld. paper.—

Window Curtains of the same for two Windows; with either Papier Maché Cornish to them, or Cornish cover'd with the Cloth.

1 fine Bed Coverlid to match the Curtains. 4 Chair bottoms of the same; that is, as much Covring suited to the above furniture as will go over the seats of 4 Chairs (which I have by me) in order to make the whole furniture of this Room uniformly handsome and genteel.

1 Fashionable Sett of Desert Glasses, and Stands for Sweet Meats Jellys &ca. together with Wash Glasses and a proper Stand for these also.—

2 Setts of Chamber, or Bed Carpets—Wilton.

4 Fashionable China Branches, & Stands, for Candles.

2 Neat fire Screens

50 lbs Spirma Citi Candles

6 Carving knives and Forks—handles of Stain'd Ivory and bound with Silver.

A pretty large Assortment of Grass Seeds—amongst which let there be a good deal of Lucerne & St. Foin, especially the former, also a good deal of English, or bleu Grass Clover Seed I have.—

1 Large, neat, and easy Couch for a Passage.

50 yards of best Floor Matting.—

2 pair of fashionable mixd, or Marble Cold. Silk Hose.

6 pr. of finest Cotton Ditto.

6 pr. of finest thread Ditto

6 pr. of midling Do. to cost abt. 5/.

6 pr. Worsted Do of the best sorted—2 pr of w'ch. to be White. N. B. All the above Stockings to be long, and tolerably large.

1 piece of finest and most fashionable Stock Tape.

1 Suit of Cloaths of the finest Cloth, & fashionable colour made by the
Inclos'd measure.—

The newest, and most approv'd Treatise of Agriculture—besides this,
send me a small piece in Octavo—call'd a New System of Agriculture, or a Speedy Way to grow Rich.

Longley's Book of Gardening.—

Gibson, upon Horses the latest Edition in Quarto—

Half a dozn. pair of Men's neatest Shoes and Pumps, to be made by one
Didsbury on Colo. Baylors Last; but a little larger than this and
to have high Heels.

6 pr. Mens riding Gloves rather large than the middle size.

One neat Pocket Book, capable of receiving Memorandoms & small Cash
Accts. to be made of Ivory, or any thing else that will admit of
cleaning.—

Fine Soft Calf Skin for a pair of Boots—

Ben leathr. for Soles.

Six Bottles of Greenhows Tincture.

Order from the best House in Madeira a Pipe of the best Old Wine, and
let it be Secur'd from Pilferers.

· Richard Corbin to James Semple

Mr. James Semple: 1 Jan. 1759.

As it 'will be necessary to say something to you and to suggest
to you my thoughts upon the business you have undertaken, I shall
endeavor to be particular & circumstantial.

1st. The care of negroes is the first thing to be recommended that
you give me timely notice of their wants that they may be provided with
all Necessarys: The Breeding wenches more particularly you must Instruct the Overseers to be Kind and Indulgent to, and not force them
when with Child upon any service or hardship that will be injurious to
them & that they have every necessary when in that condition that is
needful for them, and the children to be well looked after and to give
them Spring & Fall the Jerusalem Oak seed for a week together & that
none of them suffer in time of sickness for want of proper care.

Observe a prudent and watchful conduct over the overseers that
they attend their business with diligence, keep the negroes in good
order, and enforce obedience by the example of their own industry,
which is a more effectual method in every respect of succeeding and
making good crops than Hurry & Severity; The ways of industry are
constant and regular, not to be in a hurry at one time and do nothing
at another, but to be always usefully and steadily employed. A man
who carries on business in this manner will be prepared for every in-

cident that happens. He will see what work may be proper at the distance of some time and be gradually & leisurely providing for it, by this foresight he will never be in confusion himself and his business instead of a labor will be a pleasure to him.

2nd. Next to the care of negroes is the care of stock & supposing the necessary care taken, I shall only here mention the use to be made of them for the improvement of the Tobo Grounds, Let them be constantly and regularly Pend. Let the size of the Pens be 1000 Tobo Hills for 100 Cattle, and so in proportion for a Greater or less Quantity, and the Pens moved once a week. By this practise steadily pursued a convenient quantity of land may be provided at Moss's neck without clearing, and as I intend this seat of land to be a settlement for one of my sons, I would be very sparing of the woods, and that piece of woods that lies on the left hand of the Ferry Road must not be cut down on any account. A proper use of the cattle will answer every purpose of making Tobo without the disturbance too commonly made of the Timber land & as you will see this Estate once a Fortnight, you may easily discover if they have been neglectful of Pening the Cattle and moving the Cowpens.

Take an exact account of all the Negroes & Stocks at each Plantation and send to me; & Tho once a year may be sufficient to take this account yet it will be advisable to see them once a month at least; as such an Inspection will fix more closely the overseers' attentions to these points. As complaints have been made by the negroes in respect to their provision of Corn, I must desire you to put that matter under such a Regulation as your own Prudence will dictate to you; The allowance to be Sure is Plentiful and they ought to have their Belly full but care must be taken with this Plenty that no waste is Committed; You must let Hampton know that the care of the Negroes' corn, sending it to mill, always to be provided with meal that every one may have enough & that regularly and at stated times, this is a duty as much incumbent upon him as any other. As the corn at Moss's neck is always ready money it will not be advisable to be at much Expense in raising Hogs; the shattered corn will probably be enough for this purpose. When I receive your Acct of the spare corn at Moss's Neck and Richland which I hope will be from King and Queen Court, I shall give orders to Col. Tucker to send for it.

Let me be acquainted with every incident that happens & Let me have timely notice of everything that is wanted, that it may be provided. To employ the Fall & Winter well is the foundation of a successful Crop in the Summer: You will therefore Animate the overseers to great diligence that their work may be in proper forwardness and not have that to do in the Spring that ought to be done in the Winter: there is Business sufficient for every Season of the year and to prevent the work of one Season from interfering with the work of Another depends upon the care of the overseer.

The time of sowing Tobo seed, the order the Plant Patch ought to be in, & the use of the Wheat Straw I have not touched upon, it being too obvious to be overlooked.

Supposing the Corn new laid & the Tobo ripe for Housing: To cut the Corn Tops and gather the blades in proper time is included under the care of Cattle, their Preservation in the Winter depending upon Good Fodder. I shall therefore confine myself to Tobo. Tobo hhds should always be provided the 1st week in September; every morning of the month is fit for striking & strip[p]ing; every morning therefore of this month they should strike as much Tobo as they can strip whilst the Dew is upon the Ground, and what they strip in the morning must be stem'd in the Evening: this method Constantly practised, the Tobacco will be all prised before Christmas, weigh well, and at least one hhd in Ten gained by finishing the Tobo thus early. You shall never want either for my advice or assistance. These Instructions will hold good for Poplar Neck & Portobacco & perhaps Spotsylvania too.

I now send my two Carpenters Mack & Abram to Mosses Neck to build a good barn, mend up the Quarters & get as many staves and heading as will be sufficient for next years Tobo hhds; I expect they will compleat the whole that is necessary upon that Estate by the last of March.

44. THE MERCHANTS: HENRY LAURENS, SAMUEL GALLOWAY, GERARD G. BEEKMAN: LETTERS ON TRADE, 1755–67*

By the middle of the eighteenth century, colonial merchants directed a lucrative business throughout the New and the Old World. In America they loaned money at interest, kept stores in the city and country, factored for the planters, bought and sold land, speculated in Western lands—in short, nearly anything "to advantage." In the overseas trade they exported agricultural products or dried fish in exchange for English and European manufactured goods and luxuries. Their ship

* Samuel Galloway Letters in Galloway, Maxey, Markoe Papers, Mss, Library of Congress. *The Beekman Mercantile Papers, 1746–99*, Philip L. White, ed. (New York: The New York Historical Society, 1956), Vol. I, pp. 508–9. Reprinted by permission of the publisher. Elizabeth Donnan, *Documents Illustrative of the Slave Trade to America* (Washington: The Carnegie Institution of Washington, 1935), Vol. IV, pp. 317–21. Originally published by the Carnegie Institution of Washington. Reprinted by permission of the publisher. See also *The Papers of Henry Laurens*, Philip M. Hamer, ed. (Columbia: published for the South Carolina Historical Society by the University of South Carolina Press, 1968), Vol. I, pp. 254–257, 263–265.

captains plied the trade of the towns and plantations along the Atlantic seaboard, selling many items and buying foodstuffs. These products were exchanged in the West Indies for sugar which was made into Yankee rum and traded for African Negroes.

The following business letters document their complicated operations. The first group was written to Samuel Galloway (1720–85) of Annapolis; the second was written by Gerard G. Beekman (1719–99) of New York; the third, by Henry Laurens (1724–92) of Charlestown.

1

To Mr. Samuel Galloway
Annapolis,

Lisbon 17. Septr. 1763

Sir: We never had any answer to our letter of 18th. May, 14th Aug[u]st, or 31st d[itt]o of last year, although we expected you would have given orders for our reimbursement of the r[ei]s 33$600 [in Portuguese money] we advanced Capt Belt to pay his sailours, for which he gave us his bill as 67¾, for £9.9.8 . . . [illegible] on Mr. Sylvanus Grove in London, who suffered it to be protested. We repeat our desire that you will order our said reimbursement, and being without any of your favours, we are now to acquaint you with the occurrences of this market. Staves are at present in great plenty and little or no demand, the present price for pipe is 40$000 hogshead, 26:000 barrell, 17:000 p thousand.

The harvest of wheat in most parts of Europe has fallen something short this year, particularly in this Kingdom, so that in all appearance there will be a brisk demand in the winter, and the prices begin allready to rise, English wheat being now worth 360. to 380. rs p alq[uie]r [two and one-half alquiers = bushel] which we expect will hold up unless great quantities should arrive together. From England they write that the harvest has been hurt by the very wet weather, which causes a considerable rise in the prices. Our white wine is at 44$rs p pipe. Large salt 1900.rs, Small do. 1800.rs p Moyo, [three-fourths of a ton] Lemons 4$rs p box, flour 2400.rs to 2500.rs p. quintal of 128 . . . [pounds]. Baccalhao [codfish] in little demand as it is summer time, but toward winter the consumption will increase as usual. We are with regard—Sir. . . .

Mayne, Burn and Mayne [In Lisbon].

To Samuel Galloway
Annapolis,

Octer. 31st, 1763

Dear Sir: My last was of the 18th July by Dawson; have since rec'd yours of the 29th of the same month. We have yet only three Ships come in from Maryland viz. the Jane Weldon and Sea Nymph Maynard from Patuxent [river] and the Betsey Lloyd from Eastern Shore. The Tobo sells as fast as landed tho' low. . . . The Lighter fine colours is wanted. I should not have sent so large a Ship as the Globe to Patuxent but could not get a smaller; I expect to lose by her. Ships are now much in demand and sell well. If you should have one come this year to be disposed of, don't doubt she will fetch a good price. We have lately had a considerable Mercht here stop payment wch it's thought will affect a House in Cork. You will therefore do well to be on your guard who you trust there. I thought necessary to give you this hint as you have formerly Consign'd Ships to the Port. I don't chose to venture to speak more plain especially as I imagine this is enough. When your Son was at home at Bartholomewtide he was ill of an intermitting Fever and since he went to School has had a Sore Throat but is now well. I am Dear Sir Your most affect. Friend and Obedt Servt

Silvanus Grove [in London].

To Samuel Galloway
Annapolis,

20th June 1764.
Sir: Above is Copy of my last Respects to you under the 1st Ins[tan]t wch I now confirm, and have only to add that a few days ago an oppo[rtunity] offer'd for England, by wch I forwarded your Letter to Mr. Grove and drew on him for the amt. of the Pipe of Wine I Ship'd you by Capt. Scougal. We are now overstocked wth American Produce, and Wine is become very Scarce here, on acct of the vast Quantity Ship'd off this year, so that I cannot Encourage you to Ship any thing this way, till towards Novr or Decr Next, when the Wines of the New Vintage will be fit to Ship, and your Produce Probably in better Demand here. I Shall advise you of all occurrences as oppo[rtunitie]s present, and in the Mean time am very Respectfully Sr. Your most obedt, hble Servt

John Searle [In Madeira]

To Mr. Samuel Galloway
Annapolis,

5 July 1764
Sir: Our last was 26th May and being depriv'd of your favours we have only to advise you of what further Novelty Occurr'd in our Market. Wheat having fallen to 22rs4 p fanega [1.6 bushels] and all over Italy in proportion has occasiond several Cargoes destind for those markets to Come in here so that here is a great quantity of Engsh Wheat at Market which goes off very Slowly at the Nominal price of 380 to 420

rs Alqr but there will be no real fixt price till the quantity at market is diminished and the produce of the New Crop thoroughly ascertain'd. As there is but a triffle of American Wheat at Market, it retailes for 360 to 380rs p Alquier.

A Cargoe of flour lately from Philadelphia to the Consignment of another house is offer'd at 260ors and the price will either fix there or at 250ors p Ql, but as there is some talk of a fleet going to the Brazils, as soon as it is fix'd the price will take favour as the fleet generally takes a great quantity. As more Staves are daily imported they become more and more a Drugg. . . . Your obt hble Servts

Mayne and Co [In Lisbon]

2   Beekman Letters
To Richard Sharpe, London, Jan. 16, 1767

Since my last I have to this time been afflected with a nervous Complaint in both feet and hands but not so much in my right hand tho I assure you I never Expected to Right You Again but Thank God I am Able at this time, but Still am afraid of the Consiquences as the Complaint Cant be Removed Should this be my Last and I have Not the Happiness to see you, Godbless you in All your Undertakings and do by my Son as you would be his father. Inclosed is Another bill for £81.1.8 drawn by William Park on Mr. William Smith. should it not be accepted advise me as soon As Possible, if Paid youl know how to Apply the same. I Assure you all the Cash I have sent you I have been obliged to hire on Interest and much ado to get it. I know you are troubled with so many tryfling Request that I am unwilling to be troublesom to you however as you Are to bring a Little of the very best Tea for Mrs. Sharpe add 3 or 4 lbs. Extraordinary for me. I have Wrote Commodore Loring Twice, but find he verifys the Old Proverb, Out of Sight Out of mind. make my Compliments to him and put him in mind of the dozen Pair of Under Stockings he was to Procure for me when bought his Own. My best Respects to Mr. and Mrs. Edmonds. . . . NB Remember me to Our friend Davis.

[Gerard G. Beekman, in New York].

To David Beekman, St. Croix, Jan. 24, 1767

I have Not had a Line from [you] in Sometime hope you are well. I have been Confined to the house 5 Weeks with a Strange disorder in hands and feet and how it will End God knows. Prince has at Last Induced his master to sell him and deClared he would Not Live with Any Other man but you, and is Now Come to St. De Croix with Captain

Lightborne and as the fellow has so hearty desire to Live with you, I hope he will please and that you will use him well. I gave £ 100 for him and is Reckoned Cheap, and as tools may be dear with you have bought Every thing he may Want that we Could think of and sent with him As also Some Cloaths. if I am Able and have time Shall send your account this is sudden affair and the Vessel Sails tomorrow I have Received of DeWight for your account £ 29.6.9 he sent £ 50 more to me by a man named McCormack Last November but the man has never Appeared and am fraid hell Lose his money. have also Received £ 70.8 of Mathews and no more from Any Person. have wrote Dean but Cant get Any Money Much More Answer Give Mathews Orders if he Can be sued and is Lyable [for] the debt to do it When he Comes to town, and also shreeves I a [have?] put him in away [to be Sued?] I Imagin youl find Prince a Valuable fellow I could Sell him at a proffit here. . . . 29th January Lightborn not sailing so soon as I Expected. I must Let you know that I pressed Breasted So Close for Interest money due me that I Obliged him to part with . . . the negro. he say I must give him £ 110 but I dont intend to Allow him More then £ 100 tho several persons here say he is worth £ 120 or 130 I believe Could get that for him. The Negro has done his Endeavour to Come to you I was obliged to promise him you Would not sell him at St. Croix. Garry desires his Compliments.

[Gerard G. Beekman, in New York].

To Torrans and Company, Charlestown, South Carolina, March 2, 1767

I have taken the Liberty to Consign to you with Two Punchions of Choice Old Jamaica Sperits for Pundh which I beg you will Sell for the most you Can. Should have Sent you Ten Cask but was diswaded from it by a friend who told me it would not Answer. if it will and I Can have Early advise so as to get it with you before the New Crops Comes in, Shall send the Remainder. Youl Obsarve its much Superior to new for Immediate Use. please to Send me the Net proceeds in the very best Indigo such as the sample Sent you by the Captain if none so good of the blue, then in the very best Cooper Coulered that breaks Easey will be much Obliged to you if you Will Send me samples of the four best Qualitys and the Prices of Each Number then and Keep a Sample of Each. I purpose if your Indigo will Sell here at a Proffit to Order some Annually. beg youl Let me know what Hoptons best Whole Sides of Sole Leather May be bought for in Cash per Quantity.

[Gerard G. Beekman, in New York].

3   Laurens Letters
To Smith and Clifton, St. *Christophers*
per the *Benjamin*, Capt. Dickinson

26th May 1755.

Gentn., . . . We thank you for the care of our Letters to the Gentn. in your Neighbourhood and your intention of delivering that to the Captn. of the *Pearl* immediately on her arrival. It would have given us great pleasure to have heard through Capt. Rice how he left that Vessell as she has been out on the Voyage now near 12 months. from this we might have formed some judgment of the *Emperor*, Capt. Gwynn, a Ship we are largely concern'd in. She sail'd from Cork for Malimba the 31st July and we can get no tidings of her further than that she had a short Passage to Angola. She had a Cargo out largely calculated for the purchase of 570 Slaves and we are told that one Capt. Carruthers of the *Jesse* that touched at your place in his way to Jamaica should say that Gwynn would not be able to purchase more than 350 at which rate she must make but a ragged Voyage; her Cargo and Outset was above £7000 Sterling. was she to appear soon the prices with us might be some help as Slaves just now would sell very well. We have two Guinea Vessells now in port and both under a Quarantine for the small Pox so they wont be allowd to sell in less than a month or two, between them they have not more than 240 Slaves which are but a trifle to the number wanted. could you have sent 60 or 70 fine Slaves in Compa[ny] with Mr. Crooke as you propos'd We think we must have rendered an agreeable Account of them but we cannot promise that will be the case a while hence as 'tis impossible to judge what number may arrive with us this Summer. If we see two or three months hence that our imports are but small it may be worth while to take a share with you in One or two hundred to be here in the months of October and November. our Common method of selling Slaves arrived at what time they will is for payment in January or March following, if they are a very fine parcel Purchasers often appear that will produce the ready money in order to command a preference. the engagements we enter into in the Slave Trade are these to load the Ship with such Produce as can be got, pay the Coast Commission and Mens half Wages and to remit the remainder as the payments shall grow due. We sold three Cargo's last Year after the first of July and every shilling was remitted for them by the 18th March and every preceding Year has been much the same. all our Remittances hitherto but trifles have been Bills of Exchange at 30 or 40 days sight, an entire parcel of fine negroes must enable us to remit quicker than we can for a Cargo which consists of a mixture of all sorts and sizes, for the ordinary and small Slaves we must sell on such terms of payment as we can, those which are prime enable us to pick our Customers. at some times of the Year we can advance for our Friends without any inconvenience at others when we have large orders for Produce it is very inconvenient as our Planters produce such as is fine always commands Cash down. thus we have given you the best Account we can of our African business if at any time you should be disposed to try it be assurd it shall be our endeavours to give you satisfaction. . . .

If She [ship *Sarah*] Comes down the most Certain Article we can recommend to be Sent by her is a few fine Negro Men (not Callabars). We dont know how things are just now in Jamaica be them as they will [*sic*] there may be Strange alterations before the *Sarah* can return; which is the fullest and best reply we are able to give to your favour before us. . . .

[Henry Laurens, Charlestown]

To Capt. Charles Gwynn of the *Emperor* at *Jamaica*, per Adams

12th June 1755.

Sir, We have before us your kind favour of 3d May from Jamaica the date would have pleasd us much better if it had been from Rebellion Rhoad, [Charles Town Harbour] however what cant be cur'd must be submitted to which we do on our parts as chearfully as can be expected on such an occasion and are thankfull that you are safe and that matters are no worse after such a trying Storm as you describe. to be sure if you had arrived about the middle of April or any time since we should have made a glorious Sale of your Cargo, our Planters are in full spirits for purchasing Slaves and have almost all the money hoarded up for that purpose. Indigo has kept up at a most exhorbitant price in England so has Rice and in short every Article from our Colony sells mighty well. at home our Planters in general have bent their strength to Indigo and we verily believe that many of them have planted much more than they can reap and work without an augmentation of their Slaves, relying on the importation of this Summer. from hence we expect to make a fine Sale the 24th Inst of the *Pearl's* Cargo, Capt. Jefferies. He arrivd here the 10th Inst with 251 pretty Slaves, we shall strain hard to get £40 Stg. per head for the best men 'tho we must be carefull not to break the Cord besides this Guinea Man here's only the *Matilda* from the Bight and a Sloop from Gambia both performing Quarantine for the small Pox. the latter indeed has gone through it. Our Accounts from Gambia are very bad, Slaves scarce, upward of 20 Sail in the River and the small Pox currant among them, we believe few Slaves will come from that Quarter. Capt. Timberman has lost his Ship going over the Bar of Bonny and we judge no other Vessell will come here from Angola. from all this we are of opinion our importation will not be excessive and that barring a War with France the price of Slaves will hold up here thro this Summer, good prices and quick payments. . . .

[Henry Laurens, Charlestown]

45. MECHANICS' NEWSPAPER ADVERTISEMENTS, 1733–72 *

Comprising a major part of the population of the colonial cities were the craftsmen—the small manufacturers and day laborers of early America. Although some account books and a few letters describe their work, their advertisements in newspapers are more numerous and revealing. Among the most active were the New York artisans whose advertisements are offered here, but no less busy were the shopkeepers and workers in Boston, Philadelphia, and Charleston. The distasteful competition with English manufacturers, whose products sold heavily in America, was a concern for all of them, as evidenced by the frequent statements of the colonial artisans that their products were "equal to any imported from England."

Cabinetmakers

GILBERT ASH.—For the Benefit of a Poor Widow. On Thursday the 18th Instant, will be open'd, at the City Hall, in the City of New-York, a New Organ, made by Gilbert Ash, where will be performed, A Concert of Vocal and Instrumental Musick. . . . Tickets, at Five Shillings each, to be had at Mr. Cobham's in Hanover-Square, at the Gentleman's Coffee-House, at the King's Arms, at the Province Arms, at the Bible & Crown in Queenstreet, and at Mr. Ash's joining Mr. Willet's in Wall-street; who continues the Business of Organ Building, by whom Gentlemen and Ladies, may be furnished with noble Instrument, in a convenient Time after it is bespoke.—*The New-York Mercury*, March 15, 1756.

John Brinner, Cabinet and Chair-Maker, from London; at the Sign of the Chair, opposite Flatten Barrack-Hill, in the BroadWay, New York: Where every Article in the Cabinet, Chair-making, Carving and Gilding Business, is executed on the most reasonable Terms, with the utmost neatness and Punctuality. He carves all sorts of Architectural, Gothic and Chinese Chimney Pieces, Glass and Picture Frames, Slab Frames, Gerondoles, Chandaliers, and all kinds of Mouldings and Front-ispieces, &c. &c. Desk and Book-Cases, Library Book-Cases, writing and

* *The Arts and Crafts in New York, 1726–1776: Collections of The New York Historical Society*, Rita Susswein Gottesman, ed. (New York: The New York Historical Society, 1938), Vol. LXXXII, pp. 109, 110, 193, 218, 358–59. Reprinted by permission of the publisher.

Reading Tables, Commode and Bureau Dressing Tables, Study Tables, China Shelves and Cases, Commode and Plain Chest of Drawers, Gothic and Chinese Chairs; all Sorts of plain or ornamental Chairs, Sofa Beds, Sofa Settees, Couch and easy Chair Frames, all kinds of Field Bedsteads, &c. &c.

N.B. He has brought over from London six Artificers, well skill'd in the above Branches.—*The New-York Mercury,* May 31, 1762.

House Carpenters

A CARPENTER'S DAY MADE EASY.—Mr. [Peter] Zenger: I am a Carpenter by Trade and can read English, therefore I some Times borrow your paper. My fellow Trades Men say, that you are to print every Thing that is good and bad in the Country, and to reward all Men according to their Deserts. I hear that some Body has put a Clapper into the Fort Bell, and that it is to ring at Morning, Noon and Night, as in the old Times. I am heartily glad of it. It will produce a great Reformation. We shall breakfast, dine, and sup, according to Rule and Compass, and know how to square our Work as in the Days of our Forefathers. I assure you, Mr. Zenger, that is a good deed, and ought not to be slighted: Therefore I and the Rest of the Day Labourers in Town, intend very speedily to pay our Thanks to that worthy Artist, in a very Handsome Address of which pray take Notice in your Papers. I am Bob Chizel.—*The New-York Weekly Journal,* January 7, 1733.

HOUSE CARPENTER.—To Be Sold, By Peter Hendrick's House carpenter, near the new dutch Church, several sorts of Cordials which cures the Hestirk Fitts; Children of Worms; pangs in the stomach, chollick, and several other Ailments.—*The New-York Evening Post,* December 19, 1748.

WAGE.—For the Encouragement of Ship-Carpenters, able Seamen, and Labourers, in the Country, and the neighbouring Provinces, to repair to the City of New-York, The Merchants of this City have agreed to give to Ship-Carpenters, Eight shillings per Day, able Seamen, Five shillings; and Labourers Four shillings; with the usual Allowance of Provisions; and no other or greater Wages whatsoever. And all Persons liking the above Proposals, may be certain of constant Employment.—*The New York Gazette or the Weekly Post-Boy,* September 18, 1758.

SOCIETY OF HOUSE CARPENTERS.—To the Public, The Society of House Carpenters, in this City, having fixed on the House of Mr. David Philips, at which to hold their stated Meetings, and transact the Business of the Society, beg Leave to take this Method to acquaint the Public therewith, and to desire the favour of such Gentlemen who shall have Occasion to employ them, either in drawing Plans, Elevations, and Estimates, or to execute any Carpenters Work, that they would be pleased to apply to said Philip's, where they will meet with the Workmen, who will faithfully, and on reasonable Terms, perform the different Kinds of Work which they shall undertake; and will with Gratitude acknowledge any Favours received from their Employers.—*The New-York Gazette and the Weekly Mercury,* November 18, 1771.

Ironmongers

STERLING IRON WORKS.—W. Hawxhurst, Still carries on the Sterling iron works, and gives the best encouragement for founders, miners, mine burners, pounders, and furnace fillers, bank's-men, and stock takers, finers of pigg, and drawers of bar; smiths, and anchor smiths, carpenters, colliers, woodcutters, and common labourers; They will be paid ready cash for their labour, and will be supplied with provisions there, upon the best terms. . . .—*The New-York Gazette and the Weekly Post-Boy, Supplement* for November 3, 1763, dated November 4, 1763.

THE STERLING ANCHORY Which was burnt down in May, 1767, is rebuilt, and carried on by Noble and Townsend; all Gentlemen, Merchants, and others, that will be kind enough to apply to William Hawxhurst, in New-York, may be supplied with Anchors warranted for a Year, made out of refin'd Iron wrought from the Sterling Pigs. . . . —*The New-York Gazette and the Weekly Mercury,* April 17, 1769.

TANTON FORGE.—A New Forge or Bloomery, called Tanton, is now finished on a Stream never failing nor subject to Back-Water or hasty Freshes, about sixteen Miles from Burlington, and the same Distance from Philadelphia, in a Country remarkably healthy, and has a good Stock of Coal housed.

Good sober Workmen are wanted to carry her on, and extraordinary Encouragement will be given to One who will have a more general Oversight, and shall come well recommended, with or without a Family.

Good Master Colliers to Coal by the Load, bringing Recommendations with them, will be encouraged at Tanton and Atsion Forges, which are near to each other, and where the Business of Coaling has every Convenience possible. Wood Cutters are also wanted. For further Particulars, enquire of Charles Read, Esq; at Burlington.—*The New-York Gazette and the Weekly Post-Boy,* December 25, 1766.

UNION IRON WORKS.—To be sold, two tracts of land, one of 750 acres, part in the county of Hunterdon, and part in the County of Morris, divided by a run called Spruce-Run (which run turns the Union-Iron-Works) is about 8 miles from said works, about the same distance from Johnson's furnace, and about 12 miles from Robinson's works. . . .—*The New-York Mercury,* August 22, 1757.

Coachmakers

WILLIAM DEANE, Coach-maker, Informs the public in general and his customers in particular, that he carries on his business as usual in Broad-street where he makes all sorts of coaches, landaus, phaetons, curricles, chairs and chaises; likewise all sorts of harness and saddlers work, as also painting, guilding and japanning, in the neatest and most elegant manner. And as he finishes all carriages whatever in his own shop without applying to any other, He is likewise determined to make them as good, sell them as cheap, and be as expeditious as there is a posibility. And to convince the public of the truth of what he asserts, he will make any piece of work that is required, EQUAL to any imported from England, and will sell it at the prime cost of that imported, by which means those who are pleased to favour him with their custom will save the freight, insurance, and expences naturally attending in putting the carriages to rights after they arrive. And as a further inducement, he will engage his work for a year after it is delivered, that is, if any part gives way or fails by fair usage, he will make it good at his own expence. Those advantages cannot be obtained on carriages imported. He has now a considerable stock of the best of all materials fit for making carriages. For the above reasons, he most humbly requests the encouragement of the public, which will be most gratefully acknowledged by him.

Said Deane paints and repairs all manner of old work very reasonably, and has for sale just finished, a new phaeton, and four new chairs.—*The New-York Journal or the General Advertiser,* June 4, 1772.

6

Political Philosophy
and Government

46. JOHN WISE, *A VINDICATION OF THE GOVERNMENT OF THE NEW ENGLAND CHURCHES*, 1717[*]

John Wise (1652–1725), clergyman and philosopher, was born in Roxbury, Massachusetts, and was graduated from Harvard. He was pastor of the Second Congregational Church during his entire career, and was one of America's earliest political liberals. An advocate of the prerogatives of the Assembly over the Crown, he was jailed during the Edmund Andros regime for refusing to pay an "unconstitutional" tax.

In 1690, Wise was chaplain to the Massachusetts forces which marched against Quebec. Later he became involved in the paper money controversy, advocating cheap money to relieve poor debtors. When Cotton and Increase Mather attempted to establish associations of clergymen to perform functions formerly decided by individual churches, Wise effectively destroyed their proposal and protected independent congregationalism in two far-reaching pamphlets: The Churches' Quarrell Espoused *and* A Vindication of the Government of New England Churches. *For the latter, sections of which follow, he derived his ideas largely from Baron von Puffendorpf. Wise develops a "humane" rights philosophy of government, based on the compact theory, one not deduced from the Scriptures. Though his immediate concern in these essays is with church government, his arguments have broader applicability to the relationship between an individual and his government.*

[*] John Wise, *A Vindication of the Government of New England Churches* ... (Boston: J. Allen, 1721), pp. 32–51, 53–54.

On Man and Government
Chap II

I Shall disclose several Principles of Natural Knowledge; plainly discovering the Law of Nature; or the true sentiments of Natural Reason, with Respect to Mans Being and Government. And in this Essay I shall peculiarly confine the discourse to two heads, viz.

1. Of the Natural [in distinction to the Civil] and then,

2. Of the Civil Being of Man. And I shall Principally take Baron Puffendorff for my Chief Guide and Spokes-man.

1. I shall consider Man in a state of Natural Being, as a Free-Born Subject under the Crown of Heaven, and owing Homage to none but God himself. It is certain Civil Government in General, is a very Admirable Result of Providence, and an Incomparable Benefit to Man-kind, yet must needs be acknowledged to be the Effect of Humane Free-Compacts and not from any direct Orders of Infinite Wisdom, in any positive Law wherein is drawn up this or that Scheme of Civil Government. Government [says the Lord Warrington] is necessary—in that no Society of Men can subsist without it; and that Particular Form of Government is necessary which best suits the Temper and Inclination of a People. Nothing can be Gods Ordinance, but what he has particularly Declared to be such; there is no particular Form of Civil Government described in Gods Word, neither does Nature prompt it. The Government of the Jews was changed five Times. Government is not formed by Nature, as other Births or Productions; If it were, it would be the same in all Countries; because Nature keeps the same Method, in the same thing, in all Climates. If a Common Wealth be changed into a Monarchy, is it Nature that forms, and brings forth the Monarch? Or if a Royal Family be wholly Extinct (as in Noah's Case, being not Heir Apparent from Descent from Adam) is it Nature that must go to work (with the King Bees, who themselves alone preserve the Royal Race in that Empire) to Breed a Monarch before the People can have a King, or a Government sent over them? And thus we must leave Kings to Resolve which is their best Title to their Crowns, whether Natural Right, or the Constitution of Government settled by Humane Compacts, under the Direction and Conduct of Reason. But to proceed under the head of a State of Natural Being, I shall more distinctly Explain the State of Humane Nature in its Original Capacity, as Man is placed on Earth by his Maker, and Cloathed with many Investitures, and Immunities which properly belong to Man separately considered. As,

1. The Prime Immunity in Mans State, is that he is most properly the Subject of the Law of Nature. He is the Favourite Animal on Earth; in that this Part of Gods Image, viz. Reason is Congenate with his

Nature, wherein by a Law Immutable, Instampt upon his Frame, God
has provided a Rule for Men in all their Actions, obliging each one to
the performance of that which is Right, not only as to Justice, but likewise as to all other Moral Vertues, the which is nothing but the Dictate
of Right Reason founded in the Soul of Man. *Motloy, De Mao,*

Praef. That which is to be drawn from Mans Reason, flowing
from the true Current of that Faculty, when unperverted, may be said
to be the Law of Nature; on which account, the Holy Scriptures declare
it written on Mens Hearts. For being indowed with a Soul, you may
know from your self, how, and what you ought to act, Rom. 2. 14. These
having not a Law, are a Law to themselves. So that the meaning is,
when we acknowledge the Law of Nature to be the dictate of Right
Reason, we must mean that the Understanding of Man is Endowed with
such a power, as to be able, from the Contemplation of humane Condition to discover a necessity of Living agreeably with this Law: And
likewise to find out some Principle, by which the Precepts of it, may be
clearly and solidly Demonstrated. The way to discover the Law of
Nature in our own state, is by a narrow Watch, and accurate Contemplation of our Natural Condition, and propensions. Others say this is
the way to find out the Law of Nature.

Scil.[*icet:* namely] If a Man any ways doubts, whether what he is
going to do to another Man be agreeable to the Law of Nature, then
let him suppose himself to be in that other Mans Room; And by this Rule
effectually Executed. A Man must be a very dull Scholar to Nature not
to make Proficiency in the Knowledge of her Laws. But more Particularly in pursuing our Condition for the discovery of the Law of Nature,
this is very obvious to view, viz.

1. A Principle of Self-Love, & Self-Preservation, is very predominant in every Mans Being.

2. A Sociable Disposition.

3. An Affection or Love to Man-kind in General. And to give
such Sentiments the force of a Law, we must suppose a God who takes
care of all Mankind, and has thus obliged each one, as a Subject of
higher Principles of Being, then meer Instincts. For that all Law properly
considered, supposes a capable Subject, and a Superiour Power; And the
Law of God which is Binding, is published by the Dictates of Right
Reason as other ways: Therefore says Plutarch, To follow God and
obey Reason is the same thing. But moreover that God has Established
the Law of Nature, as the General Rule of Government, is further illus-
trable from the many Sanctions in Providence, and from the Peace and
Guilt of Conscience in them that either obey, or violate the Law of
Nature. But moreover, the foundation of the Law of Nature with relation
to Government, may be thus Discovered.

Scil. Man is a Creature extreamly desirous of his own Preservation; of himself he is plainly Exposed to many Wants, unable to secure his own safety, and Maintenance without the Assistance of his fellows: and he is also able of returning Kindness by the furtherance of mutual Good; But yet Man is often found to be Mailicious, Insolent, and easily Provoked, and as powerful in Effecting mischief, as he is ready in designing it. Now that such a Creature may be Preserved, it is necessary that he be Sociable; that is, that he be capable and disposed to unite himself to those of his own species, and to Regulate himself towards them, that they may have no fair Reason to do him harm; but rather incline to promote his Interests, and secure his Rights and Concerns. This then is a Fundamental Law of Nature, that every Man as far as in him lies, do maintain a Sociableness with others, agreeable with the main end and disposition of humane Nature in general. For this is very apparent, that Reason and Society render Man the most potent of all Creatures. And Finally, from the Principles of Sociableness it follows as a fundamental Law of Nature, that Man is not so Wedded to his own Interest, but that he can make the Common good the mark of his Aim: And hence he becomes Capacitated to enter into a Civil State by the Law of Nature; for without this property in Nature, viz. Sociableness, which is for Cementing of parts, every Government would soon moulder and dissolve.

2. The Second Great Immunity of Man is an Original Liberty Instampt upon his Rational Nature. He that intrudes upon this Liberty, Violates the Law of Nature. In this Discourse I shall wave the Consideration of Mans Moral Turpitude, but shall view him Physically as a Creature which God has made and furnished essentially with many Enobling Immunities, which render him the most August Animal in the World, and still, whatever has happened since his Creation, he remains at the upperend of Nature, and as such is a Creature of a very Noble Character. For as to his Dominion, the whole frame of the Lower Part of the Universe is devoted to his use, and at his Command; and his Liberty under the Conduct of Right Reason, is equal with his trust. Which Liberty may be briefly Considered, Internally as to his Mind, and Externally as to his Person.

1. The Internal Native Liberty of Mans Nature in general implies, a faculty of Doing or Omitting things according to the Direction of his Judgment. But in a more special meaning, this Liberty does not consist in a loose and ungovernable Freedom, or in an unbounded Licence of Acting, Such Licence is disagreeing with the condition and dignity of Man, and would make Man of a lower and meaner Constitution then Bruit Creatures; who in all their Liberties are kept under a better and more Rational Government, by their Instincts. Therefore as Plutarch says, These Persons only who live in Obedience to Reason, are worthy to be accounted free; They alone live as they Will, who have Learnt what they ought to Will. So that the true Natural Liberty of Man, such

as really and truely agrees to him, must be understood, as he is Guided and Restrained by the Types of Reason, and Laws of Nature; all the rest is Brutal, if not worse.

2. Mans External Personal, Natural Liberty, Antecedent to all Humane parts, or Alliances must also be considered. And so every Man must be conceived to be perfectly in his own Power and disposal, and not to be controuled by the Authority of any other. And thus every Man, must be acknowledged equal to every Man, since all Subjection and all Command are equally banished on both sides; and considering all Men thus at Liberty, every Man has a Prerogative to Judge for himself, viz. What shall be most for his Behoof, Happiness and Well-being.

3. The Third Capital Immunity belonging to Mans Nature, is an equality amongst Men; Which is not to be denied by the Law of Nature, till Man has Resigned himself with all his Rights for the sake of a Civil State; and then his Personal Liberty and Equality is to be cherished, and preserved to the highest degree, as will consist with all just distinctions amongst Men of Honour, and shall be agreeable with the publick Good. For Man has a high valuation of himself, and the passion seems to lay its first foundation (not in Pride, but) really in the high and admirable Frame and Constitution of Humane Nature. The Word Man, says my Author, is thought to carry somewhat of Dignity in its sound; and we commonly make use of this as the most proper and prevailing Argument against a rude Insulter, viz. I am not a Beast or a Dog, but am a Man as well as your self. Since then Humane Nature agrees equally with all persons; and since no one can live a Sociable Life with another that does not own or Respect him as a Man; It follows as a Command of the Law of Nature, that every Man Esteem and treat another as one who is naturally his Equal, or who is a Man as well as he. There be many popular, or plausible Reasons that greatly Illustrate this Equality, viz. that we all Derive our Being from one stock, the same Common Father of humane Race. On this Consideration Boethius checks the pride of the Insulting Nobility,

> Quid Genus et Proavos Strepitis
> Si Primordia Vestra,
> Arteremque Deum Spectas,
> Nullus Degener Extat
> Nist vitiis Pejura sovens,
> Preprium Deserat Orturn.

> Fondly our first Descent we Boast;
>   If whence at first our Breath we Drew,
>   The common springs of Life we view,
> The airy Notion soon is Lost.

> The Almighty made us equal all;
> But he that slavishly complyes
> To do the Drudgery of Vice,
> Denyes his high Original.

And also that our Bodies are Composed of matter, frail, brittle, and lyable to be destroyed by thousand Accidents; we all owe our Existence to the same Method of propagation. The Noblest Mortal in his Entrance on to the Stage of Life, is not distinguished by any pomp or of passage from the lowest of Mankind; and our Life hastens to the same General Mark: Death observes no Ceremony, but Knocks as loud at the Barriers of the Court, as at the Door of the Cottage. This Equality being admitted, bears a very great force in maintaining Peace and Friendship amongst Men. For that he who would use the Assistance of others, in promoting his own Advantage, ought as freely to be at their service, when they want his help on the like Occasions. One Good turn Requires another, is the Common Proverb; for otherwise he must need esteem others unequal to himself, who constantly demands their Aid, and as constantly denies his own. And whoever is of this Insolent Temper, cannot but highly displease those about him, and soon give Occasion of the Breach of the Common Peace. It was a Manly Reproof which Charactacus gave the Romans. *Num Si vos Omnibus &c.* What! because you desire to be Masters of all Men, does it follow therefore that all Men should desire to be your Slaves, for that it is a Command of Natures Law, that no Man that has not obtained a particular and special Right, shall arrogate to himself a Larger share than his fellows, but shall admit others to equal Priviledges with himself. So that the Principle of Equality in a Natural State, is peculiarly transgressed by Pride, which is when a Man without sufficient reason prefers himself to others. And though as Hensius, Paraphrases upon Aristotle's Politicks to this Purpose. viz. Nothing is more suitable to Nature, than that those who Excel in Understanding and Prudence, should Rule and Controul those who are less happy in those Advantages, &c. Yet we must note, that there is room for an Answer.

Scil. That it would be the greatest absurdity to believe, that Nature actually Invest the Wise with a Sovereignity over the weak; or with a Right of forcing them against their Wills; for that no Sovereignty can be Established, unless some Humane Deed, or Covenant Precede: Nor does Natural fitness for Government make a Man presently Governour over another; for that as Ulpain says, by a Natural Right all Men are born-free; and Nature having set all Men upon a Level and made them Equals, no Servitude or Subjection can be conceived without Inequality; and this cannot be made without Usurpation or Force in others, or Voluntary Compliance in those who Resign their freedom, and give away their degree of Natural Being and thus we come,

2. To consider Man in a Civil State of Being; wherein we shall observe the great difference betwen a Natural, and Political State; for in the Latter State many Great disproportions appear, or at least many obvious distinctions are soon made amongst Men; which Doctrine is to be laid open under a few heads.

1. Every Man considered in a Natural State, must be allowed to be Free, and at his own dispose; yet to suit Mans Inclinations to Society; And in a peculiar manner to gratify the necessity he is in of publick Rule and Order, he is Impelled to enter into a Civil Community; and Divests himself under Government; which amongst other things Comprehends the Power of Life and Death over Him; together with Authority to Injoyn him some things to which he may have as strong an Inclination; so that he may be often under this Authority, obliged to Sacrifice his Private, for the Publick Good. So that though Man is inclined to Society, yet he is driven to a Combination by great necessity. For that the true and leading Cause of forming Governments, and yeilding up Natural Liberty, and throwing Mans Equality into a Common Pile to be new Cast by the Rules of fellowship; was really and truly to guard themselves against the Injuries Men were lyable to Interchangeably; none so Good to Man, as Man, and yet none a greater Enemy. So that,

2. The first Humane Subject and Original of Civil Power is the People. For as they have a Power every Man over himself in a Natural State, so upon a Combination they can and do bequeath this Power unto others; and settle it according as their united discretion shall Determine. For that this is very plain, that when the Subject of Sovereign Power is quite Extinct, that Power returns to the People again. And when they are free, they may set up what species of Government they please; or if they rather incline to it, they may subside into a State of Natural Being, if it be plainly for the best. In the Eastern Country of the Mogul, we have some resemblance of the Case; for upon the Death of an absolute Monarch they live so many days without a Civil Head but in that Interregnum, those who survive the Vacancy, are glad to get into a Civil State again; and usually they are in a very Bloody Condition when they return under the Covert of a new Monarch; this project is to indear the People to a Tyranny, from the Experience they have so lately had of an Anarchy.

3. The formal Reason of Government is the Will of a Community, yielded up and surrendred to some other Subject, either of one particular Person, or more, Conveyed in the following manner.

Let us conceive in our Mind a multitude of Men, all Naturally Free & Equal; going about voluntarily, to Erect themselves into a new

Common-wealth. Now their Condition being to bring themselves into a Politick Body, they must needs Enter into divers Covenants.

1. They must Interchangeably each Man Covenant to joyn in one lasting Society, that they may be capable to concert the measures of their safety, by a Publick Vote.

2. A Vote or Decree must then nextly pass to set up some Particular species of Government over them. And if they are joyned in their first Compact upon absolute Terms to stand to the Decision of the first Vote concerning the Species of Government: Then all are bound by the Majority to acquiesce in that particular Form thereby settled, though their own private Opinion, incline them to some other Model.

3. After a Decree has specified the Particular form of Government, then there will be need of a New Covenant, whereby those on whom Sovereignty is conferred, engage to take care of the Common Peace, and Welfare. And the Subjects on the other hand, to yield them faithful Obedience. In which Covenant is Included that Submission and Union of Wills, by which I state may be conceived to be but one Person. So that the most proper Definition of a Civil State, is this. viz. A Civil State is a Compound Moral Person, whose Will (United by those Covenants before passed) is the Will of all; to the end it may Use, and Apply the strength and riches of Private Persons towards maintaining the Common Peace, Security, and Well-being of all. Which may be conceived as tho' the whole State was now become but one Man; in which the aforesaid Covenants may be supposed under Gods Providence, to be the Divine Fiat, Pronounced by God, let us make Man. And by way of resemblance the aforesaid Being may be thus Anatomized.

1. The Sovereign Power is the Soul infused, giving Life and Motion to the whole Body.

2. Subordinate Officers are the Joynts by which the Body moves.

3. Wealth and Riches are the Strength.

4. Equity and Laws are the Reason.

5. Councellors the Memory.

6. Salus Populi, or the Happiness of the People, is the End of its Being; or main Business to be attended and done.

7. Concord amongst the Members, and all Estates, is the Health.

8. Sedition is Sickness, and Civil War Death.

The Parts of Sovereignty may be considered: So,

1. As it Prescribes the Rule of Action: It is rightly termed Legislative Power.

2. As it determines the Controversies of Subjects by the Standard of those Rules. So is it justly Termed Judiciary Power.

3. As it Arms the Subjects against Foreigners, or forbids Hostility, so its called the Power of Peace and War.

4. As it takes in Ministers for the discharge of Business, so it is called the Right of Appointing Magistrates. So that all great Officers and Publick Servants, must needs owe their Original to the Creating Power of Sovereignty. So that those whose Right it is to Create, may Dissolve the being of those who are Created, unless they cast them into an Immortal Frame. And yet must needs be dissoluble if they justly forfeit their being to their Creators.

5. The Chief End of Civil Communities, is, that Men thus conjoyned, may be secured against the Injuries, they are lyable to from their own Kind For if every Man could secure himself singly; It would be great folly for him, to Renounce his Natural Liberty, in which every Man is his own King and Protector.

6. The Sovereign Authority besides that is inheres in every State as in a Common and General Subject. So farther according as it resides in some One Person, or in a Council (consisting of some Select Persons, or of all the Members of a Community) as in a proper and particular Subject, so it produceth different Forms of Common-wealths, viz. Such as either simple and regular, or mixt.

1. The Forms of a Regular State are three only, which Forms arise from the proper and particular Subject, in which the Supream Power Resides. As,

1. A Democracy, which is when the Sovereign Power is Lodged in a Council consisting of all the Members, and where every Member has the Priviledge of a Vote. This Form of Government, appears in the greatest part of the World to have been the most Ancient. For that Reason seems to shew it to be most probable, that when Men (being Originally in a condition of Natural Freedom and Equality) had thoughts of joyning in a Civil Body, would without question be inclined to Administer their common Affairs, by their common Judgment, and so must necessarily to gratifie that Inclination establish a Democracy; neither can it be rationally imagined, that Fathers of Families being yet Free and Independent, should in a moment, or little time take off their long delight in governing their own Affairs, & Devolve all upon some single Sovereign Commander; for that it seems to have been thought more Equitable, that what belonged to all, should be managed by all, when all had entered by Compact into one Community. The Original of our Government, says Plato, (speaking of the Athenian Commonwealth) was taken from the Equality of our Race. Other States there are composed of different Blood, and of unequal Lines, the Consequence of which are disproportionable Soveraignty, Tyrannical or Oligarchycal Sway; under which men live in such a manner, as to Esteem themselves partly Lords, and partly Slaves to each other. But we and our Country men, being all Born Brethren of the same Mother, do not look upon our selves, to stand under so hard a Relation, as that of Lords and Slaves; but the Parity of

our Descent incline us to keep up the like Parity by our Laids, and to yield the precedency to nothing but to Superious Vertue and Wisdom. And moreover it seems very manifest that most Civil Communities are at first from the Union of Families, that were nearly allyed in Race and Blood. And though Ancient Story make frequent mention of Kings, yet it appears that most of them were such that had an Influence rather in perswading, then in any Power of Commanding. So Justin describes that Kind of Government, as the most Primitive, which Aristotle stiles an Heroical Kingdom. viz. Such as is no ways Inconsistent with a Democratical State. De Princip. Reru. 1. L. 1. C.

A democracy is then Erected, when a Number of Free Persons, do Assemble together in Order to enter into a Covenant for uniting themselves in a Body. And such a Preparative Assembly hath some appearance already of a Democracy; it is a Democracy in Embrio properly in this Respect, that every Man hath the Priviledge freely to deliver his Opinion concerning the Common Affairs. Yet he who dissents from the Vote of the Majority, is not in the least obliged by what they determine, till by a second covenant, a Popular Form be actually Established; for not before then can we call it a Democratical Government, viz. Till the Right of Determining all matters relating to the publick Safety, is actually placed in a General Assembly of the whole People; or by their own Compact and Mutual Agreement, Determine themselves the proper Subject for the Exercise of Sovereign Power. And to compleat this State, and render it capable to Exert its Power to answer the End of a Civil State: These Conditions are necessary.

1. That a certain Time and Place be Assigned for Assembling.

2. That when the Assembly be Orderly met, as to Time and Place, that then the Vote of the Majority must pass for the Vote of the whole Body.

3. That Magistrates be appointed to Exercise the Authority of the whole for the better dispatch of Business, or every days Occurrence; who also may with more Mature diligence, search into more Important Affairs; and if in case any thing happens of greater Consequence, may report it to the Assembly; and be peculiarly Serviceable in putting all Publick Decrees into Execution. Because a large Body of People is almost useless in Respect of the last Service, and of many others, as to the more Particular Application and Exercise of Power. Therefore it is most agreeable with the Law of Nature, that they Institute their Officers to act in their Name, and Stead

2. The Second Species of Regular Government, is an Aristocracy; and this is said then to be Constituted when the People, or Assembly United by a first Covenant, and having thereby cast themselves into the first Rudiments of a State; do then by Common Decree, Devolve the Sovereign Power, on a Council consisting of some Select Members; and

these having accepted of the Designation, are then properly invested with Sovereign Command; and then an Aristocracy if formed.

3. The Third Species of a Regular Government, is a Monarchy which is settled when the Sovereign Power is confered on some one worthy Person. It differs from the former, because a Monarch who is but one Person is Natural, as well as in Moral account, & so is furnished with an Immediate Power of Exercising Sovereign Command in all Instances of Government; but the fore named must needs have Particular Time and Place assigned; but the Power and Authority is Equal in Each.

On Rebellion

In General concerning Rebellion against Government for Particular Subjects to break in upon Regular Communities duly Established, is from the premises to Violate the Law of Nature; and is a high Usurpation upon the first grand Immunities of Mankind. Such Rebels in States, and Usurpers in Churches affront the World, with a presumption that the Best of the Brotherhood are a Company of Fools, and that themselves have fairly Monopolized all the Reasons of Humane Nature. Yea, they take upon them the Boldness to assume a Prerogative of trampling under foot the natural original Equality & Liberty of their Fellows; for to push the Proprietors of Settlements out of possession of their old, and impose new Schemes upon them, is vertually to declare them in a state of Vassalage, or that they were born so; and therefore will the usurper be so gracious as to insure them they shall not be Sold at the next Market. They must esteem it a favour, for by this time all the original Prerogatives of Man's Nature are intentionally a Victim, smoaking to satiate the Usurpers ambition. It is a very tart Observation on an *English* Monarch, and where it may be proportion be applied to a Subject must needs sink very deep, and serve for evidence under this Head. It is in the Secret History of King Charles and King James II p. 2. Says my author, *Where the Constitution of a Nation is such, that the Laws of the Land are the Measures both of the Soverigns Commands, and the Obedience of the Subjects, whereby it is Provided; that as the one are not to Invade what by Concessions and Stipulations is granted to the Ruler; so the other is not to deprive them of their lawful and determined Rights and Liberties; then the Prince who strives to subvert the Fundamental Laws of the Society, is the Trayter and the Rebel and not the People, who endeavour to Preserve and Defend their own.* It's very applicable to particular Men in their Rebellions or Usurpations in Church and State.

47. THE ASSEMBLY: WILLIAM SHIRLEY TO GEORGE CLINTON, 1748[*]

William Shirley (1694–1771), Judge of the Admiralty, Advocate General, and Governor of Massachusetts (commissioned in 1714), was one of the Crown's more able placemen. Financial crises in his family motivated his journey to Massachusetts in 1731, and he quickly marked himself as a Crown "prerogative man," alive to every opportunity for himself and the Empire. He was an expansionist and an imperialist and was chiefly responsible for the capture of Louisburg in the King George's War. In 1755, with the death of Major General Edward Braddock, Shirley succeeded to the command of the Anglo-American forces in the French and Indian War. But he was a better politican than a soldier, and because of his military blunders his personal enemies secured his removal to the governorship of the Bahamas. His political astuteness and foresight are shown in this letter to George Clinton (c. 1686–1761), Governor-elect of New York. Shirley, aware of the growth of political power by the Assembly, advised Clinton to take measures to forestall it. Clinton, however, proved a weak, perhaps dishonest official, and the Assembly defeated his every move to curtail its power.

William Shirley to George Clinton

New York, August 13th 1748.

Sir,

  I am honoured with your Excellency's letter of the 5th instant in which you inform me, "That you are of opinion the present state of His Majesty's government within this Province requires the immediate attention of the Ministry" and are pleased to desire me "as His Majesty's service has brought me here, whereby I have an opportunity of fully informing myself of this matter from the Publick papers, and other information which your Excellency has directed Mr Colden to lay before me to consider the same and to represent it to the Duke of Bedford, as you believe I shall find things in such a state that I shall think it my duty to give my sentiments thereon." Upon which I am to acquaint your Excellency that according to your desire I have informed myself of the state of His Majestys government within this Colony and find that several late innovations have been introduced by the Assembly into it, and incroachments made upon His Majesty's prerogative greatly tending to weaken his government, not only in the Colony of New York but in His Majesty's other Colonies in North America, through the influence which

[*] *Documents Relative to the Colonial History of New York* E. B. O'Callaghan and others, eds. (Albany: Weed Parsons and Co., 1853–87), Vol. VI, pp. 432–37.

so bad an example (in this Colony especially) may have among them; and I now send your Excellency a particular state of the innovations and incroachments which appear to me most materially to effect His Majesty's government, with my sentiments of what may be the most adviseable measures for putting an end to them, as may either serve for your Excellency's private consideration only, or be of use to you in making a representation of them, as you shall think fit to the Duke of Bedford which I think will come more properly from your Excellency than from me.

And as I found it necessary in order to trace the beginning and growth of the several incroachments that have been made on the King's prerogative, as also to judge what might be the most proper steps for putting a stop to them, to look back into the state of the government under the Administrations of your Predecessors and compare it with the present state of it under your own, I have used the same method in drawing the following account of them, vizt.

It appears by the Acts of Assembly that at the entrance of Governours Hunter, Burnet, Montgomery, and Cosby, for about twenty eight years past, upon their respective Administrations the Extablishments for the support of His Majesty's Government were made for the term of five years, and no aplication of any part of the money arising from the supplies granted to His Majesty for that purpose, except for the payment of the Treasurer and Members of the Assembly, was made in these Acts: but there was only one general appropriation in them, vizt. *For the support of His Majesty's government*; and the money raised was thereby directed to be drawn out of the Treasury by warrants from the Governour with the advice and consent of His Majesty's Council, which it appears by the minutes of Council was done, and that £ 1560 *p* Annum, being at first and for several years afterwards equal in value to £ 1200 sterling (which sum the Govr is by His Majesty's 26th instruction directed to take out of his revenue within the Colony for his support) was constantly drawn out of the Treasury by him for that purpose, as also £ 400 *p* annum New York currency for fire wood and Candles for his Majesty's garrison there, and £ 200 *p* annum for the repairs of the fortifications; and no other grants or matters whatsoever were intermixed in the before mentioned Acts, except the Taxes and Supplies which constituted the Fund, out of which the salaries and allowances to the Governour, Judges and other Officers of the Government were to be paid.

It appears also by the minutes of Council that all other monies levied by Acts of Assembly were during that time drawn out of the Treasury by warrant from the Governour and Council.

And I find that during that time all publick warlike stores for the defence of the Colony were lodged in the King's Magazine with the Store

Keeper and issued by order of the Governour in whose sole disposal they were.

And it does not appear that within this time the Assembly assumed to themselves the appointment of such officers, as it appertain'd to the Governour to appoint, or to nominate them to him, or turn them out of their posts or to create a dependency of them upon themselves by an extraordinary manner of making grants for their subsistence.

But I find that in the year 1743 upon your Excellency's first coming to the Administration the Assembly instead of making the before mentioned Establishment for the support of His Majesty's Government for the term of five years, pass'd an Act intituled "An Act for the payment of the Salaries, Services and Contingencies therein mentioned untill the 1st of September 1744 out of the funds appropriated for the support of the Government" and have continued this method of granting salaries for the support of the Governour and other officers from year to year only, ever since; and many other innovations tending to create an intire dependency of the Governour and other Officers upon the Assembly, and to weaken His Majesty's Government in this Colony, have been occasionally introduced from year to year by that Act.

At first, many other grants are tack'd in it to those made to the Governour, among which some have been made to persons under pretence of *Extraordinary Services* done by them, but in reality (as I am informed by Mr Colden) for composing and publishing libellous papers against your Excellency's Administration, others to an officer of their own appointment for keeping the gun powder provided for the defence of the Colony, others to their Agent in England whom they have in the same Act obtruded upon your Excellency with directions for him to take his instructions from a Committee of their own house, exclusive (as it appears) to the Governour and Council, others to Committees appointed by the Act for the Payment of Officers and Soldiers raised for the defence of the Colony, the allowance of whose Muster Rolls as well as their pay has been likewise committed wholly to them by the Act. Others to the Commissioners for Indian Affairs for payment of outscouts to be raised and employed by them solely at their discretion.

2dly The Assembly have taken upon themselves contrary to the express directions of His Majesty's commission to his Governour by virtue of which their House sits, which orders "that all money raised by Acts of Assembly shall be issued out by warrants from the Governour with the Advice and Consent of the Council, and disposed of by the Governour for the support of the Government and not otherwise" to limit in the Act what sums of money thereby raised shall be drawn out of the Treasury by such warrants and all other sums of money rais'd by Act of Assembly ever since, except those specially directed by this Act, to be drawn out by warrant from the Governor in Council, have been issued out by virtue of the several Acts *without such Warrant*.

3dly. The grants to the Governor for his support and to the Chief Justice for his salary, provided in this Act, run thus (vizt) "To the Governour for administring the Government of this Colony from the 22nd of September 1743 to the first of September 1744 (and in like manner for other years) after the rate of £ 1560 *p* Annum" (which sum I observe is now according to the present exchange, sunk from its former value of £ 1200 sterling, to £ 900) "and to James DeLancey Esq. as Chief Justice of the Supreme Court &c for the same year after the rate of £ 300 *p* Annum"; and so to the other Justices of the Supreme Court and to several other officers of the Government by *name*, and in case of the death or removal of any of them within the year it is provided in the Act that no more of their salaries shall be paid than what was due at the time of their respective deaths or removals and that "the Remainder shall be kept in the Treasury 'till dispos'd of by Acts to be hereafter pass'd for that purpose." So that in case the Governour or any of those officers dye or are superseded within the year, there is no provision for the support of the Lieut Governour or President of the Council in either of *their* Administrations during the remainder of the year, and untill the appointment of a new Governour, nor for the support of the successor of any other officer dying or removed within the year. And I would observe besides, that this new method of making personal grants to the Officers for the time being, seems plainly to imply that the Assembly, in case any of the officers should dye or be removed by the Governour, will not make provision for those whom he shall appoint to succeed them 'till they know who they are and how they approve of them.

4thly. It appears by the Minutes of the Assembly's proceedings that the Acts thus made for your Excellency's annual support are pass'd the last of the Sessions, and I am informed by Mr Colden that intimations have been given (as indeed the Assemblys delaying to compleat these Acts till the others of the same Session are consented to by your Excellency, is of its self) that unless you pass the others which are lay'd before you for your Consent, the Act for your support will not be passed.

It appears likewise that since the year 1743 considerable advances have been made by the Assembly towards usurping the nomination of Officers which it appertains to the Governour to appoint, and the power of turning such as are actually appointed by him, out of their posts, and that they have proceeded so far as even to appoint an Officer to keep part of the King's warlike Stores; one instance of which is, the Speaker's acquainting your Excellency in the name and by order of the Assembly and in their presence in the Council Chamber before the Council, that they had turned out one Mr Heath commission'd by you to be Land and Tyde Waiter for the Colony imposts, and chose Mr Brass into that post, whom they desired you would accordingly commissionate; which Mr Colden assures me was done when he was present at the Council Board. Another instance is, their message to your Excellency desiring you to appoint Mr Mills Sergeant at Arms, as appears by the minutes of their proceedings: another the committing the custody of the Gunpowder provided by them for the service of the King's garrison, to a person who had no authority from your Excellency to receive it, and for which he has a grant made him by Act of Assembly out of the money raised for the support of His Majesty's Government, and paid to him by the Treasurer, by virtue of the directions in that act, without any warrant from Your Excellency; all which appears by the Act itself.

The Assembly have likewise taken the custody and disposal of the gunpowder provided for the use of the King's garrison and defence of the Colony, out of your Excellency's hands into their own; which appears from their refusal to pass an Act pursuant to the recommendation in His Majesty's 77th instruction, for imposing a powder duty on every vessel that enters and clears, for furnishing the magazines with powder for the defence of the Colony (as is the method of most other Colonies, and was used not long since in this) that they might avoid having the powder lodged in the magazine with the Store Keeper and in the disposal of your Excellency. But instead thereof purchasing gunpowder out of the publick money granted to His Majesty for the support of his government, and which they call by a new distinction *the Colony's Powder* and order to be lodged in the Colony's powder House in the custody of their own officer, and not to be issued by him without an Act of Assembly for that purpose, but to remain there subject to their own directions and disposal; and such quantities as are issued out by acts of Assembly for the service of His Majesty's forts at New York and Albany, are ordered to be delivered, not to the Store keeper there to be kept in the King's magazine, but to particular persons nominated from time to time in those Acts, by the Assembly.

And I find likewise they have taken from your Excellency the passing of the Muster Rolls of all the troops raised for the defence of the Colony (except the King's four Independent Companies) and issuing the pay for them and their officers, according to the Establishment made for that purpose, and committed it to persons specially appointed in their Acts; by which they likewise take upon them to draw money out of the Treasury for the pay, without warrant from the Governour.

And they have likewise taken upon them not only to give the like power to the Commissioners for Indian Affairs, with regard to the payment of outscouts, but even a power to raise and employ them at discretion.

I find also that since 1743, they have assumed the power of erecting, by Acts of Assembly, fortifications and ordering *in what manner* they should be raised, and committed the *execution* of this to the conduct and direction of persons specially appointed for that purpose, in their Act.

And they have still proceeded farther in your Excellency's absence at Albany and without your consent or privity, to take upon themselves in conjunction with the Council to fortify part of the City of New York with stockades and Blockhouses, as your self informed me.

Upon all which innovations and encroachments I shall only observe in general, that the Assembly seems to have left scarcely any part of His Majesty's prerogative untouched, and that they have gone great lengths towards getting the government, military as well as civil, into their hands.

I have omitted to take notice to your Excellency of the stile of the Colony Acts, which runs thus: "Be it enacted by His Excellency the Governour, the Council and the General Assembly *and it is hereby enacted by the Authority of the same*" as a designed incroachment; because I apprehend the latter part of it is not inserted in their acts with a view of claiming an independency of His Majesty in the passing of their laws or excluding His Majesty's royal authority to disallow them; but is a mere impropriety in them; However as the latter part of the enacting clause is not the proper stile of a subordinate government, and nothing should be permitted to be put into the Provincial Acts which may have a tendency to accustom the Assemblys to consider their power of passing laws, as compleat, without His Majesty's allowance of them, it should be omitted.

As to what may be the most adviseable measures for your Excellency to take in the present situation of affairs within your government, I think no time should be lost for letting the Assembly know you expect that for the future they should provide for the support of His Majesty's government in the same manner which former Assemblies used to do it in, except as to having the sums proposed to be drawn out of the Treasury for the Governours salary and other Allowances, and for the maintenance of the several officers, ascertained in the Act or Acts themselves (which I am of opinion the Assembly have a right to do) instead of intrusting it with the Governour and Council, as was the former method; also that your Excellency should insist in general to have His Majesty's government within the Province restored to its former state. And I think your Excellency will have an advantage for effecting this beyond any other person, as the innovations and incroachments have arisen under your administration (what was done in Mr Clark's time who was only an occasional Commander in Chief upon the death of Mr Cosby and till the appointment of a New Governour, I think can not be regarded in the case) and therefore that it must seem reasonable to the Assembly for you to insist upon putting a stop to them; whereas should a Lieut Governour or President of the Council attempt this in your Excellency's absence from your government, I can not think he would have the least weight with the Assembly for altering what the Chief Governour has yielded to; and should not this reformation of the government be made during your Excellency's administration, your successor will I fear find that the continuance of these innovations and incroachments during the whole time of *that*, will be a considerable barr to his getting the government restored to it's former state and make the Assembly more tenacious of these incroachments than they will probably be now.

I shall only add that as your Excellency must expect at first to meet with some reluctancy and opposition in the Assembly to giving up the points they have gained I would recommend it to your consideration whether if you could procure His Majesty's disallowance of one or more of the late Acts of Assembly, by which these innovations have been introduced, and an additional instruction for restraining you from giving your assent to the like for the future, to be transmitted you, it might not strengthen your Excellency's hands and facilitate your resettling the King's government upon it's former foot: I think it would go far towards it. Wishing your Excellency all possible success in this affair, I have the honour to be with the most perfect regard, Sir,

Your Excellency's most Obedient
and most humble Servt.
W. Shirley.

Selected Bibliography: Provincial Society

ADAMS, James T. *Provincial Society*. New York: The Macmillan Company, 1927.

ALDRIDGE, Alfred Owen. *Jonathan Edwards. Great American Thinkers Series.* New York: Washington Square Press, 1966.*

ANDREWS, Charles McLean. *Colonial Folkways: A Chronicle of American Life in the Reign of the Georges*. New Haven: Yale University Press, 1919.

BEER, George Louis. *The Old Colonial System 1660–1754*. 2 Vols. New York: Peter Smith Publisher, 1933.

BIDWELL, W., and FALCONER, John D. *History of Agriculture in the Northern United States 1620–1860*. Washington: Carnegie Institution of Washington, 1925.

BRIDENBAUGH, Carl. *Metre and Scepter: Transatlantic Faiths, Ideas, Personalities, and Politics 1689–1775*. New York: Oxford University Press, 1962.*

———. *Myths and Realities: Societies of the Colonial South*. Baton Rouge: Louisiana State University Press, 1952.*

* Denotes availability in a paperbound edition.

270 *Provincial Society, 1713–63*

CADY, Edwin H. *John Woolman: The Mind of a Quaker Saint. Great American Thinkers Series.* New York: Washington Square Press, 1966.*

CAREY, Lewis James. *Franklin's Economic Views.* New York: Doubleday, Doran & Company, Inc., 1929.

CLARK, Elmer, and others (eds.) *The Journal and Letters of Francis Asbury.* 3 Vols. Nashville: Abingdon Press, 1958.

COHEN, I. Bernard (ed.) *Benjamin Franklin's Experiments.* Cambridge: Harvard University Press, 1942.

————. *Franklin and Newton: An Inquiry into Speculative Newtonian Science.* Philadelphia: American Philosophical Society, 1956.

DICKERSON, Oliver M. *American Colonial Government, 1646–1765.* Cleveland: Arthur Clark Company, 1912.

DORFMAN, Joseph. *The Economic Mind in American Civilization.* Vol. I. New York: Viking Press, 1946.

FRANKENA, William K. (ed.) *The Nature of True Virtue by Jonathan Edwards.* Ann Arbor: The University of Michigan Press, 1960.

FREEMAN, Douglas Southall. *George Washington, A Biography.* Vol. III, *George Washington: Planter and Patriot.* New York: Charles Scribner's Sons, 1951.

GAUSTED, Edwin Scott. *The Great Awakening in New England.* New York: Harper & Brothers, 1957.

GEWEHR, Wesley M. *The Great Awakening in Virginia.* Durham, N.C.: The Duke University Press, 1930.

GRAY, Lewis Cecil. *History of Agriculture in the Southern United States to 1860.* Vol. I. Washington: Carnegie Institution of Washington, 1933.

GREENE, Evarts Boutwell. *The Provincial Governor.* Cambridge: Harvard University Press, 1906.

HARPER, Francis (ed.) *William Bartram: Travels.* New Haven: Yale University Press, 1958.

HEDGES, James Blaine. *The Browns of Providence Plantations.* Cambridge: Harvard University Press, 1952.

HEIMERT, Alan. *Religion and the American Mind, from the Great Awakening to the Revolution.* Cambridge: Harvard University Press, 1966.

HINDLE, Brooke. *David Rittenhouse.* Princeton: Princeton University Press, 1964.

————. *The Pursuit of Science in Revolutionary America: 1735–1789.* Chapel Hill: The University of North Carolina Press for the Institute of Early American History and Culture, 1956.*

————. *Technology in Early America . . .* Chapel Hill: The University of North Carolina Press for the Institute of Early American History and Culture, 1966.

HORNBERGER, Theodore. *Scientific Thought in the American Colleges 1638–1800.* Austin: University of Texas Press, 1945.

ILLICK, Joseph E. *William Penn the Politician.* New York: Cornell University Press, 1965.

JENSEN, Arthur L. *The Maritime Commerce of Colonial Philadelphia.* Madison: The University of Wisconsin Press, 1963.

JOHNSON, Emory R., and others. *History of the Domestic and Foreign Policy* of the United States 1620–1860. Washington: Carnegie Institution of Washington, 1915.

JOHNSON, Herbert Alan. *The Law Merchant and Negotiable Instruments in Colonial New York, 1664–1730*. Chicago: Loyola University Press, 1966.

KELLEY, J. Reaney. "Tulip Hill, Its History and Its People," *Maryland Historical Magazine*, LX (December, 1965), pp. 349–403.

KEYS, Alice Mapelsden. *Cadwallader Colden: A Representative Eighteenth Century Official*. New York: Columbia University Press, 1906.

KLEIN, Milton Martin. (ed.) *The Independent Reflector* . . . Cambridge: The Belknap Press, Harvard University Press, 1963.

KOCH, Adrienne. "Pragmatic Wisdom and the American Enlightenment," *William and Mary Quarterly*, 3rd ser., XVIII (July, 1961), pp. 313–29.

KRAUS, Michael. *Inter-colonial Aspects of American Culture* . . . New York: Columbia University Press, 1928.

LABAREE, Leonard W. *Conservatism in Early America*. New York: New York University Press, 1959.*

————. *Royal Government in America*. New Haven: Yale University Press, 1934.

MAKINSON, David H. Barbados. *A Study of North American-West Indian Relations: 1739–1789*. The Hague: Mouton & Co., 1964.

MAXSON, C. H. *The Great Awakening in the Middle Colonies*. Chicago: The University of Chicago Press, 1920.

MERRENS, Harry Roy. *Colonial North Carolina in the Eighteenth Century*. Chapel Hill: The University of North Carolina Press, 1964.

MIDDLETON, Arthur Pierce. *Tobacco Coast: A Maritime History of Chesapeake Bay*. Newport News, Va.: Mariners' Museum, 1953.

MORTON, Richard Lee. *Colonial Virginia*. Vol. II. Chapel Hill: The University of North Carolina Press for the Virginia Historical Society, 1960.

NETTELS, Curtis P. *The Money Supply of the American Colonies, before 1720*. Madison: The University of Wisconsin Press, 1934.

NEWMAN, Eric P. *Early Paper Money of America*. Racine, Wis.: Whitman Publishing Co., 1967.

OSGOOD, Herbert Levi. *The American Colonies in the Eighteenth Century*. 4 Vols. New York: Peter Smith Publisher, 1958.

RAND, B. *Berkeley's American Sojourn*. Cambridge: Harvard University Press, 1932.

RILEY, I. W. *American Philosophy: The Early Schools*. New York: Dodd, Mead, & Company, Inc., 1907.

SAVELLE, Max. *Seeds of Liberty: The Genesis of the American Mind*. New York: Alfred A. Knopf, Inc., 1948.*

SCHNEIDER, Herbert and Carroll (eds.). *Samuel Johnson: His Career and Writings*. 4 Vols. New York: Columbia University Press, 1929.

SCHUTZ, John A. *William Shirley: King's Governor of Massachusetts*. Chapel Hill: The University of North Carolina Press for the Institute of Early American History and Culture, 1961.

SHIPTON, Clifford K. *New England Life in the Eighteenth Century*. Cambridge: Harvard University Press, 1963.

SMITH, William. *Historical Memoirs, Historian of the Province of New York*.

Edited by William H. W. SABINE. New York: New York Public Library, 1956.

SWEET, William Warren. *Religion in Colonial America.* New York: Charles Scribner's Sons, 1942.

TYLER, Moses Coit. *History of American Literature: 1687–1765.* Vol. II. G. P. Putnam's Sons, 1879.

WALLACE, David Duncan. *The Life of Henry Laurens.* New York: G. P. Putnam's Sons, 1915.

WERTENBAKER, Thomas Jefferson. *The Golden Age of Colonial Culture.* 2nd ed. New York: New York University Press, 1949.*

————. *The Old South.* New York: Charles Scribner's Son's, 1942.

WHITE, Philip L. *The Beekmans of New York in Politics and Commerce.* New York: New York Historical Society, 1956.

WINSLOW, Ola Elizabeth. *Jonathan Edwards: 1703–1758.* New York: Collier Books, 1961.

WRIGHT, Louis B. *The First Gentlemen of Virginia: Intellectual Qualities of the Early Colonial Ruling Class.* San Marino, Calif.: Huntington Library, 1940.*

————. (ed.) *The Prose Works of William Byrd of Westover: Narratives of a Colonial Virginian.* Cambridge: Harvard University Press, 1966.

THREE

The Revolutionary Era
1763–89

INTRODUCTION

Some observers of the Revolutionary era emphasized the differences between the colonies, the political and social divisions between frontier and coast, and the rifts between classes; nevertheless, on the eve of the Revolution there existed a burgeoning nationalism, which bound the diverse elements into one society. At the time of the Stamp Act crisis, Christopher Gadsden, the outspoken radical from South Carolina, declared, "There ought to be no New England man, no New Yorker etc. known on the continent but all of us Americans." Prophetically, a French traveler observed in the same year, "This country Can not be long subjected to great Britain, nor indeed to any Distant power, its Extent is so great [,] the Daily Encrease of its Inhabitants So Considerable, and haveing every thing necessary within themselves for (more than) their own Defense, that no Nation seems beter Calculated for Independency."

The religious revivalism of the previous generation and continuing interest in science cut across provincial boundaries. The old colonial colleges and the more recently founded institutions, such as Princeton, Columbia, and Brown, began to serve an intercolonial student body and produce an American-educated leadership. And the numerous colonial newspapers exchanged continental news, literary items, and political essays by American authors.

Travel and communication between the colonies had greatly improved. What had a century before been narrow paths between nearly isolated villages had become passable roads linking cities—roads were increasingly used by post-riders, businessmen, itinerants, craftsmen, teachers, preachers, and peddlers, who carried their particular wares or skills, plus the inevitable news and gossip, from one colony to another.

A more unified commercial interest developed. Larger and more numerous ships facilitated intercolonial travel and trade. Localism and old prejudices eroded as Yankee, Yorker, or Philadelphian ship captains carried Virginia tobacco or Carolina rice and indigo to market. American merchants established intercolonial branches in ports all along the coast and often employed trusted friends or relatives in another city as agents to broaden business.

England's narrow-minded politicians, by too often confusing imperial interests with their own national interests, buoyed up the forces of American nationalism. Their attempts at reorganization and taxation brought on arguments in the colonies over the nature and utility of the Empire, and evoked colonial declarations of rights. Parliamentary legislation raised colonial resentment and then resistance to English rule.

As John Adams commented, the Revolution began "in the minds and *hearts of the people." Its effect on the already vigorous American intellectual life was awesome. "The war," historian David Ramsay stated, "not only required but created talents. Men whose Minds were warmed with the love of liberty, and whose abilities were improved by daily exercise, and sharpened with a laudable ambition to serve their distressed country, spoke, wrote, and acted with an energy far surpassing all expectations."*

1

The American People
on the Eve of the Revolution

48. ANDREW BURNABY, *TRAVELS THROUGH
NORTH AMERICA*, BOSTON AND ITS
ENVIRONS, 1760*

Andrew Burnaby (c. 1734–1812) was born in England, one of a long line of Anglican ministers. Shortly after being graduated from Cambridge, he came to America and toured the "Middle Settlements," describing his travels in the invaluable Observations on the State of the Colonies. *Although written in 1760, it was first published in 1775, during the height of the Revolutionary crisis. Burnaby seems not to have added to his original impressions except for one passing reference to a hard-pressed economy in tax-burdened Boston. However, in the Preface he states his hopes for a reconciliation between the mother country and her colonies, whose people he generally liked. He abhorred slavery when he saw it in Virginia, and later in England he wrote against the slave trade (1788).*

Burnaby was a noteworthy man of letters in his day, producing other writings, chiefly on religious subjects, and a Journal of a Tour to Corsica (1805), *as well as* Observations, *which went into three editions. A contemporary critic wrote of him: "His Sermons and Charges are excellent compositions, as well in a literary point of view, as in their able support of our present religious establishment; and in his Travels, . . . he relates what he saw with great fidelity."*

* Andrew Burnaby, *Travels Through North America*, Rufus Rockwell Wilson, ed. (New York: A. Wessels Co., 1904), pp. 132–43. This is the third edition (1798). See John Nichols, *Literary Anecdotes of the Eighteenth Century* . . . (London: Printed for the Author, 1815), vol. IX, pp. 278–80.

[September–October] Boston, the metropolis of Massachusetts Bay, in New England, is one of the largest and most flourishing towns in North America. It is situated upon a peninsula, or rather an island joined to the continent by an isthmus or narrow neck of land half a mile in length, at the bottom of a spacious and noble harbour, defended from the sea by a number of small islands. The length of it is nearly two miles, and the breadth of it half a one; and it is supposed to contain 3,000 houses, and 18 or 20,000 inhabitants. At the entrance of the harbour stands a very good lighthouse; and upon an island, about a league from the town, a considerable castle, mounting near 150 cannon: there are several good batteries about it, and one in particular very strong, built by Mr. Shirley. There are also two batteries in the town, for 16 or 20 guns each; but they are not, I believe, of any force. The buildings in Boston are in general good; the streets are open and spacious, and well paved; and the whole has much the air of some of our best country towns in England. The country round about it is exceedingly delightful; and from a hill, which stands close to the town, where there is a beacon to alarm the neighbourhood in case of any surprise, is one of the finest prospects, the most beautifully variegated, and richly grouped, of any without exception that I have ever seen.

The chief public buildings are, three churches; thirteen or fourteen meeting-houses; the governor's palace; the court-house, or exchange; Faneuil Hall; a linen manufacturing-house; a workhouse; a bridewell; a public granary; and a very fine wharf, at least half a mile long, undertaken at the expense of a number of private gentlemen, for the advantage of unloading and loading vessels. Most of these buildings are handsome: the church, called King's Chapel, is exceedingly elegant; and fitted up in the Corinthian taste. There is also an elegant private concert-room highly finished in the Ionic manner. I had reason to think the situation of Boston unhealthy, at least in this season of the year, as there were frequent funerals every night during my stay there.

The situation of the province of Massachusetts Bay, including the district of Plymouth, is between the 41st and 43d degree of north latitude, and about 72 degrees west longitude. The climate, soil, natural produce, and improved state of it, are much the same as of Rhode Island. It is divided into counties, and townships; and each township, if it contains forty freeholders, has a right to send a member to the assembly; the present number of representatives amounts to between 130 and 140, of which Boston sends four.

The number of souls in this province is supposed to amount to 200,000; and 40,000 of them to be capable of bearing arms. They carry on a considerable traffic, chiefly in the manner of the Rhode Islanders; but have some material articles for exportation, which the Rhode Islanders have not, except in a very trifling degree: these are salt fish, and vessels. Of the latter they build annually a great number, and send them, laden with cargoes of the former, to Great Britain, where they sell them. They clear out from Boston, Salem, Marblehead, and the different ports in this province. Exclusive of these articles, their manufactures are not large; those of spirits, fishoil, and iron, are, I believe, the most considerable. They fabricate beaver-hats, which they sell for a moidore apiece; and some years ago they erected a manufactory, with a design to encourage the Irish settlers to make linens; but at the breaking out of the war the price of labour was enhanced so much, that it was impossible to carry it on. Like the rest of the colonies they also endeavour to make woollens; but they have not yet been able to bring them to any degree of perfection; indeed it is an article in which I think they will not easily succeed; for the American wool is not only coarse, but in comparison of the English, exceedingly short. Upon the best inquiry I could make, I was not able to discover that any one had ever seen a staple of American wool longer than seven inches; whereas in the counties of Lincoln and Leicester, they are frequently twenty-two inches long. In the southern colonies, at least in those parts where I travelled, there is scarcely any herbage; and whether it is owing to this, or to the excessive heats, I am ignorant, the wool is short and hairy. The northern colonies have indeed greater plenty of herbage, but are for some months covered with snow; and without a degree of attention and care in housing the sheep, and guarding them against accidents, and wild beasts, which would not easily be compensated, it would be very difficult to increase their numbers to any great amount. The Americans seem conscious of this fact, and, notwithstanding a very severe prohibition, contrive to procure from England every year a considerable number of rams, in order to improve and multiply the breed. What the lands beyond the Allegheny and upon the banks of the Ohio may be, I do not know; they are said to be very rich: but the climate I believe is not less severe; and I think, upon collating different accounts, that the severity of heat and cold is not much abated by cultivation. The air becomes dryer and more wholesome, in proportion as the woods are cut down, and the ground is cleared and cultivated; but the cold is not less piercing, nor the snow less frequent. I think therefore upon the whole, that America, though it may with particular care and attention, produce small quantities of tolerably good wool, will yet never be able to produce it in such plenty and of such a quality as to serve for the necessary consumption of its inhabitants.

The government of this province is lodged in the hands of a governor or lieutenant-governor, appointed by the king; a council of twenty-eight persons, chosen annually, with the governor's approbation, by the general assembly; and a house of representatives annually elected by the freeholders. The governor commissions all the militia, and other military officers; and, with consent of the council, also nominates and appoints all civil officers, except those that are concerned in the revenue. He calls and adjourns the assembly, and has in every respect a very extensive authority. His salary, with perquisites, amounts to about 1,300 £. sterling per year. The governor and council together have the probate of wills, and the power of granting administrations and divorces.

There are several courts of judicature. All actions under twenty shillings sterling are cognizable by a justice of peace, from whose determination there lies an appeal to the inferior county court of common-pleas; and from hence to the superior provincial court in its circuits, which is also a court of oyer and terminer in criminal affairs, and is held by a chief justice and some assistant judges. In this court, if the determination is not satisfactory, a rehearing of the cause may be had with a different jury; and even, by petition to the general assembly, a second rehearing: the dernier resort is to his majesty in council, but this only in cases of 300 £. sterling value: and the appeal must be made within fourteen days after judgment.

The established religion here, as in all the other provinces of New England, is that of the Congregationalists; a religion, different in some trifling articles, though none very material, from the Presbyterian. There are, besides these however, great numbers of people of different persuasions, particularly of the religion of the Church of England, which seems to gain ground, and to become more fashionable every day. A church has been lately erected at Cambridge, within sight of the college; which has greatly alarmed the Congregationalists, who consider it as the most fatal stroke that could possibly have been levelled at their religion. The building is elegant, and the minister of it (the Reverend Mr. Apthorpe,) is a young man of shining parts, great learning, and pure and engaging manners. (This gentleman, I have heard, afterward met with so much opposition and persecution from the Congregationalists, that he was obliged to resign his cure, to quit the colony, and has since lived in England upon a living, [I believe in Surrey] which was given him by the late Archbishop Secker.)

Arts and Sciences seem to have made a greater progress here, than in any other part of America. Harvard College has been founded above a hundred years; and although it is not upon a perfect plan, yet it has produced a very good effect. The arts are undeniably forwarder in Massachusetts Bay than either in Pennsylvania or New York. The public buildings are more elegant; and there is a more general turn for music, painting, and the belles lettres.

The character of the inhabitants of this province is much improved, in comparison of what it was: but Puritanism and a spirit of persecution is not yet totally extinguished. The gentry of both sexes are hospitable, and good-natured; there is an air of civility in their behaviour, but it is constrained by formality and preciseness. Even the women, though easiness of carriage is peculiarly characteristic of their nature, appear here with more stiffness and reserve than in the other colonies. They are formed with symmetry, are handsome, and have fair and delicate complections; but are said universally, and even proverbially, to have very indifferent teeth.

The lower class of the people are more in the extreme of this character; and, which is constantly mentioned as singularly peculiar to them, are impertinently curious and inquisitive. I was told of a gentleman of Philadelphia, who, in travelling through the provinces of New England, having met with many impertinences from this extraordinary turn of character, at length fell upon an expedient almost as extraordinary, to get rid of them. He had observed, when he went into an ordinary, that every individual of the family had a question or two to propose to him relative to his history; and that, till each was satisfied, and they had conferred and compared together their information, there was no possibility of procuring any refreshment. He, therefore, the moment he went into any of these places, inquired for the master, the mistress, the sons, the daughters, the men-servants and the maid-servants; and having assembled them all together, he began in this manner: "Worthy people, I am B.[enjamin] F.[ranklin] of Philadelphia, by trade a _____, and a bachelor; I have some relations at Boston, to whom I am going to make a visit: my stay will be short, and I shall then return and follow my business, as a prudent man ought to do. This is all I know of myself, and all I can possibly inform you of; I beg therefore that you will have pity upon me and my horse, and give us both some refreshment."

Singular situations and manners will be productive of singular customs; but frequently such as upon slight examination may appear to be the effects of mere grossness of character, will, upon deeper research, be found to proceed from simplicity and innocence. A very extraordinary method of courtship, which is sometimes practised amongst the lower people of this province, and is called Tarrying, has given occasion to this reflection. When a man is enamoured of a young woman, and wishes to marry her, he proposes the affair to her parents, (without whose consent no marriage in this colony can take place); if they have no objection, they allow him to tarry with her one night, in order to make his court to her. At their usual time the old couple retire to bed, leaving the young ones to settle matters as they can, who, after having sat up as long as they think proper, get into bed together also, but without pulling off their under-garments, in order to prevent scandal. If the parties agree, it is all very well; the banns are published, and they are married without delay. If not, they part, and possibly never see each other again; unless, which is an accident that seldom happens, the forsaken fair-one prove pregnant, and then the man is obliged to marry her, under pain of excommunication. (A gentleman some time ago travelling upon the frontiers of Virginia, where there are few settlements, was obliged to take up his quarters one evening at a miserable plantation; where, exclusive of a negro or two, the family consisted of a man and his wife, and one daughter about sixteen years of age. Being fatigued, he presently desired them to shew him where he was to sleep; accordingly they pointed to a bed in a corner of the room where they were sitting. The gentleman was a little embarrassed but, being excessively weary, he retired, half undressed himself, and got into bed. After some time the old gentlewoman came to bed to him, after her the old gentleman, and last of all the young lady. This, in a country excluded from all civilized society, could only proceed from simplicity and innocence: and indeed it is a general and true observation that forms and observances become necessary and are attended to, in proportion as manners became corrupt, and it is found expedient to guard against vice, and that design and duplicity of character, which, from the nature of things, will ever prevail in large and cultivated societies.)

The province of Massachusetts Bay has been for some years past, I believe, rather on the decline. Its inhabitants have lost several branches of trade, which they are not likely to recover again. They formerly supplied, not only Connecticut, but other parts of the continent, with dry goods, and received specie in return: but since the introduction of paper currency they have been deprived of great part of this commerce. Their ship trade is considerably decreased, owing to their not having been so careful in the construction of vessels as formerly: their fisheries too have not been equally successful: they have had also a considerable number of provincial troops (Between six and seven thousand, I believe.) in pay during the course of the present war, and have been burthened with heavy taxes. These have been laid upon estates, real and personal. Some merchants in Boston, I have been credibly informed, have paid near 400 £. sterling annually. Assessments are made by particular officers, who, with the selectmen, constables, overseers, and several others, are elected annually by the freemen, for the direction and management of each particular township.

There is less paper money in this colony, than in any other of America: the current coin is chiefly gold and silver: and Boston is the only place, I believe, where there ever was a mint to coin money.

I was told of a very impolitic law in force in this province, which forbids any master, or commander of a vessel, to bring strangers into the colony, without giving security that they shall not become chargeable to it. However, notwithstanding what has been said, Massachusetts Bay is a rich, populous, and well-cultivated province.

49. PETER KALM, *TRAVELS INTO NORTH AMERICA*, NEW YORK, 1748–61*

Peter Kalm (1716–79), botanist, was born in Sweden. At the urging of his friend and colleague, Carolus Linnaeus, he voyaged to the colonies to study the natural life of North America and made an extensive tour through the northern colonies between 1748 and 1752. He did not confine himself merely to classifying the flora and fauna of America, but also made keen and impartial observations about the people—their manners and customs, their commerce, their religions, and their general characteristics. His En Risa til Norra America *was published in 1761 and translated into English a decade later.*

1749
November the 3rd

The inhabitants of this town [Albany] are as a whole all Dutch or of Dutch extraction, descended from those who first came to settle this part of the country. Both sexes dress now very nearly like the English. In their homes and between themselves they always speak Dutch, so that rarely is an English word heard. They are so to speak permeated with a hatred toward the English, whom they ridicule and slander at every opportunity. This hatred is said to date back to the time when the English took this country away from the Dutch. Nearly all the books found in the homes are Dutch and it is seldom that an English book is seen. They are also more thrifty in their homes than the English. They are more frugal when preparing food, and seldom is more of it seen on the table than is consumed, and sometimes hardly that. They are careful not to load up the table with food as the English are accustomed to do. They are not so given to drink as the latter, and the punch bowl does not make a daily round in their households. When the men go out of doors, they frequently have only a white cap under the hat and no wig. Here are seen many men who make use of their own hair, cut short without a braid or knot, as both of the latter are considered a mark and characteristic of a Frenchman. The vast majority, in fact almost everyone here, carries on a business, though a great many have in addition their houses and farms in the country, close to or at some distance from the town. They have there good country estates, several sawmills and in many places even flour mills. The servants in this

* From *Peter Kalm's Travels in North America:* The English Version of 1770. Revised and edited by Adolph B. Benson. Dover Publications, Inc., New York, 1966. Vol. II, pp. 613–15, 615–16, 620–25, 626–27, 628–29. Reprinted through permission of the publisher.

town are nearly all negroes. The children are instructed in both the English and Dutch languages. The English accuse the inhabitants here of being big cheats and worse than the Jews.

November the 4th

The *Province of New York*, it was said, was not nearly as well populated and cultivated as the other English provinces here in America. The reason was said to be that for the most part the inhabitants were Dutch who in the past had acquired large stretches of land. Most of them are now very wealthy and their feeling of jealously toward the English prevents their selling a piece of land unless they are able to get for it much more than it is worth. As the English as well as persons of other nations can buy land at a far more reasonable price in the other provinces here, they gladly allow the inhabitants of New York to keep their land. Moreover, in Pennsylvania there are greater advantages to be gained than here in New York. Because of this it so happens that people come from Germany every year to settle in this country. They come sometimes from London by boat to New York, but they hardly come ashore before they leave here for Pennsylvania. It is a fact that Pennsylvania alone has now almost more inhabitants than Virginia, Maryland and New York put together, due to the generous privileges which the sagacious Penn wrote into his wise laws and constitution for Pennsylvania. The inhabitants of New York console themselves with the thought that when once all the land in Pennsylvania has been filled up with inhabitants, the remainder will of necessity come hither, and then they can set whatever price they wish upon their land. But it is the general opinion that they will have to wait a long time.

November 8. In New York

The current prices on products in New York for this autumn were those given in the New York *Gazette* of November 13, 1749, as follows:

Wheat, per bush.	6 s.	Molasses,	1 s. 9 d. per Gal.
Flour, per c.	18 s.	Westindia Rum	3 s. 9 d.
Milk bread,	39 s.	New England d:o	2 s. 6 d.
White d:o	29 s.	Beef, per Bus.	36 s.
Middling,	24 s.	Pork	21.18 s.
Brown	18 s.	Flax-seed	10 s.
Single refined Sugar	16 d.	Bohea Tea,	6 s. 6 d. per Box
Muscovado Sugar, per C.	50 s.	Indigo	7 s.
Salt, per Bush.	2 s. 6 d.	Chocolate	2 s. by the doz.

The *Copper mine* which is located nine to twelve miles from New York on the side toward Philadelphia is as yet the only one known in this country. At least none of that ore is mined elsewhere. Nearly all the owners of it live in New York. The mine was worked previous to the last war. The ore from it is said to be of the best obtainable. Following an act of the Parliament in England the inhabitants here are no longer allowed to smelt and refine the silver and copper ores which they find, but are obliged to send them to England in their original state and have them smelted there. This ore has been so rich that they have sent it to England and sold it at a profit in spite of the high freight charges incurred. During the last war the work in the mine was abandoned, as it was not safe to send the ore over the seas to England for the privateers to seize. It was at this time that the mine became full of the water which is still in it. Now the owners intend to send to London for engines to pump the water out of it.

November the 9th

The Dutch Church, the Service, etc.—*Hunc diem perdidi* (This day I have spent uselessly) I can in a certain way say about this day because I spent the morning in one of the Dutch churches and the afternoon in the other. I listened to two sermons, one of which lasted two hours, the other two and a half, and in neither instance could I understand much, because I was so far away from the pulpit; and even if I had understood all of it, I could not have remembered so long a sermon. But nevertheless, for the mere pleasure of it, I shall here record the ceremonies which are used here, a description of the church, etc. The morning service began exactly at ten A. M. and was to-day especially noteworthy, inasmuch as it was fifty years to-day since the minister preached his first sermon in that church. The fact was also stressed that the sum total of those who had heard his first (installation) sermon and were now present in the church, could not be very great. The church service was conducted as follows: first, the bell was sounded two or three times (they had here [in America] only one bell in each church tower) and this was rung by means of a rope which reached way down to the floor of the church, where it was customary to stand when ringing, or more correctly speaking, when tolling the bell. Then the cantor began to sing one of David's psalms rendered into verse. Only a few stanzas thereof were sung, and it seemed to me that nearly all of their hymns had similar tunes. While this hymn was being sung the minister mounted the pulpit, hung his hat on a peg, took off his robe and also hung that there, since the old fellow was eighty years of age and could not endure wearing his robe for two hours. He sat down on a chair and when the singing ceased, he stood up and preached for a while; then he read a lot of prayers, after which he began preaching again. At that time two men came forward, took the contribution bags and placed themselves before the pulpit, holding the handles upright, with the bags at the top. After the minister had mentioned a few facts about church work, they went about taking the offering. It was the custom here that everyone contributed, but no one was asked to contribute more than once during the same service. When the minister had finished the sermon, the clerk passed a note to him. He had put the note in a split at the end of a cane and thus passed it up to the minister from the place where he stood below the pulpit, saving himself the trouble of going up into it. It was the license to have the banns of marriage announced of those who were to be married. Finally he finished his sermon with the Lord's Prayer, announced the hymn to be sung, which was another from the Psalms of King David, and when he had finished, the cantor began to sing it. They had also in the church several boards on which were indicated what hymns were to be sung before the sermon: e. g. to-day the following words were on the boards: "Psalm 18 pause"; but no post-sermon hymn had been indicated. The minister remained seated in the pulpit during the singing, and when this was finished he pronounced the benediction, after which everyone departed. No mass was said and no altar devotions with gospel, epistle, etc. were held. Even if they had had this chanting service at the altar, it could not have been performed since there were no altars in the Dutch churches here, but just a pulpit.

The church where I to-day attended morning worship was the so called New Dutch Church. I shall now describe the building. It is a large structure built of stone like the ordinary church, with a tower and bell. The church is located nearly in the direction of S.S.W. and N.N.E. with the tower at the latter end. Here I wish to note that the churches in this town are not constructed to face any particular direction, one standing east and west [for instance] in the customary way, as was almost true of the English church. The others were set north and south, the direction generally followed by the Lutheran and Reformed or Presbyterian churches, etc. Quite a large churchyard surrounds the temple, and about it are planted trees which give it the appearance of an enclosure. The church has several doors and large, high windows on all sides. Within there is not a sign of a painting or figure, only white walls and ceiling and an unpainted pulpit. The church is not vaulted, but has a ceiling built of boards in the form of a vault. There is no balcony in it. There are pews everywhere in the church, also several aisles; but both are rather narrow. The pews are made like ours except in the manner hereafter described. The backs of our pews extend perpendicularly from the top to the floor, while here the back extends from the top to the seat only. Then there is another perpendicular partition which is not in line with the back of the pew but placed a little ways under the seat of the pew so that a person can place his feet under the pew in front of him. The number of the pew is painted on its door. There are no chandeliers and no candlesticks in the church. There is no sacristy and no other room to take its place.

The ministers are dressed in black with a gown and collar like those of our ministers except that the gown is not quite as long. During the week when there is no service in the church, the shutters are closed. In the tower is a clock, which strikes the hour, the only one of its kind in the city, as far as I know.

The church was filled to-day with people who came out of curiosity to hear a man begin his fifty-first year as minister. For this reason more had flocked hither than usual. The men were dressed like the English; the majority wore wigs, but a few had their own hair, which was not very long, was not powdered, and had no more curls than nature had bestowed. A few elderly persons had worsted caps on and three or four wore hats. Perhaps they were Quakers whom curiosity had driven hither. The women as a rule had black velvet caps which they could fasten on by tying at the ears. Others wore the ordinary English gowns and short coats of broadcloth of various colors. Nearly everyone had her little container, with the glowing coals of which I have spoken before, under her skirt in order to keep warm. The negroes or their other servants accompanied them to church mornings carrying the warming pans. When the minister had finished his sermon and the last hymn had been sung, the same negroes, etc. came and removed the warming pans and carried them home.

In the afternoon I went to the so called Old Dutch Church. The service began there at two P.M. and was performed in exactly the same manner as the morning worship which I attended. There was singing before the sermon and the latter was preached in the same way. It ended with the Lord's Prayer, followed by a final hymn and the benediction. I observed one ceremony here which I did not see during the morning service, namely, the christening of a child. The service was as follows: as soon as the sermon was finished and the minister had read a few prayers, a woman carrying a child on her arm came forward to the pulpit. Then the minister began to read from there all the prayers contained in the Dutch prayer book, and when he had finished she took the child to the rector, who sat in his pew, and let him christen it. This was performed, as we do in baptism, by putting water upon the child's head. After this the other minister in the pulpit talked briefly on the significance of the christening and then ended the service with the Lord's Prayer.

This church was also of stone with two pillars in the center which supported the wooden roof built in the form of a vault. Some of the windows had colored glass, but they were not old, since "City of New

York" was inscribed upon them. There was a small organ, the gift of former Governor Burnet. The pulpit and vault were painted, but without any figures on them. There was not a single figure or painting in the church, only several coats-of-arms had been hung there. There were large balconies, and it was the custom here that the men sat there while the women occupied the ground floor, except the pews against the walls which were reserved for the men. There were many chandeliers here. The examination in the Catechism was held late at night by candle-light.

November 10

French Refinement vs. the Dutch. I have already told in my journal of the good breeding of the French in Canada. Now I must emphasize one item before I forget it: namely, that the inhabitant of Canada, even the ordinary man, surpasses in politeness by far those people who live in these English provinces, especially the Dutch. I just recently came from Canada and left behind me in the vicinity of Saratoga the French who had brought me to the English colonies. When I reached Saratoga and came in contact with the first English inhabitants who were of Dutch descent, I noticed a vast difference in the courtesy shown me in comparison with that shown me by the French; it was just as if I had come from the court to a crude peasant. Yet I must grant that although they [the Dutch] showed a lack of breeding in their speech, their intentions were of the best. I noticed that when they believed, or were persuaded to believe, that a person did not understand Dutch, they amused themselves by censuring the manners which differed [from their own]. The women, especially in the towns, had this habit, for they did not like the French mode of living at all. But never have I seen folks more ashamed than they when a person let them know that he understood every word they said. Some of them did not dare show themselves again.

The King of England's birthday was celebrated in town to-day, but the people did not make a great fuss over it. A cannon was fired at noon and the warships were decorated with many flags. In the evening there were candles in some windows and a ball at the governor's. Some drank until they became intoxicated, and that was all.

November 11

Dutch was generally the language which was spoken in Albany, as before mentioned. In this region and also in the places between Albany and New York the predominating language was Dutch. In New York were also many homes in which Dutch was commonly spoken, especially by the elderly people. The majority, however, who were of

Dutch descent, were succumbing to the English language. The younger generation scarcely ever spoke anything but English, and there were many who became offended if they were taken for Dutch, because they preferred to pass for English. Therefore it also happened that the majority of the young people attended the English church, although their parents remained loyal to the Dutch. For this same reason many deserted the Reformed and Presbyterian churches in favor of the English.

Lodgings, food, wood etc. were in this town much more expensive than in Philadelphia. The rooms were said to have grown more costly since so many people from Albany had lived here during the last war and thus brought about a shortage of living quarters. The prices paid then were still in force. Food was high-priced because so much flour, corn and other food stuffs had been exported in great quantities to the West Indies, and even to New England. The farming region round about here is not so well populated that it can supply the town in such quantity as is the case in Philadelphia, where the whole countryside is thickly inhabited by the Germans and others who have settled there. On the other hand, it is the general opinion that broadcloth and other merchandise can be had here at a more reasonable price than in Philadelphia.

November 14

Dutch Customs. In New York I had lodgings with Mrs. van Wagenen, a woman of Dutch extraction whose dwelling was opposite the new Dutch church. She as well as everyone in her house was quite polite and kind. It is true that the Dutch both in speech and outward manners were not as polite and well-bred as the English, and still less so than the French, but their intentions were good and they showed their kindly spirit in all they did. When a Frenchman talks about a man in his presence and even in his absence he always uses "monsieur": e.g. "*donnez à monsieur* etc.". An Englishman says: "give the gentleman etc." while the Dutch always said: "*giw dese man*". The women were treated in the same way without ceremony, and yet the Dutchman always had the same good intentions as he who used more formality. If several persons of Dutch extraction should come into a house at this time of the year, as many as could be accommodated would sit down about the fire. Then if any others should happen in, they pretended not to see them. Even though they saw them and conversed with them, they did not consider it wise to move from the fire and give the others a little room, but they sat there like lifeless statues. The French and English always made room by moving a little. When one spoke of refinement as the word is now used, and in applying it to the French and Dutch, it was just as if the one had lived a long time at the court while the other, a peasant, had scarcely ever visited the city. The difference between the English and the Dutch was like that of a refined merchant in the city and a rather crude farmer in the country. But it is well to remember that there are exceptions to every rule.

I have lived now for almost a week in a house with a good-sized family. There was the same perpetual evening meal of porridge made of corn meal. (The Dutch in Albany as well as those in New York called this porridge *Sappaan.*) It was put into a good-sized dish and a large hole made in its center into which the milk was poured, and then one proceeded to help oneself. When the milk was gone, more was added until all the porridge had been consumed. Care was usually taken that there should be no waste, so that when all had eaten, not a bit of porridge should remain. After the porridge one ate bread and butter to hold it down. I had observed from my previous contacts with people of Dutch extraction that their evening meal usually consisted of this "Sappaan". For dinner they rarely had more than one dish, meat with turnips or cabbage; occasionally there were two [dishes]. They never served more than was consumed before they left the table. Nearly all women who had passed their fortieth year smoked tobacco; even those who were considered as belonging to the foremost families. I frequently saw about a dozen old ladies sitting about the fire smoking. Once in a while I discovered newly-married wives of twenty and some years sitting there with pipes in their mouths. But nothing amused me more than to observe how occupied they were with the placing of the warming pans beneath their skirts. In a house where there were four women present it was well nigh impossible to glance in the direction of the fire without seeing at least one of them busily engaged in replacing the coals in her warming pan. Even their negro women had acquired this habit, and if time allowed, they also kept warming pans under their skirts.

50. JOURNAL OF A FRENCH TRAVELLER IN THE COLONIES, PHILADELPHIA, 1765*

In 1765, an unidentified Frenchman visited the American colonies and carefully noted down what he saw. Scholars believe that because his observations have a military cast this man was an agent sent by his government to spy on the Anglo-Americans. He was especially interested in the city of Philadelphia, the most populous city in America on the eve of the Revolution, and soon to become a hotbed of the revolutionary movement.

* This journal is priceless not only for its descriptive qualities but also because of its report on the speech of Patrick Henry against the Stamp Act during the Frenchman's visit to Williamsburg. The document was found in the archives of the Service Hydrographique de la Marine and translated and published in the *American Historical Review*, Oct., 1920–July, 1921 Part I, Vol. XXVI, pp. 726–47; Oct. 1921–July, 1922 excerpt from Part II, Vol. XXVII, pp. 77–81.

1765

[*July*] *the 28th*. from Mr. Chews to New Castle on the Delawar. this is a prety town Consisting of about 500 Dwelling houses. it is looked upon as the next to philadelphia In the province. it is about 30 from this last, S.W., on the north side of said river. there was two Kings Fregates of[f] the town to visit the vessels going in and out therby to hinder foreign trade. from New castle to wilmington, 6 miles. crossed the fery at Christeen river [Christiana Creek]. this is a small but very well situated litle town, on the side of sd. river. large ships Can Come up this river to the town. it is about 1 mile Dist. from the Bay, on which the town has a fine prospect, being on the side of a hill. this place is so near the City that there is but litle trade Caryed on. tavern Keeping is the best business that is Caryed on in all those small towns, therfore are they well stocked with taverns. here I lay.

July the 29th. Set out Early for Chester, 12 miles. the weather Extremly hot. the horsses had great Difficulty to Dr[a]gg me along. Chester is on Priest Creek [Ridley Creek] about 15 miles from philad. the roads from willmington are very hilly and stoney which seemd odd at first. being so long acustomed to fine level roads. I met here a number of gentlemen and ladys who Came out from the City on a party of pleasure. I Dined in their Company and wee all Set out together after Dinner. arrived at p[h]ilad. at 6½ and took lodgeings at the widow Gradens in Second Street, which is the only genteel lodgeing in town. we Crossed sculkill fery about 3 miles from town, from whence the road to philada. is Beautifull, the Country one Continuall farm and several prety litle Country houses.

August the 3d. went to a fishing party on sculkill river in Company with Samuel Mifflin Esqr., Messrs. Willing and moris (to whom I had a letter of recommend'n from Beans and Cuthbert In Jamaica) and severall other of the first people in the town, where we Spent the Day.

Do. the 5th. went [to] German town with another Company to see the stocking manufacture. this is a Small place setled by Germans and Dutch who are all stocking weavers and manufacture great quantitys of thread and woolen.

Do. 7th. went again with another Company to Sculkill falls which are not Considerable wheras boats and flats Can Come Down without any great Dangour. there is here what they Call a museum or a room where they have a Colection of all the Curiossitys they can pick up in the Country, which Consists in Different sorts of fowls, fishes, shels, sneaks, and other Curious anymals, also Indian dresses and Diff't ornaments. there were a few miners here Blowing up the rocks of the fall to facilitate the passage for Boats over it, for when once over the falls they Can go a Considerable way up the Country. we Dined at a tavern that is here, a large Company of both sexes.

August the 10th. Mr. Mifflin introduced me to the Governor, [John Penn] with whom we Dined. he is nephew to Mr. Pen the proprietor. there are two brothers of them here.

Do. 12th. went with Mr. harden [the Rev. Robert Harden, S.J.] the roman Catholique missionary to Dine with Messrs. mead and fitsimons also roman.

Do. 16th. went on second party on sculkill river.

Philadelphia Capital of pensilvania is situated on a neck of land at the Confluence of the two fine rivers, Delawar and Schulkil. it is layed out in the form of a paralelogram or long square and Designed when finished, to extend two miles, from river to river, and to Compose eight long streets which are to be intersected at right angles by sixteen others Each a mile in length, broad, spacious and Even, with proper spaces left for the public buildings Churches and market places, in the Center is a Square of 10 acres, round which the public buildings are to be Disposed. the two principal streets, called high Street, [High Street, now Market Street] and Broad Street, are each one hund'd feet in Breadth, the others 60, and most of the houses have a small garden or orchard. there are great numbers of wharfs, the principal an hund'd. foot wide, and water enough for ships of 500 tuns burthen to load and unload alongside them. the ware houses are numerous and commodious, and the Docks for ship building are well adapted and Convenient. there is now twenty Vessels on the Stocks, great and small, some of the former three hund. tuns Burthen. the City exclusive of warehouses Consists of about 3,000 houses or more, the number of inhabitants, Computed to be about 30,000. the original of the town which I have Described here is far from being Completed, but is more advanced than any town whatsoever Ever was in so short a time, and encreasses Daily very considerably. there is a number of very rich merchants in this City. their trade is considerable to all westindia Islands, also the madeiras, spain, portugal, England, Ireland, and holland, there is a Surprising quantity of all kind of grain raised in the province Espec'y wheat, with which the[y] suplied England and Ireland abundantly this year, where it was very scarce, they have all kinds of provisions great plenty of vegetables, all this is brought Down the rivers Delawar and Sculkill. the Dutch [*i.e.* Germans] Employ the product of their farms to philadelph[ia] market. there has been 300 Vessels Cleard out of this port in one year, and as many Enter'd. between 8 and 900 thd. wagons drawn with four horsses Each In bringing their Chief Exportations, are, grain, lumber, Iron, of which there is plenty, Beef, pork, flaxseed, some hemp and furs the hemp theyl find use amongst themselves as the[y] have now many roperies and make very good Canvas or Duck. their Importations from the westindies Consists in sugar, rum, Cofee, Coten, and Molasses, sometimes Cash. they have set up several looms of late where there is a very good linnen made, and no Doubt but the Stamp Duty will augment their aplication that way. they send great quantitys of flaxseed to Ireland yearly, in return for which they have Irish linnens. the established religion was quaker formerly, but all believers in Christ are tolarated, the quakers seem to Dwindle very fast, there is a roman Church here [St. Mary's] to which resorts about 1200 people, many of which are Dutch, they are in generall poor. there are several good churches of protestants and presbiterens. the state house is a very good building, also the hospital. there are three public liberaries [the Library Company, the Logonian Library, and the American Philosophical]. they have two market Days in the week, wednesdays, and saturdas. It is amazeing the quantity of meat (which is exceed fine) and all kinds of provisions vegitables and fruits, that abounds at this market, and the number of people of both sexes, that Comes to buy provisions on those Days.

The Climate of Pensilvania is very agreable, and the air sweet and Clean. the fall or autumn begins about the 20th 8bre [October] and lasts to the Begining of Xbre [December], when the winter sets in, which Continues til march, frosty weather and extreme Cold seasons, are very Common here, so that the river Delawar tho broad and rapid, is often froze over, but then the weather is Dry and healthy. the spring lasts from march to June, and the Sumer in July, august, and September, Dureing which, the heats are Excessive, particularly in the night, more Disagreably so, than In the Island of hispaniola in the hotest time, this I have experienced.

the Soil of this province is in some places a black or yellow sand, in some light and gravelly, and in the vales along rivers sides a fat mould. the earth is very fruitful and easy to be laboured, it is prety well watered, well furnished with timber and Iron. In Short there is no part of america in a more flourishing Condition than pensilvania. great numbers of people abound to it, in some years more have transported themselves into this province, then into all the others besides. In the year 1729, 6208 perssons Came as passengers and servants, to setle here, four fifths of whom were from Ireland. they Continue still Comeing, to avoid the misery of their own Country, where they are a thousand times worse than guinea Slaves.

the Chief Inland town in pensilvania is lancaster, Sixty miles from philada. back in the Country. here they renew their treaties with the Indians, there is a prety Considerable trade Caryed on here with the back setlers. the Inhabitants of this province are a well Disposed people of a moderate Jenius, strong and well looking. they are more shie of strangers than in the other provs. and litle Curious of getting acquainted with them, or shewing any civilitys Except they have very good recommendations, this they say themselves, is owing to tricks put upon them by strangers, but I belive to be more owing to the reservedness of the quakers, which seems to have infused itself into all the Inhabit's,

August the 20th. Set out this morning for New York. breakfastd at fronkfort, 6 miles, a Small vilage. Dined at the red Lion tavern, 7 miles; [Torresdale] and slept at the Delawar fery tavern, 16 m., where I met with young Thoms. Mifflin and others.

Do. 21st. Crossed the Delawar near the falls. went thorough trenton i m. [*In margin:* There [are] Baraks by Trent[on] to hold 600 men.] and breakf'd at princetown. this is a prety Country town situated in a fine fruitful agreable Country. there is a good Colege here large Enough to hold 400 people, there is now 160 scholars. princetown is 10 m from trenton. from here to [New] Brunswick, 14 miles. here I Dined. there is also a Barack here. the road is very fine hithertoo, the Country well inhabited. this side the Delawar Is new Jersys. it [is] well cultivated, great plenty of all Sorts of fruits on each side, with which they faten the hogs in the season. indeed all the Catle like it beter than grass. they make great quantitys of Cider here but not Extraordinary in quality. after Dinner Crossed the fery and continued to amboy, 12 m. this is the Capital of East Jersy, Consisting of about 200 houses. it is well situated and has a comod[iou]s harbour there is Barracks here also. the Jerseys are Divided into East and west, amboy is Capitl of the first, and Burlington (which is on the Delawr, 20m. above philadelphia) Capital of west Jersy. the Governor resides 6 months in one place and 6 in the other. this Colony is well Inhabited and Cultivated. the climate is healthy and temperate. its general produce is, all sorts of Grain, horsses, black Catle, hogs, skins and pipe Staves, the[y] Catch some whale on the Coast.

they Export Bread, Corn, flower, Beef, pork, hams, fish, some buter, and bar Iron, to west Indies for which they receive, sugar molasses and rum in return; they send to England skins, pitch, tar, whale bone, etc. and oyl, for which the[y] have furniture and Cloath'g.

As the towns generally ly up in the Country the trade is Chiefly over land to new York.

There are from 100 to 200 familys in one place, great part of which are Dutch. the number of Inhabitants is computed at 65,000 of all ages and sexes, of which 6000 are men fit to Cary arms, and about 200 Indians. There is no Considerable town in the Jersys, amboy being the most so of any.

August the 22d. Crossed the fery from amboy to Staten Island which is about a mile broad, from hence to watsons fery at the other Extremity of the Island, 16 miles. here I Broke fast. this Island is in the province of new York, Distance about 9 m. N.W. [S.W.] from the metropolis. it is about [13] miles in length, and 6 or 7 in breadth. on the

South side is a Considerable tract of good level land, but the Island in general is rough and the hills prety high and stoney. the Inhabitants are principally Dutch [in fact, not German] and some french.

51. LORD ADAM GORDON, JOURNAL, CHARLESTON, 1764*

Lord Adam Gordon (c. 1726–1801) was a British colonel stationed in the West Indies. In 1764, he went as far north as Boston and kept a journal of his travels. After his return to England, he became an adviser to the Crown on conditions in the colonies. He was a member of Parliament between 1754 and 1768, and during the Revolution commanded forces in Scotland. The Charleston of Gordon's day had become the largest center of commerce and culture in the colonial South, and its influential, wealthy merchants, planters, and mechanics would direct the revolutionary movement from this metropolis.

I arrived at Charlestown, the Metropolis of South Carolina, *on the 8th Decemr.* 1764, having landed at Beaufort in Port Royal Island, some days before from Savannah river, which divides it from Georgia, as an imaginary Line does this Province from North Carolina.

It is of all the Southern Provinces the most considerable, on account of the Number of Inhabitants, the quantity and the variety of its productions and Exports, and the good condition of its Inhabitants. There seems in general to be but two Classes of people—the planters who are the proprietors, and the Merchants who purchase and Ship the produce.

Rice and Indigo are the two grand Staples of this Province, of which very great quantities are annually made and Exported to Europe and elsewhere. It has been augmenting annually in Numbers, wealth and Industry, since the Crown purchas'd out the Lords proprietors, and as none of its Exports or productions, interfere with those of the Mother Country, it will be prudent in her to give this Province all possible encouragement.

Almost every family of Note have a Town residence, to which they repair on publick occasions, and generally for the three Sickly months in the fall, it being a certainty, that the Town of Charles Town, is at present the most healt[h]y spot in the Province; fevers and other disorders are both less frequent in it, and less virulent in their Symptons; this is attributed to the Air being mended by the Number of Fires in

* From *Travels in the American Colonies*, Newton D. Mereness, ed. (New York: Macmillan, 1916), pp. 397–400. Reprinted by permission of The National Society of the Colonial Dames of America. A transcript of the original journal is in the Library of Congress, No. 213, King's Manuscripts, British Museum.

Town, as much as to its cool Situation, on a point, at the junction of the two navigable Streams, called Ashley and Cowper [Cooper] Rivers.

The Inhabitants are courteous, polite and affable, the most hospitable and attentive to Strangers, of any I have yet seen in America, very clever in business, and almost all of them, first or last, have made a trip to the Mother-Country. It is the fashion indeed to Send home all their Children for education, and if it was not owing to the nature of their Estates in this Province, which they keep all in their own hands, and require the immediate overlooking of the Proprietor, I am of opinion the most opulent planters, would prefer a home [English] life. It is in general believed, that they are more attached to the Mother Country, than those Provinces which lie more to the Northward, and which having hardly any Staple Commodities of their own growth, except Lumber, Stock and Horses, depend mostly on Smuggling Molasses and other Contraband Commodities.

The Town of Charlestown is very pleasantly Seated, at the conflux of two pretty rivers, from which all the Country product is brought down, and in return all imported goods are sent up the Country. The Streets are Straight, broad and Airy, the Churches are handsome; The other places of Worship are commodious, and many of the houses belonging to Individuals, are large and handsome, having all the conveniencies one sees at home. There is a Law against building houses of Wood, which like other Laws in other Countries no body observes, however, the most considerable buildings are of Brick, the others of Cypress and yellow Pine. The houses now are about fifteen hundred, but increase annually in a very surprizing manner.

Their Bar, which is very intricate, seems their only defence, for tho' they have a Fort below the Town, and a kind of earthen Rampart, with some Tabby works, round particular parts of Charlestown, yet it would not be tenible, against attacks of Shipping, or from the land, and therefore must fall a prey to any Enemy, the moment we lose our Superiority at Sea. A Forty Gun Ship has been in, but small Frigates and Sloops are generally employed on that Station.

The Town of Beaufort, Situated on Port Royal Island and Sound, has more depth of water on its Bar, but being on an Island there is a difficulty of bringing down the exportable Commodities, which will for ever prevent its Rivalling Charlestown, in wealth or grandeur.

On the Northern part of South Carolina, Stands George-Town, a pretty little Town near Wynyaw river, and not far from Pedee, Black river and Wakama, which river, I should think, would make a more Sure and Commodious boundary, between the two Carolinas, than any limits they now have.

The back Country towards the Cherokee Mounts and Nation, is all healthy and fertile land, producing large Oak, and other deciduous timber, and is finely watered, without much Sand or Pine-barren, but is not yet fully peopled;—In general what part of South Carolina is planted, is counted unhealthy, owing to the Rice-dams and Swamps, which as they occasion a great quantity of Stagnated water in Summer, never fails to increase the Number of Insects, and to produce fall fevers and Agues, dry gripes and other disorders, which are often fatal to the lower set of people, as well White as Black.

Within these two or three last years, a pretty considerable quantity of Flax and Hemp, has been raised by the Germans and other back settlers, which, as well as the produce of a considerable part of North Carolina, comes down to Charlestown in Waggons, drawn with four Horses, two abreast—perhaps at the distance of three hundred Miles— this would appear extraordinary at home, but it must be remember'd that they live at no more expence when travelling than they would at home, since the[y] lie in the woods all night, make a good fire to dress their Bacon, and turn their Horses loose near them, 'till day light, after which they proceed on their Journey, and carry back in Return what goods they stand in need of themselves, or for their neighbours in the back Settlements.

It is pretty singular to remark, that the Number of White Inhabitants, fit to bear Arms in one of their back Counties, called Craven County,—does,—at present exceed what was the Number of fighting Men, in all the Province Seven years ago,—from this—I conclude that the farther you go back from the Sea Board in America, the more fertile the land is, and the more healthy the Climate, for there the people increase and breed, and rear up more Children than towards the Pine barren and Sandy Shores.

The Tide Swamp land in these Southern Provinces is by much the most valuable, since, when they are properly banked in, and your trunks and dams in perfect good order, by a judicious use of these advantages, it is alternately equally capable and fit to produce the two great Staple Commodities—Vizt Rice and Indigo, the first requiring an uncommon degree of moisture or Water, and the last, dry and rich land, altho' the light land very near the Shore, will fetch very Surprizing Crops of Indigo, for two or three years, but it must then be thrown out, and left to time to recover its fertility.

Poultry and Pork, particularly Hams are excellent here. Beef and Mutton middling, and Fish very rare and dear; the general drink of the better people is Punch and Madeira Wine, and many prefer Grog and Toddy. All the poor, and many of the Rich, eat Rice for Bread, and give it even a preference; they use it in their Cakes, called Journey Cakes and boiled, or else boiled Indian corn, which they call Hominy, and of this they have two sorts, the great and small—the last I think the best.

Upon the whole, this is undoubtedly one of the most opulent, and most increasing Colonies in America, and bids fair to exceed all the others, if it advances in the like proportion as it has done for forty years past.

The unhappy differences which have Subsisted for some years past, between the Governour and the Commons House of Assembly, and are not yet set to rights, have been the means of this Country not standing so well at home, as otherways they would have done, and as they really deserve to do. [*See below*, The Gadsden-Boone Controversy, No. 57.]

52. THE WEST: SERMON BOOK OF CHARLES WOODMASON, 1770*

Charles Woodmason (fl. 1720–1776) was a planter, storekeeper, and Anglican preacher. Despite his Tory leanings, he became a self-styled spokesman for the back-country people of South Carolina, who held only small property and were politically underprivileged. His journal, sermons, and letters describe a rough frontier folk who possessed neither the social graces nor the refinements and education of the tide-water aristocrats. Woodmason soon became persona non grata *to the tidewater revolutionaries because of his Toryism and his outspoken statements on the underrepresentation of the West. The following sermon was delivered at the High Hills of Santee.*

Behavior in Church

Always contrive to come before Service begins—Which You may do, as We begin so late. 'Tis but putting and getting things in Order over Night—Whereas many will hardly set about it till Sunday Morning. Contrive too, to go as early as possible to rest on Saturday Night so that You may rise early and refresh'd on the Lords day and not be hurry'd in dressing, and ordering Matters. The coming late to Sermon discourages People, for lack of Company—and coming in after Service is begun is very troublesome—Disturb both me and ev'ry One and should be avoided as much as possible—But if it is unavoidable, pray enter leisurely—tread softly—nor disturb any who are on their Knees or are intent on their Devotions. Bring no Dogs with You—they are very troublesome—and I shall inform the Magistrate of those who do it, for it is an Affront to the Divine Presence which We invoke, to be in the midst of Us, and to hear our Prayers, to mix unclean things with our Services.

When You are seated—do not whisper, talk, gaze about—shew

* Richard J. Hooker, ed., *The Carolina Backcountry on the Eve of The Revolution: The Journal and Other Writings of Charles Woodmason . . .* (Chapel Hill: University of North Carolina Press, and The Institute of Early American History and Culture, 1953), pp. 88–89. Reprinted by permission of the publisher.

light Airs, or Behaviour—for this argues a wandering Mind and Ir-
reverence towards God; is unbecoming Religion, and may give Scandal
and Offence to weak Christians:—Neither sneeze or Cough, if You can
avoid it—and do not practise that unseemly, rude, indecent Custom of
Chewing or of spitting, which is very ridiculous and absurd in Public,
expecially in Women and in Gods House. If you are thirsty—Pray drink
before you enter or before Service begins, not to go out in midst of
Prayer, nor be running too and fro like Jews in their Synagogues—except
Your necessary Occasions should oblige You—Do You see anything like
it in Charles Town or among Well bred People. Keep Your Children as
quiet as possible. If they will be fractious, Carry them out at once for I
will not have Divine Worship *now* consider'd by You, as if I was offici-
ating in a private House. . . .

Many among you possibly prefer Extempore Sermons, to those
which are Premeditated, and may call my Mode of Delivery, rather
Reading than *Preaching.* 'Tis true, extempore Discourses have their
peculiar Merit—but there is hardly one Man in the World, but will speak
better and more useful Sense, premediately than Extempore. . . .

Ev'ry Sunday Afternoon, I purpose catechising as Many of You,
Young and old, as can possibly attend. . . .

When Banns are published—Don't make it a Matter of Sport; but
let it stir You up to put up a Petition to Heav'n for a Blessing of God
upon the Parties.

53. THE PAXTON BOYS, *A DECLARATION AND REMONSTRANCE OF THE DISTRESSED AND BLEEDING FRONTIER INHABITANTS OF . . . PENNSYLVANIA,* 1764*

*The Paxton Boys, frontiersmen from western Pennsylvania, were
Scots-Irish Rangers who had fought in the French and Indian War and
battled Pontiac during his conspiracy. Nurturing a hatred for the redman,
they demanded (unsuccessfully) a bounty on scalps from the Pennsylvania government. Their fury erupted in the massacre of a community
of peaceful Indians at Conestoga. Several of the Paxton Boys were arrested, but the governor was unable to obtain convictions from juries or
justices who sympathized with the accused.*

*In 1764, some six hundred Paxton Boys marched on Philadelphia
to cast their votes against Pennsylvania's eastern, Quaker politicians
who had been niggardly in appropriating funds for frontier defense and*

* *A Declaration and Remonstrance of the Distressed and Bleeding Frontier
Inhabitants of the Province . . . of Pennsylvania* (Philadelphia: William Bradford,
1764), pp. 10–18.

who had failed to accord equitable representation to the western counties. The following petition to the governor states the frontiersmen's grievances. There were similar troubles in South Carolina and especially North Carolina, where in 1771 bitter feelings exploded in military conflict between East and West.

To the Honourable JOHN PENN, Esquire, Governor of the Province of *Pennsylvania*, and of the Counties of *New-Castle, Kent* and *Sussex*, on *Delaware*; and to the Representatives of the Free-Men of said Province, in Assembly met.

We *Matthew Smith*, and *James Gibson*, in behalf of ourselves, and his Majesty's faithful and loyal Subjects, the Inhabitants of the Frontier Counties of *Lancaster, York, Cumberland, Berks*, and *Northampton*, humbly beg Leave to remonstrate, and to lay before you, the following Grievances, which we submit to your Wisdom for Redress.

1st. WE apprehend, that as Free-Men and *English* Subjects, we have an indisputable Title to the same Privileges and Immunities with his Majesty's other subjects, who reside in the interior Counties of *Philadelphia, Chester* and *Bucks*, and therefore ought not be excluded from an equal Share with them in the very important Privilege of Legislation. Nevertheless, contrary to the Proprietors Charter, and the acknowledged principles of Common Justice and Equity, our five Counties are restrained from electing more than ten Representatives, viz, Four for *Lancaster*, Two for *York*, Two for *Cumberland*, One for *Berks*, and one for *Northhampton*; while the Three Counties (and City) of *Philadelphia, Chester*, and *Bucks*, elect Twenty-six; this we humbly conceive is oppressive, unequal and unjust, the Cause of many of our Grievances, and an infringement of our natural Privileges of Freedom and Equality, wherefore we humbly pray, that we may be no longer deprived of an equal Number with the Three aforesaid Counties, to represent us in Assembly.

2dly. WE understand that a Bill is now before the House of Assembly, wherein it is Provided, that such Persons as shall be charged with killing any *Indians* in *Lancaster* County, shall not be tried in the County where the Fact was committed, but in the Counties of *Philadelphia, Chester*, or *Bucks*. This is manifestly to deprive *British* Subjects of their known Privileges, to cast an eternal Reproach upon whole Counties, as if they were unfit to serve their Country in the Quality of Jury-Men, and to contradict the well known Laws of the *British* Nation, in a point whereon Life, Liberty, and Security essentially depend: Namely, that of being tried by their Equals in the Neighbourhood where their own, their Accusers, and the Witnesses Character and Credit, with the Circumstances of the Fact are best known, and instead thereof, putting their

Lives in the Hands of Strangers, who may as justly be suspected of Partiality to, as the Frontier Counties can be of Prejudices against Indians; and this too in favour of Indians only, against his Majesty's faithful and loyal Subjects. Besides it is well known that the Design of it is to comprehend a Fact committed before such a Law was thought of. And if such Practices were tollerated, no man could be secure in his most invaluable Interests. We are also informed to our great Surprize, that this Bill has actually received the Assent of a Majority of the House, which we are persuaded could not have been the Case, had our Frontier Counties been equally represented in Assembly: However, we hope, that the Legislator of this Province will never enact a Law of so dangerous a tendency, or take away from his Majesty's good Subjects, a Privilege so long esteemed sacred by *English Men.*

3dly. DURING the late and present *Indian* Wars, the Frontiers of this Province have been repeatedly attacked and ravaged by Skulking parties of the Indians, who have with the most savage Cruelty, murdered Men, Women and Children, without distinction; and have reduced near a Thousand Families to the most extream Distress. It grieves us to the very Heart, to see such of our Frontier Inhabitants as have escaped from savage Fury, with the loss of their Parents, their Children, their Husbands, Wives, or Relatives, left destitute by the Public, and exposed to the most cruel Poverty and Wretchedness; while upwards of One Hundred and Twenty of the Savages, who are with great Reason suspected of being guilty of these horrid Barbarities, under the Mask of Friendship, have procured themselves to be taken under the Protection of the Government, with a view to elude the Fury of the brave Relatives of the Murdered; and are now maintained at the public Expence. . . .

4thly. WE humbly conceive that it is contrary to the Maxims of good Policy and extreamly dangerous to our Frontiers, to suffer any *Indians* of what Tribe soever, to live within the inhabited Parts of this Province, while we are engaged in an *Indian* War; as Experience has taught us that they are all Perfidious, and their Claim to Freedom and Independency puts it in their Power to act as Spies, to entertain and give Intelligence to our Enemies, and to furnish them with Provisions and warlike Stores. To this fatal Intercourse between our pretended Friends and open Enemies we must ascribe the greatest Part of the Ravages and Murders that have been committed in the Course of this and the last *Indian* War. We therefore pray that this Grievance be taken under consideration and remedied.

5th. WE cannot help lamenting that no Provision has been hitherto made, that such of our Frontier Inhabitants as have been wounded in defence of the Province, their Lives and Liberties, may be taken care of and cured of their Wounds at public Expence. We therefore pray that this Grievance may be redressed.

6thly. IN the late *Indian* War this Province, with other of his Majesty's Colonies gave rewards for *Indian* Scalps, to encourage the seeking them in their own Country, as the most likely Means of destroying or reducing them to reason. But no such Encouragement has been given in this War, which has damped the Spirits of many brave Men, who are willing to venture their Lives in Parties against the Enemy. We therefore pray that public Rewards may be proposed for *Indian* Scalps, which may be adequate to the Dangers attending Enterprises of this Nature.

7th. WE daily lament that Numbers of our nearest and dearest Relatives are still in Captivity amongst the savage Heathen, to be trained up in all their ignorance and Barbarity, or be tortured to death with all the Contrivances of Indian cruelty, for attempting to make their Escape from Bondage. We see they pay no regard to the many solemn Promises which they made to restore our Friends, who are in Bondage amongst them; we therefore earnestly pray that no Trade may hereafter be permitted to be carried on with them, untill our Brethren and Relatives are brought home to us.

8thly. WE complain that a certain Society of People in this Province in the late *Indian* War and at several Treaties held by the Kings Representatives, openly loaded the *Indians* with Presents and that I[srael] P[emberton] a Leader of the said Society, in defiance of all Government not only abetted our *Indian* Enemies, but kept up a private Intelligence with them, and publickly received from them a Belt of Wampum, as if he had been our Governor or authorized by the King to treat with his Enemies. By this Means the *Indians* have been taught to dispise us as a weak and disunited People and from this fatal Source have arose many of our Calamities under which we groan. We humbly pray therefore this Grievance may be redressed and that no private Subject be hereafter permitted to treat with or carry on a Correspondence with our Enemies.

9thly. WE cannot but observe with sorrow that Fort *Augusta* which has been very expensive to this Province, has afforded us but little assistance, during this or the last War. The Men that were stationed at that Place neither helped our distressed Inhabitants to save their Crops, nor did they attack our Enemies in their Towns, or patrole on our Frontiers. We humbly request, that proper Measures may be taken to make that Garrison more serviceable to us in our Distress, if it can be done. . . .

54. LABORING AND DEPENDENT CLASSES, 1762–72[*]

Many commoners besides Westerners felt uncomfortable in the social organization of British colonial society, among them the small farmer, the mechanic, and the indentured servant. There is abundant material describing the lives and viewpoints of the great merchants, planters, and politicians; by comparison the plebeians are voiceless. They did not write letters—many could not write—and they did not keep journals. But an occasional letter to the local newspaper editor, a comment in an advertisement, or a writer's observations of common folk give insight into their interests. In the following selections, the common people indicate which side they are likely to take in the revolutionary struggle. Mechanics often made up the mobs who rioted against the British on the eve of the revolt. Farmers joined the forces of Washington, Greene, or Marion. Some elected to remain loyal and went home to England or managed to remain and somehow survive the ordeal of loyalism during and after the war.

The Farmer

To the Printer of the PROVIDENCE GAZETTE and COUNTRY JOURNAL:

SIR,

    I Am one of your Country Subscribers, and although I have no Learning myself, more than what I obtained from my own Industry, without Instruction, I value it in others. There is generally too much Reflection cast on Country People for being illiterate and aukward; but if the Authors of such Reflections had any Candour, they would make all proper Allowances for narrow Circumstances, the constant Attendance which we and our Children are obliged to give in the Execution of our laborious Callings, the dispersed Manner of our Living, and the Want of Schools. It is impracticable under these Circumstances to become learned, or acquainted with the Fashions of the World, which is called being polite, as a Merchant's Clerk, or a Printer, to become an able General of an Army, or an expert Seaman; all these Cases require Leisure, Instruction, and Experience. Printing is the greatest Means of promoting Learning that ever was invented; and I hope that the setting up of that Business near us, may contribute to our Instruction, and be

[*] "The Farmer" from the *Providence Gazette* and *Country Journal*, October 30, 1762; "The Mechanic" from the *South Carolina Gazette*, February 2, 1765. The Indentured servant from *Woodstock Letters*, Vol. XXXV, (1906), pp. 53–54. The originals are in the Georgetown University Archives.

one means of improving the rising Generation, and in wiping out the
Odium cast on us, of being ignorant, rude, and unpolished.

Smithfield,   *Your Well-wisher,*

Oct. 25. 1762   A COUNTRYMAN

The Mechanic

To the South Carolina Gazette:

CHARLES-TOWN January 30, 1765

Mr. Timothy,

If there is a Curse heavier than another, let it fall with fourfold
Vengance upon the Head of a FORESTALLER, who is a Wretch that,
Tyger-like, preys, with the same unrelenting Heart, on the Vitals of the
Small and Great, and gluts his Avarice, that he may wallow for a Time,
in ill-gotten Pelf.

The Character of the HIGHWAYMAN is more respectable than
an INGROSSER's; for a Man may stand on his Defence against the
former; but neither Courage nor Prudence can shield him from the in-
iquitous Imposition of the other; who, as much in him lies, defeats the
gracious designs of Providence, in showering down its Blessings abundantly; but alas! the Multitude have not wherewithal to purchase them
from the *Extortioner*.

He that forestalls the Necessaries of Life, *insults* his God, by
making an artificial *Scarcity*, though Plenty surrounds us; and in broad
Day, he tramples upon the Bonds of Society, by plundering the Affluent,
and *grinding* the Faces of *the* POOR with impunity. He knows indeed
that Loads of Imprecations are poured forth against him both in Public
and in private; but his whole Soul is so engrossed by the Desire of Gain,
that he is deaf to every Thing else, and a reasonable Profit will not
content him.

When the Measure of some Men's Consciences will be full, no one
can say. But it seems *Time*, and I am sure it is *necessary*, to set Bounds
to them, or we shall soon be obliged to build *more* ALMSHOUSES, to
receive our poor distressed Inhabitants; for it is past a Doubt, that an
industrious man, who does not earn more then *Thirty* or *Forty Shillings*
in the Day (and *few* do that) cannot possibly pay House-Rent, cloath
and feed his Family, and pay FIVE POUNDS out of his poor Pittance,
to purchase a CORD OF FIREWOOD, and that *ill-measured* too; an
Article which he must have, either in small or greater Quantity: His
Family therefore, must either be worse clothed, worse fed, or both, if
they will enjoy the Comfort of a Fire; so that one Way or the other,
they must be pinched or half starved; and in Consequence Sickness and
Distress must multiply.

ROUZE then, FELLOW-CITIZENS! and root out those Pests from the Community; for, be the *Affluent* ever so passive, under such barefaced Extortion, the Condition of the MANY who are placed by Providence in lower Stations, surely deserves *some Consideration.*

Let us therefore directly *instruct* our REPRESENTATIVES; *petition* the GENERAL ASSEMBLY for a proper Law; *apply* for an Act TO INCORPORATE THE TOWN, or do *any Thing* else that becomes us, to extirpate this Evil of the blackest Dye.

Never was a more proper Time; for we may be assured, from *past experience*, that our present worthy GOVERNOR will most chearfully concur in whatever Measure can be proposed to relieve from Distress, a People whom he rules with the Tenderness of an indulgent Parent; nor need we doubt, that our present ASSEMBLY, who have done so many good Things, and in all Respects shown themselves deserving of the Trust reposed in them, will readily protect us from the Hardships we already suffer, and others which are daily gaining Ground on us.

A TRADESMAN

The Indentured Servant

Joseph Mosley [S.J.] Tuckahoe, [Maryland] to Mrs. Dunn Junior of Northumberland June 5, 1772

Dear Sister:

. . . .

I must give you an insight of the nature of an imported servant, indented here to be sold. 1st. An indented servant must be publicly sold, for a slave, for the term of years signed in his indenture, which brings him for that term of years on a footing with our Negro slaves. 2ndly. They have no choice of masters; but, the highest bidder, at public sale, carries them off, to be used at his mercy, without any redress at law. 3rdly. These masters (as they are chiefly accustomed to negroes, a stubborn, dull set of mortals, that do nothing but by driving) are, in general, cruel, barbarous, and unmerciful—some worse than others. 4thly. The servants' labour is chiefly in the fields, with an ox, plow, or hoe, with an overseer by them, armed with a cudgel, to drive them on with their work. 5thly. Their diet is mean and poor, chiefly some composition of our Indian corn, which at best is very strong, and ill-savoured to an European taste, and, I think, more fit for horses and hogs, than Christians; although in my Missions, I've made many a hearty meal of it. Lastly, and which is yet worst of all, for Roman Catholics: by the law of Maryland every indented servant must take the oaths on landing, or the captains of ships pay £ 5 for each recusant, a law invented to prevent the importation of Catholic servants. The captains of ships, before landing, use the utmost rigor with them, to bring them to it. Many have told me, that they have, for trifling faults, been severely whipped to bring them to that one point. Most are brought to it by threats and promises, before they come to anchor. I beg of you to use all your interest, to hinder any of your acquaintance, especially of our [Roman Catholic] persuasion, from shipping themselves to America: they will bitterly regret it, when it is too late. Masters of ships may sing them fine Canterbury stories of this wild country, but as a friend they may believe me, as being an eye-witness of what I say and advance. It has been a fine poor man's country, but now it is well peopled, the lands are all secured, and the harvest for such is now all over. The Lands are mostly worked by the landlords' negroes, and, of consequence, white servants, after their term of bondage is out, are strolling about the country without bread. [His nephew] if he is careful and industrious, may do well at Annapolis, as his business is little known, and much courted by the ladies, who are fond of dress, and particularly of a nice head of hair. I think I've said enough on this head, for you to give your advice, where it may be asked and wanted. . . .

2

Conservative Thought in the Revolution

55. THOMAS POWNALL, *THE ADMINISTRATION OF THE AMERICAN COLONIES*, 1765*

Thomas Pownall (1722–1805) was a student of colonial administration. His experiences as secretary to the governor of New York, aide to Lord Loudon (commander of Anglo-American forces during the French and Indian War), and later advised to William Pitt impressed him with the need for imperial reform. In 1765, he published his Administration of the American Colonies, *revising it four times during the following decade in accordance with changing political conditions. In many respects he was an advanced political thinker, advocating the extension of natural rights throughout the Empire. But his ideas for centralization through a commercial dominion under which all provincial governments would be uniform and tightly bound to the king were unacceptable to the increasingly nationalistic Americans. James Otis, a Massachusetts radical, responded to Pownall's proposals by averring, "This never will nor can be done, without making the colonists vassals of the crown."*

. . . I do not think it would be impertinent just to make the idea of colonies, and their special circumstances, which makes it a measure in commercial governments, to establish, cultivate, and maintain them.

The view of trade in general, as well as of manufactures in particular, terminates in securing an extensive and permanent vent; or to speak more precisely, (in the same manner as shop-keeping does) in

---

* Thomas Pownall, *The Administration of the American Colonies* (London: J. Walter, 1768), pp. 38–52. The 1765 edition (pp. 25–39) is in the Library of Congress but its condition rendered it unusable for this editor's purposes. The sections which were excerpted are the same, however.

having many and good customers: the wisdom, therefore, of a trading
nation, is to gain, and to create, as many as possible. Those whom we
gain in foreign trade, we possess under restrictions and difficulties, and
may lose in the rivalship of commerce: those that a trading nation can
create within itself, it deals with under its own regulations, and makes its
own, and cannot lose. In the establishing colonies, a nation creates people
whose labour, being applied to new objects of produce and manufacture,
opens new channels of commerce, by which they not only live in ease
and affluence within themselves, but, while they are labouring under
and for the mother country, (for there all their external profits center)
become an increasing nation, of appropriated and good customers to the
mother country. These not only increase our manufactures, encrease our
exports, but extend our commerce; and if duly administered, extend the
nation, its powers, and its dominions, to wherever these people extend
their settlements. This is, therefore, an interest which is, and ought to
be dear to the mother country: this is an object that deserves the best
care and attention of government: and the people, who through various
hardships, disasters, and disappointments; through various difficulties and
almost ruinous expences, have wrought up this interest to such an important object, merit every protection, grace, encouragement, and privilege, that are in the power of the mother country to grant. It is on this
valuable consideration . . . that they have a right to the grants, charters,
privileges and protection which they receive; and also on the other
hand, it is from these grants, charters, privileges and protection given to
them, that the mother country has an exclusive right to the external
profits of their labour, and to their custom. As it is the right, so it becomes the duty of the mother country to nourish and cultivate, to
protect and govern the colonies: which nurture and government should
precisely direct its care to two essential points. 1st, That all the profits
of the produce and manufactures of these colonies center finally in the
mother country: and 2dly, That the colonies continue to be the sole and
proper customers of the mother country. To these two points, collateral
with the interests, rights and welfare of the colonies, every measure of
administration, every law of trade should tend: I say collateral, because,
rightly understood, these two points are mutually coincident with the
interests, rights and welfare of the colonies.

It has been often suggested, that care should be taken in the administration of the plantations; lest, in some future time, these colonies
should become independent of the mother country. But perhaps it may
be proper on this occasion, nay, it is justice to say it, that if, by becoming
independent is meant a revolt, nothing is further from their nature, their
interest, their thoughts. If a defection from the alliance of the mother
country be suggested, it ought to be, and can be truly said, that their
spirit abhors the sense of such; their attachment to the protestant suces-

sion in the house of Hanover will ever stand unshaken; and nothing can eradicate from their hearts their natural, almost mechanical, affection to Great Britain, which they conceive under no other sense, nor call by any other name, than that of *home*. Besides, the merchants are, and must ever be, in great measure allied with those of Great Britain; their very support consists in this alliance, and nothing but false policy here can break it. If the trade of the colonies be protected and directed from hence, with the true spirit of the act of navigation, that spirit under which it has risen, no circumstances of trade could tempt the Colonists to certain ruin under any other connections. The liberty and religion of the British colonies are incompatible with either French or Spanish government; and they know full well, that they could hope for neither liberty nor protection under a Dutch one. Any such suggestion, therefore, is a false and unjust aspersion of their principles and affections; and can arise from nothing but an intire ignorance of their circumstances. Yet again, on the other hand, while they remain under the support and protection of the government of the mother country; while they profit of the beneficial part of its trade; while their attachment to the present royal family stands firm, and their alliance with the mother country is inviolate, it may be worth while to inquire, whether they may not become and act independent of the *government and laws* of the mother country:—and if any such symptoms should be found, either in their government, courts, or trade, perhaps it may be thought high time, even now, to inquire how far these colonies are or are not arrived, at this time, at an independency of the government of the mother country:—and if any measure of such independency, formed upon precedents unknown to the government of the mother country at the time they were form'd, should be insisted on, when the government of the mother country was found to be so weak or distracted at home, or so deeply engaged abroad in Europe, as not to be able to attend to, and assert its right in America, with its own people:—perhaps it may be thought, that no time should be lost to remedy or redress these deviations—if any such be found; or to remove all jealousies arising from the idea of them, if none such really exist.

If the colonies are to be possessed, as of right, and governed by the crown, as demesnes of the crown, by such charters, commissions, instructions, &c. as the crown shall, from time to time, grant or issue; then a revision of these charters, commissions, instructions, so as to establish the rights of the crown, and the privileges of the people, as thereby created, is all that is necessary. But while the crown may, perhaps justly and of right, *in theory*, consider these lands, and the plantations thereon, as its demesnes, and as of special right properly belonging to it; not incorporated and of common right with the dominions and realm of Great Britain: in consequence of which theory, special rights of the

crown are there established; and from which theory, the special modification under which the people possess their privileges is derived.—While
this is the idea on one hand, the people on the other say, that they could
not forfeit, nor lose the common rights and privileges of Englishmen, by
adventuring under various disasters and difficulties, under heavy expences, and every hazard, to settle these vast countries, to engage in un-
tried channels of labour, thereby increasing the nation's commerce, and extending its dominions; but that they must carry with them, whereever they
go, the right of being governed only by the laws of the realm; only by
laws made with their own consent:—that they must ever retain with
them the right of not being taxed without their own consent, or that
of their representatives; and therefore, as it were by nature divided off
from the share of the general representation of the nation, they do not
hold, by tenor of charter or temporary grant, in a commission, but by an
inherent, essential right, the right of representation and legislature, with
all its powers and privileges, as possessed in England. It is, therefore, that
the people do, and ever will, until this matter be settled, exercise these
rights and privileges after the precedents formed here in England, and
perhaps carried, in the application, even further, than they ever were in
England; and not under the restriction of commissions and instructions:
and it is therefore also, in matters where laws, made since their establishment, do not extend to them by special proviso, that they claim the right
of directing themselves by their own laws. While these totally different
ideas of the principles, whereon the government and the people found
their claims and rights, remain unsettled and undetermined, there can
be nothing but discordant jarring, and perpetual obstruction in the
exercise of them;—there can be no government, properly so called, but
merely the predominancy of one faction or the other, acting under the
mask of the forms of government. This is the short and precise abstract of
the long and perplexed history of the governments and administrations
of the colonies, under the various shapes with which their quarrels have
vexed themselves, and seized government here in Britain.

If this idea of the crown's right to govern these as demesnes be
just, and be as right in fact, as it is supposed to be in theory, let it be
settled and fixed by some due and sufficient authority, what it is, and
how far it extends. But this is not all; let it be so established, that where
it ought, it may actually, and in practice, be carried into execution also.
If this right be doubted; or is, being allowed, it finds itself in such
circumstances as not to be able to carry its powers into execution, it will
then become an object of government, to see that these colonies be
governed, and their affairs administered some other way. There is no
doubt in the theory of our constitution of the king's right, in time of war
and array, to exercise martial law: and yet in practice it has been found

right, (and would not otherwise be permitted) that this martial law should be confirmed by parliament.

If, therefore, the several points wherein the crown, or its governors acting under its instructions, differ with the people be considered, and it be once determined what, in order to maintain the subordination of the government of the colonies to the government of Great Britain, is necessary to be done,—the mode of doing that will be easily settled. If it be a point determined, that it lies wholly with the crown to fix and actuate this order of government—the crown will duly avail itself of that power, with which it is entrusted, to enforce its administration. But if it be found that, however this may lie with the crown as of right, yet the crown is not in power to establish this right,—it will of course call in aid the power of the legislature, to confirm and establish it. But if, finally, it should appear, that these colonies, as corporations within the dominions of Great Britain, are included within the imperium of the realm of the same,—it will then of right become the duty of legislature to interpose in the case; to regulate and define their rights and privileges; to establish and order their administration; and to direct the channels of their commerce. Tho' the first of these measures should be, in strict justice, the crown's right—yet the second is the only next practicable one: and altho' the second, as such, may most likely be adopted—yet the third is the only wise and sure measure. In the second case, the crown, having formed its several general instructions for the several governments, according to their various charters, grants, and proprietaries, will order the same, in those points which it cannot influence and determine by the effect of its own negative, to be laid before parliament, to be considered and confirmed by the legislature, in the same manner as are the rules for governing the army. In the third case, the crown will order its ministry to lay before parliament, the rights and powers of the crown; the rights, privileges and claims of the people; with a general state of the colonies, their interest and operations, as related to the crown, as related to the mother country, as related to foreign powers and interests, and to the colonies of foreign powers, as related to the laws and government of the mother country;—perhaps pointing out some general plan of government, judicatory, revenue and commerce, as may become, what I hinted at in the beginning of this paper—*a leading measure to the forming Great Britain, with all its Atlantic and American possessions, into one great commercial dominion.* In the one case, the instructions of the crown, either some general form of such, or the special ones given to each governor, on each fresh nomination, will be confirm'd by parliament, as the rules and orders for governing the army are. In the other, a general bill of rights, and establishment of government and commerce on a great plan of union, will be settled and enacted: the governments of the several colonies, on the continent and in the islands, will be considered as so many corporations, holding their lands in common soccage, according to the manor of East Greenwich, united to the realm; so that, for every power, which they exercise or possess, they will depend on the government of Great Britain; so that, in every movement, they may be held, each within its proper sphere, and be drawn and connected to this center: and as forming a one system, they will be so connected in their various orbs and subordination of orders, as to be capable of receiving and communicating, from the first mover (the government of Great Britain) any political motion, in the direction in which it is given. Great Britain, as the center of this system, must be the center of attraction, to which these colonies, in the administration of every power of their government, in the exercise of their judicial powers, and the execution of their laws, and in every operation of their trade, must tend. They will be so framed, in their natural and political interests; in the rights, privileges, and protection they enjoy; in the powers of trade, which they actuate, under the predominating general commerce of the nation, that they will remain under the constant influence of the attraction of this center; and cannot move, but that every direction of such movement will converge to the same. At the same time that they all conspire in this one center, *they must be guarded against having, or forming, any principle of coherence with each other above that, whereby they cohere in this center*; having no other principle of intercommunication between each other, than that by which they are in joint communion with Great Britain as the common center of all. At the same time that they are, each in their respective parts and subordinations, so framed, as to be actuated by this first mover, —they should always remain incapable of any coherence, or of so conspiring amongst themselves, as to create any other equal force, which might recoil back on this first mover; nor is it more necessary to preserve the several governments subordinate within their respective orbs, than it is essential to the preservation of the empire to keep them disconnected and indepedent of each other: they certainly are so at present; the different manner in which they are settled, the different modes under which they live, the different forms of charters, grants and frame of government they possess, the various principles of repulsion that these create, the different interests which they actuate, the religious interests by which they are actuated, the rivalship and jealousies which arise from hence, and the impracticability, if not the impossibility of reconciling and accommodating these incompatible ideas and claims, will keep them for ever so. And nothing but a tampering activity of wrongheaded inexperience misled to be meddling, can ever do any mischief here. The provinces and colonies are under the best form as to this point, which they can be. They are under the best frame and disposition for the government of the mother country (duly applied) to take place. And as there cannot be a more just, so there cannot be a wiser measure than to leave them all in the free and full possession of their several rights and privileges, as by grant, charter, or commission given, and in the full exercise thereof, so far, and no further, than as derived therefrom. If, upon a revision, there be found any, and perhaps some one such at least, may be found, who have grossly and intentionally transgressed these bounds, such should be an exception to this rule, and be made an example also to others.

Under the guidance therefore of these principles—that the final external profits of the labour and produce of colonies should center in the mother country,—that the colonists are the appropriated special customers of the mother country,—that the colonies, in their government and trade, should be all united in communion with, the subordination to the government of the mother country, but ever disconnected and independent of each other by any other communion than what centers here:—Under the guidance of these principles, with a temper and spirit which remember that these are our own people, our brethren, faithful, good and beneficial subjects, and free-born Englishmen, or by adoption, possessing all the right of freedom:—Under the guidance of these principles, and with this temper and spirit of government,—let a revision be made of the general and several governments of the colonies, of their laws and courts of justice, of their trade, and the general British laws of trade, in their several relations in which they stand to the mother country, to the government of the mother country, to foreign countries, and the colonies of foreign countries, to one another; and then let those measures be taken, which, upon such a review, shall appear necessary; and all which government can do, or ought to do at present, will be done. . . .

56. JONATHAN BOUCHER, *A VIEW OF THE CAUSES AND CONSEQUENCES OF THE AMERICAN REVOLUTION*: CIVIL LIBERTY, 1774*

Jonathan Boucher (1738–1804), Anglican clergyman, was born in England, the third son of an alehouse keeper and tutor. Taught by his father and educated in the free schools, his talent developed despite an early life of grinding poverty. In 1759 he emigrated to Virginia and opened a school for boys. Among his pupils was "Jackie" Custis, son of Martha Custis Washington, and from this association Boucher formed a profitable friendship with George Washington.

Boucher took orders in the church in 1762 and began rising socially, settling in Annapolis where he became a literary figure and

---

* Jonathan Boucher, *A View of the Causes and Consequences of the American Revolution* (London: G. G. and J. Robinson, 1797), Discourse XII, pp. 508–60.

a patron of the theater. He strongly supported the establishment of an American episcopate and persevered as a staunch advocate of Crown and Parliamentary prerogatives as the quarrel with the colonists intensified. For his opinions he was placed under constant surveillance by the Committee of Safety, was burned in effigy by radicals, and threatened by mobs. So vehement was the feeling against him in his own parish that he felt constrained to deliver his sermons with a brace of loaded pistols resting on a nearby cushion. The following sermon was given to the parishioners of Queen Anne's Church. Boucher finally fled to England in 1775.

Civil Liberty, Passive Obedience and Non Resistance, 1774

. . . .

If the form of government under which the good providence of God has been pleased to place us be mild and free, it is our duty to enjoy it with gratitude and with thankfulness; and, in particular, to be careful not to abuse it by licentiousness. If it be less indulgent and less liberal than in reason it ought to be, still it is our duty not to disturb and destroy the peace of the community, by becoming refractory and rebellious subjects, and *resisting the ordinances of God.* However humiliating such acquiescence may seem to men of warm and eager minds, the wisdom of God in having made it our duty is manifest. For, as it is the natural temper and bias of the human mind to be impatient under restraint, it was wise and merciful in the blessed Author of our religion not to add any new impulse to the natural force of this prevailing propensity, but, with the whole weight of his authority, altogether to discountenance every tendency to disobedience.

If it were necessary to vindicate the Scriptures for this their total unconcern about a principle which so many other writings seem to regard as the first of all human considerations, it might be observed, that, avoiding the vague and declamatory manner of such writings, and avoiding also the useless and impracticable subtleties of metaphysical definitions, these Scriptures have better consulted the great general interests of mankind, by summarily recommending and enjoining a conscientious reverence for law whether human or divine. To respect the laws, is to respect liberty in the only rational sense in which the term can be used; for liberty consists in a subserviency to law. "Where there is no law," says Mr. Locke, "there is no freedom." The mere man of nature (if such an one there ever was) has no freedom: *all his lifetime he is subject to bondage.* It is by being included within the pale of civil polity and government that he takes his rank in society as a free man.

Hence it follows, that we are free, or otherwise, as we are governed by law, or by the mere arbitrary will, or wills, of any individual, or any number of individuals. And liberty is not the setting at nought and despising established laws—much less the making our own wills the rule of our own actions, or the actions of others—and not bearing (whilst yet we dictate to others) the being dictated to, even by the laws of the land; but it is the being governed by law, and by law only. . . .

"Civil liberty (says an excellent writer [Bishop Butler]) is a severe and a restrained thing; implies, in the notion of it, authority, settled subordinations, subjection, and obedience; and is altogether as much hurt by too little of this kind, as by too much of it. And the love of liberty, when it is indeed the love of liberty, which carries us to withstand tyranny, will as much carry us to reverence authority, and to support it; for this most obvious reason, that one is as necessary to the being of liberty, as the other is destructive of it. And, therefore, the love of liberty which does not produce this effect, the love of liberty which is not a real principle of dutiful behaviour towards authority, is as hypocritical as the religion which is not productive of a good life. Licentiousness is, in truth, such an excess of liberty as is of the same nature with tyranny. For, what is the difference betwixt them, but that one is lawless power exercised under pretence of authority, or by persons vested with it; the other, lawless power exercised under pretence of liberty, or without any pretence at all? A people, then, must always be less free in proportion as they are more licentious; licentiousness being not only different from liberty, but directly contrary to it—a direct breach upon it."

True liberty, then, is a liberty to do every thing that is right, and the being restrained from doing any thing that is wrong. So far from our having a right to do every thing that we please, under a notion of liberty, liberty itself is limited and confined—but limited and confined only by laws which are at the same time both it's foundation and it's support. It can, however, hardly be necessary to inform you, that ideas and notions respecting liberty, very different from these, are daily suggested in the speeches and the writings of the times; and also that some opinions on the subject of government at large, which appear to me to be particularly loose and dangerous, are advanced . . . ; and that, therefore, you will acknowledge the propriety of my bestowing some farther notice on them. . . .

It is laid down . . . as a settled maxim, that the end of government is "the common good of mankind." I am not sure that the position itself is indisputable; but, if it were, it would by no means follow that, "this common good being matter of common feeling, government must therefore have been instituted by common consent." There is an appearance of logical accuracy and precision in this statement; but it is only an appearance. The position is vague and loose; and the assertion is made without an attempt to prove it. If by men's "common feelings" we are to understand that principle in the human mind called common sense, the assertion is either unmeaning and insignificant, or it is false. In no instance have mankind ever yet agreed as to what is, or is not, "the common good." A form or mode of government cannot be named, which these "common feelings" and "common consent," the sole arbiters, as it seems, of "common good," have not, at one time or another, set up and established, and again pulled down and reprobated. What one people in one age have concurred in establishing as the "common good," another in another age have voted to be mischievous and big with ruin. The premises, therefore, that "the common good is matter of common feeling," being false, the consequence drawn from it, viz. that government was instituted by "common consent," is of course equally false.

This popular notion, that government was originally formed by the consent or by a compact of the people, rests on, and is supported by, another similar notion, not less popular, nor better founded. This other notion is, that the whole human race is born equal; and that no man is naturally inferior, or, in any respect, subjected to another; and that he can be made subject to another only by his own consent. The position is equally ill-founded and false both in it's premises and conclusions. In hardly any sense that can be imagined is the position strictly true; but, as applied to the case under consideration, it is demonstrably not true. Man differs from man in every thing that can be supposed to lead to supremacy and subjection, *as one star differs from another star in glory*. It was the purpose of the Creator, that man should be social: but, without government, there can be no society; nor, without some relative inferiority and superiority, can there be any government. A musical instrument composed of chords, keys, or pipes, all perfectly equal in size and power, might as well be expected to produce harmony, as a society composed of members all perfectly equal to be productive of order and peace. If (according to the idea of the advocates of this chimerical scheme of equality) no man could rightfully *be compelled to come in* and be a member even of a government to be formed by a regular compact, but by his own individual consent; it clearly follows, from the same principles, that neither could he rightfully be made or compelled to submit to the ordinances of any government already formed, to which he has not individually or actually consented. On the principle of equality, neither his parents, nor even the vote of a majority of the society, (however virtuously and honourably that vote might be obtained,) can have any such authority over any man. Neither can it be maintained that acquiescence implies consent; because acquiescence may have been extorted from impotence or incapacity. Even an explicit consent can bind a man no longer than he chooses to be bound. The same principle of equality that exempts him from being governed without his own consent, clearly entitles him to recall and resume that consent whenever he sees fit; and he alone has a right to judge when and for what reasons it may be resumed.

Any attempt, therefore, to introduce this fantastic system into practice, would reduce the whole business of social life to the wearisome, confused, and useless talk of mankind's first expressing, and then withdrawing, their consent to an endless succession of schemes of government. Governments, though always forming, would never be completely formed: for, the majority to-day, might be the minority tomorrow; and, of course, that which is now fixed might and would be soon unfixed. Mr. Locke indeed says, that, "by consenting with others to make one body-politic under government, a man puts himself under an obligation to every one of that society to submit to the determination of the majority, and to be concluded by it." For the sake of the peace of society, it is undoubtedly reasonable and necessary that this should be the case: but, on the principles of the system now under consideration, before Mr. Locke or any of his followers can have authority to say that it actually is the case, it must be stated and proved that every individual man, on entering into the social compact, did first consent, and declare his consent, to be concluded and bound in all cases by the vote of the majority. In making such a declaration, he would certainly consult both his interest and his duty; but at the same time he would also completely relinquish the principle of equality, and eventually subject himself to the possibility of being governed by ignorant and corrupt tyrants. Mr. Locke himself afterwards disproves his own position respecting this supposed obligation to submit to the "determination of the majority," when he argues that a right of resistance still exists in the governed: for, what is resistance but a recalling and resuming the consent heretofore supposed to have been given, and in fact refusing to submit to the "determination of the majority?" It does not clearly appear what Mr. Locke exactly meant by what he calls "the determination of the majority:" but the only rational and practical public manner of declaring "the determination of the majority," is by law: the laws, therefore, in all countries, even in those that are despotically governed, are to be regarded as the declared "determination of a majority" of the members of that community; because, in such cases, even acquiescence only must be looked upon as equivalent to a declaration. A right of resistance, therefore, for which Mr. Locke contends, is incompatible with the duty of submitting to the determination of "the majority," for which he also contends.

It is indeed impossible to carry into effect any government which, even by compact, might be framed with this reserved right of resistance. Accordingly there is no record that any such government ever was so formed. If there had, it must have carried the seeds of it's decay in it's very constitution. For, as those men who make a government (certain that they have the power) can have no hesitation to vote that they also have the right to unmake it; and as the people, in all circumstances, but more especially when trained to make and unmake governments, are at least as well disposed to do the latter as the former, it is morally impossible that there should be any thing like permanency or stability in a government so formed. Such a system, therefore, can produce only perpetual dissensions and contests, and bring back mankind to a supposed state of nature; arming every man's band, like Ishmael's, against every man, and rendering the world an *aceldama*, or field of blood. Such theories of government seem to give something like plausibility to the notions of those other modern theorists, who regard all governments as invasions of the natural rights of men, usurpations, and tyranny. On this principle it would follow, and could not be denied, that government was indeed fundamentally, as our people are sedulously taught it still is, an evil. Yet it is to government that mankind owe their having, after their fall and corruption, been again reclaimed, from a state of barbarity and war, to the conveniency and the safety of the social state: and it is by means of government that society is still preserved, the weak protected from the strong, and the artless and innocent from the wrongs of proud oppressors. It was not without reason, then, that Mr. Locke asserted, that a greater wrong cannot be done to prince and people, than is done by "propagating wrong notions concerning government."

Ashamed of this shallow device that government originated in superior strength and violence, another party, hardly less numerous, and certainly not less confident than the former, fondly deduce it from some imaginary compact. They suppose that, in the decline perhaps of some fabulous age of gold, a multitude of human beings, who, like their brother beasts, had hitherto ranged the forests, *without guide, overseer, or ruler*—at length convinced, by experience, of the impossibility of living either alone with any degree of comfort or security, or together in society, with peace, without government, had (in some lucid interval of reason and reflection) met together in a spacious plain, for the express purpose of framing a government. Their first step must have been the transferring to some individual, or individuals, some of those rights which are supposed to have been inherent in each of them: of these it is essential to government that they should be divested; yet can they not, rightfully, be deprived of them, otherwise than by their own consent. Now, admitting this whole supposed assembly to be perfectly equal as to rights, yet all agreed as to the propriety of ceding some of them, on what principles of equality is it possible to determine, either who shall relinquish such a portion of his rights, or who shall be invested with such new accessory rights? By asking another to exercise jurisdiction over me, I clearly confess that I do not think myself his equal; and by his consenting to exercise such authority, he also virtually declares that he thinks himself superior. And, to establish this hypothesis of a compact, it is farther necessary that the whole assembly should concur in this opinion—a concurrence so extremely improbable, that it seems to be barely possible. The supposition that a large concourse of people, in a rude and imperfect state of society, or even a majority of them, should thus rationally and unanimously concur to subject themselves to various restrictions, many of them irksome and unpleasant, and all of them contrary to all their former habits, is to suppose them possessed of more wisdom and virtue than multitudes in any instance in real life have ever shewn.

3

The Radicals

57. CHRISTOPHER GADSDEN, *TO THE GENTLEMEN ELECTORS OF ST. PAUL'S PARISH*, 1763*

Christopher Gadsden (1724–1804), Charleston merchant and statesman, was one of the earliest advocates of independence. He gave the Revolution its first impetus in South Carolina during his heated controversy with Governor Thomas Boone. The Governor had challenged the validity of Gadsden's election to the Commons House of Assembly in 1762, and tried to remove him from that body, occasioning Gadsden's address on the prerogatives of colonial legislatures and the inherent rights of Englishmen, which follows. Gadsden carried his views to the Stamp Act Congress of 1765, and voiced them again in the Continental Congresses, where he also pleaded for armed colonial union.

Inherent Not Promissive Rights

[A writer asserts that] a governor under the *present* happy establishment, "[should] merit his majesty's highest commendation" for denying that an assembly "have the sole and inherent right of judging of the validity of the election of their own members!" Is not a parliament or assembly supposed by the constitution to be an *independent* branch of the legislature? Is it not then a flat contradiction in terms to suppose this and at the same time suppose, that a governor can be any, much less the ultimate judge of the matter?

Thank God! we have as good a king upon the throne as ever

* Reprinted from *The Writings of Christopher Gadsden*, Richard Walsh, ed. (The University of South Carolina Press, 1966) by permission of the publishers. Copyright © 1966 by the University of South Carolina Press. Pp. 30–33, 48–50.

graced it, who has given the earliest and most endearing signs of his tenderest regard for the liberties and privileges of his subjects, and has thereby manifestly shown, his inclination is, to reign solely *in* the hearts of *free* people, not over a parcel of *slaves*; *free* men I *say*, who have an *inherent* not *promissive* right to be so. And does not the act of settlement shew this, where it *says*, that "the laws of England are the birth-right of the people thereof." Does not the act too, declaring the rights and liberties of the subject, and settling the succession of the crown, expressly accuse King James the 2d of having "violated the freedom of elections of members to serve in parliament?" And does not the same act expressly declare, "that elections of members of parliament ought to be free?" How can they be so, if any but the people of their representatives are judges of the pretensions of any to be such? This right is so unalienable and inherent in the people, that they can be no longer denominated a free people when it is parted with; because all their *freedom* as British subjects most essentially depends upon it. The parliament of Great Britain, and the general assembly (or parliament) of this or any American province, though they differ widely with regard to the extent of their different spheres of action, and the latter's may be called a sphere within the former's, yet they differ not an iota when only the point in dispute is disregarded. "Tis, in fact, so much the *sine qua non* of any real parliament or assembly, that without it, what might be *called*, such, would be just like the French parliament, a mere *rex et praeterea nihil* [king and a windy promise].

Will it be asserted by any friend to the natural liberties of British subjects, that, in order to retain those liberties, a man must never stir out of Britain, where they are *indisputably* and essentially his; or that the moment he sets foot on American ground, he has bid farewell to the *dearest* of them? If this had been the doctrine formerly, the sons of Britain would have been thinly, very thinly, scattered on this side the Atlantic ocean. It might indeed have been *then* fixed on, *very properly*, as a place to transport her convicts to, but surely no free men, on such conditions, would have ever thought of coming to America. Those nations only, who were already enslaved, therefore could lose nothing by the bargain, would certainly have been found almost, if not altogether, the only adventurers this way.

That the being *freely* represented in parliament, by men altogether first and last of the people's *own* chusing, without any interfering whatever, is the most essential and inherent right the British subjects residing in Great-Britain are possessed of, I believe none will be so hardy as to deny. That none of the British subjects residing in America have given their votes for any member of parliament of Great-Britain, cannot be denied also. Are then the British Americans to be represented nowhere? Shall their several hundred thousands, by which industry and spirit the nation has been greatly assisted to arrive at that conspicuous figure she now so extensively makes, Taken Collectively, be deprived of that birth-right and most characteristical privilege, that Every, even the lowest Individual Man, of her *domestic* subjects, *may be*, and most of them *actually are*, intitled unto, that of voting for a member of parliament[?]

What difference can there be between the subjects residing in Britain and America, but that of latitude and climate? Have these any natural or rational connection with the matter? How can, or ought, they then to affect it?

Freedom of the Assembly

Again, if the British subjects in America are permitted to send no members to the British parliament, but may be capable, or have a natural right, to be represented somewhere, which surely will not be disputed, the next question is, where can that somewhere be, but in America? If they but have this capacity or right, 'tis not a farthing matter with regard to the argument, whether they send their representatives to one general assembly to all parts (supposing that practicable) or whether, as at present, each colony has an assembly of its own. In all cases, whether the sphere of action for parliaments or assemblies be ever so extensive, or ever so much limited and contracted, by divisions and sub-divisions, still the *smallest* within its own sphere *must be free*, and in order to be so, be the *sole* judges of the elections of its *own* members, or else it can be no *free* assembly at all, but a *mockery* of the people.

Now let us see how this reasoning can be farthar supported by fact, in regard to ourselves.

First, we have a charter, by which "the natural rights of free men of this province, to be represented in general assembly, is confirmed to them."

We have also a law now in force, passed in December 1712, entitled "An act to put in force, in this province, the several statutes of the kingdom of England or South-Britain therein particularly mentioned; wherein, after such particular English statutes are expressly taken notice of by their titles, that are to be of force here, beginning with the Great Charter of Henry the Third, and ending with an act passed in the eighth year of queen Anne." That act, in its third, and part of its fourth section, goes on, and says thus:

III. And be it further enacted, by the authority aforesaid: that all the statutes of the kingdom of England, *relating to the allegiance of the people to her present majesty queen Anne, and her lawful* successors, and the several public oaths, and subscribing the tests required of the people of England in general by any of the said statutes as relates to the above mentioned particulars of the allegiance of the people to their sovereign, the public oaths, and subscribing the tests required of them, and the declaring and securing the rights and liberties of the subjects, *are hereby enacted and declared to extend to, and to be of full force in this province*, as if particularly enumerated in this act.

IV. And, for the better putting force and execution of all and every the before enumerated statutes, paragraphs, sections, or numbers of paragraphs of statutes, be it further enacted, by the authority aforesaid, and it is hereby enacted and declared, *that the general assembly, for that part of this province that lies south and west of Cape Fear, and the several members thereof, shall have the* Same Power *and authority in* Any *matter or thing* Relating TO *the said statutes, that is given by the same to the* Parliament Of England, *or the members thereof.*

Nothing can be more express than the above words of our act; they manifestly allude to the act of settlement, and that other act already mentioned; and refer likewise to so much of All Other Acts Then Passed In England, wherein the rights and liberties of the subjects are declared, and better secured.

Now certainly it must be granted, that nothing Can Concern the security of the rights and liberties of the British subjects more *essentially*, than those laws that relate to the securing of the Freedom of parliament, which is the essence of the thing; to which *every particular manner* and form appointed is intended to be subservient, and ought to be so, not to be construed into a destruction of it.

The last mentioned statute then, which may be called the basis of the present establishment, says expressly, "that elections of members of parliament ought to be free." This must at least be called free, in *the first step*, the choice of the electors; and with regard to *the last step*, that is an examination of the returns or credentials of all that pretend to a seat in parliament, can any act more plainly and carefully secure it solely to the collective body of *free men elected in parliament*, than the statute of the 7th and 8th of William the Third, wherein it is enacted, "That in case any person or persons shall return any member to serve in parliament for any county, *etc.* contrary to the last determination of the house of commons of the right of election in such county, *etc.* "that such return so made, shall, and is hereby adjudged, to be a false return;" and that the clerk of the crown is not to alter any return without order of the house of commons, *etc.* which certainly implies he may and is to alter it with such order, and that they, and only they, have to do with them.

Will any person here say, that those parts of these acts here quoted, by a fair and equitable construction, are not, and ought not to be, of force here, by virtue of our own law just mentioned, so far as to corroborate and ascertain these two grand and natural points, which is all we want?

1st. That our assemblies ought to be freely chosen by the people.

2dly. That the returns ought to be *solely* examined by such assembly so chosen.

The Source of the Present Trouble

What is the grand cause from whence spring many of the complaints against American assemblies? The history of the colonies will tell us. Instances of inexperienced governors can be produced, who (dizzied with a little power, not giving themselves time to attend to the plainest and most essential fundamentals of the constitution, impatient of the least contradiction, and depending solely and absolutely on their own interest and connections to bear them out in every thing) have been too apt to attempt such dangerous innovations as assemblies could not submit to, and of course must differ with them or betray their trust. Such governors too, if they happen to be of warm disposition and an arbitrary turn contracted perhaps from a larger acquaintance in the military than the civil life, are more apt to be surprised and duped into such wrong measures, by the sly insinuations, and misrepresentations, of artful flatterers of specious talents, with voluble time serving tongues and vain heads, always ready, with the utmost expedition, to carry or notify to them *all*, and perhaps, *more than all* that stirs, in order to magnify their own importance.

Weak servants are very apt to judge of their masters by themselves, a greater stretch of power they want; if then they can kill 2 birds with one stone, by acquiring a greater power to themselves at the same time obtain it for their masters, nothing to be sure, in their opinion, can contribute so much to secure and enlarge their interest, and so effectually recommend their own extraordinary abilities, as such notable management. This is but too often the case, and had assemblies but the same chance of introducing their story as *early*, and with as great advantages, as governors can theirs, there is no doubt, they would not be so often looked upon in the bad light they seem to be at present.

Would but all governors permit us, who reside in America, to enjoy the same privileges, that our fellow-subjects residing in Great-Britain do, we claim, we *pretend to* no more. Would they listen to no vain or subtle proposals from busy tale-bearers, to sap the very foundation upon which such privileges stand, they would find no people more docile, more tractable . . .

'Tis well known how dangerous precedents are, especially of the nature of that in dispute. Let me remind you of what an English parliament thought of them upon a very similar occasion. They told King James I: "that if the chancellor" (which with us is, as has been said already, the governor And Council, not the governor or council, who, by virtue of acting in that character alone, issue our writs and receives the returns) "only could examine returns, then, upon every surmise, whether it were true or false, the chancellor might send a second writ, and cause a new election to be made; and thus the *free* election of the county should be abrogated, which would be too dangerous to the common-wealth, for by such means, *the King and his council might make any man, whom* They *would, to be of the parliament house*, Against The Great Charter And The Liberties Of England." And in a famous remonstrance, printed and directed to the king in 1604, they roundly assert, "That the prerogative of princes *may* easily, and *do* daily grow and encrease—but the privileges of subjects are, for the most part, *at an everlasting stand; they may*, by good providence and care, *be preserved*, but being *once lost*, are not to be recovered but with much disquiet and disorder."

If an English parliament thought *thus*, what must be the case with us, should such a misfortune happen? Would they not be lost, without a miracle, for ever? How watchful ought we then to be? How careful of shewing precedents?

58. RICHARD BLAND, *AN INQUIRY INTO THE RIGHTS OF THE BRITISH COLONIES*, 1766*

Richard Bland (1710–76) of Virginia, member of the House of Burgesses, the Committee of Safety, and the Continental Congress, was one of the most effective pamphleteers to defend American rights. Widely read, his writings were reprinted by radicals in other provinces to buttress their own arguments. His contemporaries considered him an excellent authority on legislative history, and Thomas Jefferson thought him "the most learned and logical man of those who took prominent lead in public affairs, profound in constitutional lore"—even though "a most ungracious speaker."

The Question is whether the Colonies are represented in the *British* Parliament or not? You affirm it to be an indubitable Fact that they are represented, and from thence you infer a Right in the Parliament to impose Taxes of every Kind upon them. You do not insist upon the *Power*, but upon the *Right* of Parliament to impose Taxes upon the Colonies. This is certainly a very proper Distinction, as *Right* and *Power* have very different Meanings, and convey very different Ideas: For had you told us that the Parliament of *Great Britain* have *Power*, by the Fleets and Armies of the Kingdom, to impose Taxes and to raise Contri-

* Richard Bland, *An Inquiry into the Rights of the British Colonies* . . . (Williamsburg: Alexander Purdie & Co., 1766), pp. 4–12.

butions upon the Colonies, I should not have presumed to dispute the Point with you; but as you insist upon the *Right* only, I must beg Leave to differ from you in Opinion, and shall give my Reasons for it.

But I must first recapitulate your Arguments in Support of this Right in the Parliament. You say "the Inhabitants of the Colonies do not indeed choose Members of Parliament, neither are nine Tenths of the People of *Britain* Electors; for the Right of Election is annexed to certain Species of Property, to peculiar Franchises, and to Inhabitancy in some particular Places. But these Descriptions comprehend only a very small Part of the Lands, the Property and People of *Britain*; all Copy-Hold, all Lease-Hold Estates under the Crown, under the Church, or under private Persons, though for Terms ever so long; all landed Property in short that is not Free hold, and all monied Property whatsoever, are excluded. The Possessors of these have no Votes in the Election of Members of Parliament; Women and Persons under Age, be their Property ever so large, and all of it Freehold, have none: The Merchants of *London*, a numerous and respectable Body of Men, whose Opulence exceeds all that *America* can collect; the Proprietors of that vast Accumulation of Wealth, the Publick Funds; the Inhabitants of *Leeds*, of *Halifax*, *Birmingham*, and of *Manchester*, Towns that are each of them larger than the largest in the Plantations; many of lesser Note, that are incorporated; and that great Corporation the *East India* Company, whose Rights over the Countries they possess fall very little short of Sovereignty, and whose Trade and whose Fleets are sufficient to constitute them a maritime Power, and all in the same Circumstances: And yet are they not represented in Parliament? Is their vast Property subject to Taxation without their Consent? Are they all arbitrarily bound by Laws to which they have not agreed? The Colonies are exactly in the same Situation; all *British* Subjects are really in the same; none are actually, all are virtually, represented in Parliament: For every Member of Parliament sits in the House not as a Representative of his own Constituents, but as one of that august Assembly by which all the Commons of *Great Britain* are represented."

This is the Sum of what you advance, in all the Pomp of Parliamentary Declamation, to prove that the Colonies are represented in Parliament, and therefore subject to their Taxation; but notwithstanding this Way of reasoning, I cannot comprehend how Men who are excluded from voting at the Election of Members of Parliament can be represented in that Assembly, or how those who are elected do not sit in the House as Representatives of their Constituents. These Assertions appear to me not only paradoxical, but contrary to the fundamental Principles of the *English* Constitution.

To illustrate this important Disquisition, I conceive we must recur to the civil Constitution of *England*, and from thence deduce and ascertain the Rights and Privileges of the People at the first Establishment of the Government, and discover the Alterations that have been made in them from Time to Time; and it is from the Laws of the Kingdom, founded upon the Principles of the Law of Nature, that we are to show the Obligation every Member of the State is under to pay Obedience to its Institutions. From these Principles I shall endeavour to prove that the Inhabitants of *Britain*, who have no Vote in the Election of Members of Parliament, are not represented in that Assembly, and yet that they owe Obedience to the Laws of Parliament; which, as to them, are constitutional, and not arbitrary. As to the Colonies, I shall consider them afterwards.

Now it is a Fact, as certain as History can make it, that the present civil Constitution of *England* derives its Original from those *Saxons* who, coming over to the Assistance of the *Britons* in the Time of their King *Vortigern*, made themselves Masters of the Kingdom, and established a Form of Government in it similar to that they had been accustomed to live under in their native Country; as similar, at least, as the Difference of their Situation and Circumstances would permit. This Government, like that from whence they came, was founded upon Principles of the most perfect Liberty: The conquered Lands were divided among the Individuals in Proportion to the Rank they held in the Nation (Caesar, *Gallic Wars*; Tacitus, *de Germ.*); and every Freeman, that is, every Freeholder, was a Member of their Wittinagemot, or Parliament. The other Part of the Nation, or the Non-Proprietors of Land, were of little Estimation. They, as in *Germany*, were either Slaves, mere Hewers of Wood and Drawers of Water, or Freedmen; who, being of foreign Extraction, had been manumitted by their Masters, and were excluded from the high Privilege of having a Share in the Administration of the Commonwealth, unless they became Proprietors of Land (which they might obtain by Purchase or Donation) and in that Case they had a Right to sit with the Freemen, in the Parliament or sovereign Legislature of the State.

How long this Right of being personally present in the Parliament continued, or when the Custom of sending Representatives to this great Council of the Nation, was first introduced, cannot be determined with Precision; but let the Custom of Representation be introduced when it will, it is certain that every Freeman, or, which was the same Thing in the Eye of the Constitution, every Freeholder, had a Right to vote at the Election of Members of Parliament, and therefore might be said, with great Propriety, to be present in that Assembly, either in his own Person or by Representation. This Right of Election in the Freeholders is evident from the Statute 1st *Hen.* 5. Ch. 1st, which limits the Right of Election to those Freeholders only who are resident in the Counties the Day of the Date of the Writ of Election; but yet every resident Freeholder indiscriminately, let his Freehold be ever so small, had a Right to vote at the Election of Knights for his County, so that they were actually represented: And this Right of Election continued until it was taken away by the Statute 8th *Hen.* 6. Ch. 7. from those Freeholders who had not a clear Freehold Estate of forty Shillings by the Year at the least.

Now this Statute was deprivative of the Right of those Freeholders who came within the Description of it; but of what did it deprive them, if they were represented notwithstanding their Right of Election was taken from them? The mere Act of voting was nothing, of no Value, if they were represented as constitutionally without it as with it: But when by the fundamental Principles of the Constitution they were to be considered as Members of the Legislature, and as such had a Right to be present in Person, or to send their Procurators or Attornies, and by them to give their Suffrage in the supreme Council of the Nation, this Statute deprived them of an essential Right; a Right without which, by the ancient Constitution of the State, all other Liberties were but a Species of Bondage.

As these Freeholders then were deprived of their Rights to Substitute Delegates to Parliament, they could not be represented, but were placed in the same Condition with the Non-Proprietors of Land, who were excluded by the original Constitution from having any Share in the Legislature, but who, notwithstanding such Exclusion, are bound to pay Obedience to the Laws of Parliament, even if they should consist of nine Tenths of the People of *Britain*; but then the Obligation of these Laws does not arise from a quite different Reason.

Men in a State of Nature are absolutely free and independent of one another as to soverign Jurisdiction, (*Vattel's Law of Nature. Locke on Civil Govern. Wollaston's Rel. of Nat.*) but when they enter into a Society, and by their own Consent become Members of it, they must submit to the Laws of the Society according to which they agree to be governed; for it is evident, by the very Act of Association, that each Member subjects himself to the Authority of that Body in whom, by common Consent, the legislative Power of the State is placed: But though they must submit to the Laws, so long as they remain Members of the Society, yet they retain so much of their natural Freedom as to have a Right to retire from the Society, to renounce the Benefits of it, to enter into another Society, and to settle in another Country; for their Engagements to the Society, and their Submission to the publick Authority of the State, do not oblige them to continue in it longer than they find it will conduce to their Happiness, which they have a natural Right to promote. This natural Right remains with every Man, and he cannot justly be deprived of it by any civil Authority. Every Person therefore who is denied his Share in the Legislature of the State to which he had

an original Right, and every Person who from his particular Circumstances is excluded from this great Privilege, and refuses to exercise his
natural Right of quitting the Country, but remains in it, and continues to
exercise the Rights of a Citizen in all other Respects, must be subject to
the Laws which by these Acts he *implicitly*, or to use your own Phrase,
virtually consents to: For Men may subject themselves to Laws, by consenting to them *implicitly*; that is, by conforming to them, by adhering to
the Society, and accepting the Benefits of its Constitution, as well, as
explicitly and directly, in their own Persons, or by their Representatives
substituted in their Room (Wollaston's Rel. of Nat.). Thus, if a Man
whose Property does not entitle him to be an Elector of Members of
Parliament, and therefore cannot be represented, or have any Share in
the Legislature, "inherits or takes any Thing by the Laws of the Country
to which he has no indubitable Right in Nature, or which, if he has a
Right to it, he cannot tell how to get or keep without the Aid of the Laws
and the Advantage of Society, then, when he takes this Inheritance, or
whatever it is, *with* it he takes and owns the Laws that gave it him. And
since the Security he has from the Laws of the Country, in Respect of his
Person and Rights, is the *Equivalent* for his Submission to them, he cannot accept *that* Security without being obliged, in Equity, to pay *this*
Submission: Nay his very continuing in the Country shows that he either
likes the Constitution, or likes it better, notwithstanding the Alteration
made in it to his Disadvantage, than any other; or at least thinks it
better, in his Circumstances, to conform to it, than to seek any other;
that is, he is content to be comprehended in it."

From hence it is evident that the Obligation of the Laws of Parliament upon the People of Britain who have no Right to be Electors does
not arise from their being *virtually* represented, but from a quite different
Principle; a Principle of the Law of Nature, true, certain, and universal,
applicable to every Sort of Government, and not contrary to the common
Understandings of Mankind.

If what you say is a real Fact, the nine Tenths of the People of
Britain are deprived of the high Privilege of being Electors, it shows a
great Defect in the present Constitution, which has departed so much
from its original Purity; but never can prove that these People are
even *virtually* represented in Parliament. And here give me Leave to
observe that it would be a Work worthy of the best patriotick Spirits in
the Nation to effectuate an Alteration in this putrid Part of the Constitution; and, by restoring it to its pristine Perfection, prevent any "Order or
Rank of the Subjects from imposing upon or binding the rest without
their Consent." But, I fear, the Gangrene has taken too deep Hold to be
eradicated in these Days of Venality.

59. SAMUEL ADAMS, *ON THE BOSTON MASSACRE*, 1770[*]

Samuel Adams (1722–1803), plebeian leader, politician, and lawyer, was a close friend of Christopher Gadsden. He was an inveterate opponent of Great Britain and a consistent advocate of independence from the mother country. A master politician and propagandist, he headed one of the first political clubs in America and was in frequent correspondence with nearly every radical in the American colonies. He publicized every British affront, real or imagined.

Adams' newspaper piece reprinted below is a typical, highly partisan account of the Boston Massacre, which received its dramatic name from Adams and his friends. One colleague, Paul Revere, the coppersmith, silversmith, and engraver, prepared a widely circulated picture of the British slaughtering innocent civilians. But in fact these civilians comprised an unruly mob; on the evening of March 5, 1770, they so provoked a British sentry that his superior, Captain Thomas Preston, and a squad went to his rescue. In the confusion, several of the soldiers fired on the mob, killing five and wounding eight. The soldiers were tried locally and defended by John Adams, cousin of Samuel, who despite the highly charged atmosphere, secured the release of Preston and six of his men. Two were found guilty of manslaughter, branded on the hand, and released. To placate public opinion, the home government removed two regiments of troops whose presence had consistently inflamed the city. This action was of no avail, however, thanks to Samuel Adams, who continued to kindle the fires of resistance and revolution at every opportunity.

To the Printers.

In the late trials of Preston and the Soldiers, it was observ'd that the Court constantly from day to day adjourn'd at noon and at sun-set. Our enemies, who are fruitful in their inventions, may possibly from hence take occasion to represent that it was dangerous for the Court to sit in the tumultuous town of Boston after dark. At the first view it may perhaps bear this complexion in the eye of a prejudiced stranger; for such adjournments in capital causes it may be were never before known here: But the representation would be without the least foundation in truth. It is possible that among other reasons this might be one, that the judges are all of them, to use the words of a good old Patriarch, well stricken in years, and one of them labours under infirmities of Body. I

[*] *The Writings of Samuel Adams*, Harry Alonzo Cushing, ed. (New York: Putnam, 1904–6), Vol. II, pp. 89–98.

have another observation to make on this occasion, but I reserve it till a future opportunity.

I have already said that the Soldiers in coming down from the main-guard to the custom-house behaved with an haughty air—that they abused the people as they pass'd along—pushing them with their bayonets—and damning them; and when they had got to their post, they in like manner abused and struck innocent persons there who offer'd them no injury—and all this was even before they form'd, in doing which it does not appear that they were obstructed; and as the witnesses declared, before the people press'd upon them, if they did at all, and when there did not appear to be danger to them or any one else. These facts, I think were prov'd, if we may believe persons of good credit, who declared them upon their oaths in Court:—And that they came down under a pretence of suppressing a riot, without a civil magistrate or peace officer, which ought always to be remembered, no one will dispute.

There was indeed a sort of evidence bro't into Court, which, if it is at all to be rely'd upon, may serve to invalidate in some measure what has been said—namely the declaration of one of the deceas'd persons, as it was related by the gentleman who dress'd his wounds, and to whom he is said to have declared it. This man, as the doctor testified, told him among many other things, that he saw some Soldiers passing from the main-guard to the custom-house and the people pelted them as they went along. But whether these Soldiers were Preston and his party; or other Soldiers who are mention'd by another witness, as going from the main-guard towards the Centry, having short coats and arm'd with bayonets, swords or sticks, and one of them with a pair of kitchen tongs, chasing the people as they went, must remain an uncertainty. If he meant the former, it is somewhat strange that among all the witnesses on both sides, no one saw the people pelting them as they went along but he. This man confess'd to the doctor that he was a fool to be there—was surprized at the forbearance of the soldiers; believed that they fired in their own defence & freely forgave the man that shot him. But it is to be observed, he did not declare this under oath nor before a magistrate: It was however the dying speech, very affecting and all, true no doubt; altho' no one knew the character of this believing penitent either in point of veracity or judgment. By the testimony of his land-lady in Court, one would not form the best opinion of him; but de mortuis nil nisi bonum [of the dead speak nothing but good].

There were others ready to be sworn, if the Council for the crown had thought it worth while to have bro't them forward, that they also could relate what this man had told them, viz. that his doctors had encouraged him that he would soon recover of his wounds, and he hoped to live to be a swift witness against the soldiers. Great stress was laid by some upon the simple declaration of this man, who in all probability died in the faith of a roman catholick. This however, I am apt to think, will not disparage his declaration in the opinion of some great men at home, even tho' he did not make his confession to a ghostly physician.

Before I proceed to enquire into the danger the Soldiers were in, if they were in any at all, and who were in fault, I will take the liberty to lead the reader back to a consideration of the temper the Soldiers in general discovered, and their correspondent conduct, for some considerable time before the fatal tragedy was acted. It is well known indeed that from their first landing, their behavior was to a great degree insolent; and such as look'd as if they had enter'd deeply into the spirit of those who procur'd them,—and really believed, that we were a country of rebels and they were sent here to subdue us. But for some time before the fifth of March, they more frequently insulted the inhabitants who were quietly passing the streets; and gave out many threats, that on that very night the blood would run down the streets of Boston, and that many who would dine on Monday would not breakfast on Tuesday; and to show that they were in earnest they forewarn'd their particular acquaintance to take care of themselves. These things were attested before the magistrates by credible persons under oath. Accordingly when the Monday evening came on, they were early in every part of the town arm'd with bludgeons, bayonets and cutlasses, beating those whom they could, and assaulting and threatning others. By the way, I will just observe for the information of a certain honorable gentleman, that the name of bludgeons was unheard of in this town till the Soldiers arrived. This behavior put the inhabitants in mind of their threatenings; and was the reason that those of them who had occasion to walk the streets, came out arm'd with canes or clubs. Between eight and nine o'clock, the Soldiers in Murray's barracks in the centre of the town rush'd out with their naked cutlasses insulting, beating and wounding the inhabitants who were passing along: This, in so frequented a street, naturally collected numbers of people who resented the injury done and an affray ensued. About the same time a difference arose in King-street, between a centry there and a barber's boy, who said to his fellowapprentice in the hearing of the centry "there goes Capt. _____ who has not paid my master for dressing his hair:" The centry foolishly resented it, and words took place; and the boy answering him with pertness, & calling him a name, the centry struck him. Here was the first assault in King-street. But for what reason the evidence of this matter was not bro't into Court, at the last trial, as it had been at the trial of Preston, the reader if he pleases may conjecture. At the same time a gentleman not living far from the custom-house, and hearing as he tho't a distant cry of murder, came into the street, which he had just before left perfectly still, and to use his own words, "never clearer": He there saw a party of Soldiers issue from the mainguard, and heard them say, damn them where are they, by Jesus let them come; and presently after another party rush'd thro' Quaker-land into the street, using much such expressions:—Their arms glitter'd in the moon-light. These cried fire, and ran up the street and into Cornhill which leads to Murray's barracks; in their way they knocked down a boy of twelve years old, a son of Mr. Appleton, abused and insulted several gentlemen at their doors and others in the street: Their cry was, damn them, where are they, knock them down; and it is suppos'd they join'd in the affray there, which still continued. They also then cried fire, which one of the witnesses took to be their watch-word.

By this time the barber's boy had return'd to the centry with a number of other boys to resent the blow he had received: The centry loaded his gun and threatened to fire upon them, and they threatened to knock him down. The bells were ringing as for fire: Occasion'd either by the Soldiers crying fire as is before mention'd, for it is usual in this town when fire is cried, for any one who is near a church to set the bells a ringing; or it might be, to alarm the town, from an apprehension of some of the inhabitants, that the Soldiers were putting their former threats into execution, and that there would be a general massacre: It is not to be wonder'd at, that some persons were under such apprehensions; when even an officer at Murray's barracks, appeared to encourage the Soldiers and headed them, as it was sworn before the magistrate. This officer was indicted by the grand jury, but he could not be found afterwards. Some other officers, and particularly lieutenants Minchen and Dickson, discovered a very different temper.

The ringing of the bells alarmed the town, it being suppos'd by the people in general there was fire; and occasion'd a concourse in King-street which is a populous part of it. As the people came into the street, the barber's boy told them that the centry had knock'd him down—and a person who had come into the street thro' Royal-exchange lane, which leads from Murray's barracks, (and possibly had observ'd the behavior of the Soldiers there) and seeing the centry, cried here's a Soldier. Various were the dispositions and inclinations of the people according to their various "feelings" no doubt; for mankind, it is said, "act · from their feelings more than their reason:" The cooler sort advis'd to go home: The curious were willing to stay and see the event, and those whose feelings were warmer, perhaps partook of the boys resentment. So it had been before at Murray's barracks, and so it always will be among a multitude: At the barracks some, to use the expression of one of the witnesses, called out home, home; while some in their heat cried, huzza for the main-guard—there is the nest. This was said by a person of distinction in court, to savour of treason Tho' it was allow'd on both sides, that the main-guard was not molested thro' the whole evening.

I would here beg the reader's further patience, while I am a little more particular, in relation to the affray at Murray's barracks; for it may be of importance to enquire how it began there. Mr. Jeremiah Belknap, an householder of known good reputation, had been sworn before the magristrate; and why he was not bro't in as a witness at the trial, is not my business to say, and I shall not at present even conjecture. Mr. Belknap, who lived in Cornhill near Murray's barracks, testified, that on the first appearance of the affray there, hearing a noise he ran to his door, and heard one say he had been struck by a Soldier: he presently saw eight or nine Soldiers arm'd with clubs and cutlasses, come out of Boylston's alley, which is a very short passage leading from Murray's barracks into the street—he desired them to retire to the barracks—one of them with a club in one hand and a cutlass in the other, with the latter, made a stroke at him: Finding no prospect of stopping them, he ran to the mainguard and called for the officers of the guard—he was inform'd, there was no officer there—he told the Soldiers, that if a party was not sent down there would be bloodshed; upon which he was attacked by two Soldiers, with drawn cutlasses, who he suppos'd were of the party from Murray's barracks—Another gentleman, one of the prisoners witnesses, swore in Court, that a little after eight o'clock he saw at his own door, which is very near the barracks, several Soldiers passing and repassing, some with clubs, others with bayonets: And then he related the noise & confusion he afterwards heard, & the squabble he saw two Soldiers, each at a different time, present his gun at the people, threatning to make a lane through them; but the officers drove them in. The tragedy was compleated very soon in King-street. The firing was reserv'd for another party of Soldiers, not much if at all to their discredit in the judgment of some, and under the command of an officer who did not restrain them. The witness heard the report of the first gun soon after the people cried home, home; and declared that he tho't they had fired upon the main guard, for he heard the drum at the main guard beat to arms. Another, who was sworn in Court, a witness for the Crown declared, that about nine o'clock, passing near Draper's (or Boylston's) alley, which leads into Murrary's barracks, and thro' which he intended to go, he heard some boys huzzaing—he judged there were not more than six or seven, and they were small; they ran thro' dock-square towards the Market. Presently after he saw two or three persons in the alley with weapons—a number of Soldiers soon sallied out, arm'd with large naked cutlasses, assaulting every body coming in their way—that he himself narrowly escaped a cut from the foremost of them who pursued him; and that he saw a man there, who said he was wounded by them and he felt of the wound. The wounded man stopped, and this occasioned the people who were passing to gather round him—Thinking it dangerous for him to proceed, the witness returned home—A Captain of the 14th, one of the prisoners witnesses was also sworn in Court: He testified that in Cornhill he saw a mob collected at the pass (Boylston's alley) leading to Murray's barracks—the people were pelting the Soldiers and they were defending themselves—one of the Soldiers he tho't had a fire-shovel—as soon as they knew him, he prevailed on them to go to the bottom of the pass, and with some difficulty he got down. This witness, it seems, must have been later than the others; and Mr. Belknap, perhaps gives as early an account of it, as any can, but the Soldiers themselves.

I would only ask how it came to pass that the Soldiers, on that particular evening, should be seen abroad, in every part of the town, contrary to the rules of the army, after eight o'clock. If the officers, who should have restrain'd them, were careless of their duty, whence was so general a carelessness among the officers at that juncture? It was said, there was no officer at the main-guard, which may in part account for it. Or, if the Soldiers were all at once ungovernable by their officers, and could not be restrain'd by them, a child may judge from the appearance they made, that there had been a general combination, agreable to their former threats, on that evening to put in execution some wicked and desperate design.

Dec. 18th   VINDEX.

60. THOMAS PAINE, *COMMON SENSE*, 1776*

Thomas Paine (1737–1809) was born in England and came to America in 1774. By trade a staymaker, he had displayed a genius for journalism in England during a controversy over higher wages between Parliament and its excise agents. This incident brought him to the attention of Benjamin Franklin, who envisioned his usefulness and recommended him to friends in the colonies. In Philadelphia, Paine's writings moved Dr. Benjamin Rush to suggest that he compose a pamphlet supporting independence. The result was Common Sense, in which Paine represented the American cause as mankind's. After digesting every radical thought—those of the delegates at the Congress as well as of people in drawing rooms and taverns—and assimilating radical pamphlets and philosophical tracts on natural rights, Paine developed a powerful case for American freedom from Great Britain which proved effective for militants both in America and Europe.

Of Monarchy and Hereditary Succession

Mankind being originally equal in the order of creation, the equality could only be destroyed by some subsequent circumstance: the distinctions of rich and poor may in a great measure be accounted for,

* Thomas Paine, *Common Sense* (Philadelphia: R. Bell, 1776), pp. 12–29.

and that without having recourse to the harsh ill-sounding names of oppression and avarice. Oppression is often the consequence, but seldom or never the means of riches; and though avarice will preserve a man from being necessitously poor, it generally makes him too timorous to be wealthy.

But there is another and greater distinction for which no truly natural or religious reason can be assigned, and that is the distinction of men into KINGS and SUBJECTS. Male and female are the distinctions of nature, good and bad the distinctions of heaven; but how a race of men came into the world so exalted above the rest, and distinguished like some new species, is worth inquiring into, and whether they are the means of happiness or of misery to mankind.

In the early ages of the world, according to the scripture chronology there were no kings; the consequence of which was, there were no wars; it is the pride of kings which throws mankind into confusion. Holland, without a king hath enjoyed more peace for this last century than any of the monarchial governments in Europe. Antiquity favors the same remark; for the quiet and rural lives of the first Patriarchs have a happy something in them, which vanishes when we come to the history of Jewish royalty.

Government by kings was first introduced into the world by the heathens, from whom the children of Israel copied the custom. It was the most prosperous invention the devil ever set on foot for the promotion of idolatry. The heathens paid divine honors to their deceased kings, and the Christian world has improved on the plan by doing the same to their living ones. How impious is the title of sacred majesty applied to a worm, who in the midst of his splendor is crumbling into dust!

As the exalting one man so greatly above the rest cannot be justified on the equal rights of nature, so neither can it be defended on the authority of scripture; for the will of the Almighty as declared by Gideon, and the prophet Samuel, expressly disapproves of government by kings. All anti-monarchial parts of scripture, have been very smoothly glossed over in monarchial governments, but they undoubtedly merit the attention of countries which have their governments yet to form. Render unto Cesar the things which are Cesar's, is the scripture doctrine of courts, yet it is no support of monarchial government, for the Jews at that time were without a king, and in a state of vassalage to the Romans.

Near three thousand years passed away, from the Mosaic account of the creation, till the Jews under a national delusion requested a king. Till then their form of government (except in extraordinary cases where the Almighty interposed) was a kind of Republic, administered by a judge and the elders of the tribes. Kings they had none, and it was held sinful to acknowledge any being under that title but the Lord of Hosts. And when a man seriously reflects on the idolatrous homage which is paid to the persons of kings, he need not wonder that the Almighty, ever jealous of his honor, should disapprove a form of government which so impiously invades the prerogative of heaven.

Monarchy is ranked in scripture as one of the sins of the Jews, for which a curse in reserve is denounced against them. The history of that transaction is worth attending to.

The children of Israel being oppressed by the Midianites, Gideon marched against them with a small army, and victory through the divine interposition decided in his favor. The Jews, elated with success, and attributing it to the generalship of Gideon, proposed making him a king, saying, Rule thou over us, thou and thy son, and thy son's son. Here was temptation in its fullest extent; not a kingdom only, but an hereditary one; but Gideon in the piety of his soul replied, I will not rule over you, neither shall my son rule over you. THE LORD SHALL RULE OVER YOU. Words need not be more explicit; Gideon doth not decline the honor, but denieth their right to give it; neither doth he compliment them with invented declarations of his thanks, but in the positive style of a prophet charges them with disaffection to their proper sovereign, the King of Heaven.

About one hundred and thirty years after this, they fell again into the same error. The hankering which the Jews had for the idolatrous customs of the heathens, is something exceedingly unaccountable; but so it was, that laying hold of the misconduct of Samuel's two sons, who were intrusted with some secular concerns, they came in an abrupt and clamorous manner to Samuel, saying, Behold thou art old, and thy sons walk not in thy ways, now make us a king to judge us like all the other nations. And here we cannot but observe that their motives were bad, viz. that they might be like unto other nations, i.e. the heathens, whereas their true glory lay in being as much unlike them as possible. But the thing displeased Samuel when they said, give us a king to judge us; and Samuel prayed unto the Lord, and the Lord said unto Samuel, hearken unto the voice of the people in all that they say unto thee, for they have not rejected thee, but they have rejected me, THAT I SHOULD NOT REIGN OVER THEM. According to all the works which they have done since the day that I brought them up out of Egypt even unto this day, wherewith they have forsaken me, and served other Gods: so do they also unto thee. Now therefore hearken unto their voice, howbeit, protest solemnly unto them and show them the manner of the king that shall reign over them, i.e. not of any particular king, but the general manner of the kings of the earth whom Israel was so eagerly copying after. And notwithstanding the great distance of time and difference of manners, the character is still in fashion. And Samuel told all the words of the Lord unto the people, that asked of him a king. And he said, This shall be the manner of the king that shall reign over you. He will take your sons and appoint them for himself for his chariots and to be his horsemen, and some shall run before his chariots (this description agrees with the present mode of impressing men) and he will appoint him captains over thousands and captains over fifties, will set them to ear his ground and to reap his harvest, and to make his instruments of war, and instruments of his chariots. And he will take your daughters to be confectionaries, and to be cooks, and to be bakers (this describes the expense and luxury as well as the oppression of kings) and he will take your fields and your vineyards, and your olive yards, even the best of them, and give them to his servants. And he will take the tenth of your see, and of your vineyards, and give them to his officers and to his servants (by which we see that bribery, corruption, and favouritism, are the standing vices of kings) and he will take the tenth of your men servants, and your maid servants, and your goodliest young men, and your asses, and put them to his work: and he will take the tenth of your sheep, and ye shall be his servants, and ye shall cry out in that day because of your king which ye shall have chosen, AND THE LORD WILL NOT HEAR YOU IN THAT DAY. This accounts for the continuation of monarch; neither do the characters of the few good kings which have lived since, either sanctify the title, or blot out the sinfulness of the origin; the high encomium given of David takes no notice of him officially as a king, but only as a man after God's own heart. Nevertheless the people refused to obey the voice of Samuel, and they said, Nay but we will have a king over us, that we may be like all the nations, and that our king may judge us, and go out before us and fight our battles. Samuel continued to reason with them but to no purpose; he set before them their ingratitude, but all would not avail; and seeing them fully bent on their folly, he cried out, I will call unto the Lord, and he shall send thunder and rain (which was then a punishment, being in the time of wheat harvest) that ye may perceive and see that your wickedness in great which ye have done in the sight of the Lord, IN ASKING YOU A KING. So Samuel called unto the Lord, and the Lord sent thunder and rain that day, and all the people greatly feared the Lord and Samuel. And all the people said unto Samuel, Pray for thy servants unto the Lord thy God that we die not, for WE HAVE ADDED UNTO OUR SINS THIS EVIL, TO ASK A KING. These portions of scripture are direct and positive. They admit of no equivocal construction. That the Almighty hath here entered his protest against monarchical government is true, or the scripture is false. And a man hath good reason to believe that there is as much of kingcraft as priestcraft in withholding the scripture from the public in popish countries. For monarchy in every instance is the popery of government.

　　To the evil of monarchy we have added that of hereditary succession; and as the first is a degradation and lessening of ourselves, so the second, claimed as a matter of right, is an insult and imposition on posterity. For all men being originally equals, no one by birth could have a right to set up his own family in perpetual preference to all others for ever, and though himself might deserve some decent degree of honors of his contemporaries, yet his descendants might be far too unworthy to inherit them. One of the strongest natural proofs of the folly of hereditary right in kings, is that nature disapproves it, otherwise she would not so frequently turn it into ridicule, by giving mankind an ass for a lion.

Secondly, as no man at first could possess any other public honors than were bestowed upon him, so the givers of those honors could have no power to give away the right of posterity, and though they might say "We choose you for our head," they could not without manifest injustice to their children say "that your children and your children's children shall reign over ours forever." Because such an unwise, unjust, unnatural compact might (perhaps) in the next succession put them under the government of a rogue or a fool. Most wise men in their private sentiments have ever treated hereditary right with contempt; yet it is one of those evils which when once established is not easily removed: many submit from fear, others from superstition, and the more powerful part shares with the king the plunder of the rest.

This is supposing the present race of kings in the world to have had an honorable origin: whereas it is more than probable, that, could we take off the dark covering of antiquity and trace them to their first rise, we should find the first of them nothing better than the principal ruffian of some restless gang; whose savage manners or pre-eminence in subtilty obtained him the title of chief among plunderers: and who by increasing in power and extending his depredations, overawed the quiet and defenceless to purchase their safety by frequent contributions. Yet his electors could have no idea of giving hereditary right to his descendants, because such a perpetual exclusion of themselves was incompatible with the free and unrestrained principles they professed to live by. Wherefore, hereditary succession in the early ages of monarchy could not take place as a matter of claim, but as something casual or complemental; but as few or no records were extant in those days, and traditionary history stuff'd with fables, it was very easy, after the lapse of a few generations, to trump up some superstitious tale conveniently timed, Mahomet-like, to cram hereditary right down the throats of the vulgar. Perhaps the disorders which threatened, or seemed to threaten, on the decease of a leader and the choice of a new one (for elections among ruffians could not be very orderly) induced many at first to favor hereditary pretensions; by which means it happened, as it hath happened since, that what at first was submitted to as a convenience was afterwards claimed as a right.

England since the conquest hath known some few good monarchs, but groaned beneath a much larger number of bad ones; yet no man in his senses can say that their claim under William the Conqueror is a very honorable one. A French bastard landing with an armed banditti and establishing himself king of England against the consent of the natives, is in plain terms a very paltry rascally original. It certainly hath no divinity it it. However it is needless to spend much time in exposing the folly of hereditary right; if there are any so weak as to believe it, let them promiscuously worship the ass and the lion, and welcome, I shall neither copy their humility, nor disturb their devotion.

Yet I should be glad to ask how they suppose kings came at first? The question admits but of three answers, viz. either by lot, by election, or by usurpation. If the first king was taken by lot, it establishes a precedent for the next, which excludes hereditary succession. Saul was by lot, yet the succession was not hereditary, neither does it appear from that transaction that there was any intention it ever should. If the first king of any country was by election, that likewise establishes a precedent for the next; for to say, that the right of all future generations is taken away, by the act of the first electors, in their choice not only of a king but of a family of kings for ever, hath no parallel in or out of scripture but the doctrine of original sin, which supposes the free will of all men lost in Adam; and from such comparison, and it will admit of no other, hereditary succession can derive no glory. For as in Adam all sinned, and as in the first electors all men obeyed; as in the one all mankind were subjected to Satan, and in the other to sovereignty; as our innocence was lost in the first, and our authority in the last; and as both disable us from reassuming some former state and privilege, it unanswerably follows that original sin and hereditary succession are parallels. Dishonorable rank! inglorious connection! yet the most subtle sophist cannot produce a juster simile.

As to usurpation, no man will be so hardy as to defend it; and that William the Conqueror was an usurper is a fact not to be contradicted. The plain truth is, that the antiquity of English monarchy will not bear looking into.

But it is not so much the absurdity as the evil of hereditary sucession which concerns mankind. Did it insure a race of good and wise men it would have the seal of divine authority, but as it opens a door to the foolish, the wicked, and the improper, it has in it the nature of oppression. Men who look upon themselves born to reign, and others to obey, soon grow insolent. Selected from the rest of mankind, their minds are early poisoned by importance; and the world they act in differs so materially from the world at large, that they have but little opportunity of knowing its true interests, and when they succeed to the government are frequently the most ignorant and unfit of any throughout the dominions.

Another evil which attends hereditary succession is, that the throne is subject to be possessed by a minor at any age; all which time the regency acting under the cover of a king have every opportunity and inducement to betray their trust. The same national misfortune happens when a king worn out with age and infirmity enters the last stage of human weakness. In both these cases the public becomes a prey to every miscreant who can tamper successfully with the follies either of age or infancy.

The most plausible plea which hath ever been offered in favor of hereditary succession is, that it preserves a nation from civil wars; and were this true, it would be weighty; whereas it is the most bare-faced falsity ever imposed upon mankind. The whole history of England disowns the fact. Thirty kings and two minors have reigned in that distracted kingdom since the conquest, in which time there has been (including the revolution) no less than eight civil wars and nineteen rebellions. Wherefore instead of making for peace, it makes against it, and destroys the very foundation it seems to stand upon.

The contest for monarchy and succession, between the houses of York and Lancaster, laid England in a scene of blood for many years. Twelve pitched battles besides skirmishes and sieges were fought between Henry and Edward. Twice was Henry prisoner to Edward, who in his turn was prisoner to Henry. And so uncertain is the fate of war and the temper of a nation, when nothing but personal matters are the ground of a quarrel, that Henry was taken from a prison to a palace, and Edward obliged to fly from a palace to a foreign land; yet, as sudden transitions of temper are seldom lasting, Henry in his turn was driven from the throne, and Edward re-called to succeed him. The Parliament always following the strongest side.

This contest began in the reign of Henry the Sixth, and was not entirely extinguished till Henry the Seventh, in whom the families were united. Including a period of 67 years, viz. from 1422 to 1489.

In short, monarchy and succession have laid (not this or that kingdom only) but the world in blood and ashes. 'Tis a form of government which the word of God bears testimony against, and blood will attend it.

If we inquire into the business of a king, we shall find that in some countries they may have none; and after sauntering away their lives without pleasure to themselves or advantage to the nation, withdraw from the scene, and leave their successors to tread the same idle round. In absolute monarchies the whole weight of business civil and military lies on the king; the children of Israel in their request for a king urged this plea, "that he may judge us, and go out before us and fight our battles." But in countries where he is neither a judge nor a general, as in England, a man would be puzzled to know what is his business.

The nearer any government approaches to a Republic, the less business there is for a king. It is somewhat difficult to find a proper name for the government of England. Sir William Meredith calls it a Republic; but in its present state it is unworthy of the name, because the corrupt influence of the crown, by having all the places in its disposal, hath so effectually swallowed up the power, and eaten out the virtue of the House of Commons (the republican part in the Constitution) that the government of England is nearly as monarchial as that of France or Spain. Men fall out with names without understanding them. For 'tis the republican and not the monarchial part of the Constitution of England which Englishmen glory in, viz. the liberty of choosing an House of Commons from out of their own body—and it is easy to see that when republican virtues fail, slavery ensues. Why is the Constitution of England sickly, but because monarchy hath poisoned the Republic; the crown has engrossed the Commons.

In England a king hath little more to do than to make war and give away places; which, in plain terms, is to empoverish the nation and set it together by the ears. A pretty business indeed for a man to be allowed eight hundred thousand sterling a year for, and worshipped into the bargain! Of more worth is one honest man to society, and in the sight of God, than all the crowned ruffians that ever lived.

4

The Literature of the Revolution: Nationalism and Romanticism

61. TIMOTHY DWIGHT, *COLUMBIA*, 1777[*]

Timothy Dwight (1752–1817) was one of the Connecticut Wits, a group of Hartford intellectuals who urged Americans to develop a national literature in keeping with the spirit of a free and independent people. During the early part of the Revolution, while serving as an army chaplain, Dwight wrote the following war song. He later resigned from the army, and spent his life as an educator, minister, essayist, and poet. In the new progressive spirit he established a school to educate both sexes, and later became president of Yale. An influential Federalist leader, he joined those who considered efforts to push the Revolution beyond independence from England as a threat to true liberty.

COLUMBIA, Columbia, to glory arise,
The queen of the world, and the child of the skies!
Thy genius commands thee; with rapture behold,
While ages on ages thy splendors unfold.
Thy reign is the last, and the noblest of time,
Most fruitful thy soil, most inviting thy clime;
Let the crimes of the east ne'er encrimson thy name,
Be freedom and science, and virtue thy fame.

To conquest and slaughter let Europe aspire;
Whelm nations in blood, and wrap cities in fire;
Thy heroes the rights of mankind shall defend,

[*] *Library of American Literature,* Edmund C. Stedman and Ellen Mackay Hutchinson, eds. (New York: Charles Webster and Co., 1890), Vol. III, pp. 480–81.

And triumph pursue them, and glory attend.
A world is thy realm: for a world be thy laws,
Enlarged as thine empire, and just is thy cause;
On Freedom's broad basis, that empire shall rise,
Extend with the main, and dissolve with the skies.

Fair Science her gates to thy sons shall unbar,
And the east see thy morn hide the beams of her star.
New bards, and new sages, unrivalled shall soar.
To fame unextinguished, when time is no more;
To thee, the last refuge of virtue designed,
Shall fly from all nations the best of mankind;
Here, grateful to heaven, with transport shall bring
Their incense, more fragrant than odors of spring.

Nor less shall thy fair ones to glory ascend,
And genius and beauty in harmony blend;
The graces of form shall awake pure desire,
And the charms of the soul ever cherish the fire;
Their sweetness unmingled, their manners refined,
And virtue's bright image, instamped on the mind,
With peace and soft rapture shall teach life to glow.
And light up a smile in the aspect of woe.

Thy fleets to all regions thy power shall display,
The nations admire, and the oceans obey;
Each shore to thy glory its tribute unfold,
And the east and the south yield their spices and gold.
As the dug-spring unbounded, thy splendor shall flow,
And earth's little kingdoms before thee shall bow:
While the ensigns of union, in triumph unfurled,
Hush the tumult of war, and give peace to the world.

Thus, as down a lone valley, with cedars o'erspread,
From war's dread confusion I pensively strayed—
The gloom from the face of fair heaven retired;
The winds ceased to murmur; the thunders expired;
Perfumes, as of Eden, flowed sweetly along,
And a voice, as of angels, enchantingly sung:
"Columbia, Columbia, to glory arise,
The queen of the world, and the child of the skies."

62. FRANCIS HOPKINSON, *THE BATTLE OF THE KEGS*, 1778*

Francis Hopkinson (1737–91) was a lawyer, scientist, inventor, musician, composer, author, and artist. He made heraldic designs and seals for several states, and in 1777 designed what came to be the United States flag. A delegate to the Continental Congress from New Jersey, he was a member of the radical contingent and signed the Declaration of Independence.

But Hopkinson achieved his more lasting reputation as a writer. The following "Battle of the Kegs" ridiculed the redcoats occupying Philadelphia, particularly their commander, Lord William Howe; sung to the tune of "Yankee Doodle," it became very popular and received more acclaim than its artistry merited. It made the Americans laugh during the darkest days of the war, when their capital was captured, and remained popular after 1780 when the South came close to falling to the British.

This ballad was occasioned by a real incident. Certain machines, in the form of kegs, charged with gunpower, were sent down the river to annoy the British shipping then at Philadelphia. The danger of these machines being discovered, the British manned the wharfs and shipping, and discharged their small-arms and cannons at everything they saw floating in the river during the ebb-tide.—[Hopkinson's] *Note*

> Gallants attend and hear a friend
>   Trill forth harmonious ditty,
> Strange things I'll tell which late befell
>   In Philadelphia city.
>
> 'Twas early day, as poets say,
>   Just when the sun was rising.
> A soldier stood on a log of wood,
>   And saw a thing surprising.
>
> As in amaze he stood to gaze,
>   The truth can't be denied, sir,
> He spied a score of kegs or more
>   Come floating down the tide, sir.
>
> A sailor too in jerkin blue,
>   This strange appearance viewing,
> First damned his eyes, in great surprise,
>   Then said, "Some mischief's brewing."

* *Ibid.*, Vol. III, pp. 244–46.

"These kegs, I'm told, the rebels hold,
  Packed up like pickled herring;
And they're come down to attack the town,
  In this new way of ferrying."

The soldier flew, the sailor too,
  And scared almost to death, Sir,
Wore out their shoes, to spread the news,
  And ran till out of breath, sir.

Now up and down throughout the town,
  Most frantic scenes were acted;
And some ran here, and others there,
  Like men almost distracted.

Some fire cried, which some denied,
  But said the earth had quaked;
And girls and boys, with hideous noise,
  Ran through the streets half naked.

Sir William he, snug as a flea,
  Lay all this time a snoring.
Nor dreamed of harm as he lay warm,
  In bed with Mrs. Loring.

Now in a fright, he starts upright,
  Awaked by such a clatter;
He rubs both eyes, and boldly cries,
  "For God's sake, what's the matter?"

At his bedside he then espied,
  Sir Erskine at command, sir,
Upon one foot he had one boot,
  And th' other in his hand, sir.

"Arise, arise," Sir Erskine cries,
  "The rebels—more's the pity,
Without a boat are all afloat,
  And ranged before the city."

"The motley crew, in vessels new,
  With Satan for their guide, sir,
Packed up in bags, or wooden kegs,
  Come driving down the tide, sir."

"Therefore prepare for bloody war,
  These kegs must all be routed,

Or surely we despised shall be,
 And British courage doubted."

The royal band now ready stand
 All ranged in dread array, sir,
With stomach stout to see it out,
 And make a bloody day, sir.

The cannons roar from shore to shore,
 The small arms make a rattle;
Since wars began I'm sure no man
 E'er saw so strange a battle.

The rebel dales, the rebel vales,
 With rebel trees surrounded,
The distant woods, the hills and floods,
 With rebel echoes sounded.

The fish below swam to and fro,
 Attacked from every quarter;
Why sure, thought they, the devil's to pay,
 'Mongst folks above the water.

The kegs, 'tis said, though strongly made,
 Of rebel staves and hoops, sir,
Could not oppose their powerful foes,
 The conquering British troops, sir.

From morn to night these men of might
 Displayed amazing courage;
And when the sun was fairly down,
 Retired to sup their porridge.

A hundred men with each a pen,
 Or more upon my word, sir,
It is most true would be too few,
 Their valor to record, sir.

Such feats did they perform that day,
 Against these wicked kegs, sir,
That years to come, if they get home,
 They'll make their boasts and brags, sir.

63. PHILIP FRENEAU, *POEMS*, 1779–88[*]

Philip Freneau (1752–1832) was born in New York of French Huguenot parents and educated at Princeton. He was a strong champion of the broader principles of the Declaration of Independence and of Jeffersonian republicanism. He so incensed President Washington by his anti-Federalist barbs that he was tabbed "that rascal Freneau," and during John Adams' Presidency, when Freneau was editor of the National Gazette *of Philadelphia, he was jailed under the Sedition Act.*

Freneau was the first important poet of the new nation; indeed, most literary historians accord him a place among the great American poets. A highly talented satirist like Hopkinson, he was also a true lyricist who in his poetry ennobled the soldiers of the Revolution. He was acutely aware of European literary movements and through his poetry anticipated the rise of romanticism.

The House of Night, 1779

[The following poem, written in the Romantic Gothic style, concerns a young man who in the "House of Night" meets Death, and seeing all of its horrors, gains a deeper understanding of life.—Editor's Note]

103

Scarce had he spoke, when on the lofty dome
Rush'd from the clouds a hoarse resounding blast—
Round the four eaves so loud and sad it play'd
As though all music were to breathe its last.

104

Warm was the gale, and such as travelers say
Sport with the winds on Zaara's barren waste;
Black was the sky, a mourning carpet spread,
Its azure blotted, and its stars o'ercast!

105

Lights in the air like burning stars were hurl'd,
Dogs howl'd, heaven mutter'd, and the tempest blew,
The red half-moon peeped from behind a cloud
As if in dread the amazing scene to view.

[*] *The Poems of Philip Freneau* . . . (Philadelphia: Francis Bailey, 1786), pp. 118–23; *Poems Written and Published During the American Revolutionary War* (Philadelphia: Lydia R. Bailey, 1809), Vol. I, pp. 141–42; *Poems Relating to the American Revolution*, Everet A. Duyckinek, ed. (New York: W. J. Widdleton, Publisher, 1809), Vol. I, pp. 134–35.

106

The mournful trees that in the garden stood
Bent to the tempest as it rush'd along,
The elm, the myrtle, and the cypress sad
More melancholy tun'd its bellowing song.

107

No more that elm its noble branches spread,
The yew, the cypress, or the myrtle tree,
Rent from the roots the tempest tore them down,
And all the grove in wild confusion lay.

108

Yet, mindful of his dread command, I part
Glad from the magic dome—nor found relief;
Damps from the dead hung heavier round my heart,
While sad remembrance rous'd her stores of grief.

109

O'er a dark field I held my dubious way
Where Jack-a-lanthorn walk'd his lonely round,
Beneath my feet substantial darkness lay,
And screams were heard from the distemper'd ground.

110

Nor look'd I back, till to a far off wood,
Trembling with fear, my weary feet had sped—
Dark was the night, but at the inchanted dome
I saw the infernal windows flaming red.

111

And from within the howls of Death I heard,
Cursing the dismal night that gave him birth,
Damning his ancient sire, and mother sin,
Who at the gates of hell, accursed, brought him forth.

112

(For fancy gave to my enraptur'd soul
An eagle's eye, with keenest glance to see,
And bade those distant sounds distinctly roll,
Which, waking, never had affected me.)

113

Oft his pale breast with cruel hand he smote,
And tearing from his limbs a winding sheet,

Roar'd to the black skies, while the woods around,
As wicked as himself, his words repeat.

114

Thrice tow'rd the skies his meagre arms he rear'd,
Invok'd all hell, and thunders on his head,
Bid light'nings fly, earth yawn, and tempests roar,
And the sea wrap him in its oozy bed.

115

"My life for one cool draught!—O, fetch your springs,
"Can one unfeeling to my woes be found!
"No friendly visage comes to my relief,
"But ghosts impend, and spectres hover round.

116

"Though humbled now, dishearten'd and distrest,
"Yet, when admitted to the peaceful ground,
"With heroes, kings, and conquerors I shall rest,
"Shall sleep as safely, and perhaps as sound."

117

Dim burnt the lamp, and now the phantom Death
Gave his last groans in horror and despair—
"All hell demands me hence,"—he said, and threw
The red lamp hissing through the midnight air.

118

Trembling, across the plain my course I held,
And found the grave-yard, loitering through the gloom,
And, in the midst, a hell-red, wandering light,
Walking in fiery circles round the tomb.

119

Among the graves a spiry building stood,
Whose tolling bell, resounding through the shade,
Sung doleful ditties to the adjacent wood,
And many a dismal drowsy thing it said.

120

This fabrick tall, with towers and chancels grac'd,
Was rais'd by sinners' hands, in ages fled;
The roof they painted, and the beams they brac'd,
And texts from scripture o'er the walls they spread:

121

But wicked were their hearts, for they refus'd
To aid the helpless orphan, when distrest,
The shivering, naked stranger they misus'd,
And banish'd from their doors the starving guest.

122

By laws protected, cruel and profane,
The poor man's ox these monsters drove away:—
And left *Distress* to attend her infant train,
No friend to comfort, and no bread to stay.

123

But heaven look'd on with keen, resentful eye,
And doom'd them to perdition and the grave,
That as they felt not for the wretch distrest,
So heaven no pity on their souls would have.

124

In pride they rais'd this building tall and fair,
Their hearts were on perpetual mischief bent,
With pride they preach'd, and pride was in their prayer,
With pride they were deceiv'd, and so to hell they went.

125

At distance far approaching to the tomb,
By lamps and lanthorns guided through the shade,
A coal-black chariot hurried through the gloom,
Spectres attending, in black weeds array'd.

126

Whose woeful forms yet chill my soul with dread,
Each wore a vest in Stygian chambers wove,
Death's kindred all—Death's horses they bestrode,
And gallop'd fiercely, as the chariot drove.

127

Each horrid face a grizly mask conceal'd,
Their busy eyes shot terror to my soul
As now and then, by the pale lanthorn's glare,
I saw them for their parted friend condole.

128

Before the hearse Death's chaplain seem'd to go,
Who strove to comfort, what he could, the dead;

Talk'd much of *Satan*, and the land of woe,
And many a chapter from the scriptures read.

129

At last he rais'd the swelling anthem high,
In dismal numbers seem'd he to complain;
The captive tribes that by *Euphrates* wept,
Their song was jovial to this dreary strain.

130

That done, they plac'd the carcase in the tomb,
To dust and dull oblivion now resign'd,
Then turn'd the chariot tow'rd the House of Night,
Which soon flew off, and left no trace behind.

131

But as I stoop'd to write the appointed verse,
Swifter than thought the airy scene decay'd;
Blushing the morn arose, and from the east
With her gay streams of light dispell'd the shade.

132

What is this *Death*, ye deep read sophists, say?—
Death is no more than one unceasing change;
New forms arise, while other forms decay,
Yet all is *LIFE* throughout creation's range.

133

The towering *Alps*, the haughty *Apennine*,
The Andes, wrapt in everlasting snow,
The *Apalachian* and the *Ararat*
Sooner or later must to ruin go.

134

Hills sink to plains, and man returns to dust,
That dust supports a reptile or a flower;
Each changeful atom by some other nurs'd
Takes some new form, to perish in an hour.

135

Too nearly join'd to sickness, toils, and pains,
(Perhaps for former crimes imprison'd here)
True to itself the immortal soul remains,
And seeks new mansions in the starry sphere.

136

When Nature bids thee from the world retire,
With joy thy lodging leave, a fated guest;
In Paradise, the land of thy desire,
Existing always, always to be blest.

Eutaw Springs
To the Memory of the
Brave Americans
Under General Greene, in South
Carolina, Who Fell in the
Action of September 8, 1781

At Eutaw Springs the valiant died;
   Their limbs with dust are covered o'er—
Weep on, ye springs, your tearful tide;
   How many heroes are no more!

If in this wreck of ruin, they
   Can yet be thought to claim a tear,
O smite your gentle breast, and say
   The friends of freedom slumber here!

Thou, who shalt trace this bloody plain,
   If goodness rules thy generous breast,
Sigh for the wasted rural reign;
   Sigh for the shepherds, sunk to rest!

Stranger, their humble graves adorn;
   You too may fall, and ask a tear;
'Tis not the beauty of the morn
   That proves the evening shall be clear.—

They saw their injured country's woe;
   The flaming town, the wasted field;
Then rushed to meet the insulting foe;
   They took the spear—but left the shield.

Led by thy conquering genius, Greene,
   The Britons they compelled to fly;
None distant viewed the fatal plain,
   None grieved, in such a cause to die—

But, like the Parthian, famed of old,
   Who, flying, still their arrows threw,

These routed Britons, full as bold,
  Retreated, and retreating slew.

Now rest in peace, our patriot band;
  Though far from nature's limits thrown,
We trust they find a happier land,
  A brighter sunshine of their own.

The Wild Honey Suckle, 1786

Fair flower, that dost so comely grow,
Hid in this silent, dull retreat,
Untouched thy honied blossoms blow,
Unseen thy little branches greet:
    No roving foot shall crush thee here,
    No busy hand provoke a tear.

By nature's self in white arrayed,
She bade thee shun the vulgar eye,
And planted here the guardian shade,
And sent soft waters murmuring by,
    Thus quietly thy summer goes,
    Thy days declining to repose.

Smit with those charms, that must decay,
I grieve to see your future doom;
They died—nor were those flowers more gay,
The flowers that did in Eden bloom;
    Unpitying frosts, and autumn's power
    Shall leave no vestige of this flower.

From morning suns and evening dews
At first thy little being came;
If nothing once, you nothing lose,
For you die you are the same;
    The space between is but an hour,
    The frail duration of a flower.

The Indian Burying Ground, 1787

The North American Indians bury their dead in a sitting posture; decorating the corpse with wampum, the images of birds, quadrupeds, etc. and (if that of a warrior) with bows, arrows, tomahawks, and other military weapons. [Freneau's Note]

    In spite of all the learned have said,
    I still my old opinion keep;

The *posture*, that we give the dead,
Points out the souls' eternal sleep.

Not so the ancients of these lands—
The Indian, when from life released,
Again is seated with his friends,
And shares again the joyous feast.

His imaged birds, and painted bowl,
And venison, for a journey dressed,
Bespeak the nature of the soul,
ACTIVITY, that knows no rest.

His bow, for action ready bent,
And arrows, with a head of stone,
Can only mean that life is spent,
And not the old ideas gone.

Thou stranger, that shall come this way,
No fraud upon the dead commit—
Observe the swelling turf, and say
They do not *lie*, but here they *sit*.

Here still a lofty rock remains,
On which the curious eye may trace
(Now wasted, half, by wearing rains)
The fancies of a ruder race.

Here still an aged elm aspires,
Beneath whose far-projecting shade
(And which the shepherd still admires)
The children of the forest played!

There oft a restless Indian queen
(Pale *Shebah*, with her braided hair)
And many a barbarous form is seen
To chide the man that lingers there.

By midnight moons, o'er moistening dews,
In habit for the chase arrayed,
The hunter still the deer pursues,
The hunter and the deer, a shade!

And long shall timorous fancy see
The painted chief, and pointed spear,
And Reason's self shall bow the knee
To shadows and delusions here.

64. THE CONNECTICUT WITS,
THE ANARCHIAD, 1786–87*

*The Connecticut Wits were a group of writers and men of affairs
identified with Hartford, Connecticut, and with Yale. For a brief period
in the 1780's, they formed an informal literary club and collaborated in
writing several poems, including "The Anarchiad." Using the heroic
couplet, the group commented on the immediate postwar period and
stated their belief in the need for union accompanied by liberty and
order. During this unsettled period many of the leaders of the Revolution
feared the numerous riots and cries against authority and aristocracy
which seemed a prelude to anarchy. The Connecticut Wits, mostly
political conservatives, were unnecessarily fearful. Connected with the
Washington Administration and active during the zenith of federalism,
the group included Richard Alsop (1761–1815), a financier and the leading
Wit, though he did not participate in writing this poem; Benjamin
Trumball (1735–1820), clergyman and historian; Lemuel Hopkins (1750–
1801), physician; David Humphreys (1752–1812), soldier and diplomat;
Joel Barlow (1754—1812) poet, diplomat, and political philosopher; and
Timothy Dwight.*

Faction

Behold those veterans worn with want and care,
　　Their sinews stiffened silvered o'er their hair,
Weak in their steps of age, they move forlorn,
Their toils forgotten by the sons of scorn;
This hateful truth still aggravates the pain,
In vain they conquered, and they bled in vain.

Go then, ye remnants of inglorious wars,
Disown your marks of merit, hide your scars,
Of lust, of power, of titled pride accused,
Steal to your graves dishonored and abused.
　　For see, proud Faction waves her flaming brand,
And discord riots o'er the ungrateful land;
Lo, to the North a wild adventurous crew
In desperate mobs the savage state renew;
Each felon chief his maddening thousands draws,

* From, "American Antiquities No. X," *New Haven Gazette and Con-
necticut Magazine* (May 24, 1787). See also Vernon Louis Parrington, ed., *The
Connecticut Wits* (Hamden, Conn., London: Archon Books, 1963; New York:
Harcourt, Brace, 1926), pp. 458–62.

And claims bold license from the bond of laws;
In other states the chosen sires of shame,
Stamp their vile knaveries with a legal name;
In honor's seat the sons of meanness swarm,
And senates base, the work of mobs perform,
To wealth, to power the sons of union rise,
While foes deride you and while friends despise.

    Stand forth, ye traitors, at your country's bar,
Inglorious authors of intestine war,
What countless mischiefs from their labors rise!
Pens dipped in gall, and lips inspired with lies!
Ye sires of ruin, prime detested cause
Of bankrupt faith, annihilated laws,
Of selfish systems, jealous, local schemes,
And unioned empire lost in empty dreams;
Your names, expanding with your growing crime,
Shall float disgustful down the stream of time,
Each future age applaud the avenging song,
And outraged nature vindicate the wrong.

    Yes, there are men, who, touched with heavenly fire,
Beyond the confines of these climes aspire,
Beyond the praises of a tyrant age,
To live immortal in the patriot page;
Who greatly dare, though warning worlds oppose,
To pour just vengeance on their country's foes.

      .   .   .   .

    Yet what the hope? the dreams of congress fade,
The federal union sinks in endless shade,
Each feeble call, that warns the realms around,
Seems the faint echo of a dying sound,
Each requisition wafts in fleeting air,
And not one state regards the powerless prayer.

    Ye wanton states, by heaven's best blessings cursed,
Long on the lap of fostering luxury nursed,
What fickle frenzy raves, what visions strange,
Inspire your bosoms with the lust of change?
And frames the wish to fly from fancied ill,
And yield your freedom to a monarch's will?

    Go view the lands to lawless power a prey,
Where tyrants govern with unbounded sway;
See the long pomp in gorgeous state displayed,
The tinselled guards, the Squadroned horse parade;

See heralds gay with emblems on their vest,
In tissued robes tall beauteous pages drest;
Where moves the pageant, throng unnumbered slaves,
Lords, dukes, and princes, titulary knaves
Confusedly shine, the purple gemmed with stars,
Sceptres, and globes, and crowns, and rubied cars,
On gilded orbs the thundering chariots rolled,
Steeds snorting fire, and champing bits of gold,
Prance to the trumpet's voice—while each assumes
A loftier gait, and lifts his neck of plumes.
High on the moving throne, and near the van,
The tyrant rides, the chosen scourage of man;
Clairons, and flutes, and drums his way prepare,
And shouting millions rend the conscious air;
Millions, whose ceaseless toils the pomp sustain,
Whose hour of stupid joy repays an age of pain.
        From years of darkness springs the regal line,
Hereditary kings by right divine:
'Tis theirs to riot on all nature's spoils,
For them with pangs unblest the peasant toils,
For them the earth prolific teems with grain,
Theirs, the dread labors of the devious main,
Annual for them the wasted land renews
The gifts oppressive, and extorted dues.
For them when slaughter spreads the gory plains,
The life-blood gushes from a thousand veins,
While the dull herd, of earth-born pomp afraid,
Adore the power that coward meanness made.

                        .   .   .   .

        Nor less abhorred the certain woe that waits
The giddy rage of democratic states;
Whose popular breath, high blown in restless tide,
No laws can temper, and no reason guide;
An equal sway their mind indignant spurns,
To wanton change the bliss of freedom turns,
Led by wild demagogues the factious crowd,
Mean, fierce, imperious, insolent and loud,
Nor fame nor wealth nor power nor system draws,
They see no object and perceive no cause,
But feel by turns, in one disastrous hour,
The extremes of license and the extremes of power.
        What madness prompts, or what ill-omened fates,

Your realm to parcel into petty states?
Shall lordly Hudson part contending powers?
And broad Potomac lave two hosile shores?
Must Allegany's sacred summits bear
The impious bulwarks of perpetual war?
His hundred streams receive your heroes slain?
And bear your sons inglorious to the main?
Will states cement by feebler bonds allied?
Or join more closely as they more divide?
Will this vain scheme bid restless factions cease?
Check foreign wars or fix internal peace?
Call public credit from her grave to rise?
Or gain in grandeur what they lose in size?
In this weak realm can countless kingdoms start,
Strong with new force in each divided part?
While empire's head, divided into four,
Gains life by severance of disminished power?
So when the philosophic hand divides
The full grown polypus in genial tides,
Each severed part, informed with latent life,
Acquires new vigor from the friendly knife,
O'er peopled sands the puny insects creep,
Till the next wave absorbs them in the deep.
      What then remains? must pilgrim freedom fly
From these loved regions to her native sky?
When the fair fugitive the orient chased,
She fixed her seat beyond the watery wast;
Her docile sons (enough of power resigned,
And natural rites in social leagues combined)
In virtue firm, though jealous in her cause,
Gave senates force and energy to laws,
From ancient habit local powers obey,
You feel no reverence for one general sway,
For breach of faith no keen compulsion feel,
And feel no interest in the federal weal.
But know, ye favored race, one potent head,
Must rule your states, and strike your foes with dread,
The finance regulate, the trade control,
Live through the empire, and accord the whole.
      Ere death invades, and night's deep curtain falls,
Through ruined realms the voice of Union calls,
Loud as the trump of heaven through darkness roars,
When gyral gusts entomb Caribbean towers,

When nature trembles through the deeps convulsed,
And ocean foams from craggy cliffs repulsed,
On you she calls! attend the warning cry,
"Ye live united, or divided die."

5

The Philosophy of
Religion and Reason

65. ETHAN ALLEN, *REASON THE ONLY ORACLE OF MAN*, 1784*

Ethan Allen (1737–89), the almost legendary revolutionary soldier, politician, and philosopher was born in Litchfield, Connecticut. At about age thirty, after indifferent financial success in iron smelting and mining, he moved into the Vermont frontier and purchased lands from New Hampshire. Following a decision by the Crown awarding Vermont to New York, that province's high court declared the land claims of Allen and other settlers invalid; to protect his investment Allen organized the men of the region into the fabled Green Mountain Boys. Their violent protests caused Governor Tryon of New York to declare Allen an outlaw and to put a price of twenty pounds on his head.

At the outbreak of the Revolution, Allen and his companions became heroes by capturing Fort Ticonderoga, whose heavy guns enabled General Washington to lay siege to Boston. Allen was not so fortunate in a subsequent attempt to invade Canada. The American army, with which he had joined forces, suffered defeat, and he was captured and held until 1778. Although then commissioned a brevet colonel by Washington, he fought no more, but busied himself with the task of Vermont independence. His goal of statehood for Vermont was achieved two years after his death.

Allen was well educated in his youth and apparently much in-

---

* Ethan Allen, *Reason the Only Oracle of Man: or a Compendious System of Natural Religion* (New York: G. W. and A. I. Matsell, 1836), Ch. I.

fluenced by Thomas Young, an itinerant physician, from whom many of his ideas emanate. Brought up in the deeply Calvinistic traditions of Connecticut, Allen later reacted against these religious and philosophical precepts. Though most of his writings are political, he also wrote Reason: the Only Oracle of Man. *He was the first to systematize the philosophy of reason and spurn the idealism of the previous age. First editions of his book are rare—the contents so frightened the printer that he burned all of them.*

Though *"none by searching can find out God, or the Almighty to perfection,"* yet I am persuaded, that if mankind would dare to exercise their reason as freely on those divine topics, as they do in the common concerns of life, they would in a great measure, rid themselves of their blindness and superstition, gain more exalted ideas of God and their obligations to him and one another, and be proportionably delighted and blessed with the views of his moral government, make better members of society, and acquire many powerful incentives to the practice of morality, which is the last and greatest perfection that human nature is capable of.

Of the Being of a God

The Laws of Nature having subjected mankind to a state of absolute dependence on something out of, and manifestly beyond themselves, or the compound exertion of their natural powers, gave them the first conception of a superior principle existing; otherwise they could have had no possible conception of a superintending power. But this sense of dependancy, which results from experience and reasoning on the facts which every man cannot fail to produce, has uniformly established the knowledge of our dependance to every individual of the species who are rational, which necessarily involves, or contains in it the idea of a ruling power, or that there is a God, which ideas are synonymous.

The globe with its productions the planets in their motions, and the starry heavens in their magnitudes, surprise our senses and confound our reason, in their munificent lessons of instruction concerning God, by means whereof, we are apt to be more or less lost in our ideas of the object or divine adoration, though at the same time every one is truly sensible that their being and preservation is from God. We are too apt to confound our ideas of God with his works, and take the latter for the former. Thus barbarous and unlearned nations have imagined, that inasmuch as the sun in its influence is beneficial to them in bringing forward the spring of the year, causing the production of vegetation, and food for their subsistence, that therefore it is their God: while others have located other parts of creation, and ascribe to them the prerogatives of God; and mere creatures and images have been substituted for gods by the wickedness or weakness of man, or both together. It seems that mankind in most ages and parts of the world have been fond of corporeal Deities with whom their outward senses might be gratified, or as fantastically diverted from the just apprehension of the true God, by a supposed supernatural intercourse with invisible and mere spiritual beings, to whom they ascribe divinity, so through one means or other, the character of the true God has been neglected, to the great detriment of truth, justice and morality in the world; nor is it possible, that mankind can be uniform in their religious opinions, or worship God according to knowledge, except they can form a consistent arrangement of ideas of the Divine character.

Although we extend our ideas retrospectively ever so far upon the succession,—yet no one cause in the extended order of succession, which depends upon another prior to itself, can be the independent cause of all things: nor is it possible to trace the order of the succession of causes back to that self-existing cause, inasmuch as it is eternal and infinite, and therefore cannot be traced out by succession, which operated according to the order of time, consequently can bear no more proportion to the eternity and infinity of God, than time itself may be supposed to do, which has no proportion at all; as the succeeding arguments respecting the eternity and infinity of God will evince. But notwithstanding the series of the succession of causes cannot be followed in a retrospective succession up to the self-existent or eternal cause, it is nevertheless a perpetual and conclusive evidence of a God. For a succession of causes considered collectively, can be nothing more than effects of the independent causes, and as much dependent on it, as those dependant causes are upon one another; so that we may with certainty conclude that the system of nature, which we call by the name of natural causes, is as much dependent on a self-existent cause, as an individual of the species in the order of generation is dependent on its progenitors for existence. Such part of the series of nature's operations, which we understand has a regular and necessary connection with, and dependence on its parts, which we denominated by the names of cause and effect. From hence we are authorised from reason to conclude, that the vast system of causes and effects are thus necessarily connected, (speaking of the natural world only) and the whole regularly and necessarily dependant on a self-existent cause, and ascribe self-existence to it, otherwise it could not be independent and consequently not a God. But the eternity or manner of the existence of a Self-existent and independent being is to all finite capabilities utterly incomprehensible; yet this is so far from an objection against the reality of such a being, that it is essentially necessary to support the evidence of it; for if we could comprehend that being whom we call God, he would not be God, but must have been finite, and that in the same degree as those may be supposed to be who could comprehend him; therefore so certain as God is, we cannot comprehend his essence, eternity, or manner of existence.

This should always be premised, when we assay to reason on the being, perfection, eternity and infinity of God, or of his creation and providence. As far as we understand nature, we are become acquainted with the character of God, for the knowledge of nature is the revelation of God. If we form in our imagination a compendious idea of the harmony of the universe, it is the same as calling God by the name of harmony, for there could be no harmony without regulation, and no regulation without a regulator, which is expressive of the idea of a God. Nor could it be possible, that there could be an order or disorder, except we admit of such a thing as creation, and creation contains in it the idea of a creator, which is another appellation for the Divine Being, distinguishing God from his creation. Furthermore there could be no proportion, figure or motion, without wisdom and power: wisdom to plan, and power to execute, and these are perfections, when applied to the works of nature, which signify the agency or superintendency of God. If we consider nature to be matter, figure and motion, we include the idea of God in that of motion; for motion implies a mover, as much as creation does a creator. If from the composition, texture and tendency of the universe in general, we form a complex idea of general good resulting there from to mankind, we implicitly admit a God by the name of good, including the idea of his providence to man. And from hence arises our obligations to love and adore God, because he provides for, and is beneficent to us: abstract the idea of goodness from the character of God, and it would cancel all our obligations to him, and excite us to hate and detest him as a tyrant; hence it is, that ignorant people are superstitiously misled into a conceit that they hate God, when at the same time it is only the idol of their own imagination, which they truly ought to hate and be ashamed of; but were such persons to connect the ideas of power, wisdom, goodness, and all possible perfection in the character of God, their hatred towards him would be turned into love and adoration.

By extending our ideas in a larger circle, we shall perceive our dependance on the earth and waters of the globe which we inhabit, and from which we are bountifully fed and gorgeously arrayed, and next extend our ideas to the sun, whose fiery mass darts its brilliant rays of light to our terraqueous ball with amazing velocity, and whose region of inexhaustible fire supplies it with fervent heat, which causes vegetation and gilds the various seasons of the year with ten thousand charms: this is not the achievement of man, but the workmanship and providence of God. But how the sun is supplied with materials, thus to perpetuate its kind influences, we know not. But will any one deny the reality of those beneficial influences, because we do not understand the manner of the perpetuality of that fiery world, or how it became such a body of fire; or will any one deny the reality of nutrition of food, because we do not understand the secret operation of the digesting powers of animal nature, or the minute particulars of its cherishing influence. None will be so stupid as to do it. Equally absurd would it be for us to deny the providence of God, by "whom we live, move, and have our being," because we cannot comprehend it.

We know that earth, water, fire and air, in their various compositions subserve us, and we also know that these elements are devoid of reflection, reason or design; from whence we may easily infer, that a wise, understanding, and designing being has ordained them to be thus subservient. Could blind chance constitute order and decorum, and consequently a providence? That wisdom, order and design should be the production of non-entity, or of chaos, confusion and old night, is too absurd to deserve a serious confutation, for it supposeth that there may be effects without a cause, viz: produced by non-entity, or that chaos and confusion could produce the effects of power, wisdom and goodness; such absurdities as these we must assent to, or subscribe to the doctrine of a self-existent and providential being.

Speculations on the Doctrine of the depravity of Human Reason

In the course of our speculations on divine providence we proceed next to the consideration of the doctrine of the depravity of human reason; a doctrine derogatory to the nature of man, and the rank and character of being which he holds in the universe, and which, if admitted to be true overturns knowledge and science and renders learning, instruction and books useless and impertinent; inasmuch as reason, depraved or spoiled, would cease to be reason; as much as the mind of a raving mad-man would of course cease to be rational: admitting the depravity of reason, the consequence would unavoidably follow, that as far as it may be supposed to have taken place in the midst of mankind, there could be no judges of it, in consequence of the supposed depravity; for without the exercise of reason, we could not understand what reason is, which would be necessary for us previously to understand, in order to understand what it is not; or to distinguish it from that which is its reverse. But for us to have the knowledge of what reason is, and the ability to distinguish it from that which is depraved, or is irrational, is incompatible with the doctrine of the depravity of our reason, inasmuch as to understand what reason is, and to distinguish it from that which is marred or spoiled, is the same to all intents and purposes, as to have, exercise, and enjoy, the principle of reason itself, which precludes its supposed depravity: so that it is impossible for us to understand what reason is, and at the same time determine that our reason is depraved; for this would be the same as when we know that we are in possession and exercise of reason, to determine that we are not in possession or exercise of it.

It may be, that some who embrace the doctrine of the depravity of human reason, will not admit, that it is wholly and totally depraved, but that it is in a general measure marred or spoiled. But the foregoing arguments are equally applicable to a supposed depravity in parts, as in the whole; for in order to judge whether reason be depraved in part or not, it would be requisite to have an understanding of what reason may be supposed to have been, previous to its premised depravity; and to have such a knowledge of it, would be the same as to exercise and enjoy it in its lustre and purity; which would preclude the notion of a depravity in part, as well as in the whole; for it would be utterly impossible for us to judge of reason undepraved and depraved, but by comparing them together. But for depraved reason to make such a comparison, is contradictory, and impossible; so that, if our reason had been depraved, we could not have had any conception of it any more than the beast. Men of small faculties in reasoning cannot comprehend the extensive reasonings of their superiors, how then can a supposed depraved reason, comprehend that reason, which is uncorrupted and pure? To suppose that it could, is the same as to suppose that depraved and undepraved reason is alike, and if so there needs no further dispute about it.

There is a manifest contradiction in applying the term *depraved*, to that of reason, the ideas contained in their respective definitions will not admit of their association together, as the terms convey heterogeneous ideas; for reason spoiled, marred, or robbed of its perfection, ceaseth to be rational, and should not be called reason; inasmuch as it is promised to be depraved, or degenerated from a rational nature; and in consequence of the deprevation of its nature, should also be deprived of its name, and called subterfuge, or some such like name, which might better define its real character.

Those who invalidate reason, ought seriously to consider, "*whether they argue against reason, with or without reason; if with reason, then they establish the principle, that they are laboring to dethrone:*" but if they argue without reason, (which in order to be consistent with themselves, they must do) they are out of the reach of rational conviction, nor do they deserve a rational argument.

We are told that the knowledge of the depravity of reason, was first communicated to mankind by the immediate inspiration of God. But inasmuch as reason is supposed to be depraved, what principle could there be in the human irrational soul, which could receive or understand the inspiration, or on which it could operate, so as to represent, to those whom it may be supposed were inspired, the knowledge of the depravity of (their own and mankind's) reason (in general:) For a rational inspiration must consist of rational ideas; which pre-supposes, that the minds of those who were inspired, were rational, previous to the inspiration itself; the import of which was to teach the knowledge of the depravity of human reason, which without reason could not be understood, and with reason it would be understood, that the inspiration was false.

66. THOMAS PAINE, *THE AGE OF REASON*, 1794*

The Age of Reason, the bible of deism, was published in 1794, after Paine's misadventures in the French Revolution, and became one of the most controversial books in American literature. The equally controversial Paine, once regarded as a hero of the Revolution, was mistakenly accused of atheism and roundly maligned. The Age of Reason offers much insight into the thinking of the religious rationalist of the period.

An Investigation of True and of Fabulous Theology

It has been my intention, for several years past, to publish my thoughts upon religion. I am well aware of the difficulties that attend the subject, and from that consideration, had reserved it to a more advanced period of life. I intended it to be the last offering I should make to my fellow-citizens of all nations, and that at a time when the purity of the motive that induced me to it could not admit of a question, even by those who might disapprove the work. . . .

I believe in one God, and no more; and I hope for happiness beyond this life.

I believe in the equality of man; and I believe that religious duties consist in doing justice, loving mercy, and endeavoring to make our fellow-creatures happy.

But, lest it should be supposed that I believe many other things in addition to these, I shall, in the progress of this work, declare the things I do not believe, and my reasons for not believing them.

I do not believe in the creed professed by the Jewish Church, by the Roman Church, by the Greek Church, by the Turkish Church, by the Protestant Church, nor by any church that I know of. My own mind is my own church.

All national institutions of churches, whether Jewish, Christian or

* From Thomas Paine, *The Age of Reason* (New York: T. & J. Swords, for J. Fellow, 1794), pp. 7, 8–18, 67–74, 132–34; 138–43. See also *The Complete Writings of Thomas Paine,* Philip S. Foner, ed. (New York: Citadel, 1945), Vol. II, pp. 463ff.

Turkish, appear to me no other than human inventions, set up to terrify and enslave mankind, and monopolize power and profit.

I do not mean by this declaration to condemn those who believe otherwise; they have the same right to their belief as I have to mine. But it is necessary to the happiness of man that he be mentally faithful to himself. Infidelity does not consist in believing, or in disbelieving; it consists in professing to believe what he does not believe.

It is impossible to calculate the mortal mischief, if I may so express it, that mental lying has produced in society. When a man has so far corrupted and prostituted the chastity of his mind as to subscribe his professional belief to things he does not believe he has prepared himself for the commission of every other crime. He takes up the trade of a priest for the sake of gain, and in order to *qualify* himself for that trade he begins with a perjury. Can we conceive any thing more destructive to morality than this?

Soon after I had published the pamphlet *Common-Sense*, in America, I saw the exceeding probability that a revolution in the system of government would be followed by a revolution in the system of religion. The adulterous connection of state and church, wherever it has taken place, whether Jewish, Christian or Turkish, has so effectually prohibited by pains and penalties every discussion upon established creeds, and upon first principles of religion, that until the system of government should be changed, those subjects could not be brought fairly and openly before the world; but that whenever this should be done, a revolution in the system of religion would follow. Human inventions and priestcraft would be detected; and man would return to the pure, unmixed and unadulterated belief of one God, and no more.

Every national church or religion has established itself by pretending some special mission from God, communicated to certain individuals. The Jews have their Moses; the Christians their Jesus Christ, their apostles and saints; and the Turks their Mahomet, as if the way to God was not open to every man alike.

Each of those churches show certain books, which they call *revelation*, or the Word of God. The Jews say their Word of God was given by God to Moses, face to face; the Christians say that their Word of God came by divine inspiration; and the Turks say that their Word of God (the Koran) was brought by an angel from heaven. Each of those churches accuses the other of unbelief; and for my own part, I disbelieve all of them.

As it is necessary to affix right ideas to words, I will, before I proceed further into the subject, offer some observations on the word *revelation*. Revelation, when applied to religion, means something communicated *immediately* from God to man.

No one will deny or dispute the power of the Almighty to make such a communication, if He pleases. But admitting, for the sake of a case, that something has been revealed to a certain person, and not revealed to any other person, it is revelation to that person only. When he tells it to a second person, a second to a third, a third to a fourth, and so on, it ceases to be a revelation to all those persons. It is revelation to the first person only, and *hearsay* to every other, and consequently they are not obliged to believe it.

It is a contradiction in terms and ideas, to call anything a revelation that comes to us at second-hand, either verbally or in writing. Revelation is necessarily limited to the first communication—after this it is only an account of something which that person says was a revelation made to *him*; and though he may find himself obliged to believe it, it cannot be incumbent on me to believe it in the same manner; for it was not a revelation made to *me*, and I have only his word for it that it was made to him.

When Moses told the children of Israel that he received the two tables of the commandments from the hands of God, they were not obliged to believe him, because they had no other authority for it than his telling them so; and I have no other authority for it than some historian telling me so. The commandments carry no internal evidence of divinity with them; they contain some good moral precepts, such as any man qualified to be a lawgiver, or a legislator, could produce himself, without having recourse to supernatural intervention. (It is, however, necessary to except the declaration which says that God *visits the sins of the fathers upon the children*. It is contrary to every principle of moral justice.)

When I am told that the Koran was written in heaven and brought to Mahomet by an angel, the account comes too near the same kind of hearsay evidence and second-hand authority as the former. I did not see the angel myself, and, therefore, I have a right not to believe it.

When also I am told that a woman called the Virgin Mary, said, or gave out, that she was with child without any cohabitation with a man, and that her betrothed husband, Joseph, said that an angel told him so, I have a right to believe them or not; such a circumstance required a much stronger evidence than their bare word for it; but we have not even this—for neither Joseph nor Mary wrote any such matter themselves; it is only reported by others that *they said so*. It is hearsay upon hearsay, and I do not choose to rest my belief upon such evidence.

It is, however, not difficult to account for the credit that was given to the story of Jesus Christ being the Son of God. He was born at a time when the heathen mythology had still some fashion and repute in the world, and that mythology had prepared the people for the belief of such a story. Almost all the extraordinary men that lived under the heathen mythology were reputed to be the sons of some of their gods. It was not a new thing, at that time, to believe a man to have been celestially begotten; the intercourse of gods with women was then a matter of familiar opinion. Their Jupiter, according to their accounts, had cohabited with hundreds; the story, therefore had nothing in it either new, wonderful or obscene; it was conformable to the opinions that then prevailed among the people called Gentiles, or Mythologists, and it was those people only that believed it. The Jews, who had kept strictly to the belief of One God, and no more, and who had always rejected the heathen mythology, never credited the story.

It is curious to observe how the theory of what is called the Christian Church sprung out of the tail of the heathen mythology. A direct incorporation took place in the first instance, by making the reputed founder to be celestially begotten. The trinity of gods that then followed, was no other than a reduction of the former plurality, which was about twenty or thirty thousand; the statue of Mary succeeded the statue of Diana of Ephesus; the deification of heroes changed into the canonization of saints; the Mythologists had gods for everything; the Christian mythologists had saints for everything; the Church became as crowded with the one as the Pantheon had been with the other, and Rome was the place of both. The Christian theory is little else than the idolatry of the ancient Mythologists, accommodated to the purposes of power and revenue; and it yet remains to reason and philosophy to abolish the amphibious fraud.

·   ·   ·   ·

The only idea man can affix to the name of God, is, that of a *first cause*, the cause of all things. And incomprehensible and difficult as it is for a man to conceive what a first cause is, he arrives at the belief of it from the tenfold greater difficulty of disbelieving it. It is difficult beyond description to conceive that space can have no end; but it is more difficult to conceive an end. It is difficult beyond the power of man to conceive an eternal duration of what we call time; but it is more impossible to conceive a time when there shall be no time. In like manner of reasoning, everything we behold carries in itself the internal evidence that it did not make itself. Every man is an evidence to himself that he did not make himself; neither could his father make himself, nor his grandfather, nor any of his race; neither could any tree, plant or animal make itself; and it is the conviction arising from this evidence that carries us on, as it were, by necessity to the belief of a first cause eternally existing, of a nature totally different to any material existence we know of, and by the power of which all things exist; and this first cause man calls God.

It is only by the exercise of reason that man can discover God.

Take away that reason, and he would be incapable of understanding anything; and, in this case, it would be just as consistent to read even the book called the Bible to a horse as to a man. How, then, is it that people pretend to reject reason?

Almost the only parts of the book called the Bible that convey to us any idea of God are some chapters in Job and the 19th Psalm; I recollect no other. Those parts are true *deistical* compositions, for they treat of the *Deity* through His works. They take the book of creation as the Word of God, they refer to no other book, and all the inferences they make are drawn from that volume.

I insert in this place the 19th psalm, as paraphrased into English verse by Addison. I recollect not the prose, and where I write this I have not the opportunity of seeing it.

> The spacious firmament on high,
> With all the blue etherial sky,
> And spangled heavens, a shining frame
> Their great original proclaim.
> The unwearied sun, from day to day,
> Does his Creator's power display;
> And publishes to every land
> The work of an Almighty hand.
>
> Soon as the evening shades prevail,
> The moon takes up the wondrous tale,
> And nightly to the list'ning earth
> Repeats the story of her birth;
> While all the stars that round her burn,
> And all the planets in their turn,
> Confirm the tidings as they roll,
> And spread the truth from pole to pole.
>
> What, though in solemn silence all
> Move round this dark, terrestial ball?
> What though no real voice, nor sound,
> Amidst their radiant orbs be found?
> In reason's ear they all rejoice
> And utter forth a glorious voice,
> Forever singing, as they shine
> THE HAND THAT MADE US IS DIVINE.

What more does man want to know than that the hand or power that made these things is divine, is omnipotent? Let him believe this with the force it is impossible to repel, if he permits his reason to act, and his rule of moral life will follow of course.

The allusions in Job have, all of them, the same tendency with this Psalm; that of deducing or proving a truth that would be otherwise unknown, from truths already known.

I recollect not enough of the passages in Job to insert them correctly; but there is one occurs to me that is applicable to the subject I am speaking upon. "Canst thou by searching find out God? Canst thou find out the Almighty to perfection?"

I know not how the printers have pointed this passage, for I keep no Bible; but it contains two distinct questions that admit of distinct answers.

First, Canst thou by searching find out God? Yes. Because, in the first place, I know I did not make myself, and yet I have existence; and by *searching* into the nature of other things, I find that no other thing could make itself; and yet millions of other things exist; therefore it is, that I know, by positive conclusion resulting from this search, that there is a power superior to all those things, and that power is God.

Secondly, Canst thou find out the Almighty to *perfection*? No. Not only because the power and wisdom He has manifested in the structure of the creation that I behold is to be incomprehensible; but because even this manifestation, great as it is, is probably but a small display of that immensity of power and wisdom by which millions of other worlds, to me invisible by their distance, were created and continued to exist.

It is evident that both these questions were put to the reason of the person to whom they are supposed to have been addressed; and it is only by admitting the first question to be answered affirmatively that the second could follow. It would have been unnecessary, and even absurd, to have put a second question, more difficult than the first, if the first question had been answered negatively. The two questions have different objects; the first refers to the existence of God; the second to His attributes; reason can discover the one, but falls infinitely short in discovering the whole of the other.

I recollect not a single passage in all the writings ascribed to the men called apostles that conveys any idea of what God is. Those writings are chiefly controversial; and the subjects they dwell upon, that of a man dying in agony on a cross, is better suited to the gloomy genius of a monk in a cell, by whom it is not impossible they were written, than to any man breathing the open air of the creation. The only passage that occurs to me that has any reference to the works of God, by which only His power and wisdom can be known, is related to have been spoken by Jesus Christ as a remedy against distrustful care. "Behold the lilies of the field, they toil not, neither do they spin." This, however, is far inferior to the allusions in Job and in the 19th Psalm; but it is similar in idea, and the modesty of the imagery is corresponding to the modesty of the man.

.   .   .   .

Religion, therefore, being the belief of a God and the practise of moral truth, cannot have connection with mystery. The belief of a God, so far from having anything of mystery in it is, of all beliefs the most easy, because it arises to us, as is before observed, out of necessity. And the practise of moral truth, or in other words, a practical imitation of the moral goodness of God, is no other than our acting toward each other as He acts benighly towards all. We cannot *serve* God in the manner we serve those who cannot do without such service; and, therefore, the only idea we can have of serving God is that of contributing to the happiness of the living creation that God has made. This cannot be done by retiring ourselves from the society of the world and spending a recluse life in selfish devotion.

The very nature and design of religion, if I may so express it, prove even to demonstration that it must be free from everything of mystery, and unencumbered with everything that is mysterious. Religion, considered as a duty, is incumbent upon every living soul alike, and, therefore, must be on a level with the understanding and comprehension of all.

Man does not learn religion as he learns the secrets and mysteries of a trade. He learns the theory of religion by reflection. It arises out of the action of his own mind upon the things which he sees, or upon what he may happen to hear or to read, and the practise joins itself thereto.

When men, whether from policy or pious fraud, set up systems of religion incompatible with the word or works of God in the creation, and not only above, but repugnant to human comprehension, they were under the necessity of inventing or adopting a word that should serve as a bar to all questions, inquiries and speculations. The word *mystery* answered this purpose, and thus it has happened that religion, which is in itself without mystery, has been corrupted into a fog of mysteries.

.   .   .   .

Of all the modes of evidence that ever were invented to obtain belief to any system or opinion to which the name of religion has been given, that of miracle, however successful the imposition may have been, is the most inconsistent. For, in the first place, whenever recourse is had to show, for the purpose of procuring that belief (for a miracle, under any idea of the word, is a show), it implies a lameness or weakness in the doctrine that is preached. And, in the second place, it is degrading the Almighty into the character of a showman, playing tricks to amuse and make the people stare and wonder. It is also the most equivocal sort of evidence that can be set up; for the belief is not to depend upon the thing called a miracle, but upon the credit of the reporter who says that he saw it; and, therefore, the thing, were it true, would have no better chance of being believed than if it were a lie.

Suppose, I were to say, that when I sat down to write this book a hand presented itself in the air, took up the pen and wrote every word that is herein written; would anybody believe me? Certainly they would not. Would they believe me a whit more if the thing had been a fact? Certainly they would not. Since, then, a real miracle, were it to happen, would be subject to the same fate as the falsehood, the inconsistency becomes the greater of supposing the Almighty would make use of means that would not answer the purpose for which they were intended even if they were real.

If we are to suppose a miracle to be something so entirely out of the course of what is called nature that she must go out of that course to accomplish it, and we see an account given of such miracle by the person who said he saw it, it raises a question in the mind very easily decided, which is, is it more probable that nature should go out of her course or that a man should tell a lie? We have never seen, in our time, nature go out of her course; but we have a good reason to believe that millions of lies have been told in the same time; it is, therefore, at least millions to one that the reporter of a miracle tells a lie.

The story of the whale swallowing Jonah, though a whale is large enough to do it, borders greatly on the marvelous; but it would have approached nearer to the idea of a miracle if Jonah had swallowed the whale. In this, which may serve for all cases of miracles, the matter would decide itself, as before stated, namely, is it more probable that a man should have swallowed a whale or told a lie?

But supposing that Jonah had really swallowed the whale, and gone with it in his belly to Nineveh and, to convince the people that it was true, had cast it up in their sight, of the full length and size of a whale, would they not have believed him to have been the devil instead of a prophet? Or, if the whale had carried Jonah to Nineveh, and cast him up in the same public manner, would they not have believed the whale to have been the devil, and Jonah one of his imps?

The most extraordinary of all the things called miracles, related in the New Testament, is that of the devil flying away with Jesus Christ, and carrying him to the top of a high mountain, and to the top of the highest pinnacle of the temple, and showing him and promising to him *all the kingdoms of the world.* How happened it that he did not discover America, or is it only with *kingdoms* that his sooty highness had any interest?

I have too much respect for the moral character of Christ to believe that he told this whale of a miracle himself; neither is it easy to account for what purpose it could have been fabricated, unless it were to impose upon the connoisseurs of miracles as is sometimes practised upon the connoisseurs of Queen Anne's farthings or collectors of relics

and antiquities; or to render the belief of miracles ridiculous by out-
doing miracles, as Don Quixote outdid chivalry; or to embarrass the
belief of miracles by making it doubtful by what power, whether of God
or of the devil, anything called a miracle was performed. It requires, however, a great deal of faith in the devil to believe this miracle.

6

The Fruits of the Revolution

67. STATE-MAKING AND THE REVOLUTIONARY SPIRIT: CONSTITUTIONS OF VIRGINIA, PENNSYLVANIA, AND MASSACHUSETTS, 1776–90[*]

The events of 1776 and the following years made essential the formation of new governments on both national and state levels. For the most part, the revolutionaries' approach to state-making was moderate and evolutionary. In some instances the colonial forms were reconstituted with some new governmental structures embodying revolutionary ideas. The states differed, but all of the state-makers were in quest of freedom and tried to write the natural rights of the citizen into concrete law. The hallmark of the revolutionary generation was its willingness to experiment; no generation has altered its machinery on all levels of government so much and so often.

The Constitution of Virginia—1776

[The Virginia Bill of Rights of 1776 was the model for similar bills in other constitutions and for the federal Bill of Rights.—Editor's Note]

Declaration of Rights

A declaration of rights made by the representatives of the good people of Virginia, assembled in full and free convention; which rights do pertain to them and their posterity, as the basis and foundation of government.

SECTION 1. That all men are by nature equally free and independ-

[*] *Federal and State Constitutions, Colonial Charters and Other Organic Laws,* Francis Newton Thorpe, ed. (Washington: Government Printing Office, 1909), Vol. III, 1888–89, 1906–7; Vol. V, 3084–92; Vol. VII, 3812–14.

ent, and have certain inherent rights, of which, when they enter into a state of society, they cannot, by any compact, deprive or divest their posterity; namely, the enjoyment of life and liberty, with the means of acquiring and possessing property, and pursuing and obtaining happiness and safety.

SEC. 2. That all power is vested in, and consequently derived from, the people; that magistrates are their trustees and servants, and at all times amenable to them.

SEC. 3. That government is, or ought to be, instituted for the common benefit, protection, and security of the people, nation, or community; of all the various modes and forms of government, that is best which is capable of producing the greatest degree of happiness and safety, and is most effectually secured against the danger of maladministration; and that, when any government shall be found inadequate or contrary to these purposes, a majority of the community hath an indubitable, inalienable, and indefeasible right to reform, alter, or abolish it, in such manner as shall be judged most conducive to the public weal.

SEC. 4. That no man, or set of men, are entitled to exclusive or separate emoluments or privileges from the community, but in consideration of public services; which, not being descendible, neither ought the offices of magistrate, legislator, or judge to be hereditary.

SEC. 5. That the legislative and executive powers of the State should be separate and distinct from the judiciary; and that the members of the two first may be restrained from oppression, by feeling and participating the burdens of the people, they should, at fixed periods, be reduced to a private station, return into that body from which they were originally taken, and the vacancies be supplied by frequent, certain, and regular elections, in which all, or any part of the former members, to be again eligible, or ineligible, as the laws shall direct.

SEC. 6. That elections of members to serve as representatives of the people, in assembly, ought to be free; and that all men, having sufficient evidence of permanent common interest with, and attachment to, the community, have the right of suffrage, and cannot be taxed or deprived of their property for public uses, without their own consent, or that of their representatives so elected, nor bound by any law to which they have not, in like manner, assembled, for the public good.

SEC. 7. That all power of suspending laws, or the execution of laws, by any authority, without consent of the representatives of the people, is injurious to their rights, and ought not to be exercised.

SEC. 8. That in all capital or criminal prosecutions a man hath a right to demand the cause and nature of his accusation, to be confronted with the accusers and witnesses, to call for evidence in his favor, and to a speedy trial by an impartial jury of twelve men of his vicinage, without whose unanimous consent he cannot be found guilty; nor can he be compelled to give evidence against himself; that no man be deprived of his liberty, except by the law of the land or the judgment of his peers.

SEC. 9. That excessive bail ought not to be required, nor excessive fines imposed, nor cruel and unusual punishments inflicted.

SEC. 10. That general warrants, whereby an officer or messenger may be commanded to search suspected places without evidence of a fact committed, or to seize any person or persons not named, or whose offence is not particularly described and supported by evidence, are grievous and oppressive, and ought not to be granted.

SEC. 11. That in controversies respecting property, and in suits between man and man, the ancient trial by jury is preferable to any other, and ought to be held sacred.

SEC. 12. That the freedom of the press is one of the great bulwarks of liberty, and can never be restrained but by despotic governments.

SEC. 13. That a well-regulated militia, composed of the body of the people, trained to arms, is the proper, natural, and safe defence of a free State; that standing armies, in time of peace, should be avoided, as dangerous to liberty; and that in all cases the military should be under strict subordination to, and governed by, the civil power.

SEC. 14. That the people have a right to uniform government; and therefore, that no government separate from, or independent of the government of Virginia, ought to be erected or established within the limits thereof.

SEC. 15. That no free government, or the blessings of liberty, can be preserved to any people, but by a firm adherence to justice, moderation, temperance, frugality, and virtue, and by frequent recurrence to fundamental principles.

SEC. 16. That religion, or the duty which we owe to our Creator, and the manner of discharging it, can be directed only by reason and conviction, not by force or violence; and therefore all men are equally entitled to the free exercise of religion, according to the dictates of conscience; and that it is the mutual duty of all to practise Christian forbearance, love, and charity towards each other. . . .

Constitution of Pennsylvania—1776

[The Pennsylvania Constitution of 1776 was the most radical of all of the revolutionary constitutions because of its technique of referendum, rotation in office, and its unique Council of Censors. Its self-denying ordinances regarding the repetition of officeholding and other features made for much instability, and in 1790 Pennsylvanians wrote a new constitution, mitigating the radicalism of the earlier one.—Editor's Note]

Plan or Frame of Government for the Commonwealth
or State of Pennsylvania

SECTION 1. The commonwealth or state of Pennsylvania shall be governed hereafter by an assembly of the representatives of the freemen of the same, and a president and council, in manner and form following—

SECT. 2. The supreme legislative power shall be vested in a house of representatives of the freemen of the commonwealth or state of Pennsylvania.

SECT. 3. The supreme executive power shall be vested in a president and council.

SECT. 4. Courts of justice shall be established in the city of Philadelphia, and in every county of this state.

SECT. 5. The freemen of this commonwealth and their sons shall be trained and armed for its defence under such regulations, restrictions, and exceptions as the general assembly shall by law direct, preserving always to the people the right of choosing their colonels and all commissioned officers under that rank, in such manner and as often as by the said laws shall be directed.

SECT. 6. Every freemen of the full age of twenty-one years, having resided in this state for the space of one whole year next before the day of election for representatives, and paid public taxes during that time, shall enjoy the right of an elector: Provided always, that sons of freeholders of the age of twenty-one years shall be intitled to vote although they have not paid taxes.

SECT. 7. The house of representatives of the freemen of this commonwealth shall consist of persons most noted for wisdom and virtue, to be chosen by the freemen of every city and county of this commonwealth respectively. And no person shall be elected unless he has resided in the city or county for which he shall be chosen two years immediately before the said election; nor shall any member, while he continues such, hold any other office, except in the militia.

SECT. 8. No person shall be capable of being elected a member to serve in the house of representatives of the freemen of this commonwealth more than four years in seven.

SECT. 9. The members of the house of representatives shall be chosen annually by ballot, by the freemen of the commonwealth, on the second Tuesday in October forever, (except this present year,) and shall meet on the fourth Monday of the same month, and shall be stiled, *The general assembly of the representatives of the freemen of Pennsylvania,* and shall have power to choose their speaker, the treasurer of the state, and their other officers; sit on their own adjournments; prepare bills and enact them into laws; judge of the elections and qualifications of their own members; they may expel a member, but not a second time for the same cause; they may administer oaths or affirmations on examination of witnesses; redress grievances; impeach state criminals; grant charters of incorporation; constitute towns, boroughs, cities, and counties; and shall have all other powers necessary for the legislature of a free state or commonwealth: But they shall have no power to add to, alter, abolish, or infringe any part of this constitution.

SECT. 10. A quorum of the house of representatives shall consist of two-thirds of the whole number of members elected; and having met and chosen their speaker, shall each of them before they proceed to business take and subscribe, as well the oath or affirmation of fidelity and allegiance hereinafter directed. . . .

And each member, before he takes his seat, shall make and subscribe the following declaration, viz:

I do believe in one God, the creator and governor of the universe, the rewarder of the good and the punisher of the wicked. And I do acknowledge the Scriptures of the Old and New Testament to be given by Divine inspiration.

And no further or other religious test shall ever hereafter be required of any civil officer or magistrate in this State.

SECT. 11. Delegates to represent this state in congress shall be chosen by ballot by the future general assembly at their first meeting, and annually forever afterwards, as long as such representation shall be necessary. Any delegate may be superseded at any time, by the general assembly appointing another in his stead. No man shall sit in congress longer than two years successively, nor be capable of reelection for three years afterwards: and no person who holds any office in the gift of the congress shall hereafter be elected to represent this commonwealth in congress.

SECT. 12. If any city or cities, county or counties shall neglect or refuse to elect and send representatives to the general assembly, two-thirds of the members from the cities or counties that do elect and send representatives, provided they be a majority of the cities and counties of the whole state, when met, shall have all the powers of the general assembly, as fully and amply as if the whole were present.

SECT. 13. The doors of the house in which the representatives of the freemen of this state shall sit in general assembly, shall be and remain open for the admission of all persons who behave decently, except only when the welfare of this state may require the doors to be shut.

SECT. 14. The votes and proceedings of the general assembly shall be reprinted weekly during their sitting, with the yeas and nays, on any question, vote or resolution, where any two members require it, except when the vote is taken by ballot; and when the yeas and nays are so taken every member shall have a right to insert the reasons of his vote upon the minutes, if he desires it.

SECT. 15. To the end that laws before they are enacted may be more maturely considered, and the inconvenience of hasty determinations as much as possible prevented, all bills of public nature shall be printed for the consideration of the people, before they are read in general assembly the last time for debate and amendment; and, except on occasions of sudden necessity, shall not be passed into laws until the next session of assembly; and for the more perfect satisfaction of the public, the reasons and motives for making such laws shall be fully and clearly expressed in the preambles. . . .

SECT. 17. The city of Philadelphia and each county of this commonwealth respectively, shall on the first Tuesday of November in this present year, and on the second Tuesday of October annually for the two next succeeding years, *viz.* the year one thousand seven hundred and seventy-seven, and the year one thousand seven hundred and seventy-eight, choose six persons to represent them in general assembly. But as representation in proportion to the number of taxable inhabitants is the only principle which can at all times secure liberty, and make the voice of a majority of the people the law of the land; therefore the general assembly shall cause complete lists of the taxable inhabitants in the city and each county in the commonwealth respectively, to be taken and returned to them, on or before the last meeting of the assembly elected in the year one thousand seven hundred and seventy-eight, who shall appoint a representation to each, in proportion to the number of taxables in such returns; which representation shall continue for the next seven years afterwards at the end of which, a new return of the taxable inhabitants shall be made, and a representation agreeable thereto appointed by the said assembly, and so on septennially forever. The wages of the representatives in general assembly, and all other state charges shall be paid out of the state treasury.

SECT. 18. In order that the freemen of this commonwealth may enjoy the benefit of election as equally as may be until the representation shall commence, as directed in the foregoing section, each county at its own choice may be divided into districts, hold elections therein, and elect their representatives in the county, and their other elective officers, as shall be hereafter regulated by the general assembly of this state. And no inhabitant of this state shall have more than one annual vote at the general election for representatives in assembly.

SECT. 19. For the present the supreme executive council of this state shall consist of twelve persons chosen in the following manner: The freemen of the city of Philadelphia, and of the counties of Philadelphia, Chester, and Bucks, respectively, shall choose by ballot one person for the city, and one for each county aforesaid, to serve for three years and no longer, at the time and place for electing representatives in general assembly. The freemen of the counties of Lancaster, York, Cumberland, and Berks, shall, in like manner elect one person for each county respectively, to serve as counsellors for two years and no longer. And the counties of Northampton, Bedford, Northumberland and Westmoreland, respectively, shall, in like manner, elect one person for each county, to serve as counsellors for one year, and no longer. And at the expiration of the time for which each counsellor was chosen to serve, the freemen of the city of Philadelphia, and of the several counties in this state, respectively, shall elect one person to serve as counsellor for three years and no longer; and so on every third year forever. By this mode of election and continual rotation, more men will be trained to public business, there will in every subsequent year be found in the council a number of persons acquainted with the proceedings of the foregoing years, whereby the business will be more consistently conducted, and moreover the danger of establishing an inconvenient aristocracy will be effectually prevented. All vacancies in the council that may happen by death, resignation, or otherwise, shall be filled at the next general election for representatives in general assembly or delegate in congress, shall be chosen a member of the council. The president and vice-president shall be chosen annually by the joint ballot of the general assembly and council, of the members of the council. Any person having served as a counsellor for three successive years, shall be incapable of holding that office for four years afterwards. Every member of the council shall be a justice of the peace for the whole commonwealth, by virtue of his office.

In case new additional counties shall hereafter be erected in this state, such county or counties shall elect a counsellor, and such county or counties shall be annexed to the next neighbouring counties, and shall take rotation with such counties.

The council shall meet annually, at the same time and place with the general assembly.

The treasurer of the state, trustees of the loan office, naval officers, collectors of customs or excise, judge of the admiralty, attornies general, sheriffs, and prothonotaries, shall not be capable of a seat in the general assembly, executive council, or continental congress.

Sect. 20. The president, and in his absence the vice-president, with the council, five of whom shall be a quorum, shall have power to appoint and commissionate judges, naval officers, judge of the admiralty, attorney general and all other officers, civil and military, except such as are chosen by the general assembly or the people, agreeable to this frame of government, and the laws that may be made hereafter; and shall supply every vacancy in any office, occasioned by death, resignation, removal or disqualification, until the office can be filled in the time and manner directed by law or this constitution. They are to correspond with other states, and transact business with the officers of government, civil and military; and to prepare such business as may appear to them necessary to lay before the general assembly. They shall sit as judges, to hear and determine on impeachments, taking to their assistance for advice only, the justices of the supreme court. And shall have power to grant pardons, and remit fines, in all cases whatsoever, except in cases of impeachment; and in cases of treason and murder, shall have power to grant reprieves, but not to pardon, until the end of the next sessions of assembly; but there shall be no remission or mitigation of punishments on impeachments, except by act of the legislature; they are also to take care that the laws be faithfully executed; they are to expedite the execution of such measures as may be resolved upon by the general assembly; and they may draw upon the treasury for such sums as shall be appropriated by the house: They may also lay embargoes, or prohibit the exportation of any commodity, for any time, not exceeding thirty days, in the recess of the house only: They may grant such licences, as shall be directed by law, and shall have power to call together the general assembly when necessary, before the day to which they shall stand adjourned. The president shall be commander in chief of the forces of the state, but shall not command in person, except advised thereto by the council and then only so long as they shall approve thereof. The president and council shall have a secretary, and keep fair books of their proceedings, wherein any counsellor may enter his dissent, with his reasons in support of it.

.   .   .   .

SECT. 22. Every officer of state, whether judicial or executive, shall be liable to be impeached by the general assembly, either when in office, or after his resignation or removal for mal-administration: All impeachments shall be before the president or vice-president and council, who shall hear and determine the same.

SECT. 23. The judges of the supreme court of judicature shall have fixed salaries, be commissioned for seven years only, though capable of re-appointment at the end of that term, but removable for misbehaviour at any time by the general assembly; they shall not be allowed to sit as members in the continental congress, executive council, or general assembly, nor to hold any other office civil or military, nor to take or receive fees or perquisities of any kind.

SECT. 24. The supreme court, and the several courts of common pleas of this commonwealth, shall, besides the powers usually exercised by such courts, have the powers of a court of chancery, so far as relates to the perpetuating testimony, obtaining evidence from places not within this state, and the care of the persons and estates of those who are *non compotes mentis*, and such other powers as may be found necessary by future general assemblies, not inconsistent with this constitution.

SECT. 25. Trials shall be by jury as heretofore: And it is recommended to the legislature of this state, to provide by law against every corruption or partiality in the choice, return, or appointment of juries.

SECT. 26. Courts of sessions, common pleas, and orphans courts shall be held quarterly in each city and county; and the legislature shall have power to establish all such other courts as they may judge for the good of the inhabitants of the state. All courts shall be open, and justice shall be impartially administered without corruption or unnecessary delay: All their officers shall be paid an adequate but moderate compensation for their services: And if any officer shall take greater or other fees than the law allows him, either directly or indirectly, it shall ever after disqualify him from holding any office in this state.

. . . .

SECT. 28. The person of a debtor, where there is not a strong presumption of fraud, shall not be continued in prison, after delivering up, *bona fide*, all his estate real and personal, for the use of his creditors, in such manner as shall be hereafter regulated by law. All prisoners shall be bailable by sufficient sureties, unless for capital offences, when the proof is evident, or presumption great.

SECT. 29. Excessive bail shall not be exacted for bailable offences: And all fines shall be moderate.

SECT. 30. Justices of the peace shall be elected by the freeholders of each city and county respectively, that is to say, two or more persons may be chosen for each ward, township, or district, as the law shall hereafter direct. . . .

SECT. 31. Sheriffs and coroners shall be elected annually in each city and county, by the freemen; that is to say, two persons for each office, one of whom for each, is to be commissioned by the president in council. No person shall continue in the office of sheriff more than three successive years or be capable of being again elected during four years afterwards. . . .

SECT. 32. All elections, whether by the people or in general assembly, shall be by ballot, free and voluntary: And any elector, who shall receive any gift or reward for his vote, in meat, drink, monies, or otherwise, shall forfeit his right to elect for that time, and suffer such other penalties as future laws shall direct. And any person who shall directly or indirectly give, promise, or bestow any such rewards to be elected, shall be thereby rendered incapable to serve for the ensuing year.

. . . .

SECT. 35. The printing presses shall be free to every person who undertakes to examine the proceedings of the legislature, or any part of government.

SECT. 36. As every freeman to preserve his independence, (if without a sufficient estate) ought to have some profession, calling, trade or farm, whereby he may honestly subsist, there can be no necessity for, nor use in establishing offices of profit, the usual effects of which are dependence and servility unbecoming freemen, in the possessors and expectants; faction, contention, corruption, and disorder among the people. But if any man is called into public service, to the prejudice of his private affairs, he has a right to a reasonable compensation: And whenever an office, through increase of fees or otherwise, becomes so profitable as to occasion many to apply for it, the profits ought to be lessened by the legislature.

SECT. 37. The future legislature of this state, shall regulate entails in such a manner as to prevent perpetuities.

SECT. 38. The penal laws as heretofore used shall be reformed by the legislature of this state, as soon as may be, and punishments made in some cases less sanguinary, and in general more proportionate to the crimes.

·　·　·　·

SECT. 42. Every foreigner of good character who comes to settle in this state, having first taken an oath or affirmation of allegiance to the same, may purchase, or by other just means acquire, hold, and transfer land or other real estate; and after one year's residence, shall be deemed a free denizen thereof, and entitled to all the rights of a natural born subject of this state, except that he shall not be capable of being elected a representative until after two years residence.

·　·　·　·

SECT. 44. A school or school shall be established in each county by the legislature, for the convenient instruction of youth, with such salaries to the masters paid by the public, as may enable them to instruct youth at low prices: And all useful learning shall be duly encouraged and promoted in one or more universities.

SECT. 45. Laws for the encouragement of virtue, and prevention of vice and immorality, shall be made and constantly kept in force, and provision shall be made for their due execution: And all religious societies or bodies of men heretofore united or incorporated for the advancement of religion or learning, or for other pious and charitable purposes, shall be encouraged and protected in the enjoyment of the privileges, immunities and estates which they were accustomed to enjoy, or could of right have enjoyed, under the laws and former constitution of this state.

SECT. 46. [A] declaration of rights is hereby declared to be a part of the constitution of this commonwealth, and ought never to be violated on any pretence whatever.

SECT. 47. In order that the freedom of the commonwealth may be preserved inviolate forever, there shall be chosen by ballot by the freemen in each city and county respectively, on the second Tuesday in October, in the year one thousand seven hundred and eighty-three, and on the second Tuesday in October, in every seventh year thereafter, two persons in each city and county of this state, to be called the COUNCIL OF CENSORS; who shall meet together on the second Monday of November next enusing their election; the majority of whom shall be a quorum in every case, except as to calling a convention, in which two-thirds of the whole number elected shall agree: And whose duty it shall be to enquire whether the constitution has been preserved inviolate in every part; and whether the legislative and executive branches of government have performed their duty as guardians of the people, or assumed to themselves, or exercised other or greater powers than they are intitled to by the constitution: They are also to enquire whether the public taxes have been justly laid and collected in all parts of this commonwealth, in what manner the public monies have been disposed of, and whether the laws have been duly executed. For these purposes they shall have power to send for persons, papers, and records; they shall have authority to pass public censures, to order impeachments, and to recommend to the legislature the repealing such laws as appear to them to have been enacted contrary to the principles of the constitution. These powers they shall continue to have, for and during the space of one year from the day of their election and no longer: The said council of censors shall also have power to call a convention, to meet within two years after their sitting, if there appear to them an absolute necessity of amending any article of the constitution which may be defective, explaining such as may be thought not clearly expressed, and of adding such as are necessary for the preservation of the rights and happiness of the people: But the articles to be amended, and the amendments proposed, and such articles as are proposed to be added or abolished, shall be promulgated at least six months before the day appointed for the election of such convention, for the previous consideration of the people, that they may have an opportunity of instructing their delegates on the subject.

Passed in Convention the 28th day of September, 1776, and signed by their order.

Constitution or Form of Government for the
Commonwealth of Massachusetts—1780

[*The Massachusetts Constitution of 1780 was chiefly the work of John Adams. It contained the ideas then current of "mixed-government" and of the separation of powers to avoid political tyranny. Like other states, Massachusetts moved toward religious toleration. Its ideas on state responsibility for the support of education and knowledge differed from other constitutions, yet this was very much in the Puritan tradition as cited by the framers—Editor's Note*]

Preamble

The end of the institution, maintenance, and administration of government, is to secure the existence of the body politic, to protect it, and to furnish the individuals who compose it with the power of enjoying in safety and tranquillity their natural rights, and the blessings of life: and whenever these great objects are not obtained, the people have a right to alter the government, and to take measures necessary for their safety, prosperity, and happiness.

The body politic is formed by a voluntary association of individuals: it is a social compact, by which the whole people covenants with each citizen, and each citizen with the whole people, that all shall be governed by certain laws for the common good. It is the duty of the people, therefore, in framing a constitution of government, to provide for an equitable mode of making laws, as well as for an impartial interpretation and a faithful execution of them; that every man may, at all times, find his security in them.

We, therefore, the people of Massachusetts, acknowledging, with grateful hearts, the goodness of the great Legislator of the universe, in affording us, in the course of His providence, an opportunity, deliberately and peaceably, without fraud, violence, or surprise, of entering into an original, explicit, and so solemn compact with each other; and of forming a new constitution of civil government, for ourselves and posterity; and devoutly imploring His direction in so interesting a design, do agree upon, ordain, and establish, the following *Declaration of Rights, and Frame of Government*, as the CONSTITUTION OF THE COMMONWEALTH OF MASSACHUSETTS.

Part the First
A Declaration of the Rights of the Inhabitants of
the Commonwealth of Massachusetts

ARTICLE I. All men are born free and equal, and have certain natural, essential, and unalienable rights; among which may be reckoned the right of enjoying and defending their lives and liberties; that of acquiring, possessing, and protecting property; in fine, that of seeking and obtaining their safety and happiness.

II. It is the right as well as the duty of all men in society, publicly, and at stated seasons, to worship the SUPREME BEING, the great Creator and Preserver of the universe. And no subject shall be hurt, molested, or restrained, in his person, liberty, or estate for worshipping GOD in the manner and season most agreeable to the dictates of his own conscience; or for his religious profession of sentiments; provided he doth not disturb the public peace, or obstruct others in their religious worship.

. . . .

The University at Cambridge and Encouragement of Literature, etc
Section I.—The University

ARTICLE I. Whereas our wise and pious ancestors, so early as the year one thousand six hundred and thirty-six, laid the foundation of Harvard College, in which university many persons of great eminence have, by the blessing of GOD, been initiated in those arts and sciences which qualified them for public employments, both in church and state; and whereas the encouragement of art and sciences, and all good literature, tends to the honor of GOD, the advantage of the Christian religion, and the great benefit of this and the other United States of America,— it is declared, that the PRESIDENT AND FELLOWS OF HARVARD COLLEGE, in their corporate capacity, and their successors in that capacity, their officers and servants, shall have, hold, use, exercise, and enjoy, all the powers, authorities, rights, liberties, privileges, immunities, and franchises, which they now have, or are entitled to have, hold, use, exercise, and enjoy; and the same are hereby ratified and confirmed unto them, the said president and fellows of Harvard College, and to their successors, and to their officers and servants, respectively, forever.

II. And whereas there have been at sundry times, by divers persons, gifts, grants, devises of houses, lands, tenements, goods, chattels, legacies, and conveyances, heretofore made, either to Harvard College in Cambridge, in New England, or to the president and fellows of Harvard College, or to the said college by some other description, under several charters, successively; it is declared, that all the said gifts, grants, devises, legacies, and conveyances, are hereby forever confirmed unto the president and fellows of Harvard College, and to their successors in the capacity aforesaid, according to the true intent and meaning of the donor or donors, grantor or grantors, devisor or devisors.

III. And whereas, by an act of the general court of the colony of Massachusetts Bay, passed in the year one thousand six hundred and forty-two, the governor and deputy-governor, for the time being, and all the magistrates of that jurisdiction, were, with the president, and a number of the clergy in the said act described, constituted the overseers of Harvard College; and it being necessary, in this new constitution of government to ascertain who shall be deemed successors to the said governor, deputygovernor, and magistrates; it is declared, that the governor, lieutenant-governor, council, and senate of this commonwealth, are, and shall be deemed, their successors, who, with the president of Harvard College, for the time being, together with the ministers of the congregational churches in the towns of Cambridge, Watertown, Charlestown, Boston, Roxbury, and Dorchester, mentioned in the said act, shall be, and hereby are, vested with all the powers and authority belonging, or in any way appertaining to the overseers of Harvard College; provided, that nothing herein shall be construed to prevent the legislature of this commonwealth from making such alterations in the government of the said university, as shall be conducive to its advantage, and the interest of the republic of letters, is as full a manner as might have been done by the legislature of the late Province of the Massachusetts Bay.

Section II.—The Encouragement of Literature

Wisdom and knowledge, as well as virtue, diffused generally among the body of the people, being necessary for the preservation of their rights and liberties; and as these depend on spreading the opportunities and advantages of education in the various parts of the country, and among the different orders of the people, it shall be the duty of legislatures and magistrates, in all future periods of this commonwealth, to cherish the interests of literature and the sciences, and all seminaries of them; especially the university at Cambridge, public schools and grammar schools in the towns; to encourage private societies and public institutions, rewards and immunities, for the promotion of agriculture, arts, sciences, commerce, trades, manufactures, and a natural history of the country. . . .

68. THOMAS JEFFERSON, *NOTES ON THE STATE OF VIRGINIA*, 1784*

Thomas Jefferson (1743–1826), responding to several queries about the States made by the Frenchman François Marbois, published his Notes on the State of Virginia *in 1784, while he was minister to France. Eager to inform the French nation about the United States, particularly his*

* From Thomas Jefferson's *Notes on the State of Virginia*, 2nd American ed. (Philadelphia: Matthew Carey, 1794), pp. 198–201; 212–17. See also *Notes on the State of Virginia*, William Peden, ed. (Chapel Hill: University of North Carolina Press for the Institute of Early American History and Culture, 1955), pp. 136–49.

*Virginia, and about the steps needed to change the old dominion from
royalism to republicanism, Jefferson had begun accumulating the material
for these answers as early as 1780. One of the most important assessments
of American society in the immediate postwar period, the book describes
the conditions, accomplishments, and aims of the new country as seen
by the author of the Declaration of Independence.*

Republican Laws; Slavery; and Education

Many of the laws which were in force during the monarchy being
relative merely to that form of government, or inculcating principles inconsistent with republicanism, the first assembly which met after the
establishment of the commonwealth appointed a committee to revise the
whole code, to reduce it into proper form and volume, and report it to
the assembly. This work has been executed by three gentlemen, and
reported; but probably will not be taken up till a restoration of peace
shall leave to the legislature leisure to go through such a work.

The plan of the revisal was this. The common law of England,
by which is meant, that part of the English law which was anterior to
the date of the oldest statutes extant, is made the basis of the work. It
was thought dangerous to attempt to reduce it to a text: it was therefore
left to be collected from the usual monuments of it. Necessary alterations
in that, and so much of the whole body of the British statutes, and of acts
of assembly, as were thought proper to be retained, were digested into
126 new acts, in which simplicity of stile was aimed at, as far as was safe.
The following are the most remarkable alterations proposed:

To change the rules of descent, so as that the lands of any person
dying intestate shall be divisible equally among all his children, or other
representatives, in equal degree.

To make slaves distributable among the next of kin, as other move-
ables.

To have all public expences, whether of the general treasury, or
of a parish or county, (as for the maintenance of the poor, building
bridges, court-houses, &c.) supplied by assessments on the citizens, in
proportion to their property.

To hire undertakers for keeping the public roads in repair, and
indemnify individuals through whose lands new roads shall be opened.

To define with precision the rules whereby aliens should become
citizens, and citizens make themselves aliens.

To establish religious freedom on the broadest bottom.

To emancipate all slaves born after passing the act. The bill reported by the revisors does not itself contain this proposition; but an
amendment containing it was prepared, to be offered to the legislature
whenever the bill should be taken up, and further directing, that they

should continue with their parents to a certain age, then be brought up, at the public expence, to tillage, arts or sciences, according to their geniusses, till the females should be eighteen, and the males twenty-one years of age, when they should be colonized to such place as the circumstances of the time should render most proper, sending them out with arms, implements of houshold and of the handicraft arts, seeds, pairs of the useful domestic animals, &c. to declare them a free and independent people, and extend to them our alliance and protection, till they shall have acquired strength; and to send vessels at the same time to other parts of the world for an equal number of white inhabitants; to induce whom to migrate hither, proper encouragements were to be proposed. It will probably be asked, Why not retain and incorporate the blacks into the state, and thus save the expence of supplying, by importation of white settlers, the vacancies they will leave? Deep rooted prejudices entertained by the whites; ten thousand recollections, by the blacks, of the injuries they have sustained; new provocations; the real distinctions which nature has made; and many other circumstances, will divide us into parties, and produce convulsions which will probably never end but in the extermination of the one or the other race.—To these objections, which are political, may be added others, which are physical and moral. The first difference which strikes us is that of colour. Whether the black of the negro resides in the reticular membrane between the skin and scarf-skin, or in the scarf-skin itself; whether it proceeds from the colour of the blood, the colour of the bile, or from that of some other secretion, the difference is fixed in nature, and is as real as if its seat and cause were better known to us. And is this difference of no importance? Is it not the foundation of a greater or less share of beauty in the two races? Are not the fine mixtures of red and white, the expressions of every passion by greater or less suffusions of colour in the one, preferable to that eternal monotony, which reigns in the countenances, that immoveable veil of black which covers all the emotions of the other race? Add to these, flowing hair, a more elegant symmetry of form, their own judgment in favour of the whites, declared by their preference of them, as uniformly as is the preference of the Oran-ootan for the black women over those of his own species. The circumstance of superior beauty, is thought worthy attention in the propagation of our horses, dogs, and other domestic animals; why not in that of man? Besides those of colour, figure, and hair, there are other physical distinctions proving a difference of race. They have less hair on the face and body. They secrete less by the kidnies, and more by the glands of the skin, which gives them a very strong and disagreeable odour. This greater degree of transpiration renders them more tolerant of heat, and less so of cold, than the whites. . . .

Another object of the revisal is, to diffuse knowledge more generally through the mass of the people. This bill proposes to lay off every county into small districts of five or six miles square, called hundreds, and in each of them to establish a school for teaching reading, writing, and arithmetic. The tutor to be supported by the hundred, and every person in it entitled to send their children three years gratis, and as much longer as they please, paying for it. These schools to be under a visitor, who is annually to chuse the boy, of best genius in the school, of those whose parents are too poor to give them further education, and to send him forward to one of the grammar schools, of which twenty are proposed to be erected in different parts of the country, for teaching Greek, Latin, geography, and the higher branches of numerical arithmetic. Of the boys thus sent in any one year, trial is to be made at the grammar schools one or two years, and the best genius of the whole selected, and continued six years, and the residue dismissed. By this means twenty of the best geniusses will be raked from the rubbish annually, and be instructed, at the public expence, so far as the grammar schools go. At the end of six years instruction, one half are to be discontinued (from among whom the grammar schools will probably be supplied with future masters); and the other half, who are to be chosen for the superiority of their parts and disposition, are to be sent and continued three years in the study of such sciences as they shall chuse, at William and Mary college, the plan of which is proposed to be enlarged, as will be hereafter explained, and extended to all the useful sciences. The ultimate result of the whole scheme of education would be the teaching all children of the state reading, writing, and common arithmetic: turning out ten annually of superior genius, well taught in Greek, Latin, geography, and the higher branches of arithmetic: turning out ten others annually, of still superior parts, who, to those branches of learning, shall have added such of the sciences as their genius shall have led them to: the furnishing to the wealthier part of the people convenient schools, at which their children may be educated, at their own expence.—The general objects of this law are to provide an education adapted to the years, to the capacity, and the condition of every one, and directed to their freedom and happiness. Specific details were not proper for the law. These must be the business of the visitors entrusted with its execution. The first stage of this education being the schools of the hundreds, wherein the great mass of the people will receive their instruction, the principal foundations of future order will be laid here. Instead therefore of putting the Bible and Testament into the hands of the children, at an age when their judgments are not sufficiently matured for religious enquiries, their memories may here be stored with the most useful facts from Grecian, Roman, European and American history. The first elements of morality too may be instilled into their minds; such as, when further developed

as their judgments advance in strength, may teach them how to work
out their own greatest happiness, by shewing them that it does not depend on the condition of life in which chance has placed them, but is
always the result of a good conscience, good health, occupation, and
freedom in all just pursuits.—Those whom either the wealth of their
parents or the adoption of the state shall destine to higher degrees of
learning, will go on to the grammar schools, which constitute the next
stage, there to be instructed in the languages. The learning Greek and
Latin, I am told, is going into disuse in Europe. I know not what their
manners and occupations may call for: but it would be very ill-judged in
us to follow their example in this instance. There is a certain period of
life, say from eight to fifteen or sixteen years of age, when the mind, like
the body, is not yet firm enough for laborious and close operations. If
applied to such, it falls an early victim to premature exertion; exhibiting
indeed at first, in these young and tender subjects, the flattering appearance of their being men while they are yet children, but ending in reducing them to be children when they should be men. The memory—is then
most susceptible and tenacious of impressions; and the learning of
languages being chiefly a work of memory, it seems precisely fitted to
the powers of this period, which is long enough too for acquiring the
most useful languages antient and modern. I do not pretend that language is science. It is only an instrument for the attainment of science.
But that time is not lost which is employed in providing tools for future
operation: more especially as in this case the books put into the hands
of the youth for this purpose may be such as will at the same time im-
press their minds with useful facts and good principles. If this period be
suffered to pass in idleness, the mind becomes lethargic and impotent, as
would the body it inhabits if unexercised during the same time. The
sympathy between body and mind during their rise, progress and decline,
is too strict and obvious to endanger our being misled while we reason
from the one to the other.—As soon as they are of sufficient age, it is
supposed they will be sent on from the grammar schools to the university, which constitutes our third and last stage, there to study those
sciences which may be adapted to their views.—By that part of our
plan which prescribes the selection of the youths of genius from among
the classes of the poor, we hope to avail the state of those talents which
nature has sown as liberally among the poor as the rich, but which perish
without use, if not sought for and cultivated.—But of all the views of this
law none is more important, none more legitimate, than that of rendering
the people the safe, as they are the ultimate, guardians of their own
liberty. For this purpose the reading in the first stage, where *they* will
receive their whole education, is proposed, as has been said, to be
chiefly historical. History by apprising them of the past will enable them

to judge of the future; it will avail them of the experience of other times and other nations; it will qualify them as judges of the actions and designs of men; it will enable them to know ambition under every disguise it may assume; and knowing it, to defeat its views. In every government on earth is some trace of human weakness, some germ of corruption and degeneracy, which cunning will discover, and wickedness insensibly open, cultivate, and improve. Every government degenerates when trusted to the rulers of the people alone. The people themselves therefore are its only safe depositories. And to render even them safe their minds must be improved to a certain degree. This indeed is not all that is necessary, though it be essentially necessary. An amendment of our constitution must here come in aid of the public education. The influence over government must be shared among all the people. If every individual which composes their mass participates of the ultimate authority, the government will be safe; because the corrupting the whole mass will exceed any private resources of wealth: and public ones cannot be provided but by levies on the people. In this case every man would have to pay his own price. The government of Great-Britain has been corrupted, because but one man in ten has a right to vote for members of parliament. The sellers of the government therefore get ninetenths of their price clear. It has been thought that corruption is restrained by confining the right of suffrage to a few of the wealthier of the people: but it would be more effectually restrained by an extension of that right to such numbers as would bid defiance to the means of corruption.

Lastly, it is proposed, by a bill in this revisal, to begin a public library and gallery, by laying out a certain sum annually in books, paintings, and statutes.

69. WILLIAM THOMPSON, SOCIAL EQUALITY, 1784*

Captain William Thompson (fl. 1776–85) was a soldier in the Revolution, and after the war, innkeeper of the City Tavern of Charleston. He considered himself a democrat and saw the aim of the Revolution as not only the achievement of independence but also the destruction of the ruling colonial aristocracy. In 1783 and 1784, violence and antigovernment riots tore war-weary Charleston; Thompson's City Tavern seems to have been the center of these activities. Thompson became involved in an argument with the former governor John Rutledge, a member of the upper class. For his "insults" to Rutledge, he was arrested by the House of Representatives. Released pending good behavior, Thompson nevertheless published the following inflammatory statements in the newspaper.

* *Gazette of the State of South Carolina* (April 29, 1784).

Mr. William Thompson's STATE of FACTS, Respecting the origin, progress and event of a late controversy between him and John Rutledge, both citizens of this Commonwealth.

Mr. Thompson's affidavit on that head.

Personally appeared before me, John Troup.

William Thompson, who maketh oath on the Holy Evangelists of Almighty God, that, on St. Patrick's day last, when the City-Artillery were about discharging their pieces, in rejoicement for the happy event of Peace, by a ratification of the Definitive treaty,—A Negro woman named Beck, (not then known to the Deponent as the slave or servant of Mr. John Rutledge in particular,) had come to the Deponent's house, and asked him through the bar window, (the Deponent being then within the bar,) for his permission to go up stairs, to see the Artillery firing.— The Deponent, (provoked at the insolence of such a request, from one of her colour, and not announcing a message or authority from any master,) ordered her to be gone, execrating her for her impertinence. In a short space of time afterwards, the Deponent, (not suspecting in the least, that she had any message from her owner, or that he could have given him, or any man, cause of offense by such refusal,) received a peremptory requisition, (by Mr. John Rutledge's younger son,) intimating, that Mr. Rutledge desired to speak to him . . .

The Deponent, on his entrance, [to the Rutledge home] saluted the Gentlemen, to which Mr. Rutledge did not deign to make the smallest complimentary return. He rose from his seat, and advancing towards the window, took therefrom a stick or ratan—and thus he advanced towards the Deponent. Mr. Rutledge then ordered in his wench to confront the Deponent. Have you not, (says he to the wench,) delivered my message to THIS MAN—The wench replied, I have. She has never, Sir, (answered the Deponent,) delivered any message from you to me . . . Hold your tongue, (says Mr. Rutledge,) I BELIEVE HER BEFORE YOU, and I will teach you, Sir, to treat ME with more respect. You have been insolent to some GENTLEMEN on the nights of the dancing assemblies. Mr. Manigault, (says he,) informs me that you had been very impudent to severall GENTLEMEN—Mr. Manigault lies, (replied the Deponent,) and if he offers this to my face, BY THE ETERNAL GOD I WILL KICK HIS A____ E____.

William Thompson

Mr. Thompson's Address to the Public, respecting the above Transaction, and the ulterior Events which flowed therefrom.

Friends and Fellow Citizens,

I owe a deference to the general opinion, and I must submit to it. It is at your instance, that I proceed to a Statement of further FACTS;

of FACTS not less irksome to my feelings as a Man, than they are hostile to your Liberties, as Freemen.

It is a pungent evil indeed, that, in the infancy of our Commonwealth, Republicans should be forced to coalesce into one society with men, who detest Republicanism, and are detested. The NABOBS of this State, their servile Toad-eaters the BOBS,—and the servilely-servile tools and lick-spittles of Power to both, the BOBBETS are the lofty criminals I allude to . . . those howling wolves of the wilderness either desolate or menace all around you. When, in a free land, (by intermarriage or otherwise,) signal opulence and influence conspicuously unite, in swelling the ambition, as they enlarge the consequences of a few families; it then behoves, (and it is a maxim of sound policy to do so,) all free and independent minds, to regard them as men calculated to subvert Republicanism, who ought therefore to be opposed. If they aspire to be great Citizens, let them rise to it by being good, able, useful and friends to social equality. Consequence is from the public opinion, and not from private fancy. Public opinion [esteem] is the gift of the people, freely granted and given, and will not be extorted.

On my departure from Mr. Rutledge's presence, I began to recollect his conduct of a similar nature towards some, and of a worse complexion towards others. Accustomed to a Republican government where no inequality exists, but that of magistracy; and imbided from my infancy with those principles of honour which quicken sensibility, and enliven the sense of a gross injury, I found the insult debasing me.

Believing him a man of honour, and not doubting of his spirit, I stated his insult by letter, and demanded satisfaction. On the enusing day, his reply was handed to me in writing. It contained much, said little; but an apology was demanded of me in the close, with a threat, in case of refusal, of submitting my letter to be discussed before the House of Representatives, of which he was a member.

I was then sentenced, not only to apologize to the House for a breach of privilege, but also to solicit pardon of my enemy, as though I had been the aggressor; And that in case I should refuse compliance with this humiliating injunction, I was to be kept within close confinement within the common gaol, during the remainder of that session. Every means of defence was refused me, but an implicit compliance with every act of the House's Requisition.

Guilty or not guilty of a breach of that House's privileges, I thought it no dishonor, to comply with the first part of their sentence. But it was not, it seems, the privilege of the House which one active Framer, at least, of the report had so much in view, as the humiliation of a Publican, stranger, a wretch of no higher rank in the Commonwealth than that of a Common-Citizen; for having dared to dispute with a John

Rutledge, or any of the NABOB Tribe, on the subject of consequence . . . Those self-exalted characters, who affect to compose the grand hierarchy of the State, were not to be controuled . . . by any of the lower orders; and I, as one of those, was pitched upon, so to suffer in their presence, as to deter others from ever rebelling again against their petty Majesties. The cause I contended for was, equally, the birth-right of every Citizen. I acknowledged no higher order of men in any Commonwealth. The process then against me, I considered as against you and each of you. I felt a citizen's right, and as a Citizen I resisted and suffered.

I thought proper, however, as a Citizen, to discharge my duty to the House. I informed that Honourable Body, that, as such, I never intended to offend them . . . That my controversy was only with the man, and not with the Member. Mr. Rutledge expressed that he thought this matter had already been settled; that he, for his part, sought not any citizen's apology; and so hurried himself out of the room.

Your sentiments, my fellow citizens, on the aggregate of these proceedings, lie with yourselves. For your rights, so glaringly invaded in my person have I suffered. To you, therefore, (in whom ultimately resides the Sacred Majesty of this Commonwealth and the high tribinitial authority of discriminating those servants who represent from those who, from principle, misrepresent you,) do I submit this, your own case perhaps soon to be, and mine already passed.

William Thompson

Charleston, April 27, 1784.

70. EZRA STILES, *THE UNITED STATES ELEVATED TO HONOR AND GLORY*, 1785[*]

Ezra Stiles (1727–95) was a Congregational minister and scholar. As president of Yale during the inflationary and speculative war years, he saved that institution from bankruptcy. He was an ardent, idealistic patriot and an early abolitionist who wrote much but published little. Among his published works is the following sermon which takes a utopian view of the new nation and forecasts some international consequences of the Revolution.

A free tenure of lands, and equable distribution of property, enters into the foundations of a happy State; so far as I mean that body of people may have it in their power, by industry, to become possessed of real freehold fee simple estate. For connected with this will be a general spirit and principle of self-defense of our *property, liberty, country*. This

[*] Ezra Stiles, *The United States Elevated to Honor and Glory* . . . (Worcester, Mass.: Isaiah Thomas, 1785), pp. 10–11, 84–87.

has been singularly verified in New England; where we have realized the capital ideas of Harrington's *Oceana*. . . .

. . . .

This war has decided, not by the *jus maritimum* of *Rhodes, Oleron,* or *Britain,* but on the principles of commercial utility and public right, that *the navigation of the Atlantic Ocean shall be free*: and so probably will be that of all the oceans of the terraqueous globe. All the European powers will henceforth, from national and commercial interests, naturally become an united and combined guaranty for the free navigation of the Atlantic and free commerce with America. Interest will establish a free access for all nations to our shores and for us to all nations. The *armed neutrality* will disarm even war itself of hostilities against trade; will form a new chapter in the laws of nations, and preserve a free commerce among powers at war. Fighting armies will decide the fate of empires by the sword without interrupting the civil, social, and commercial intercourse of subjects. The want of anything to take will prove a natural abolition of privateering when the property shall be covered with neutral protection. Even the navies will, within a century, become useless. A generous and truly liberal system of national connection, in the spirit of the plan conceived and nearly executed by the great *Henry IV., of France,* will almost annihilate war itself.

We shall have a communication with all nations in *commerce, manners,* and *science,* beyond anything heretofore known in the world. Manufacturers and artisans, and men of every description may, perhaps, come and settle among us. They will be few indeed in comparison with the annual thousands of our natural increase, and will be incorporated with the prevailing hereditary complexion of the first settlers. We shall not be assimilated to them, but they to us; especially in the second and third generations. This fermentation and communion of nations will doubtless produce something very new, singular, and glorious. Upon the conquest of *Alexander* the great, *statuary, painting, architecture, philosophy,* and the other fine arts were transplanted in perfection from *Athens* to *Tarsus,* from Greece to Syria, where they immediately flourished in even greater perfection than in the parent state. Not in Greece herself are there to be found specimens of a sublimer or more magnificent architecture, even in the Grecian style, than in the ruins of *Baalbec* and *Palmyra.* So all the arts may be transplanted from *Europe* and *Asia,* and flourish in *America* with an augmented lustre; not to mention the augment of the sciences from American inventions and discoveries, of which there have been as capital ones here, the last half century, as in all *Europe.*

The rough, sonorous diction of the English language may here take its Athenian polish, and receive its Attic urbanity; as it will probably become the vernacular tongue of more numerous millions than ever yet spake one language on earth. It may continue for ages to be the prevailing and general language of *North America.* The intercommunion of the *United States* with all the world in *travels, trade,* and *politics,* and the infusion of letters into our infancy, will probably preserve us from the provincial dialects risen into inexterminable habit before the invention of printing. The Greek never became the language of the Alexandrine, nor the Turkish of the Ottoman conquests, nor yet the Latin that of the Roman empire. The Saracenic conquests have already lost the pure and elegant Arabic of the *Koreish* tribe, or the family of *Ishmael,* in the corrupted dialects of Egypt, Syria, Persia, and Hindostan. Different from these, the English language will grow up with the present American population into great purity and elegance, unmutilated by the foreign dialects of foreign conquests.

71. NOAH WEBSTER, EDUCATIONAL NATIONALISM, 1788*

Noah Webster (1758–1843), philologist, lexicographer, and educator, was both a product of the Revolution and a disseminator of its ideas. In the postwar years, anything that suggested aristocracy was anathematized. Echoing Washington, Jefferson, and many of the other Founding Fathers, Webster felt that American youth should be trained in republican ideals uncorrupted by European and particularly English influences. He therefore wrote the following article for the newly inaugurated American Magazine, *in which he criticizes the practice of sending young men abroad for their formal education, a custom of the well-to-do and aristocratic families of colonial society.*

I beg leave to make some remarks on a practice which appears to be attended with important consequences; I mean that of sending boys to Europe for an education, or sending to Europe for teachers. That this was right before the revolution will not be disputed; at least so far as national attachments were concerned; but the propriety of it ceased with our political relation to Great Britain.

In the first place, our honor as an independent nation is concerned in the establishment of literary institutions, adequate to all our own purposes; without sending our youth abroad, or depending on other nations for books and instructors. It is very little to the reputation of America to

* Edgar W. Knight and Clifton L. Hall, *Readings in American Educational History* (New York: Appleton-Century-Crofts, 1951), pp. 93–96. Reprinted by permission of the publisher. *The American Magazine* (May, 1788), pp. 370–73.

have it said abroad, that after the heroic achievements of the late war, this independent people are obliged to send to Europe for men and books to teach their children ABC.

But in another point of view, a foreign education is directly opposite to our political interests and ought to be discountenanced, if not prohibited.

Every person of common observation will grant, that most men prefer the manners and the government of that country where they are educated. Let ten American youths be sent, each to a different European kingdom, and live there from the age of twelve to twenty, & each will give the preference to the country where he has resided.

The period from twelve to twenty is the most important in life. The impressions made before that period are commonly effaced: those that are made during that period *always* remain for many years, and *generally* thro' life.

Ninety-nine persons of a hundred, who pass that period in England or France, will prefer the people, their manners, their laws, and their government to those of their native country. Such attachments are injurious, both to the happiness of the men, and to the political interests of their own country. As to private happiness, it is universally known how much pain a man suffers by a change of habits in living. The customs of Europe are and ought to be different from ours; but when a man has been bred in one country, his attachments to its manners make them in a great measure, necessary to his happiness; on changing his residence, he must therefore break his former habits, which is always a painful sacrifice; or the discordance between the manners of his own country and his habits, must give him incessant uneasiness; or he must introduce, into a circle of his friends, the manners in which he was educated. All these consequences may follow at the same time, and the last, which is inevitable, is a public injury. The refinement of manners in every country should keep pace exactly with the increase of its wealth—and perhaps the greatest evil America now feels is, an improvement of taste and manners which its wealth cannot support.

A foreign education is the very source of this evil—it gives young gentlemen of fortune a relish for manners and amusements which are not suited to this country; which, however, when introduced by this class of people, will always become fashionable.

But a corruption of manners is not the sole objection to a foreign education; An attachment to a *foreign* government, or rather a want of attachment to our *own*, is the natural effect of a residence abroad, during the period of youth. It is recorded of one of the Greek cities, that in a treaty with their conquerors, it was required that they should give a certain number of *male children* as hostages for the fulfilment of their engagements. The Greeks absolutely refused, on the principle that these children would imbibe the ideas and embrace the manners of foreigners, or lose their love for their own country: But they offered the same number of *old* men, without hesitation. This anecdote is full of good sense. A man should always form his habits and attachments in the country where he is to reside for life. When these habits are formed, young men may travel without danger of losing their patriotism. A boy who lives in England from twelve to twenty, will be an *Englishman* in his manners and his feelings; but let him remain at home till he is twenty, and form his attachments, he may then be several years abroad, and still be an *American*. There may be exceptions to this observation; but living examples may be mentioned, to prove the truth of the general principle here advanced, respecting the influence of habit.

It may be said that foreign universities furnish much better opportunities of improvement in the sciences than the American. This may be true, and yet will not justify the practice of sending young lads from their own country. There are some branches of science which may be studied to much greater advantage in Europe than in America, particularly chymistry. When these are to be acquired, young gentlemen ought to spare no pains to attend the best professors. It may, therefore, be useful, in some cases, for students to cross the Atlantic to *complete* a course of studies; but it is not necessary for them to go early in life, nor to continue a long time. Such instances need not be frequent even now; and the necessity for them will diminish in proportion to the future advancement of literature in America.

It is, however, much questioned whether, in the ordinary course a study, a young man can enjoy greater advantages in Europe than in America. Experience inclines me to raise a doubt, whether the danger to which a youth must be exposed among the sons of dissipation abroad, will not turn the scale in favor of our American colleges. Certain it is, that four fifths of the great literary characters in America never crossed the Atlantic.

But if our universities and schools are not so good as the English or Scotch, it is the business of our rulers to improve them—not to endow them merely; for endowments alone will never make a flourishing seminary—but to furnish them with professors of the first abilities and most assiduous application, and with a complete apparatus for establishing theories by experiments. Nature has been profuse to the Americans, in genius, and in the advantages of climate and soil. If this country, therefore, should long be indebted to Europe for opportunities of acquiring any branch of science in perfection, it must be by means of a criminal neglect of its inhabitants.

The difference in the nature of the American and European governments, is another objection to a foreign education. Men form modes of reasoning or habits of thinking on political subjects, in the country where they are bred—these modes of reasoning may be founded on fact in all countries—but the same principles will not apply in all governments, because of the infinite variety of national opinions and habits. Before a man can be a good Legislator, he must be intimately acquainted with the temper of the people to be governed. No man can be thus acquainted with a people, without residing amongst them and mingling with all companies. . . .

It is therefore of infinite importance that those who direct the councils of a nation, should be educated in that nation. Not that they should restrict their personal acquaintance to their own country, but their first ideas, attachments and habits should be acquired in the country which they are to govern and defend. When a knowledge of their own country is obtained, and an attachment to its laws and interests deeply fixed in their hearts, then young gentlemen may travel with infinite advantage and perfect safety. I wish not therefore to discourage travelling, but, if possible, to render it more useful to individuals and to the community. My meaning is, that *men* should travel, and not *boys*.

But it is time for the Americans to change their usual route, and travel thro a country which they never think of, or think beneath their notice.—I mean the United States.

While these States were a part of the British Empire, our interest, our feelings, were those of English men—our dependence led us to respect and imitate their manners—and to look up to them for our opinions. We little thought of any national interest in America—and while our commerce and government were in the hands of our parent country, and we had no common interest, we little thought of improving our acquaintance with each other or of removing prejudices, and reconciling the discordant feelings of the inhabitants of the different Provinces. But independence and union render it necessary that the citizens of different States should know each others characters and circumstances—that all jealousies should be removed—that mutual respect and confidence should succeed—and a harmony of views and interests be cultivated by a friendly intercourse. . . .

Americans, unshackle your minds, and act like independent beings. You have been children long enough, subject to the control, and subservient to the interest of a haughty parent. You have now an interest of your own to augment and defend—you have an empire to raise and support by your exertions—and a national character to establish and extend by your wisdom and virtues. To effect these great objects, it is necessary to frame a liberal plan of policy, and to build it on a broad system of education. Before this system can be formed and embraced, the Americans must *believe* and *act* from the belief, that it is dishonorable to waste life in mimicking the follies of other nations, and basking in the sunshine of foreign glory.

72. DAVID RAMSAY, VIEW OF THE UNITED STATES, 1781–89[*]

David Ramsay (1749–1815), statesman, physician, and historian, was born in Lancaster, Pennsylvania, and educated at Princeton and the College of Pennsylvania. In 1772 he went to Charleston to practice medicine and became deeply involved in the revolutionary politics and activities of his adopted state, as a result of which he was imprisoned by the British in 1780. After the war he was a member of the state legislature and of the state's ratifying convention in 1788. An avid believer in the principles of the Revolution, he lost an election in 1788 because he was "an enemy to slavery." Ramsay's histories were highly esteemed by his contemporaries, and in recent years his work has enjoyed a revival, chiefly because he was an observant, philosophical witness to the events of his day.

On the Confederation

. . . .

[In the] formation and establishment of the American constitutions, we behold our species in a new situation. In no age before, and in no other country, did man ever possess an election of the kind of government, under which he would choose to live. The constituent parts of the ancient free governments were thrown together by accident. The freedom of modern European governments was, for the most part, obtained by the concessions, or liberality of monarchs or military leaders. In America alone, reason and liberty concurred in the formation of constitutions. It is true, from the infancy of political knowledge in the United States, there were many defects in their forms of governments: but in one thing they were all perfect. They left to the people the power of altering and amending them, whenever they pleased. In this happy peculiarity they placed the science of politics on a footing with the other sciences, by opening it to improvements from experience, and the discoveries of future ages. By means of this power of amending American constitutions, the friends of mankind have fondly hoped that oppression will one day be no more; and that political evil will at least be prevented or restrained with as much certainty, by a proper combination or separation of power, as natural evil is lessened or prevented, by the application of the knowledge or ingenuity of man to domestic purposes. No part of the history of ancient or modern Europe can furnish a single fact that militates against this opinion; since, in none of its governments, have the principles of

[*] David Ramsay, *History of the United States* (Philadelphia: M. Carey and Son, 1819), Vol. III, 51–55, 180–83.

equal representation and checks been applied, for the preservation of freedom. On these two pivots are suspended the liberties of most of the states. Where they are wanting, there can be no security for liberty: where they exist, they render any further security unnecessary.

From history the citizens of the United States had been taught, that the maxims, adopted by the rulers of the earth, that society was instituted for the sake of the governors; and that the interests of the many were to be postponed to the convenience of the privileged few, had filled the world with bloodshed and wickedness; while experience had proved, that it is the invariable and natural character of power, whether entrusted or assumed, to exceed its proper limits, and, if unrestrained, to divide the world into masters and slaves. They therefore began upon the opposite maxims, that society was instituted, not for the governors, but the governed; that the interest of the few, should, in all cases, give way to that of the many; that exclusive and hereditary privileges were useless and dangerous institutions in society; and that entrusted authorities should be liable to frequent and periodical recalls. With them the sovereignty of the people was more than a mere theory. The characteristic of that sovereignty was displayed by their authority in written constitutions.

The rejection of British sovereignty not only involved a necessity of erecting independent constitutions, but of cementing the whole United States by some common bond of union. The act of independence did not hold out to the world thirteen sovereign states, but a common sovereignty of the whole in their united capacity. It therefore became necessary to run the line of distinction, between the local legislatures, and the assembly of states in congress. A committee was appointed for digesting articles of confederation, between the state or united colonies, as they were then called, at the time the propriety of declaring independence was under debate, and some weeks previously to the adoption of that measure: but the plan was not for sixteen months after so far digested, as to be ready for communication to the states, till nearly three years more had elapsed. In discussing its articles, many difficult questions occurred. One was, to ascertain the ratio of contributions from each state. Two principles presented themselves; numbers of people, and the value of lands. The last was preferred, as being the truest barometer of the wealth of nations: but from an apprehended impracticability of carrying it into effect, it was soon relinquished, and recurrence had to the former. That the states should be represented in proportion to their importance, was contended by those who had extensive territory: but those, who were confined to small dimensions, replied, that the states confederated as individuals in a state of nature, and should therefore have equal votes. The large states yielded the point, and consented that each state should have an equal suffrage.

It was not easy to define the power of the state legislatures, so as to prevent a clashing between their jurisdiction, and that of the general government. It was thought proper, that the former should be abridged of the power of forming any other confederation or alliance; of laying on any imposts or duties that might interfere with treaties made by congress; of keeping up any vessels of war, or granting letters of marque or reprisal. The powers of congress were also defined. Of these, the principal were as follows: To have the sole and exclusive right of determining on peace or war; of sending or receiving embassadors; of entering into treaties and alliances; of granting letters of marque and reprisal in times of peace; to the last resort on appeal, in all disputes between two or more states; to have the sole and exclusive right of regulating the alloy and value of coin; of fixing the standard of weights and measures; regulating the trade and managing all affairs with the Indians; establishing and regulating post offices; to borrow money, or emit bills, on the credit of the United States; to build and equip a navy; to agree upon the number of land forces; and to make requisitions from each state for its quota of men, in proportion to the number of its white inhabitants.

No coercive power was given to the general government, nor was it invested with any legislative power over individuals, but only over states in their corporate capacity. A power to regulate trade, or to raise a revenue from it, though both were essential to the welfare of the union, made no part of this first federal system. To remedy this and all other defects, a door was left open for introducing further provisions, suited to future circumstances.

The articles of confederation were proposed at a time when the citizens of America were young in the science of politics, and when a commanding sense of duty, enforced by the pressure of a common danger, precluded the necessity of a power of compulsion. The enthusiasm of the day gave such credit and currency to paper emissions, as made the raising of supplies an easy matter. The system of federal government was, therefore, more calculated for what men then were, under those circumstances, than for the languid years of peace, when selfishness usurped the place of public spirit, and when credit no longer assisted, in providing for the exigencies of government.

The experience of a few years, after the termination of the war, proved . . . that a radical change of the whole system was necessary to the good government of the United States.

On the Constitution

The people of the United States gave no new powers to their rulers; but made a more judicious arrangement of what they had formerly ceded. They enlarged the powers of the general government, not by taking from the people, but from the state legislatures. They took from the latter the power of levying duties on the importation of merchandise from foreign countries, and transferred it to Congress, for the common benefit of the Union. They also invested the general government with a power to regulate trade, and levy taxes and internal duties on the inhabitants. That these enlarged powers might be used only with caution and deliberation, Congress, which formerly consisted of one body, was made to consist of two; one of which was to be chosen by the people in proportion to their numbers, the other by the state legislatures. The executive power was committed to a supreme magistrate, with the title of President.

The constitution, of which these were the principal features, was submitted to the people for ratification. Animated debates took place on the propriety of establishing or rejecting it! Some states, which, from their local situation, were benefited by receiving impost duties into their treasuries, were unwilling to give them up to the Union. Others, which were consuming but not importing states, had an interested inducement of an opposite kind, to support the proposed new constitution. The prospects of increased employment for shipping, and the enlargement of commerce, weighed with those states which abounded in sailors and ships, and also with seaport towns, to advocate the adoption of the new system; but those states, or parts of states, which depended chiefly on agriculture, were afraid that zeal for encouraging an American marine, by narrowing the grounds of competition among foreigners, for purchasing and carrying their produce, would lessen their profits. Some of this description therefore conceived that they had a local interest in refusing the new system.

Individuals who had great influence in state legislatures, or who held profitable places under them, were unwilling to adopt a government which, by diminishing the power of the states, would eventually diminish their own importance: others, who looked forward to seats in the general government, or for officers under its authority, had the same interested reason for supporting its adoption. Some, from jealousy of liberty, were afraid of giving too much power to their rulers; others, from an honest ambition to aggrandize their country, were for paving the way to national greatness, by melting down the separate states into a national mass. The former feared the new constitution; the latter gloried in it. Almost every passion which agitates the human breast, operated on states and individuals, for and against the adoption of the proposed plan of government. Some whole classes of people were in its favour. The mass of public creditors expected payment of their debts, from the establishment of an efficient government, and were therefore decidedly for its adoption. Such as lived on salaries, and those who, being clear of debt, wished for a fixed medium of circulation, and the free course of law, were the friends of a constitution which prohibited the issuing of paper money, and all interference between debtor and creditor. In addition to these, the great body of independent men, who saw the necessity of an energetic general government, and who, from the jarring interests of the different states, could not foresee any probability of getting a better one than was proposed, gave their support to what the national convention had projected, and their influence effected its establishment. After a full consideration, and thorough discussion of its principles, it was ratified by the conventions of eleven of the original thirteen states. The accession of the other two soon followed. The ratification of it was celebrated, in most of the capitals of the states, with elegant processions, which far exceeded any thing of the kind ever before exhibited in America.

The adoption of this constitution was a triumph of virtue and good sense, over the vices and follies of human nature. In some respects, the merit of it is greater than that of the declaration of independence. The worst of men can be urged on to make a spirited resistance to invasions of their rights: but higher grades of virtue are requisite to induce freemen, in the possession of a limited sovereignty, voluntarily to surrender a portion of their natural liberties; to impose on themselves those restraints of good government, which bridle the ferocity of man, compel him to respect the claims of others, and to submit his rights and his wrongs to be decided upon by the voice of his fellow citizens. The instances of nations, which had vindicated their liberty by the sword, are many; of those which made a good use of their liberty when acquired, are comparatively few. In this particular the Americans had learned wisdom from the mistakes of their English ancestors. The people of that gallant nation, about the middle of the seventeenth century, with their swords rescued their liberties from the hands of a tyrant king; but formed no constitutional security, for their preservation. In less than twenty years, they bowed their necks unconditionally to the son of their late sovereign, whom they had brought to the block. Arbitrary power recommenced, and was carried on with a high hand: and nothing but a revolution, or another civil war, could have prevented the rivetting of their chains.

To analyse this constitution, and explain how it combines law with liberty, energy with safety, the freedom of a small state with the strength of a great empire, would require a volume, and lead the author from the objects of history. It may, nevertheless, be remarked, that its tendency to promote justice is its most prominent feature. Two circumstances doubtless contributed to this useful trait in its character. The colonies were settled under the arbitrary reigns of the James's and the Charles's: and the cruelties exercised, under the colour of law, on subjects in that disgraceful period of English history were well known in America. The constitution was adopted at the close of the revolutionary war, in the course of which much legal iniquity had been practiced. To guard against the repetition of similar evils, this honest constitution restrained all future legislators, by the solemn ties of oaths, from "emitting bills of credit; making any thing but gold or silver a tender in payment of debts; passing ex post facto laws, or laws impairing the obligation of contracts." It in like manner ordained that "no bill of attainder should be passed; that treason against the United States should consist only in levying war against them, or in adhering to their enemies, giving them aid and comfort; and that no person should be convicted of treason, unless on the testimony of two witnesses to the same overt act, or on confession in open court." From the want of similar laws, much of the best blood in England had been formerly shed for trifles or venial offences, falsely called treason. There had been also a great wreck of property and much injustice committed in the United States. To correct faults is highly praiseworthy in individuals: but for sovereign states to prevent their recurrence, by constitutional prohibition, is truly magnanimous.

The new constitution having been ratified by eleven of the states, and senators and representatives having been chosen agreeably to the articles thereof, they met at New York, and commenced proceedings under it. The old congress and confederation, like the continental money, expired without a sigh or groan. A new congress, with more ample powers, and a new constitution, partly national and partly federal, succeeded in their place, to the great joy of all who wished for the happiness of the United States.

Though great diversity of opinions had prevailed about the new constitution, there was but one opinion about the person who should be appointed the supreme executive officer. The people, as well antifederalists as federalists, for by these names the parties for and against the new constitution were called, unanimously turned their eyes on the late commander of their armies, as the most proper person to be their first president. Perhaps there was not a well-informed individual in the United States, Washington himself only excepted, who was not anxious that he should be called to the executive administration of the new government. Unambitious of further honours, he had retired to his farm in Virginia, and hoped to be excused from all further public service; but his country called him by an unanimous vote to fill the highest station in its gift. That honest zeal for the public good, which had uniformly influenced him to devote both his time and talents to the service of his country, got the better of his love of retirement, and induced him once more to engage in the great business of making a nation happy.

73. JOHN ADAMS, *DISCOURSES ON DAVILA*, LIBERTY WITH ORDER, 1789–90*

John Adams (1735–1826), second President of the United States, revolutionary statesman, and political theorist, was minister to France and England after ending his monumental work in the Continental Congress. In 1780, as a delegate to the Massachusetts Constitutional Convention, he became the guiding spirit behind its work. In his Discourses on Davila, *written during his tenure as Vice President, he defended the new federal constitution not on the grounds of the necessity for federal power but on those of "mixed government." Aware of class struggles and the impassioned pleas for liberty by the people, he realized that government should represent all interests and maintain a balance between the commoner and the aristocrat. Adams was frequently quoted out of context by his political enemies to show him as an aristocrat, even a monarchist; but he had a more realistic view of American revolutionary society and the nature of its government than many who assailed him.*

Amidst all their exultations, Americans and Frenchmen should remember that the perfectibility of man is only human and terrestrial perfectibility. Cold will still freeze, and fire will never cease to burn; disease and vice will continue to disorder, and death to terrify mankind. Emulation next to self-preservation will forever be the great spring of human actions, and the balance of a well-ordered government will alone be able to prevent that emulation from degenerating into dangerous ambition, irregular rivalries, destructive factions, wasting seditions, and bloody, civil wars.

The great question will forever remain, *who shall work?* Our species cannot all be idle. Leisure for study must ever be the portion of a few. The number employed in government must forever be very small. Food, raiment, and habitations, the indispensable wants of all, are not to be obtained without the continual toil of ninety-nine in a hundred of mankind. As rest is rapture to the weary man, those who labor little will always be envied by those who labor much, though the latter in reality be probably the most enviable. With all the encouragements, public and private, which can ever be given to general education, and it is scarcely possibly they should be too many or too great, the laboring part of the people can never be learned. The controversy between the rich and the poor, the laborious and the idle, the learned and the ignorant, distinctions as old as the creation, and as extensive as the globe, distinctions

* John Adams, *Works: Discourses on Davila*, C. F. Adams, ed. (Boston: Charles C. Little and James Brown, 1851), Vol. VI, 279–81, 399.

which no art or policy, no degree of virtue or philosophy can ever wholly
destroy, will continue, and rivalries will spring out of them. These parties
will be represented in the legislature, and must be balanced or one will
oppress the other. There will never probably be found any other mode of
establishing such an equilibrium, than by constituting the representation
of each an independent branch of the legislature, and an independent
executive authority, such as that in our government, to be a third branch
and a mediator or an arbitrator between them. Property must be secured,
or liberty cannot exist. But if unlimited or unbalanced power of disposing
property, be put into the hands of those who have no property, France
will find, as we have found, the lamb committed to the custody of the
wolf. In such a case, all the pathetic exhortations and addresses of the
national assembly to the people, to respect property, will be regarded no
more than the warbles of the songsters of the forest. The great art of
law-giving consists in balancing the poor against the rich in the legislature, and in constituting [in] the legislative a perfect balance against
the executive power, at the same time that no individual or party can
become its rival. The essence of a free government consists in an effectual
control of rivalries. The executive and the legislative powers are natural
rivals; and if each has not an effectual control over the other, the weaker
will ever be the lamb in the paws of the wolf. The nation which will not
adopt an equilibrium of power must adopt a despotism. There is no other
alternative. Rivalries must be controlled, or they will throw all things
into confusion; and there is nothing but despotism or a balance of power
which can control them. Even in the simple monarchies, the nobility and
the judicatures constitute a balance, though a very imperfect one, against
the royalties.

     Let us conclude with one reflection more which shall barely be
hinted at, as delicacy, if not prudence, may require, in this place, some
degree of reserve. Is there a possibility that the government of nations
may fall into the hands of men who teach the most disconsolate of all
creeds, that men are but fireflies, and that this *all* is without a father?
Is this the way to make man, as man, an object of respect? Or is it to
make murder itself as indifferent as shooting a plover, and the extermination of the Rohilla nation as innocent as the swallowing of mites on a
morsel of cheese? If such a case should happen, would not one of these,
the most credulous of all believers, have reason to pray to his eternal
nature or his almighty chance (the more absurdity there is in this address the more in character) *give us again the gods of the Greeks; give us
again the more intelligible as well as more comfortable systems of
Athanasius and Calvin; nay, give us again our popes and hierarchies,
Benedictines and Jesuits, with all their superstition and fanaticism, im-
postures and tyranny.* A certain duchess, of venerable years and mascu-

line understanding, said of some of the philosophers of the eighteenth century, admirably well,—"*On ne croit pas dans le Christianisme, mais on croit toutes les sottises possibles.*"

. . . .

It has been said, that it is extremely difficult to preserve a balance. This is no more than to say that it is extremely difficult to preserve liberty. To this truth all ages and nations attest. It is so difficult, that the very appearance of it is lost over the whole earth, excepting one island and North America. How long it will be before she returns to her native skies, and leaves the whole human race in slavery, will depend on the intelligence and virtue of the people. A balance, with all its difficulty, must be preserved, or liberty is lost forever. Perhaps a perfect balance, if it ever existed, has not been long maintained in its perfection; yet such a balance as has been sufficient to liberty, has been supported in some nations for many centuries together; and we must come as near as we can to a perfect equilibrium, or all is lost. When it is once widely departed from, the departure increases rapidly, til the whole is lost. If the people have not understanding and public virtue enough, and will not be persuaded of the necessity of supporting an independent executive authority, an independent senate, and an independent judiciary power, as well as an independent house of representatives, all pretensions to a balance are lost, and with them all hopes of security to our dearest interests, all hopes of liberty.

Selected Bibliography: The Revolutionary Era

ADAMS, Randolph G. *Political Ideas of the American Revolution: Britannic-American Contributions to the Problem of Imperial Organization, 1765 to 1775.* 3rd ed. New York: Barnes & Noble, Inc., 1958.

ALDEN, John Richard. *The South in the Revolution, 1763–1789.* Baton Rouge: Louisiana State University Press, 1957.

BECKER, Carl Lotus. *The Declaration of Independence: A Study in the History of Political Ideas.* New York: Peter Smith Publisher, 1933.*

————. *The History of Political Parties in the Province of New York, 1760–1776.* Bulletin of the University of Wisconsin. Madison: The University of Wisconsin Press, 1909.*

BROWN, Richard Maxwell. *The South Carolina Regulators.* Cambridge: Harvard University Press, 1963.

BRUNHOUSE, Robert Levere. (ed.) "David Ramsay, 1749–1815. Selections from his Writings," *Transactions of the American Philosophical Society.* New Series, LV, Part 4. Philadelphia: American Philosophical Society, 1965.

COLBOURN, H. Trevor. *The Lamp of Experience; Whig History and the Intellectual Origins of the American Revolution.* Chapel Hill: The University of North Carolina Press for the Institute of Early American History and Culture, 1965.

CONWAY, Moncure Daniel. (ed.) *Writings of Thomas Paine.* 4 Vols. New York: G. P. Putnam's Sons, 1894–96.

CUNNINGHAM, Charles E. *Timothy Dwight, 1752–1817. A Biography.* New York: The Macmillan Company, 1942.

DOUGLASS. Elisha P. *Rebels and Democrats: The Struggle for Equal Political Rights and Majority Rule during the American Revolution.* Chapel Hill: The University of North Carolina Press, 1955.*

GREEN, Fletcher Melvin. *Constitutional Development in the South Atlantic States, 1776–1860.* Chapel Hill: The University of North Carolina Press, 1930.*

GREENE, Evarts Boutwell, and HARRINGTON, Virginia D. *American Population before the Federal Census of 1790.* New York: Columbia University Press, 1932.

————. *The Revolutionary Generation, 1763–1790.* New York: The Macmillan Company, 1943.

GREENE, Jack P. *The Quest for Power; The Lower House of Assembly in the Southern Royal Colonies, 1689–1776.* Chapel Hill: The University of North Carolina Press for the Institute of Early American History and Culture, 1963.

HARRINGTON, Virginia Draper. *The New York Merchant on the Eve of the Revolution.* Gloucester, Mass.: Peter Smith Publisher, 1964.

JAMESON, J. Franklin. *The American Revolution Considered as a Social Movement.* Princeton: Princeton University Press, 1926.*

JENSEN, Merrill. *The New Nation: A History of the United States during the Confederation, 1781–1789.* New York: Alfred A. Knopf, Inc., 1950.*

JERNEGAN, Marcus Wilson. *Laboring and Dependent Classes in Colonial America, 1607–1783: Studies of the Economic, Educational, and Social Significance of the Slaves, Servants, Apprentices, and Poor Folk.* Chicago: The University of Chicago Press, 1931.

KNOLLENBERG, Bernhard. *Origin of the American Revolution 1759–1766.* New York: The Macmillan Company, 1960.*

KOCH, Adrienne. *Power, Morals, and the Founding Fathers: Essays in the Interpretation of the American Enlightenment.* Ithaca, N. Y.: Great Seal Books, 1961.*

KOCH, Gustav A. *Republican Religion: The American Revolution and the Cult of Reason.* New York: Henry Holt and Company, Inc., 1933.

LAND, Aubrey C. *The Dulanys of Maryland: A Biographical Study of Daniel Dulany, the Elder (1685–1753) and Daniel Dulany, the Younger (1722–1797).* Baltimore: Maryland Historical Society, 1955.

LEARY, Lewis Gaston. *That Rascal Freneau, A Study in Literary Failure.* New Brunswick, N. J.: Rutgers University Press, 1941.

MCILWAIN, Charles Howard. *The American Revolution: A Constitutional Interpretation.* Ithaca, N. Y.: Great Seal Books, 1958.*

MAIN, Jackson Turner. *The Anti-Federalists: Critics of the Constitution, 1781–1788.* Chapel Hill: The University of North Carolina Press for the Institute of Early American History and Culture, 1961.*

———. *The Social Structure of Revolutionary America.* Princeton: Princeton University Press, 1965.

MALONE, Dumas. *Jefferson and His Time.* Boston: Little, Brown and Company, 1948.

MERIWETHER, Robert Lee. *The Expansion of South Carolina.* Kingsport, Tenn.: Southern Publishers, 1940.

MILLER, John C. *Origins of the American Revolution.* Stanford, Calif.: Stanford University Press, 1957.*

———. *Sam Adams: Pioneer in Propaganda.* Boston: Little, Brown and Company, 1936.*

———. *Triumph of Freedom, 1775–1783.* Boston: Little, Brown and Company, 1948.*

MORGAN, Edmund S. *The Gentle Puritan: A Life of Ezra Stiles.* New Haven: Yale University Press for the Institute of Early American History and Culture, 1962.

MORGAN, Edmund S. and Helen M. *The Stamp Act Crisis: A Prologue to Revolution.* Chapel Hill: The University of North Carolina Press for the Institute of Early American History and Culture, 1953.*

MORRIS, Richard Brandon. "Class Struggle and the American Revolution," *William and Mary Quarterly,* XIX (January, 1962), pp. 3–29.

———. (ed.) *The Era of the American Revolution.* New York: Columbia University Press, 1939.*

———. *Government and Labor in Early America.* New York: Columbia University Press, 1946.*

NAMIER, Sir Lewis Bernstein. *England in the Age of the American Revolution.* 2nd ed. New York: St Martin's Press, Inc., 1961.*

NEVINS, Allan. *The American States during and after the Revolution, 1775–1789.* New York: The Macmillan Company, 1924.

NYE, Russell B. *The Cultural Life of the New Nation.* New York: Harper & Brothers, 1960.

PELL, John. *Ethan Allen.* Boston: Houghton Mifflin Company, 1929.

QUARLES, Benjamin. *The Negro in the American Revolution.* Chapel Hill: The University of North Carolina Press for the Institute of Early American History and Culture, 1961.*

ROGERS, George. *Evolution of a Federalist: William Loughton Smith of Charleston.* Columbia, S. C.: The University of South Carolina Press, 1962.

SELLERS, Leila. *Charleston Business on the Eve of the American Revolution.* Chapel Hill: The University of North Carolina Press, 1934.

SELSAM, J. Paul. *Pennsylvania Constitution of 1776.* Philadelphia: University of Pennsylvania Press, 1936.

SMITH, Abbot E. *Colonists in Bondage: White Servitude and Convict Labor in America, 1607–1776.* Chapel Hill: The University of North Carolina Press for the Institute of Early American History and Culture, 1947.

SMITH, Page. *John Adams*. Garden City, N. Y.: Doubleday & Company, Inc., 1962.

SMITH, Paul Hubert. *Loyalists and Redcoats: A Study in British Revolutionary Policy*. Chapel Hill: The University of North Carolina Press for the Institute of Early American History and Culture, 1964.

SOSIN, Jack M. *The Revolutionary Frontier, 1763–83*. New York: Holt, Rinehart and Winston, Inc., 1967.

TREVELYAN, Sir George Otto. *The American Revolution*. New ed. 4 Vols. New York: Longmans, Green & Co., Inc., 1926–1929.

TYLER, Moses Coit. *The Literary History of the American Revolution, 1763–1783*. 2 Vols. Published for Facsimile Library, Inc. by Barnes & Noble. New York: Barnes & Noble, Inc., 1941.

WALSH, Richard. *Charleston's Sons of Liberty: A Study of the Artisans, 1763–1789*. Columbia, S. C.: The University of South Carolina Press, 1959.*

WARFEL, Harry R. *Noah Webster, Schoolmaster to America*. New York: The Macmillan Company, 1936.

WERTENBAKER, Thomas Jefferson. *Father Knickerbocker Rebels: New York City during the Revolution*. New York: Charles Scribner's Sons, 1948.

* Denotes availability in a paperbound edition.

Index